Clean Code in JavaScript

Develop reliable, maintainable, and robust JavaScript

James Padolsey

BIRMINGHAM - MUMBAI

Clean Code in JavaScript

Copyright © 2020 Packt Publishing

Commissioning Editor: Pavan Ramchandani
Acquisition Editor: Ashitosh Gupta
Content Development Editor: Akhil Nair
Senior Editor: Martin Whittemore
Technical Editor: Suwarna Patil
Copy Editor: Safis Editing
Project Coordinator: Kinjal Bari
Proofreader: Safis Editing
Indexer: Manju Arasan
Production Designer: Deepika Naik

First published: January 2020

Production reference: 1170120

Published by Packt Publishing Ltd.
Livery Place
35 Livery Street
Birmingham
B3 2PB, UK.

ISBN 978-1-78995-764-8

www.packt.com

`Packt.com`

Subscribe to our online digital library for full access to over 7,000 books and videos, as well as industry leading tools to help you plan your personal development and advance your career. For more information, please visit our website.

Why subscribe?

- Spend less time learning and more time coding with practical eBooks and Videos from over 4,000 industry professionals

- Improve your learning with Skill Plans built especially for you

- Get a free eBook or video every month

- Fully searchable for easy access to vital information

- Copy and paste, print, and bookmark content

Did you know that Packt offers eBook versions of every book published, with PDF and ePub files available? You can upgrade to the eBook version at `www.packt.com` and as a print book customer, you are entitled to a discount on the eBook copy. Get in touch with us at `customercare@packtpub.com` for more details.

At `www.packt.com`, you can also read a collection of free technical articles, sign up for a range of free newsletters, and receive exclusive discounts and offers on Packt books and eBooks.

Contributors

About the author

James Padolsey is a passionate JavaScript and UI engineer with over 12 years' experience. James began his journey into JavaScript as a teenager, teaching himself how to build websites for school and small freelance projects. In the early years, he was a prolific blogger, sharing his unique solutions to common problems in the domains of jQuery, JavaScript, and the DOM. He later contributed to the jQuery library itself and authored a chapter within the *jQuery Cookbook* published by *O'Reilly Media*. Over subsequent years, James has been exposed to many unique software projects in his employment at Stripe, Twitter, and Facebook, informing his philosophy on what clean coding truly means in the ever-changing ecosystem of JavaScript.

I'd like to thank the following individuals for their technical insight in the domain of JavaScript: Paul Irish, Alex Sexton, Axel Rauschmayer, John Resig, John Hann, Mathias Bynens, Ana Tudor, Steven Levithan, Juriy Zaytsev, Peter van der Zee, Addy Osmani, Jake Archibald, Dave Methvin, and Lea Verou. I would like to especially thank my family, including Victoria, Henry, George, Alice, and Lucy, and my friends Erik Lundin, Owen Barnes, and Anna Stark.

About the reviewers

Derrek Landauer teaches middle school math and mentors students in an Air Force Research Lab rocketry science program. He earned a bachelor of science in electrical engineering from the University of Texas at El Paso in 2011. His work history spans industry and academia. While attending school, he was involved in defense research projects and was also a lab instructor. He later spent a couple of years managing the network and server infrastructure across four facilities for a subsidiary of a Fortune 100 company. His software development background ranges from programming microprocessors and operating systems to full stack web development.

Dobrin Ganev is a software developer with years of experience working in various development environments, ranging from finance to business process management. In recent years, he has focused on geospatial development and data analytics using JavaScript, Python, Scala, and R. He has extensive knowledge of open source geospatial software and the ESRI platform. He is also skilled in Node.js, React.js, and GraphQL. Dobrin recently authored a video course entitled *Hands-On Full Stack Web Development with GraphQL and React*, published by *Packt*.

Packt is searching for authors like you

If you're interested in becoming an author for Packt, please visit `authors.packtpub.com` and apply today. We have worked with thousands of developers and tech professionals, just like you, to help them share their insight with the global tech community. You can make a general application, apply for a specific hot topic that we are recruiting an author for, or submit your own idea.

Table of Contents

To make the mechanic's work as simple as possible, we need to focus foremost on the familiarity of our code. It's not simple to do this because different things are familiar to different people, but, on the whole, we can take heed from the following guides:

- Don't stray too far from common design patterns
- Be consistent with syntax and presentation
- Lend clarity to unfamiliar problem domains

The last point alludes to *unfamiliar problem domains*. This is something that you, as the programmer, will have to think about when it comes to each code base you work on. To discern if something can be considered unfamiliar, you can ask yourself: *Would another programmer working within another industry be able to understand this with little introduction?*

Usability

While maintainability is predominantly about catering to other programmers, usability is about catering to *all* users, whoever they may be. We can say that there are two broad groups of users that are engaged in our service:

- People wishing to wield the power of our code via interfaces (GUIs, APIs, and so on)
- People wishing to make changes to our code to accomplish new tasks or fix bugs

Usability is about making our code, and the functions and interactions it enables, as useful and easy to use as possible for the full gamut of users. All code is written with at least one use case in mind, and so it is fair to judge code based on the extent to which it fulfills that purpose. Usability, however, goes further than this. Usability is not only about fulfillment of user requirements; it's about creating experiences that enable a user to achieve their goals with minimal hassle, time, and cognitive effort.

Usability is vital whether we are creating user interfaces on the web or deeply embedded server infrastructure that'll rarely see the light of day. In both cases, there are users we are providing for, and so we must care about usability.

Have a look at this function's signature and try to discern how you would go about using it:

```
function checkIsNewYear(
  configuration,
  filter,
  formatter,
  MDY,
  SMH
) {...}
```

This function is a real function signature from a code base I once worked on. It had no documentation and the code within it was spaghetti. It was used to calculate whether a given time could be considered a *new year* and would decide when a *Happy New Year* message would be shown to a user. It's incredibly unclear how to use it though, or how it works. Some open questions I would have upon discovering this function might be as follows:

- What is *configuration* and what is available to configure in such a simple function?
- Presumably, SMH is *seconds, minutes, and hours*, but what kind of value is it expected to be? An object?
- Presumably, MDY is *months, days, and years*, but what kind of value is it expected to be? An object?
- What year does the function compare the passed date for when discerning whether it is a *new year*?
- Would any date in the ostensible *new year* work or only, for example, January 1?
- Why are there *filter* and *formatter* arguments and what do they do? Are they optional?
- What does the function return? A Boolean? The *formatter* argument would suggest not.
- Why can't I just pass a date object instead of individual date components?

The function may do as required, but, as you can see, it's not very usable. It takes significant time and cognitive effort to figure out how it works. To figure it out fully, we'd have to study its usages in other parts of the code and try to decipher the spaghetti within. As a *user* of this function, I would personally find the entire process utterly painful.

Usability is, if anything, about avoiding this pain and burden. As programmers, we engage in the creation of abstractions to simplify complex tasks, but all the preceding code achieves is further complication of a simple problem.

User stories

Usability is the degree to which something is easy to use for a given purpose. Its purpose is defined by a well-understood model of a problem and a set of clear requirements. A useful technique for articulating these purposes is via *user stories*, made famous by Scrum and Agile methodologies. User stories typically take the following form:

As a {persona}, I want to {want}, so that {purpose}...

Here are some examples of the types of user stories you'd expect if we were designing a *Contacts* application:

- As a **user**, I want to **add a new contact** so that **I can later recall that contact from my contacts list**.
- As a **user**, I want to **delete a contact** so that **I will no longer see that contact in my contacts list**.
- As a **user**, I want to **easily find a contact by their surname** so that **I can contact them**.

User stories help to define the purposes that you are catering towards and help to focus the mind on the perspective of the user. Whether you're creating a five-line function or a ten-thousand-line system, it's always worth planning out your user stories.

Intuitive design

To design something intuitively is to design it so that users don't have to dedicate cognitive effort to figure out how something works. The idea at the core of intuitive design is that *it just works*.

When we write code, we are partaking in its design, its grand architecture, its functionality, and its line-by-line syntax. All of these are vital parts of that design. Using intuitive patterns of design is vital to crafting usable code. All users are attuned to a set of patterns that are employed on their level of abstraction. Here are some examples:

- **In a GUI**: Using an X button to indicate exiting a program or process
- **In code**: A function or method starting with *is* indicates a Boolean return value
- **In a GUI**: Using green for affirmative actions and red for negative actions
- **In code**: Upper-casing constants, for example, `VARIABLE_NAME`
- **In a GUI**: Using a floppy disk icon to indicate the concept of saving

These are the assumptions and expectations that many users carry around with them as they navigate software. Tapping into these assumptions means that your code and the interactions it facilitates can be monumentally easier to use.

Accessibility

Accessibility is a key principle within usability that states the importance of catering to all users, regardless of their abilities and circumstances. Usability tends to concern itself with the user as if they are a single entity. We usually make specific assumptions about the user, bestowing them with a set of characteristics and capabilities that may not be reflected in reality. Accessibility, however, is about the real users who will end up having to use whatever you've created. These real users are a diverse set of individuals and may have all manner of differences. When we talk about accessibility in software, we are usually concerned with types of differences that directly affect a person's ability to make use of that software. These may include the follows:

- Learning disorders or differences such as dyslexia.
- Physical disabilities. For example, limited mobility of the hands or blindness.
- Developmental disorders such as Autism and ADHD.
- Less access to technology due to mobility, economy, or infrastructure.

In addition to these, there are many other differences that span the gamut of human existence, so we should always be ready to learn and adapt according to new needs and differences that we encounter among our users.

We are engaged in the creation of web applications, both on the server and in the browser. As JavaScript programmers, we sit very close to the interfaces that are served to end users. Therefore, it's vital that we have an excellent grasp of accessibility on the web. This includes an awareness of the **Web Content Accessibility Guidelines** (**WCAG 2.0**) published by the W3C, which include the following provisions:

- Provide text alternatives for any non-text content (guideline 1.1)
- Make all functionality available from a keyboard (guideline 2.1)
- Make text content readable and understandable (guideline 3.1)

Accessibility is not only about the non-programmer end user. As mentioned, we should consider other programmers to also be our *users* in the same sense as the *end users* of GUIs or other web interfaces. It is vital that we cater to other programmers. Some programmers are blind or partially sighted. Some programmers have learning or cognitive difficulties. Not all programmers work on the latest and fastest hardware. Neither do all programmers understand all the things you may take for granted. It's important to take all of these things into consideration in the code we write.

Having now finished this chapter, you may have a sense of feeling overwhelmed by the number of tenets, principles, and guidelines. Things may seem complex, but they aren't if we follow one simple rule—**always focus on the user**. Also, remember that other programmers who may work on your code *are* your users as well.

As programmers, we sit in a position where we wield unprecedented power in helping to define the behaviors that people conduct in the execution of all manner of tasks. The original programmers who worked at Twitter, Google, or Microsoft likely did not foresee the number of times their code would run. They probably couldn't have originally imagined how many humans their code would end up affecting. We should always remain humble to this power and try in earnest to be accountable to all of the users we serve, and all the myriad tasks they seek to carry out. If you were to come away with one thing from this chapter, I hope it would be simply this: a humble and continued consideration of the user, in every line of code you write.

Summary

In this chapter, we've explored the vital tenets of reliability, efficiency, maintainability, and usability. Using these tenets as lenses through which we can look at our code bases ensures that we will be far more likely to write cleaner code. One of the most important things we've learned in this chapter is always to consider the human in the code we write. The user may be a human sitting on the other side of a GUI or a fellow programmer making use of our APIs. Either way, being constantly aware of this human is vital.

In the next chapter, we'll continue the theme of studying the underlying characteristics of clean code by looking at the enemies to be aware of, such as cargo-cult programming and ego.

3 The Enemies of Clean Code

By now, we should have a pretty clear picture of what we mean when we say *clean code*. In the previous chapter, we explored the tenets of reliability, efficiency, maintainability, and usability. Together, these guide us toward cleaner code, but if we aren't careful, we can still get caught out. In this chapter, we'll explore the *enemies* of clean code: things that may prevent us from writing code that is reliable, efficient, maintainable, or usable.

None of these enemies should be considered *your* enemies; instead, they should be thought of as agitators of clean code. We need to take a holistic view of these potentially harmful factors and keep an eye out for them in our code bases, teams, and workplaces.

Specifically, the enemies we'll be covering in this chapter include the following:

- Enemy #1 – JavaScript
- Enemy #2 – Management
- Enemy #3 – Self
- Enemy #4 – The cargo cult

Enemy #1 – JavaScript

The worst JavaScript feature is also arguably its best. It is a remarkably ubiquitous language that has had to grow and adapt at a very fast rate. The language itself and its position within browser have precipitated this ubiquity.

JavaScript is an incredibly expressive and diverse language, with functional inspiration from Lisp and Scheme, prototypical inheritance from Self, and a C-like syntax that mirrors Java. It is a language of many paradigms. Whether you want to program in a classically object-oriented way, a prototypical way, or an entirely functional way, JavaScript has you covered. JavaScript's flexibility and its position in the broader web stack also make it incredibly accommodating to beginners. You can be immediately productive with it, and this was very much Brendan Eich's original intention. It was intended to be easy to pick up by designers and programmers alike, providing them with the power to script what was once a single-purpose platform: the browser. The once humble browser, however, has since grown into an incredibly broad and complex set of complementary abstractions.

The growth of JavaScript itself and its broad set of applications on both the client and server-side (and beyond!) has meant that the language has been pushed and pulled in a thousand different directions. An overwhelming number of frameworks, libraries, spin-off languages (for example, CoffeeScript), language extensions (for example, JSX), compilers, build tools, and other abstractions have erupted and have sought to leverage JavaScript in new and unique ways. Together, these tools form the JavaScript landscape, and it is an incredibly rich and diverse one. There are countless ways to do the same thing and, as a result, we can barely hope to do anything correctly. That is why I say that JavaScript's ubiquity is both its own worst enemy and its own greatest asset.

In this book, we'll explore foundational concepts that'll teach us to think critically about the nature of clean code and will allow us to write clean code within a language and landscape that don't always cater well code cleanness. JavaScript, if wielded well, will surprise you with its efficacy and expressiveness, and given time and effort, it can be the equal of any other language in terms of its reliability and maintainability.

Enemy #2 – management

Clean code is as much about the processes and principles that foster it as it is about syntax. No matter how perfect and beautiful our code is in isolation, it is usually written as part of a project, alongside a team, and managed by fallible people and fallible processes. And only by seeing and understanding these fallibilities can we hope to prevent or avoid them.

We are all taking on more challenging work nowadays. The days of JavaScript being limited to humble brochure websites with snazzy navigation rollovers are long gone. The creators of the web have been tasked with building ever more ambitious projects. As the technological tower of abstraction grows to new heights, the complexity of these projects will only increase. Due to this, if we are to truly write clean code, we must think broadly about this complexity. We must go beyond our code bases and consider the context of the team and the organization that we work in.

Casting management as an enemy may appear to suggest that managers themselves are blameworthy, but this is not the case. What we'll discover in this section is that it is individual cultural practices that make it challenging to ship clean code. Among these is the pressure to ship, bad metrics, and a lack of ownership.

Pressure to ship

The pressure to ship code, usually because of a deadline or other managerial dictates, is an ever-present and nasty force in the world of software. To the outside stakeholder or manager, a deadline is a great thing; it seems to provide certainty and accountability, but to the people working on the project, it might only be seen as enforcing unwelcome compromises. Sometimes, the first compromise that's made is that of code quality. This does not happen intentionally but is just a natural result of prioritizing completion over quality.

 A **stakeholder**, in this context, is any individual or organization that relies on the output of your work. Usual stakeholders include project managers, other teams within the same organization, outside clients, and users.

When there are pressures to ship, there are a few ways in which code quality can slowly atrophy. These include the following:

- **Documentation**: Developers, when rushed, will not be able to take the necessary time to ensure their code and its APIs are correctly documented. Existing documentation will atrophy.
- **Architecture**: Developers will begin to focus on the most necessary changes they need to make, ignoring the larger architectural structure of the code and how it all inter-relates. Dependencies will become confused and architectures will splinter over time, eventually creating spaghetti code.

- **Consistency**: Both architecturally and in terms of syntax, consistency will begin to suffer. Multiple different developers, possibly siloed away from each other, are rushed to build things in the fastest possible way. Without intending to, they may neglect communication and the establishment of standards, leading to less consistency.
- **Testing**: Writing tests often takes time, as does refactoring tests to suit new requirements. Existing tests are liable to be disabled or deleted. New tests won't be written because there simply isn't time.
- **Best practices**: When their time is stretched, developers will begin to take shortcuts in their code, not taking the care and attention that's required to make sure their software is suited for its purpose. They'll skirt best practices and instead opt for speedy and hacked-together solutions. On the web, this can often result in a less accessible and usable UI.

The preceding items are the first to go when deadlines begin to loom. If we're not careful, we can end up with the following second-order effects:

- **Bugginess**: With testing and documentation absent, and the code's architectural foundations under threat, flaky and buggy code will begin to become the norm. Many of these bugs may be caught in the Q&A process, but many others will surface to users. The fragility of the code and its APIs and UIs will increase, putting an increased burden on users.
- **Unhappy users**: Due to the increase in the number of bugs that surface to users and the software's decreased level of usability, their level of productivity and happiness will decrease. They may begin to avoid or abandon the platform in search of a higher-quality alternative.
- **Burned-out developers**: Tired developers, having had to forgo their best principles continually, will begin to become burned out. They may become depressed at the prospect of continuing their work on the team. With their mental health and general fulfillment under threat, they will start to leave.

All of these effects, when they last long enough, can coalesce and result in the failure of a project. Therefore, it is of vital importance to address the underlying pressure that is forcing such recklessly high speed. The pressure to ship code quickly is a pressure that's usually instigated by forces that do not have a strong working knowledge of the slow degeneration that can occur in software projects. This lack of knowledge may, in part, be due to them being insulated from the long-term effects of their decisions. They may assume that, when something is shipped and meets the stakeholders' approval, that's the end of it. But as we know, just because quickly shipped code meets immediate demands doesn't mean it abides by good levels of quality. Bad-quality code can have many adverse knock-on effects that are only realized in full many weeks or months after implementation. Months later, stakeholders may find themselves annoyed at the slowdown and degradation in quality, not realizing that it was the pressure they originally applied that led to it.

The solution to this mess lies in a crucial compromise between *time to ship* and *technical debt*. Technical debt accrues over time. It describes deficits that need to be addressed to keep the code base healthy and in good working order. This may include fixing bugs, writing tests, refactoring old modules, or integrating tools to improve code quality. Fundamentally, technical debt is all work that, ideally, would be part of the natural development cycle but, because of time constraints, it is pushed aside until later. There are other factors that dictate the proliferation of technical debt, but time is the biggest one. Not paying off our technical debt is a sure way to ensure code atrophy and eventual failure of the project.

There are countless pieces of advice and processes that you can utilize when it comes to project management. I won't be going into them here, but I will share some heuristics that you can use to ensure a healthy code base:

- **Do not ship a feature or fix without tests**. Without tests, a regression could occur at any time. Tests are a defensive technique to ensure the correctness of our code on a continued basis.
- **Pay off technical debt** frequently. Possibly once a week, or twice a month, try to have everyone work on technical debt, that is, any work that's believed to increase the health of the code base.
- **Communicate regularly** with stakeholders to express constraints and costs related to code and project health. Do not over-promise shipment or under-sell problems.

We, as developers, are not always in control of the way that projects are managed. Nonetheless, we should always feel comfortable broaching concerns and advocating for processes that foster clean code. Chapter 18, *Communication and Advocacy*, goes into more detail on how we can go about this.

Bad metrics

There are seemingly no industries in the world that can escape metrics. The crazed obsession with measuring things is as much a cult-like obsession as it is a genuine need that produces necessary introspection and change. In the world of software engineering, we are not strangers to this need. As programmers, we are very interested in metrics that provide us with insights into our code:

- How many bugs are there?
- How long does this code take to run?
- How much test coverage do I have?

Managers and other stakeholders, however, will usually harbor their own interests and metrics. The more infamous among these are the metrics that attempt to measure a developer's output or productivity:

- How many lines of code or commits are there?
- How many features did we ship?
- How many lines of documentation did we write?

These are good questions if they're asked for the right reasons. For example, lines of code can be a useful metric if we're using them as a proxy for complexity when discussing whether to refactor specific classes/utilities. But many metrics are entirely divorced from the thing they are attempting to measure.

A non-technical manager or stakeholder may assume that writing a certain amount of code should always take the same amount of time. They may be confused when a developer who once wrote 200 lines of code in a single day has recently taken 10 days to commit only 10 lines of code. Their confusion, of course, demonstrates a gross misunderstanding of the programming process and its chaotic complexity. But these misunderstandings are rife, so we need to be wary of them.

The clear solution to bad metrics is to push for and create better metrics. And to create good metrics, it is essential to know what underlying question we're trying to answer and then brainstorm ways of answering that question. Let's take a look at an example:

The question	The bad metric	Example of why it's bad	A better metric or approach
Are we being productive?	Lines of code/commits	A programmer could reasonably take many days to solve a crucial bug that only requires a one-line change.	Ask developers and explore what is dragging their productivity down; have team retrospectives to discover areas of improvement.
Are we delivering value to users?	Number of features shipped	Users may receive more benefit from fewer features that are of high quality.	Build metrics or A/B experiments to judge which features are being used and enjoyed. Focus on the quality of each feature.

Are we writing useful documentation?	Lines of documentation	Developers may only end up documenting the things they know well, not the areas of the code base that are most in need of documentation.	Create a metric that tracks the usage of documentation. Discern what areas of code are under-documented by asking developers.
Do we have a well-tested code base?	Test coverage	If it only measures whether certain lines of code are called, then it could be fooled with only a handful of very broad integration tests.	Use traditional test coverage in combination with other metrics. Keep track of areas of regression where bugs often occur.
Do we have a buggy code base?	Number of bugs	A code base may have many bugs in an area of the app that is virtually unused. Bugs in certain areas may be unreported.	Don't count bugs; instead, focus on and measure user happiness and developer happiness. Prioritize bugs based on how they are affecting your users.

Fixation on bad metrics within an organization or team can lead to the wrong things being optimized. Developers who are more concerned with writing more lines of code will be less interested in the underlying quality of their code. Developers who are pushed to release more features will compromise on best practices and clean code, optimizing for speed and shipment.

It's important to ensure that any metrics we track are tempered by reality and that we do not judge success based purely on those metrics. Be especially wary when you see metrics running in opposition to our principles of clean code. Over time, as well, if a metric is chased too ambitiously, it may end up corrupting the very thing it was trying to measure. This is done via an effect known as **Goodhart's law**:

> *"When a measure becomes a target, it ceases to be a good measure."*
>
> *– Marilyn Strathern*

Lack of ownership

Ownership is a key tenet of a healthy code base and relies on individuals having a stake in the health of their code. Ownership here doesn't mean that a piece of code belongs to an individual and nobody else can work on it. Instead, it means that a piece of code is fostered by an individual or a group of people, with its ongoing health and reliability a key priority.

A lack of ownership can lead to the key tenets of clean code suffering in the following ways:

- **Reliability**: The code's correctness and stability can atrophy over time as new changes are made that unknowingly create fragility. The code's ongoing stability is not monitored or cared for.
- **Efficiency**: The code is not measured or observed directly by anyone, with an underlying assumption that it just works. Over time, its efficiency may wane.

- **Maintainability**: Having many non-owners making swift and ill-considered changes can result in a non-cohesive architecture that makes ongoing maintenance more difficult in the long run.
- **Usability**: The documentation and general usability of the code will not be thought about or monitored by anyone, leading to its atrophy and, eventually, a piece of software that is complicated and burdensome to use.

Properly applied ownership can fundamentally change the otherwise burgeoning atrophy of the preceding tenets:

- **Reliability**: The code's correctness and ongoing stability will be cared for and monitored
- **Efficiency**: The code will be measured and assessed for efficiency on an ongoing basis
- **Maintainability**: The code will retain a singular vision for its architecture and syntax
- **Usability**: Documentation will be constantly updated and the code's usability will be an ongoing concern

Fundamentally, ownership is about an individual or a team that has a level of **ongoing concern** for the code. For this to occur, a level of ego or pride is necessary. An individual or team must have some kind of stake in the ongoing health of the code. It is often the organizational or managerial culture that leads to a healthy or unhealthy level of ownership, and so, again, it is vital to properly communicate and advocate processes and dynamics that will allow us, the programmers, to ensure our code's cleanliness and health.

There are also more severe and unimagined results of a lack of ownership. Due to the lack of pride and feeling of guardianship over our work, burnout becomes more likely as programmers aren't able to actualize their need to feel a sense of pride and self-worth regarding their work. Due to no ownership, team members may not be able to foster a high level of understanding in any one area, meaning that the general knowledge of the team or organization suffers, with everyone only understanding the code base in a very shallow or cursory way.

Beware of too much ego in ownership! Ego is a delicate trait. There is always the risk of *too much ownership*, which can result in a stubborn and defensive culture where *insiders* don't let *outsiders* make changes, and where strong and self-centered opinions run rife. Beware of this. Remember the key tenets of usability and maintainability. These will guide you toward kindness and openness toward those who would wish to use your code or make changes to it.

Enemy #3 – Self

Programmers, as creators, are forever impressing their version of how something should be upon the world, so it's almost impossible to not, at times, feel a sense of pride over our work. If not kept in check, this can easily spiral into a place where we are writing code to impress people, and to boost feelings of our own superiority, without considering whether the code we're writing is maintainable or usable. But if our natural ego is not allowed to flourish, then we will have no pride in our work and no inclination to foster excellence in what we do. As such, in programming, as in other areas of life, the key is a balance of ego where we retain its good parts without letting its bad parts affect things too much.

 Ego, in this context, is our selfhood; the ways in which we identify with ourselves and how we express ourselves in the world. All programmers have an ego and its effects on the code they write are numerous.

Showing off with syntax

As a younger programmer, I found my ego getting the better of me quite often. I don't presume to say this is a general truth. This is only my experience. Whenever I discovered a new JavaScript idiosyncrasy, I would try to exploit and make use of it in my next piece of code.

One example of this is the use of bitwise operators for their flooring effects. Traditionally, to floor numbers—to round a number down to its nearest whole number—you'd use the native method provided by the language:

```
Math.floor(65.7); // => 65
```

However, at the time, I preferred using bitwise operators to achieve the same result:

```
~~65.7; // => 65
0|65.7; // => 65
```

What is happening here? Bitwise operators (including ~, &, |, and so on) are used to mutate bits on operands, but as a side-effect, they will first convert their operands into 32-bit integers. This means they'll throw away the decimal fraction. To harness this implicit conversion into an integer without changing the value of the integer, we can perform, for example, a double bitwise inversion using the double tilde (~~). This essentially inverts all the bits of the operand and then inverts them again. We could also perform a bitwise OR with a zero (0 | ...), which will always return the bits of the non-zero operand, thus producing the same effect by harnessing the side-effect (the integer conversion) without changing the underlying value.

Crucially, it's important to note that this side-effect does not functionally match the flooring behavior of `Math.floor` for negative numbers. Note how the following two expressions differ:

```
Math.floor(-25.6);  // => 26
~~(-25.6);          // => 25
```

It's easy to see what's alluring about these cryptic techniques. Their usage seems to suggest a high level of language understanding, and that very much appeals to the ego. It's similar to using needlessly long or complex words to convey simple ideas: fun to say but alienating to the listener.

Techniques like this usually result in code that is less maintainable. The maintainers of our code should not be expected to understand the inner workings of rarely used operators and should be able to trust that we would not be recklessly employing side-effects of language internals to achieve results that can clearly be achieved via more familiar and obvious approaches.

Complex or rare syntax is often a vehicle for egotistic code. Another example of this lies in the misuse of logical operators to specify control flow:

```
function showNotification(message) {
  hasUserEnabledNotifications() && (
    new Notification(message).show() &&
    logNotificationShown(message)
  );
}
```

The preceding code can be more conventionally, and clearly, expressed as an *IF* statement:

```
function showNotification(message) {
  if (hasUserEnabledNotifications()) {
    new Notification(message).show();
    logNotificationShown(message);
  }
}
```

This is far clearer, more familiar, and more readable to a larger group of people.

Some people argue that we should be able to freely use the entire language to its full capability, harnessing all its idiosyncrasies and side-effects to write code that is terser and more efficient. This is a fine attitude to take if our only goal is to write code that works. But writing *clean* code is about taking a considered approach, using techniques that allow us to provide more readability and avoiding techniques that do the opposite.

It also helps to remember that, fundamentally, code is about communicating intent. Communication is as much about the listener as it is about the speaker. Egotistic code tends to fall short in this way; it limits the familiarity of your code to an elite few who have been blessed with the same knowledge that you have. This is not ideal. We should always try to take into account the diverse knowledge and capabilities of the people who will have to read, use, and maintain our code. This concern should take precedence over our ego.

Stubborn opinions

Code is rarely written in isolation; we often work with people to bring projects to life. Clean code, therefore, depends on both your approach and the approach of the entire team. A team that owns a code base continuously decides the tools, conventions, and abstractions that they'll use to achieve their goals. As such, members of the team must be able to communicate well and share perspectives, molding these perspectives into a clear outcome. Sometimes, compromise is necessary. And compromise can often hit the ego.

JavaScript and its tools are susceptible to strong opinions. Over time, we each gain experience in working with different approaches and, often through toil and pain, end up having a set of beliefs about which approaches we think are best. These beliefs may not always match those of our colleagues, though. When there is disagreement, the path to resolution is unclear. Without resolution, the team and the code base can splinter, causing more damage.

Imagine the following scenario between Adam and Susan:

> *Adam: We should use the Foo testing framework; it's more reliable and simply better.*
> *Susan: No, we should definitely use Baz; it's far superior and has a proven track record.*

There are likely many different ways this disagreement could be resolved. We could suggest, for example, that both individuals build their case and continue to debate the various merits of each testing framework. That may resolve the issue. But equally, it may not. The argument may persist, drawing a wedge between the individuals and leaving the code base in a state of flux without a firmly chosen testing framework. The paths to resolution are not always clear in cases like this, but what is clear is that resolution is less likely if uncompromising egos are involved. If both Adam and Susan can start to see each other's perspectives, broadening their view and un-entrenching themselves from their own opinions, then the path to resolution becomes much clearer.

Imposter syndrome

Ego, as a delicate trait, is also responsible for our level of faith and belief in our own capabilities and opinions. It is no wonder that having a level of belief in ourselves is vital to the act of creation and problem-solving in programming. In the technology industry especially, **imposter syndrome** seems to be a widespread occurrence. Imposter syndrome is characterized by a feeling of being an *imposter*—that you are somehow not suitable or sufficiently capable for the role you have, while you feel as though others around you are far more capable.

It can be argued that its prevalence in the software industry is due to the inherent complexity and wealth of specialties. We can, at best, hope for a high level of proficiency in a relatively narrow area but will never be expertly knowledgeable in all areas. We are, as we move about in our day-to-day work, ever aware of all the things we don't know, and this can understandably create a level of anxiety and lack of confidence in our own humble abilities. Such a feeling can sometimes cause stress, alienation, and a lack of confidence in our own abilities.

This may yield the following negative outcomes:

- **Lack of decisiveness**: A lack of belief in our own capabilities can result in low levels of confidence when making a decision about our code's architecture; not knowing which route to take can often mean the default route is taken, which is especially liable to the cargo cults.
- **Lack of boldness**: A lack of assertiveness may result in less risk-taking and fewer bold decisions being made, but sometimes such decisions need to be made to move a project or code base forward. For example, picking a more reliable UI or testing framework can be a large and bold risk given the cost of refactoring, but can lead to overall improvements in code health.
- **Lack of communication**: Lacking confidence in our own opinions and skills can result in less vital communication occurring, for example, between a programmer and the stakeholders of a project. Communication here does not mean being outgoing or talkative, but rather identifying key concerns and being sufficiently confident in them to advocate change.

The act of programming is an act of communicating our intent, that is, of impressing upon the world, maybe in a small way, the way we believe a thing should work. It is itself a bold action and a skill that we should not take for granted. If you are reading this and are concerned that you may lack specific traits or capabilities, I offer the following advice: nobody on the planet is fully capable. Everyone has their strengths and weaknesses. It is the diversity of everyone and their varying capabilities that will define the success of a project and code base. Even if you feel a sense of imposter syndrome, acknowledge that it is natural to feel this way and that, in spite of it, you offer more than you might think.

Enemy #4 – The cargo cult

In the early 20th century, it was observed that some Melanesian cultures would carry out rituals that would emulate Western technologies and behaviors, such as building runways and control towers out of wood and clay. They were doing this in the hope that material wealth, such as food, would be delivered to them. These odd rituals arose because they had previously observed cargo being delivered via Western planes and falsely concluded that it was the runway itself that summoned the cargo.

Nowadays, within programming, we use the terms *cargo cult* or *cargo culting* to broadly describe copying patterns and behaviors without fully understanding their true purpose and functionality. When programmers search for a solution online and copy and paste the first piece of code they find without consideration as to its reliability or safety, they are partaking in act of cargo culting, seeking to accomplish some task by utilizing code that appears to be responsible for it in some other context.

Cargo culting typically entails the following process:

1. The person is embedded in a slightly unfamiliar technical context
2. The person sees the effect they wish to emulate
3. The person copies code that appears to produce the desired effect

This act can occur both organizationally and technically. Programmers, sometimes tasked with tying together disparate technical dependencies that they have little expertise in, will often be left with no other option than to cargo cult. And organizations, often without time to consider all the fundamentals, will often end up cargo culting popular behaviors and processes from other organizations.

Cargo culting code

To illustrate the act of cargo culting, let's imagine that a programmer is tasked with adding a new HTTP GET route to their Node.js server. They need to add the /about_us route. They open up the routes.js file and, among its many lines, find the following code:

```
app.use('/admin', (req, res, next) => {
  const admin = await attemptLoadAdminSection(req, res);
  if (admin) {
    next();
  } else {
    res.status(403).end('You are not authorized');
  }
});
```

This code happens to be using a Node.js framework: **Express**. Unfortunately, however, the programmer is not well versed in the Express API. They see the preceding code and seek to emulate it for their own ends:

```
app.use('/about_us', (req, res, next) => {
  attemptLoadAboutSection(req, res);
  next();
});
```

Unfortunately, as you may be able to tell, this programmer has committed the act of cargo culting. They've copied code that's used to route traffic toward the admin section and have assumed that they should use similar code to route traffic toward the about page.

There are a couple of things they've missed in doing so:

- The admin route is, in fact, middleware, which is used to block unauthorized users from accessing /admin
- The app.use() method should only be used for middleware, not for a direct GET route
- Calling next() is something only middleware should be interested in doing

If the programmer had taken the time to read the Express documentation, they would have discovered that the correct way is more akin to the following:

```
app.get('/about_us', (req, res) => {
  loadAboutSection(res);
});
```

This is a very brief example. Often, the act of cargo culting is more complex. It may not involve the direct copying of code, but maybe only the subtle copying of patterns or syntax. We may shake our head at the preceding example, sure of the knowledge that we would never do such a thing, but we likely already do, in less obvious ways.

Programmers that are engaged in a project will often rightfully inherit the naming, syntax, and whitespace conventions from the existing code base. They may do this without thought, naturally reflecting and conforming to the existing paradigms without applying their critical skills at every step. This isn't necessarily negative: it is the sensible upholding of conventions and presentational consistency. These are important qualities. But equally, the mindless copying of such things can often result in the pointless proliferation of redundant code, or worse, negative effects due to misunderstood code.

Imagine you're a first-time programmer and you wanted to add a hobby field to the following slightly bizarre object:

```
const person = {
  "name": ("James"),
  "location": ("London")
};
```

It's easy to imagine that you might be inclined to copy the existing syntax when you add your new field:

```
const person = {
  "name": ("James"),
  "location": ("London"),
  "hobby": ("kayaking")
};
```

This is an entirely reasonable thing for a first-timer to have done. They were embedded in an unfamiliar context, saw an effect they wished to emulate, and so they adopted the pattern that produced the effect. It is even an understandable act by someone experienced, who wants to make the minimal necessary changes to the code surgically and without disturbing its surroundings.

There is nothing egregiously wrong in this code. It's functional. However, if we are to write code that is maximally maintainable and efficient, then we should adopt conventions and syntax that are more widely accepted and conventional. So, in this light, there are two specific problems with the preceding code:

- Wrapping every key name in double quotes (unnecessary!)
- Wrapping every value in parentheses (unnecessary!)

The non-cargo culted version of the file might look like this:

```
const person = {
  name: "James",
  location: "London",
  hobby: "kayaking"
};
```

However, this file and object will likely live on for months and maybe years to come. Nobody will ever question or challenge its syntax as they'll assume it must be like that for a reason. There is comfort and ease in conforming to an established way of doing something. It is often easier not to challenge it. This form of cargo culting is the more insidious type and introduces a lot of inertia to projects and teams. We mindlessly adopt practices without questioning their continuing validity and suitability.

Cargo culting tools and libraries

Just as code can be mindlessly copied, so can tools. As JavaScript programmers, we are exposed to a quickly shifting landscape of tools and libraries. Every month, a new utility or tool seems to be released. The excitement and hyperbole that surrounds some of these tools creates fertile ground for cargo cults to erupt. Programmers may start to use these new tools, convinced of their merit, without building a full understanding of them or properly considering their suitability for the project at hand. Tools may be prescribed by companies or managers, with non-programmers and programmers alike weighing in based purely on a tool's popularity or novelty, without considering how it actually works or how it differs from the current approach.

The *cult* in cargo cults tends to be a very persuasive force, telling us that if we just use this approach or tool, all our problems will be solved. Naturally, this rarely comes to pass. We may only end up exchanging our current set of problems for a new set of problems. So, when deciding upon a tool, whether it is a framework, library, or any third-party abstraction or service, we should always use a considered approach where we ask ourselves the following key questions:

- **Suitability**: Is it the most suitable tool for the problem at hand?
- **Reliability**: Does it work reliably and will it continue to do so?
- **Usability**: Is it simple to use and is it well documented?
- **Compatibility**: Does it integrate well with the existing codebase?
- **Adaptability**: Is it adaptable to our changing needs?

To avoid cargo culting, we should try to abstain from anecdotes and hearsay, instead preferring detailed comparative analyses in which we compare and contrast various possibilities to find the most suitable.

Summary

In this chapter, we gained an appreciation of some of the most prevalent *enemies* of clean code. We discussed how JavaScript itself is a language that, when wielded incorrectly, can invite unclean code. We also explored the pitfalls of both teams and the individual. We learned that clean code is not merely a characteristic of code but a culture that must be fostered both throughout an organization and within our own minds.

In the next chapter, we will explore some well-known and some less well-known principles of clean code and integrate what we've learned so far into some concrete JavaScript abstractions.

4
SOLID and Other Principles

The world of software is riddled with principles and acronyms. There are many firm and entrenched ideas about how we should go about writing code. The sheer quantity of all of them can be overwhelming, making it especially hard to know which path to take when designing an abstraction. JavaScript's ability to accommodate many different paradigms is one of its strengths as a programming language, but it can also make our job harder. It's up to JavaScript programmers to implement their own paradigms.

This chapter, in the hope of making things less complicated, will take various well-known principles and break them down so we can see their underlying intent. We will explore how these principles relate to the tenets of clean code that we have already discussed, enabling us to make our own informed decisions as to what approaches to use in pursuit of clean code.

We'll be covering both object-oriented and functional programming principles. By exploring this range of principles, we'll be able to craft, for ourselves, a map of guiding ideas that will enable us to think critically about how to write clean code in whatever paradigm we're engaged in.

In this chapter, we will be covering the following topics:

- The **Law of Demeter (LoD)**
- SOLID
- The abstraction principle
- Functional programming principles

The Law of Demeter

Before we delve into the SOLID arena, it's useful to explore a less well-known principle, known as LoD, or the principle of least knowledge. This so-called law has three core ideas:

- A unit should have only limited knowledge about other units
- A unit should only talk to its immediate friends
- A unit should not talk to strangers

You may rightfully wonder what it means for a unit to *talk* to a *stranger*. A unit, in this context, is a specific coded abstraction: possibly a function, a module, or a class. And *talking* here means *interfacing with,* such as calling the code of another module or having that other module call your code.

This is a very useful and simple law to learn and then apply to all our programming, whether we're writing an individual line of code or designing an entire architecture. It is, however, often forgotten or ignored.

Let's take the example of the simple act of making a purchase in a shop. We can express this interaction with `Customer` and `Shopkeeper` abstractions:

```
class Customer {}
class Shopkeeper {}
```

Let's also say that the `Customer` class has a wallet where they store their money:

```
class Customer {
  constructor() {
    this.wallet = new CustomerWallet();
  }
}

class CustomerWallet {
  constructor() {
    this.amount = 0;
  }
  addMoney(deposit) {
    this.amount += deposit;
  }
  takeMoney(debit) {
    this.amount -= debit;
  }
}
```

A simplified version of an interaction between the `Shopkeeper` and the `Customer` may go something like the following globally:

```
class Shopkeeper {
  processPurchase(product, customer) {
    const price = product.price();
    customer.wallet.takeMoney(price);
    // ...
  }
}
```

This may look okay, but let's consider a real-life analogy of this interaction. The shopkeeper takes the wallet from the customer's pocket and then proceeds to open the wallet and take the desired amount without in any way interacting with the customer directly.

It's immediately obvious that this would never be a socially appropriate interaction in real life, of course, but crucially, the shopkeeper is making assumptions outside of their remit. The customer may wish to pay using a different mechanism, or may not even have a wallet. The nature of the customer's payment is their own business. This is what we mean when we say *only talk to friends*: you should only interface with abstractions that you should have knowledge of. The shopkeeper here should not (and would not) have knowledge of the customer's wallet and so should not be *talking* to it.

Taking this learnings on board, we can program a cleaner abstraction as follows:

```
class Shopkeeper {
  processPurchase(product, customer) {
    const price = product.price();
    customer.requestPayment(price);
    // ...
  }
}
```

This now seems more reasonable. The `Shopkeeper` is talking to the `Customer` directly. The customer, in turn, will *talk to* their `CustomerWallet` instance, retrieving the desired amount and then handing it to the shopkeeper.

We have all likely written code that somewhat violates the LoD. Of course, the code we write is not always as contrived or neatly exemplified by real-life as the interaction between a shopkeeper and a customer, but nonetheless, the LoD still applies. We can illustrate this further with a typical piece of JavaScript that is responsible for displaying a message to the user via the **document object model (DOM)**:

```
function displayHappyBirthday(name) {
  const container = document.createElement('div');
  container.className = 'message birthday-message';
```

```
container.appendChild(
    document.createTextNode(`Happy Birthday ${name}!`)
);
document.body.appendChild(container);
}
```

This is quite typical and idiomatic frontend JavaScript. To display the `Birthday` message within a document, we first construct the string ourselves and place it in a text node, which itself is appended to a `<div>` element with `message` and `birthday-message` classes. We then take this DOM tree and append it to the document so it can be viewed by the user.

 The DOM is a set of APIs that enables us to interface with a parsed HTML document, usually within the browser. The DOM, as a term, is also used to describe the tree of nodes generated by this parsing process. So, a DOM tree can be derived from a given HTML document, but we can also construct our own DOM trees and manipulate them freely.

Does the preceding code abide by the LoD? Our abstraction here, the `displayHappyBirthday` function, is concerned with the concept of a happy birthday message and is *talking* directly to the DOM. The DOM, however, is not its friend. The DOM is an implementation detail—a stranger—in the concept of a `Happy Birthday` message. The `Happy Birthday` message mechanism should not be required to have knowledge about the DOM. It would, therefore, be appropriate to build another abstraction that bridges these two strangers:

```
function displayMessage(message, className) {
    const container = document.createElement('div');
    container.className = `message ${className}`;
    container.appendChild(
        document.createTextNode(message)
    );
    document.body.appendChild(container);
}
```

Here, we have a more generic `displayMessage` function that is interfacing directly with the DOM—a friend. Our `displayHappyBirthday` function could then be changed so that it purely interacts with this `displayMessage` abstraction:

```
function displayHappyBirthday(name) {
    return displayMessage(
        `Happy Birthday ${name}!`,
        'birthday-message'
    );
}
```

This code can now be said to be more loosely coupled to the implementation of `displayMessage`. We could later decide to change the exact mechanism that we use to display messages without altering the `displayHappyBirthday` function at all. We've therefore bolstered the maintainability of code. By generalizing a common piece of functionality—displaying a message—we also make future features much more seamless—for example, displaying a `Happy New Year` message:

```
function displayHappyNewYear(name) {
  return displayMessage(
    `Happy New Year! ${name}`,
    'happy-new-year-message'
  );
}
```

The LoD, at its core, is concerned with which abstractions we feel should interface with other abstractions. It does not provide guidance as to what a *friend* or a *stranger* is or what it means for a unit to only have limited knowledge of other units. The law challenges us to define these terms for ourselves, alongside the abstractions we're building. It's our responsibility to stop and consider how our abstractions are interfacing, and whether perhaps we should design them differently.

I chose to write about this principle first as I feel it is the most memorable and most generally useful tool for writing clean code with clean abstractions.

Next, we'll be discussing SOLID and other principles that all, in their own ways, complements the LoD.

SOLID

SOLID is a commonly packaged set of principles that are useful when constructing both individual modules or larger architectures. Specifically, it is an acronym that stands for five specific **object-oriented programming (OOP)** design principles:

- **Single responsibility principle(SRP)**
- Open-closed principle
- Liskov substitution principle
- Interface segregation principle
- Dependency inversion principle

It is not vital to remember these names or even the acronym itself, but the ideas behind each of these principles are useful. In this section, we're going to explore each principle alongside JavaScript examples. It's important to note that, while SOLID relates mostly to OOP, there are deeper truths underlying it that are useful regardless of your programming paradigm.

Single responsibility principle

When we write code, we are constantly building abstractions; when doing this, we are interested in building the right ones, delineated in the right way. The SRP helps us to figure out how to delineate these abstractions by looking at their responsibilities.

Responsibility, in this context, refers to the purpose and area of concern that your abstraction encompasses. A function that validates phone numbers can be said to have a singular responsibility. A function that both validates and normalizes those numbers with their country codes, however, can be said to have two responsibilities. The SRP would tell us that we need to split that abstraction into two separate ones.

The aims of the SRP are to arrive at code that is highly cohesive. Cohesiveness is when an abstraction's parts are all functionally united in some way, where they can all be said to work together to fulfill the abstraction's purpose. A useful question about discerning singular responsibility is: *how many reasons does your abstraction's design have to change*?

We can explore this question using an example. Say that we are tasked with building a small calendar application. We might imagine, initially, that there are two distinct abstractions here:

```
class Calendar {}
class Event {}
```

The `Event` class can be said to contain time and metainformation about an event, and the `Calendar` class can be said to contain events. The basic starting premise is that you can both add and remove one or more `Event` instances to and from a `Calendar` instance. Here, we express the methods used to add and remove events from `Calendar`:

```
class Calendar {
  addEvent(event) {...}
  removeEvent(event) {...}
}
```

Over time, we have to add various other pieces of functionality to our `Calendar`, such as methods for retrieving events within specific dates, and methods to export events in various formats:

```
class Calendar {

  addEvent(event) {...}
  removeEvent(event) {...}
  getEventsBetween(stateDate, endDate) {...}

  setTimeOfEvent(event, startTime, endTime) {...}
  setTitleOfEvent(event, title) {...}

  exportFilteredEventsToXML(filter) {...}
  exportFilteredEventsToJSON(filter) {...}

}
```

Even without implementations, you can see how the addition of all of these methods has created a far more complex class. Technically, all of these methods are related to the functionality of a calendar, so there is an argument for them to remain within one abstraction, but if we go back to the question we posed—*How many reasons does our abstraction's design have to change?*—we can see that the `Calendar` class now has many possible reasons:

- The way time is defined on events may need to change
- The way titles are defined on events may need to change
- The way events are searched for may need to change
- The XML schema may need to change
- The JSON schema may need to change

Given the number of different reasons for potential change, it makes sense to split the change into more appropriate abstractions. The methods for setting the time and title of a particular event (`setTimeOfEvent`, `setTitleOfEvent`), for example, definitely make sense within the `Event` class itself, as they're highly related to the purpose of the `Event` class: to contain details regarding a specific event. And the methods that export to both JSON and XML should also be moved, perhaps into their own class that is solely responsible for the export logic. The following code shows the changes that we've made:

```
class Event {
  setTime(startTime, endTime) {...}
  setTitle(title) {...}
}
```

```
class Calendar {
  addEvent(event) {...}
  removeEvent(event) {...}
  getEventsBetween(stateDate, endDate) {...}
}

class CalendarExporter {
  exportFilteredEventsToXML(filter) {...}
  exportFilteredEventsToJSON(filter) {...}
}
```

As you can hopefully see, each of our abstractions seems inwardly cohesive, and each one encapsulates its responsibilities far more cohesively than would be the case if all of that functionality resided solely within the Calendar class.

The SRP is not only about creating abstractions that are simple to use and maintain, it also allows us to write code that is more focused on its key purpose. Being more focused in this way gives us a clearer path to optimize and test our units of code, which benefits the reliability and efficiency of our codebase. The correct delineation of cohesive abstractions, guided by the SRP, is probably one of the most significant ways you can improve the cleanness of your code.

Open–closed principle

The **open–closed principle** (**OCP**) states the following:

> *Software entities (classes, modules, functions, and so on) should be open for extension, but closed for modification*
>
> *-Meyer, Bertrand (1988)*

When crafting abstractions, we should enable them to be open to extension so that other developers can come along and build upon their behavior, adapting the abstraction to suit their needs. Extension, in this context, is best thought of as a broad term that encompasses all types of adaptation. If a module or function does not behave as we require it to, it would be ideal for us to be able to adapt it to our needs without having to modify it or create our own alternative.

Consider the following `Event` class and `renderNotification` method from our
`Calendar` application:

```
class Event {

  renderNotification() {
    return `
      You have an event occurring in
      ${this.calcMinutesUntil()} minutes!
    `;
  }

  // ...

}
```

We may wish to have a separate type of event that renders a notification prefixed with the
word `Urgent`! to ensure that the user pays more attention to it. The simplest way to
achieve this adaptation is via inheritance of the `Event` class, as follows:

```
class ImportantEvent extends Event {
  renderNotification() {
    return `Urgent! ${super.renderNotification()}`;
  }
}
```

We are prefixing our urgent message by overriding the `renderNotification` method and
calling the super class's `renderNotification` to fill in the remainder of the notification
string. Here, via inheritance, we have achieved extension, adapting the `Event` class to our
needs.

Inheritance is only one way that extension can be achieved. There are various other
approaches that we could take. One possibility is that, in the original implementation of
`Event`, we foresee the need for custom notification strings and implement a way to
configure a `renderCustomNotifcation` function:

```
class Event {

  renderNotification() {
    const defaultNotification = `
      You have an event occurring in
      ${this.calcMinutesUntil()} minutes!
    `;
    return (
      this.config.renderCustomNotification
        ? this.config.renderCustomNotification(defaultNotification)
```

```
          : defaultNotification
    );
  }

  // ...

}
```

This code presumes that there is a `config` object available. We are optionally calling the `renderCustomNotification` and passing the default notification string. If it hasn't been configured, then the default notification string is used anyway. This is crucially different from the inheritance approach in that the `Event` class itself is prescribing the itself is prescribing the possibilities possibilities extension that exist.

Providing adaptability via configuration means that users don't need to worry about the internal implementation knowledge required when extending classes. The path to adaptation is simplified:

```
new Event({
  title: 'Doctor Appointment',
  config: {
    renderCustomNotification: defaultNotification => {
      return `Urgent! ${defaultNotifcation}`;
    }
  }
});
```

This approach requires that your implementation can foresee its most likely adaptations and that those adaptations are predictably internalized into the abstraction itself. However, it is impossible to foresee all needs, and even if we tried to, we would likely end up creating such a complicated and large configuration that users and maintainers would suffer. So there is a balance to strike here: adaptability is a good thing, but we also must balance it with a focused and cohesive abstraction that has a constrained purpose.

Liskov substitution principle

The **Liskov substitution principle** states that types should be able to be replaced by their subtypes without altering the reliability of the program. This is, on the surface, an obscure principle, so it's worth explaining it in terms of a real-world analogy.

Many real-world technological innovations share this characteristic of substitution. A Volvo XC90 is a type of car, as is a Ford Focus. Both provide the common interfaces that we have come to expect from cars. For us, as human users of these vehicles, we can assume that their respective means of operation inherit from a common schema of vehicle operation, such as having a steering wheel, doors, a brake pedal, and so on.

The human assumption is that these two models of car are subtypes of the supertype *car*, and so I as a human can rely on the aspects that they each inherit from their supertype (the car). Another way of phrasing the Liskov substitution principle is: *A consumer of a type should only be concerned with the least specific type necessary to operate it reliably.* To build on the analogy, if we were to program a `Driver` abstraction in code, we would want it to interface generally with all `Car` abstractions rather than writing specific code that relies on specific models of car (such as the Volvo XC90).

To make the Liskov substitution principle a little more concrete, let's dive back into our `Calendar` application example. In the preceding section on the open-closed principle, we explored how to extend the `Event` class via inheritance with a new `ImportantEvent` class:

```
class ImportantEvent extends Event {
  renderNotification() {
    return `Urgent! ${super.renderNotification()}`;
  }
}
```

The assumption implicit in our doing this is that our `Calendar` class and its implementation will not be concerned with whether events are `Event`s or subclasses of `Event`s. We expect that it will treat them the same. The `Calendar` class may have a `notifyUpcomingEvents` method, for example, that iterates through all upcoming events and calls `renderNotification` on each event:

```
class Calendar {

  getEventsWithinMinutes(minutes) {
    return this.events.filter(event => {
      return event.startsWithinMinutes(minutes);
    });
  }

  notifiyUpcomingEvents() {
    this.getEventsWithinMinutes(10).forEach(event => {
      this.sendNotification(
        event.renderNotification()
      );
    });
  }
```

```
    // ...
  }
```

What's crucial here is that the `Calendar` implementation makes no deliberations as to the type of `Event` instance that it is dealing with. In fact, the preceding code (which doesn't account for the entire implementation) only prescribes that event objects have a `startsWithinMinutes` method and a `renderNotification` method.

Related to the Liskov substitution principle is an idea that we've already discussed: the principle of least information (LoD), which drives us to ask: what is the least information that this abstraction requires in order to fulfill its purpose? In the case of `Calendar`, it only needs to prescribe that events have the methods and properties that it will use. There is no good reason for it to make deliberations beyond that. Not only can the `Calendar` implementation now deal with subclasses of events, but it can deal with any objects that supply the desired properties and methods.

Interface segregation principle

The **interface segregation principle** is concerned with keeping interfaces highly cohesive, engaged in only one task or a set of tasks that are highly related. It states that *no client should be forced to depend on methods that it does not use.*

This principle is similar in spirit to the principle of single responsibility: its goal is to ensure that you create focused and highly-cohesive abstractions that are only concerned with a single area of responsibility. But instead of making you consider the concept of responsibility itself, it makes you look at the interfaces that you're creating and consider whether they're appropriately segregated.

Consider a local government office. They have a paper form (let's call it Form 1A) that it uses to change a person's details. It is a form that's existed for over 50 years. Via this form, a local citizen can change a number of their details, including, but not limited to, the following:

- A change of name
- A change of marital status
- A change of address
- A change of council tax discount status (student/elderly)
- A change of disability status

As you can imagine, it's a very complex and dense form, with many independent sections that a citizen must ensure they fill out correctly. We've all likely been exposed to the bureaucratic complexity of government paperwork, as shown in the following:

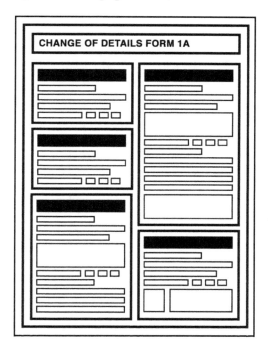

Form 1A provides a set of interfaces to the various change functions that are provided by the local government office. The interface segregation principle asks us to consider whether this form is forcing its clients to depend on methods that they don't use. In this context, the clients are the users of the form, the citizens, and the methods are all of the available functions that the form provides: the ability to register a name change, an address change, and so on.

As is hopefully obvious by now, Form 1A does not follow the interface segregation principle very well. If we were to redesign it, we would likely separate out the individual functions it serves into their own independent forms. The way we'd do this is by employing something we learned at the beginning of the chapter: the principle of least information (LoD), which asks us a very simple question: What's the least amount of information each abstraction (for example, changing one's address) requires? We can then choose to only include in each form what is needed to fulfill its function:

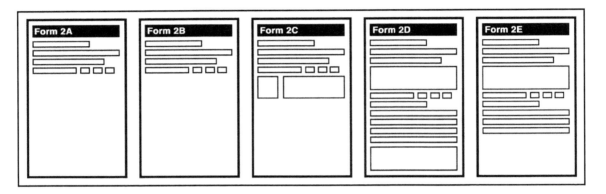

To separate out and then only include the necessary fields in paper forms such as these may seem quite obvious, but it's something programmers continually neglect to do effectively within their coded abstractions. The interface segregation principle reminds us of the importance of properly separating out our abstractions into interfaces that are distinct and internally cohesive. Doing so has the following benefits:

- **Increased reliability**: Having properly isolated interfaces that are truly decoupled makes code easier to test and verify, thereby aiding its general reliability and stability over time.
- **Increased maintainability**: Having segregated interfaces means that changes to one needn't affect the others. As we saw in the layout of Form 1A, the positioning and space available are heavily dependent on each part of the form. Once we have decouple these dependencies, however, we are free to maintain and change each one as we see fit, without worrying about the others.
- **Increased usability**: Having interfaces that are separated according to their purpose and function means that users are able to understand and navigate the interfaces with far less time and cognitive effort. The users are the consumers of our interfaces, and so are the most dependent on the interfaces being clearly delineated.

Dependency inversion principle

The dependency inversion principle states the following:

- High-level modules should not depend on low-level modules. Both should depend on abstractions (that is, interfaces)
- Abstractions should not depend on details. Details (such as concrete implementations) should depend on abstractions

The first point may remind you of the LoD. It is largely talking about the same concept: the separation of high-level from low-level.

Our abstractions should be separated (decoupled) in such a way that we can easily change low-level implementation details at a later date without having to refactor all of our code. The dependency inversion principle, in its second point, suggests that we do this via intermediary abstractions through which the high-level modules can interface with the low-level details. These intermediary abstractions are sometimes known as adapters, as they adapt a low-level abstraction for consumption by a high-level abstraction.

 Why is it called dependency inversion? A high-level module may initially depend on a low-level module. In languages that provide OOP concepts such as abstract classes and interfaces (a type of schematic for classes), such as Java, it can be said that a low-level module may end up depending upon the interface, as it is the interface that provides the scaffolding on which the low-level module is implemented. The high-level module also depends on this interface, so that it may utilize the low-level module. We can see here how the dependencies are inverted so that both high- and low-level modules depend on the same interface.

Considering our `Calendar` application once again, let's say that we wanted to implement a way to retrieve events happening within a specific radius of a fixed location. We may choose to implement a method like so:

```
class Calendar {
  getEventsAtLocation(targetLocation, kilometerRadius) {

    const geocoder = new GeoCoder();
    const distanceCalc = new DistanceCalculator();

    return this.events.filter(event => {

      const eventLocation = event.location.address
        ? geocoder.geocode(event.location.address)
        : event.location.coords;
```

```
      return distanceCalc.haversineFormulaDistance(
        eventLocation,
        targetLocation
      ) <= kilometerRadius / 1000;

    });

  }

  // ...

}
```

The `getEventsAtLocation` method here is responsible for retrieving events that are within a certain radius (measured in kilometers) from a given location. As you can see, it uses both a `GeoCoder` class and a `DistanceCalculator` class to achieve its purpose.

The `Calendar` class is a high-level abstraction, concerned with the broad concepts of a calendar and its events. The `getEventsAtLocation` method, however, contains a lot of location-related details that are more of a low-level concern. The `Calendar` class here is concerns itself with which formula to utilize on the `DistanceCalculator` and the units of measurement used in the calculation. You can see how, for example, the `kilometerRadius` argument must be divided by `1000` to get the distance in meters, which is then compared to the distance returned from the `haversineFormulaDistance` method.

All of these details should not be the business of a high-level abstraction, such as `Calendar`. The dependency inversion principle asks us to consider how we can abstract away these concerns to an intermediary abstraction that acts as a bridge between high-level and low-level. One way in which we may accomplish this is via a new class, `EventLocationCalculator`:

```
const distanceCalculator = new DistanceCalculator();
const geocoder = new GeoCoder();
const METRES_IN_KM = 1000;

class EventLocationCalculator {
  constructor(event) {
    this.event = event;
  }

  getCoords() {
    return this.event.location.address
      ? geocoder.geocode(this.event.location.address)
      : this.event.location.coords
  }
```

```
    calculateDistanceInKilometers(targetLocation) {
      return distanceCalculator.haversineFormulaDistance(
        this.getCoords(),
        targetLocation
      ) / METRES_IN_KM;
    }
  }
```

This class could then be utilized by the `Event` class in its own `isEventWithinRadiusOf`
method. An example of this is shown in the following code:

```
class Event {

  constructor() {
    // ...
    this.locationCalculator = new EventLocationCalculator();
  }
  isEventWithinRadiusOf(targetLocation, kilometerRadius) {
    return locationCalculator.calculateDistanceInKilometers(
      targetLocation
    ) <= kilometerRadius;
  }

  // ...

}
```

Therefore, all the `Calendar` class needs to concern itself with is the fact that `Event`
instances have `isEventWithinRadiusOf` methods. It needs no information and makes no
prescriptions as to the specific implementation that determines distances; the details of that
are left to our lower-level `EventLocationCalculator` class:

```
class Calendar {
  getEventsAtLocation(targetLocation, kilometerRadius) {
    return this.events.filter(event => {
      return event.isEventWithinRadiusOf(
        targetLocation,
        kilometerRadius
      );
    });
  }

  // ...

}
```

The dependency inversion principle is similar to other principles that are related to the delineation of abstractions, such as the interface segregation principle, but is specifically concerned with dependencies and how these dependencies are directed. As we design and build abstractions, we are, implicitly, setting up a dependency graph. For example, if we were to map out the dependencies for the implementation that we arrived at, then it would look something like this:

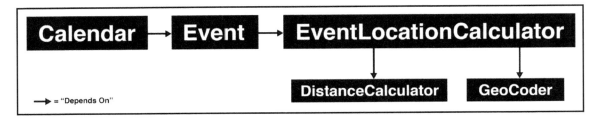

It's incredibly useful to draw dependency graphs such as these. They are a useful way to explore the true complexity of your code, and can often highlight areas of possible improvement. Most importantly, they let us observe where, if anywhere, our low-level implementations (details) impact our high-level abstractions. Only when we see such situations can we remedy them. So, as you advance through this book and beyond, always have in your mind's eye a graph of the dependencies; it'll help to steer you toward more decoupled, and thus more reliable, code.

The dependency inversion principle is the very last of the SOLID acronym, and SOLID, as we've seen, is chiefly concerned with *how* we go about building abstractions. The next principle we'll cover binds together a lot of the content we've covered so far, as it is the principle of abstraction itself. If we remember nothing else from this chapter, then we should, at least, remember the **abstraction principle**.

The abstraction principle

In the first chapter, we introduced the concept of a tower of abstractions, and the idea that every abstraction is a simplified lever to hidden complexity. The principle of abstraction within programming states the following:

Implementation should be separate from interface.

An implementation is the complex underside of an abstraction: the part that it's hiding. The interface is the simplified topside. That is why we say that abstraction is a simplified lever to hidden complexity. The craft of creating abstractions that separate implementation from interface to just the right degree is not as simple as it may seem. As such, the programming world provides two warnings for us:

- **Don't repeat yourself (DRY)**: A warning that tells us to avoid writing code that duplicates other code we have written. If you find yourself having to repeat yourself, then this indicates that you've failed to abstract something, or have under-abstracted something.
- **You aren't gonna need it (YAGNI)**: Also known as **keep it simple, stupid! (KISS)**, this warning tells us to be wary of over-abstracting code that does not need to be abstracted. It's the polar opposite of DRY, and serves to remind us that we should not attempt abstraction unless it's warranted (if we start to repeat ourselves, perhaps).

Between these two warnings, somewhere in the middle, lies the perfect abstraction. Designing abstractions so that they are maximally simple and maximally useful is a balancing act. On the one hand, we can say we have under-abstraction (DRY warns us about this) and, on the other hand, we have over-abstraction (YAGNI warns us about this).

Over-abstraction

Over-abstraction is when too much complexity has been removed or replaced, so that the underlying complexity becomes difficult to leverage. The risk with over-abstraction is that we either remove too much complexity in favor of simplicity or we add new unnecessary complexity that confuses the user of our abstraction.

For example, say that we are in need of a gallery abstraction that we want to use to display a gallery on both our website and various mobile applications. Depending on the platform, the gallery will use the interfaces available to produce the layout. On the web, it would produce HTML and DOM, but on a mobile application, it would use the various native UI SDKs available. The abstraction provides a lever to all that cross-platform complexity.

Our initial requirements for the gallery are quite simple:

- The ability to display one or more images
- The ability to display captions alongside images
- The ability to control the dimensions of individual images

An external team has created a Gallery component for us to use. We open the documentation and see that it has the following example code, showing us how to create a gallery with two images:

```
const gallery = new GalleryComponent(
  [
    new GalleryComponentImage(
      new GalleryComponentImage.PathOfImage('JPEG',
'/foo/images/Picture1.jpg'),
      new GalleryComponentImage.Options({
        imageDimensionWidth: { unit: 'px', amount: 200 },
        imageDimensionHeight: { unit: 'px', amount: 150 },
        customStyleStrings: ['border::yellow::1px']
      }),
      [
        new GalleryComponentImage.SubBorderCaptionElementWithText({
          content: { e: 'paragraph', t: 'The caption for this employee' }
        })
      ]
    }),
    new GalleryComponentImage(
      new GalleryComponentImage.PathOfImage('JPEG',
'/foo/images/Picture2.jpg'),
      new GalleryComponentImage.Options({
        imageDimensionWidth: { unit: 'px', amount: 200 },
        imageDimensionHeight: { unit: 'px', amount: 150 },
        customStyleStrings: ['border::yellow::1px']
      }),
      [
        new GalleryComponentImage.SubBorderCaptionElementWithText({
          content: { e: 'paragraph', t: 'The caption for this employee' }
        })
      ]
    })
  ]
);
```

This interface seems very complex for the basic purpose of only displaying a couple of images. Considering our simple requirements, we can say that the preceding interface is evidence of over-abstraction: instead of simplifying the underlying complexity, it has introduced a whole new realm of complexity and various features that we don't even need. It does technically fulfill our requirements, but we must navigate its realm of complexity to achieve what we want.

An abstraction like this, which encodes new complexities and prescribes its own features and naming conventions, is at risk of not only failing to reduce complexity, but also of increasing it! An abstraction has no business in increasing complexity; that is antithetical to the entire point of abstraction.

 Keep in mind that the appropriate level of abstraction is context-dependent. What may be over-abstracted for your use case may be under-abstracted for another. The driver of an F1 racing car would require different levels of abstraction over their engine than a Ford Focus driver. Abstraction, like many clean-code concepts, is audience- and user-dependent.

Over-abstraction can, curiously, also take the form of over-simplification, where levers to the underlying complexity are not made available to us. An oversimplified version of our `GalleryComponent` interface may look like the following:

```
const gallery = new GalleryComponent(
  '/foo/images/PictureOne.jpg',
  '/foo/images/PictureTwo.jpg'
);
```

This minimal interface may seem like the polar opposite of the previous code, and in some ways it is, but curiously, it is also an example of over-abstraction. Remember, abstraction is when we provide a lever to underlying complexity via an interface. In this case, the lever is just too simple, only providing very limited leverage for the complexity that we wish to harness. It does not allow us to add captions or control image dimensions; it only allows us to list a set of images, nothing more.

Having gone through the two previous examples, you've seen how over-abstraction can come in two distinct flavors: one that over-complicates and one that over-simplifies. These are both undesirable.

Under-abstraction

If over-abstraction is when *too much* complexity has been removed or replaced, then under-abstraction is when *too little* complexity has been removed or replaced. This results in a situation where the user of the abstraction then needs to concern themselves with the underlying complexity. Imagine that you have a car that you must drive without a steering wheel or dashboard. You must control it directly via the engine by pulling levers and cranking oily cogs with your bare hands while keeping an eye on the road. We can say that this car has an under-abstracted method of control.

We explored the over-abstracted versions of our gallery component, so let's see what an under-abstracted version might look like:

```
const gallery = new GalleryComponent({
  web: [
    () => {
      const el = document.createElement('div');
      el.className = 'gallery-container';
      return el;
    },
    {
      data: [
        `<img src="/foo/images/PictureOne.jpg" width=200 height=150 />
        <span>The caption</span>`,
        `<img src="/foo/images/PictureTwo.jpg" width=200 height=150 />
        <span>The caption</span>`
      ]
    }
  ],
  android: [
    (view, galleryPrepData) => {
      view.setHasFixedSize(true);
      view.setLayoutManager(new
GridLayoutManager(getApplicationContext(),2));
      return new MyAdapter(getApplicationContext(), galleryPrepData());
    },
    {
      data: [
        ['/foo/images/PictureOne.jpg', 200, 150, 'The Caption']
        ['/foo/images/PictureTwo.jpg', 200, 150, 'The Caption']
      ]
    }
  ]
});
```

This version of `GalleryComponent` seems to be forcing us to define web-specific HTML and Android-specific code. We were, ideally, depending on the abstraction to hide this complexity from us, giving us a simplified interface with which to harness—it hasn't done this. The complexity of writing platform-specific code has not been sufficiently abstracted here, and so we can therefore say that this is an example of under-abstraction.

From the previous code, you can also see that we are being made to repeat the source URL of our image and the caption text. This should remind us of one of the warnings we explored earlier: DRY, which indicates that we have not sufficiently abstracted something.

If we keep an eye out for areas in which we are forced to repeat ourselves, then we can hope to build better abstractions. But be aware that under-abstraction is not always obvious.

Various abstractions can be said to be *leaky abstractions* because they *leak* parts of their complexity upwards, through their interfaces. The previous code is an example of this: we can say that it is leaking the implementation details of its cross-platform complexities upward.

Balanced abstraction

Given what we've learned about under- and over-abstraction, we can say that a balanced abstraction is one that sits neatly in between these two undesirable opposites. The skill of creating a balanced abstraction is both an art and a science, and requires that we have a very good understanding of both the problem domain and the user's capabilities and intents. By employing many of the principles and warnings in this chapter, we can hope to remain balanced in our code building. For the previous example of a GalleryComponent, we should, once again, explore the requirements of the abstraction:

- The ability to display one or more images
- The ability to display captions alongside images
- The ability to control the dimensions of individual images

These, we can say, are the *levers* that we must provide to the underlying cross-platform complexity. Our abstraction should solely aim to expose these levers and no other unnecessary complexity. The following is an example of such an abstraction:

```
const gallery = new GalleryComponent([
  {
    src: '/foo/images/PictureOne.jpg',
    caption: 'The Caption',
    width: 200,
    height: 150
  },
  {
    src: '/foo/images/PictureTwo.jpg',
    caption: 'The Caption',
    width: 200,
    height: 150
  },
]);
```

Via this interface, we can define one or more images, set their dimensions, and define captions for each image. It fulfills all of the requirements without inviting new complexities or leaking complexities from the underlying implementation. This is, therefore, a balanced abstraction.

Functional programming principles

JavaScript allows us to program in a variety of different ways. Many of the examples we've shared so far in this book have been more inclined towards OOP, which primarily uses objects to express problem domains. Functional programming is different in that it uses mostly pure functions and immutable data to express problem domains.

 All programming paradigms are broadly interested in the same thing: making it easier to express problem domains, to communicate our intent as programmers, and to accommodate the creation of useful and usable abstractions. The best principles we adopt from one paradigm may still apply to another, so adopt an open-minded approach!

It's easiest to observe and discuss the difference between OOP and functional programming by exploring an example. Let's imagine that we wish to build a mechanism so that we can fetch paginated data from a server. To achieve this in an object-oriented way, we might create a `PaginatedDataFetcher` class:

```
// An OOP approach

class PaginatedDataFetcher {

  constructor(endpoint, startingPage) {
    this.endpoint = endpoint;
    this.nextPage = startingPage || 1;
  }

  getNextPage() {
    const response = fetch(
      `/api/${this.endpoint}/${this.nextPage}`
    );
    this.nextPage++;
    return fetched;
  }

}
```

The following is an example of how you would use the `PaginatedDataFetcher` class:

```
const pageFetcher = new PaginatedDataFetcher('account_data', 30);

await pageFetcher.getNextPage(); // => Fetches /api/account_data/30
await pageFetcher.getNextPage(); // => Fetches /api/account_data/31
await pageFetcher.getNextPage(); // => Fetches /api/account_data/32
```

As you can see, with each call to `getNextPage`, we retrieve the next page of data. The `getNextPage` method relies on the remembered state of its objects, `endpoint` and `nextPage`, in order to know which URL to request next.

 A **state** can be thought of as the underlying remembered data of any program or piece of code that its results or effects are derived from. The state of a car may mean its current upkeep, its fuel and oil levels, and so on. Likewise, the state of a running program is the underlying data that it derives its functionality from.

Functional programming, as distinct from OOP, is purely interested in the usage of functions and immutable state to achieve its goals. The first mental blocker that people usually encounter when exploring functional programming is related to states, raising questions such as *Where should I store my state?* and *How do I make things change without being able to mutate that state?* We can explore this question by looking at the functionally programmed equivalent of the paginated data fetcher.

We have created a function, `getPage`, to which we will pass an `endpoint` and a `pageNumber`, as follows:

```
// A more functional approach

const getPage = async (endpoint, pageNumber = 1) => ({
  endpoint,
  pageNumber,
  response: await fetch(`/api/${endpoint}/${pageNumber}`)
  next: () => getPage(endpoint, pageNumber + 1)
});
```

When called, the `getPage` function will return an object containing the response from the server, as well as the `endpoint` and `pageNumber` used. In addition to these properties, the object will also contain a function named `next`, which itself, if called, will fire off another request via a subsequent call to `getPage`. It can be used in the following way:

```
const page1 = await getPage('account_data');
const page2 = await page1.next();
const page3 = await page2.next();
```

```
const page4 = await page3.next();

// Etc.
```

You'll notice that, when using this pattern, we only need a reference to the last retrieved page in order to make the next request. Page 3 is retrieved via page 2's returned `next()` function. Page 4 is retrieved via page 3's returned `next()` function.

Our `getPage` function does not mutate any data: it only uses the passed data to derive new data, and therefore, it can be said that it employs immutability. It can also be said that it is a pure function as well, in that, with a given set of input parameters (an `endpoint` and a `pageNumber`), it will always return the same thing. The `next` function returned by `getPage` is also pure, as it will always return the same thing: if I call `page2.next()` a million times, it'll always fetch `page 3`.

Functional purity and immutability are among the most vital functional concepts to understand, and, usefully, are principles that are applicable to all paradigms of programming. We're not looking to thoroughly explore functional programming here, but just to cover its most applicable principles in order to bolster our abstraction-crafting abilities.

Functional purity

Functions can be said to be pure when their return value is only derived from their input values (also called **idempotence**), and when there are no side-effects. These characteristics give us the following benefits:

- **Predictability:** A function that does not have any side-effects on other areas of the program is a function that can be easily reasoned about. If a function mutates a state that it does not own, potentially creating cascades of changes in other areas of the code, it can be incredibly complicated to disentangle, creating maintenance and reliability issues.
- **Testability**: A pure function, thanks to the characteristic of always returning the same result when given the same inputs, is very easy to verify. Pure functions can become complex but, if kept pure, they will always be easily testable.

Idempotence is the characteristic of always deriving the same result when provided with a certain input. An idempotent function is therefore highly deterministic. An idempotent function may still have side-effects, so it may not always be a *pure* function, but from the perspective of an abstraction user, idempotence is highly desirable, as it means that we always know what to expect.

Often in OOP, methods on objects cannot be said to be pure since they mutate the state (on the object) or return different results with the same input parameters. Consider, for example, the following `Adder` class:

```
class Adder {
  constructor() {
    this.total = 0;
  }
  add(n) {
    return this.total += n;
  }
}

const adder = new Adder();
adder.add(10); // => 10
adder.add(10); // => 20
adder.add(5);  // => 25
```

The `add` method here is not pure. It returns different results even when given the same arguments, and it has a side-effect: mutating a state that it does not own (that is the total property of the object). We could instead create a functionally pure addition abstraction very simply:

```
const add = (a, b) => a + b;

add(10, 10); // => 20
add(10, 20); // => 30
```

This may seem contrived, but the concept behind functional purity is to, from complex needs, derive the truly pure primitives and functions that are needed to construct it. Functional purity teaches us a general lesson here: to break down functionality to its most primal parts until you have a truly testable standalone unit. We can then compose these smaller units into larger units that do more complex work.

Immutability

This chapter has largely been about how we structure and separate our abstractions, but it is equally important to consider the expectations of the data that passes *between* these abstractions.

Immutability refers to the simple idea that data should not mutate. This means that, when we initialize an object, for example, we should not add new properties to it or change existing properties over time. Instead, we should derive a brand new object and only make changes to our own copy. Immutability is a characteristic of data, but is also a general tenet of functional programming. A language can also enforce immutability by disallowing the mutation of already declared variables or objects. JavaScript's `const` is an example of this type of enforcement:

```
const name = 'James';
name = 'Samuel L. Jackson';
// => Uncaught TypeError: Assignment to constant variable.
```

Knowing that something is immutable means that we can rest assured that it will not change; we can rely on its characteristics without worrying that some other part of the program may change it without us knowing. This is especially pertinent in the asynchronous world of JavaScript, where data is shuttled between scopes and interfaces in complex ways.

Like many of the principles we've covered in this chapter, immutability does not have to be followed religiously to gain benefits from it. Immutability in some areas, and mutability in others, can be a viable approach. Imagine an official document being shuttled around a government building. Each department has the implicit assumption that the document has not been arbitrarily modified by unexpected people; a specific department may choose to make a copy of the document and then make various mutations to its own copy for its own unique purposes. A codebase is not so different from this. By crafting abstractions and letting them interdepend on each other, we are intentionally enabling them to manipulate each other's data and functionality.

Summary

In this chapter, we covered a vast amount of theory and practical skills. We covered the LoD (or principle of least information), all SOLID principles, the principle of abstraction, and a couple of key principles from the paradigm of functional programming. Even if you don't remember all of the names, you will hopefully remember the underlying knowledge and key lessons that each principle encapsulates.

Programming is as much an art as it is a science. It involves balancing all of these principles in the pursuit of crafting truly balanced abstractions. None of these principles should be considered hard-and-fast rules. They are merely guidelines that will help us on our journey.

In the next chapter, we continue this journey by exploring one of the most challenging aspects of programming, both in JavaScript and outside it: the problem of naming things.

5
Naming Things Is Hard

Names are everywhere. They are our mind's way of abstracting the complexity of the universe. In the world of software, we are always engaged in crafting new abstractions to describe our everyday realities. A common quip in the programming world is *naming things is hard*. Coming up with a name isn't always hard, but coming up with a *good* name usually is.

In the previous chapters, we have explored the principles and theory underlying abstractions. In this chapter, we'll provide the final key to the puzzle. An abstraction cannot be a good abstraction without good naming. In the names we use, we are distilling a concept, and that distillation will define how people end up understanding the concept. So, naming things isn't just the provision of arbitrary labels; it is the provision of understanding. Only via a good name can a user or other programmer be able to internalize our abstraction fully and navigate it with a full understanding.

In this chapter, we will use some examples to explore the key characteristics that make a good name. We'll also discuss the challenges of naming things in a dynamically typed language such as JavaScript. We should come away from this chapter with a clear understanding of what is involved in coming up with clean and descriptive names.

Specifically, we'll be covering the following topics:

- What's in a name?
- Naming anti-patterns
- Consistency and hierarchy
- Techniques and considerations

What's in a name?

Breaking down the key elements of a good name is difficult. It seems to be more of an art than a science. The boundary between quite a good name and a very good name is fuzzy and liable to subjective opinions.

Consider a function that is responsible for applying multiple CSS styles to a button. Imagine a scenario in which this is a standalone function. Which of the following names would you consider to be the most suitable?

- `styleButton`
- `setStyleOfButton`
- `setButtonCSS`
- `stylizeButton`
- `setButtonStyles`
- `applyButtonCSS`

You've likely picked your favorite. And there is, among those of you reading this book, bound to be disagreements. Many of these disagreements will be founded in our own biases. And many of our biases will have been conditioned by factors such as what language we speak, what programming languages we've been previously exposed to, and what types of programs we spend our time creating. There are many variances that exist between all of us and yet, somehow, we have to come up with a non-fuzzy concept for what a good or clean name is. At the very least, we can say that a good name might have the following characteristics:

- **Purpose**: What something is for and how it behaves
- **Concept**: Its core idea and how to think about it
- **Contract**: Expectations about how it works

This doesn't completely cover the complexity of naming, but with these three characteristics, we have a starting point. In the remainder of this section, we will learn how each of these characteristics is vital to the process of naming things.

Purpose

A good name indicates **purpose**. Purpose is what something does, or what something *is*. In the case of a function, its purpose is its behavior. This is why functions are typically named in the verbal form, such as `getUser` or `createAccount`, whereas things that store values are usually nouns, such as *account* or *button*.

A name that encapsulates a clear purpose will never need further explanation. It should be self-evident. If a name requires a comment to explain its purpose, then that is usually an indicator that it has not done its job as a name.

The purpose of something is highly contextual and so will, therefore, be informed by the surrounding code and the area of the codebase in which that name resides. This is why it's often okay to use a generic name as long as it is surrounded by context that helps to inform its purpose. For example, compare these three method signatures within the TenancyAgreement class:

```
class TenancyAgreement {

  // Option #1:
  saveSignedDocument(
    id,
    timestamp
  ) {}

  // Option #2:
  saveSignedDocument(
    documentId,
    documentTimestamp
  ) {}

  // Option #3:
  saveSignedDocument(
    tenancyAgreementSignedDocumentID,
    tenancyAgreementSignedDocumentTimestamp
  ) {}

}
```

There are subjectivities to this, of course, but most people would agree that, when we have a surrounding context that communicates its purpose well, we shouldn't need to granularize the naming of every variable within that context. With this in mind, we can say that Option #1 in the preceding code is too limited and may invite ambiguity and that Option #3 is needlessly verbose as parts of its argument names are already provided by its context. Option #2, however, with documentId and documentTimestamp, is just right: it sufficiently communicates the purpose of the arguments. And this is all we need.

Purpose is absolutely central to any name. Without a description or an indication of purpose, a name is merely decoration, and can often mean that users of our code are left rummaging around between documentation and other pieces of code just to figure something out. Therefore, we must remember to always consider whether our names communicate purpose well.

Concept

A good name indicates **concept**. A name's concept refers to the idea behind it, the intent in its creation, and how we should think about it. For example, a function named `relocateDeviceAccurately` not only tells us what it will do (its purpose) but informs us about the concept surrounding its behavior. From this name, we can see that devices are things that can be located and that locating such devices can be done at different levels of accuracy. A relatively simple name can arouse a rich concept within the minds of those who read it. This is part of the vital power of naming things: names are avenues to understanding.

A name's concept, like its purpose, is strongly tied to the context in which it exists. Context is the *shared space* that our names exist within. The other names that surround the name we're interested in are absolutely instrumental in helping us understand its concept. Imagine the following names together:

- `rejectedDeal`
- `acceptedDeal`
- `pendingDeal`
- `stalledDeal`

By these names, we immediately understand that a *deal* is something that can have at least four different states. It is implied that these states are mutually exclusive and cannot apply to a deal at the same time, although that is unclear at this time. We are likely to assume that there are specific conditions related to whether a deal is pending or stalled, although we're not sure what those conditions are. So, even though there is ambiguity here, we are already starting to build up a rich understanding of the problem domain. That's just by looking at names—without even reading the implementation.

We have spoken about context as a kind of *shared space* for names. In programming vernacular, we usually say that things named together in one area occupy a single namespace. A namespace can be thought of as a place where things share a conceptual area with each other. Some languages have formalized the concept of a namespace into its own language construct (often called a **package**, or simply a namespace). Even without such formal language constructs, JavaScript still makes it possible to construct namespaces via hierarchical constructs such as objects like so:

```
const app = {};
app.transactions = {};
app.transactions.dealMaking = {};
app.transactions.dealMaking.states = [
  'REJECTED_DEAL',
  'ACCEPTED_DEAL',
```

```
        'PENDING_DEAL',
        'STALLED_DEAL'
    ];
```

Most programmers tend to think of namespaces as a very formal construct, but this isn't often the case. Often, without knowing it, we are composing implied namespaces when we write functions with functions within them. Instead of being delineated by a level of an object hierarchy, the namespaces, in this case, are delineated by the scopes of our functions, as follows:

```
function makeFilteredRequest(endpoint, filterFn) {
    return fetch(`/${endpoint}/`)
      .then(response => response.json())
      .then(data => data.filter(filterFn);
}
```

Here, we are making a request to an endpoint, via `fetch`, and before we return, we are gathering the required data via tapping into the promise returned by `fetch`. To do this, we use two `then(...)` handlers.

 A **promise** is a natively provided class that provides a useful abstraction for handling asynchronous actions. You can usually identify a promise by its then method, like what we used in the preceding code. It's common practice to either use promises or callbacks when tapping into asynchronous actions. You can read more about this in Chapter 10, *Control Flow*, in the *Asynchronous control flow* section.

Our first `then(...)` handler names its argument *response*, while the second one names its argument `data`. Outside the context of `makeFilteredRequest`, these terms would be very ambiguous. However, because we are within the implied namespace of a function related to making a filtered request, the terms *response* and *data* are sufficient to communicate their concepts.

The concepts communicated by our names, much like their purposes, are heavily intertwined with the contexts in which they are specified, so it's important to consider not only the name itself but everything that surrounds it: the complex mesh of logic and behavior in which it resides. All code deals with some level of complexity, and a conceptual understanding of that complexity is crucial in being able to harness it. So, when naming something, it helps to ask yourself: *How do I want them to understand this complexity?* This is relevant if you're crafting a simple interface to be consumed by other programmers, writing a deeply embedded hardware driver, or creating a GUI for non-programmers to consume.

Contract

A good name indicates a **contract** with other parts of the surrounding abstraction. A variable, by its name, may indicate how it will be used or what type of value it contains and what general expectations we should have about its behavior. It's not usually thought about, but when we name something, we are, in fact, setting up a series of implicit expectations or *contracts* that will define how people understand and use that thing. Here are some examples of the hidden contracts that exist in JavaScript:

- A variable prefixed with *is*, for example, `isUser`, is expected to be a Boolean type (either `true` or `false`).
- A variable in all-caps is expected to be a constant (only set once and immutable), for example, `DEFAULT_USER_EXPIRY`.
- Variables named plurally (for example, elements) are expected to contain one or more items in a set-like object (for example, an array), whereas singularly named variables (for example, element) are only expected to contain one item (not in a set).
- Functions with names beginning with `get`, `find`, or `select` are usually expected to return something to you. Functions beginning with `process`, `build`, or `run` are more ambiguous and may not do so.
- Property or method names beginning with an underscore, such as `_processConfig`, are usually intended to be internal to an implementation or pseudo-private. They are not intended to be called publicly.

Whether we like it or not, all names carry with them the baggage of unavoidable expectations regarding their values and behaviors. It's important to be aware of these conventions so that we do not accidentally break the contracts that other programmers rely on. Every convention will have an exception where it doesn't apply, of course, but nonetheless, we should try to abide by them where possible.

Unfortunately, there isn't a canonical list where all of these contracts have been defined. They are usually quite subjective and will depend on the code base. Nonetheless, where we do encounter such conventions, we should follow them. As we mentioned in `Chapter 2`, *The Tenets of Clean Code*, ensuring familiarity is a great way to increase the maintainability of our code. And there is no better way to ensure familiarity than to adopt conventions that other programmers have come to adopt.

Many of these implied contracts are related to types, and JavaScript, as you may be aware, is dynamically typed. This means the types of values will be determined at runtime, and the type contained by any variable may be liable to change:

```
var something;
something = 1;     // a number
something = true;  // a boolean
something = [];    // an array
something = {};    // an object
```

The fact that a variable can refer to many different types means that the contracts and conventions implied by the names we adopt are even more important. There is no static type checker to help us. We are left alone at the chaotic whim of ourselves and other programmers.

 Later in this chapter, we'll discuss **Hungarian notation**, a type of naming that is useful in dynamically typed languages. Also, it's useful to know that there are various static type checking and type annotating tools available for JavaScript if you find dealing with its dynamism painful. These will be covered in Chapter 15, *Tools for Cleaner Code*.

Contracts are not only important because of JavaScript's dynamically typed nature. They are fundamentally useful in giving us confidence in how certain values behave and what we can expect from them throughout the runtime of our program. Imagine if there was an API with a method called getCurrentValue() that didn't always return the current value. That would break its implied contract. Seeing names through the lens of contracts is quite a mind-warper. Soon, you will begin to see contracts everywhere – contracts between variables, between interfaces, and at the integration level between entire architectures and systems.

Now that we've discussed the three characteristics of a good name (purpose, concept, contract), we can begin to explore some anti-patterns, that is, ways of naming things that we should try to avoid.

Naming anti-patterns

Much like the abstraction-building warnings of DRY and YAGNI, naming has its own warnings and anti-patterns. There are many ways to compose a bad name, and nearly all of them can be split into three broad naming anti-patterns: **needlessly short names**, **needlessly exotic names**, and **needlessly long names**.

Names are the initial lenses via which we and others will view the abstractions we build. Therefore, it is vital to know how to avoid creating lenses that only end up obscuring understanding and complicating things for other programmers. Let's begin by exploring needlessly short names and how they can end up drastically limiting our ability to understand what something does.

Needlessly short names

Names that are too short are usually employing either program-specific knowledge or domain-specific knowledge that may not generalize well to the audience of the code. A lone programmer may think it reasonable to write the following code:

```
function incId(id, f) {
  for (let x = 0; x < ids.length; ++x) {
    if (ids[x].id === id && f(ids[x])) {
      ids[x].n++;
    }
  }
}
```

We are able to discern the fact that it is related to IDs and its purpose is to conditionally increment a specific object's n property within the `ids` array. Therefore, it is possible to discern what it is doing on a functional level, but its meaning and intent are difficult to grasp. The programmer has used single-letter names (f, x, n) and has also employed an abbreviated function name (`incId`). Most of these names fail to fulfill the basic characteristics that we desire from a name: to indicate purpose, concept, and contract. We can only guess at these names' purposes and concepts by how they are being used. It would vastly help to refactor this with more meaningful names:

```
function incrementJobInstancesByIdIfFilter(id, filter) {
  for (let i = 0; i < jobs.length; i++) {
    let job = jobs[i];
    if (job.id === id && filter(job)) {
      job.nInstances++;
    }
  }
}
```

We now have a far clearer idea of what's going on. The arrays being iterated over contains jobs. The function's purpose is to find jobs with a specified ID and conditional on that job satisfying a specified filter. It increments the job's `nInstances` property by `1`. Via these new names, we already have a far richer conceptual understanding of this abstraction. We now understand that jobs are items that can have any number of instances and that the number of current instances is tracked via the `nInstances` property. Via the lenses provided by the names, we have been able to understand the underlying problem domain more clearly. Now, we can see that names are not just decoration or needless verboseness; names are the very essence of your abstractions.

A needlessly short name is, in many ways, just an insufficiently meaningful name. However, a name being short does not necessarily indicate a problem. The iterator variable, `i`, which we used in the preceding code, is perfectly fine as it is a convention that has established itself over decades. Programmers all over the world understand the conceptual and contractual implications of it: it is used only to iterate through an array and to access array elements at each stage of the iteration.

On the whole, and outside of rare exceptions such as our iteration variable, it is incredibly important to avoid the deficit in meaning that is invited by short names. They are often composed initially with haste or laziness and may even give the programmer attuned to their meaning a sense of accomplishment. After all, being able to wield obscure logic is a gift for the ego. But as we've covered, the ego is not a friend to clean code. Whenever you feel the urge to use a short name, push back on the impulse and take the time to pick a name that is richer in meaning.

Needlessly exotic names

Another avenue for the ego is in the proliferation of exotic names. Exotic names are those that draw unnecessary attention to themselves and are often obscure or elusive in meaning, like so:

```
function deStylizeParameters(params) {
  disEntangleParams(params, p => !!p.style).obliterate();
}
```

This is an ostensibly simple piece of behavior obscured by needlessly exotic names. We can, with minimal effort, make a world of difference to the comprehensibility of these abstractions with only a couple of tweaks:

```
function removeStylingFromParams(params) {
  filterParams(params, param => !!param.style).remove();
}
```

Names, on the whole, should be boring. They should not draw attention to themselves. They should sit there with only their plain meaning on display and nothing that makes fellow programmers go, *oh that's what it means!* or *hehe clever!* Our egos may have their own ideas about naming, but we should remember to limit the ego and think purely of the people who must endure the task of trying to understand our code and the interfaces we've created. On the whole, the following advice will keep us on the right track:

- **Avoid fancy or longer synonyms of regular words**: For example, using `kill` or `obliterate` instead of `delete`
- **Avoid words that don't exist**: For example, `deletify`, `elementize`, or `dedupify`
- **Avoid puns or clever insinuations**: For example, using chemical element names to refer to DOM elements

Being overly exotic risks alienating our audience. You may be able to easily understand the names you've adopted, but that does not mean they are easily understood by others. The wider programming community is incredibly diverse and has many different cultural and linguistic backgrounds. It's best to stick to names that are descriptive and boring so that your code is understandable to as many people as possible.

Needlessly long names

As we've already discovered, the needlessly short name is, in fact, a name without sufficient meaning. The needlessly long name is, therefore, a name with too much meaning. You may wonder how a name could have too much meaning. Meaning is a good thing, but too much meaning crushed into a single name can only serve to confuse; for example:

```
documentManager.refreshAndSaveSignedAndNonPendingDocuments();
```

This name is hard to understand: is it refreshing and saving documents that are signed and documents that are non-pending, or is it refreshing and saving documents that are both signed and non-pending? It's unclear.

This long name gives us a clue that the underlying abstraction is needlessly complex. We can split the name into its constituent parts to get a full grasp of its interface:

- **refresh (verb)**: The refreshing action that occurs on a document
- **save (verb)**: The saving action that occurs on a document
- **signed (adjective)**: The signed state of a document
- **non-pending (adjective)**: The non-pending state of a document
- **document (noun)**: The document itself

We have a few different things happening here. With names this long, a good guideline is to refactor the underlying abstraction so that we only need a name with, at most, one verb, one adjective, and one noun. For example, we could take our long name and split its function into four distinct functions:

```
documentManager.refreshSignedDocuments();
documentManager.refreshNonPendingDocuments();
documentManager.saveSignedDocuments();
documentManager.saveNonPendingDocuments();
```

Alternatively, if the intent is to perform actions on documents that carry multiple states (SIGNED and NON_PENDING), then we could implement a method like this for refreshing (and a similar one for the saving action):

```
documentManager.refreshDocumentsWithStates([
  documentManager.STATE_SIGNED,
  documentManager.STATE_NON_PENDING
]);
```

The point is that long names are a clue to a broken or confused abstraction. Making a name more understandable usually goes hand in hand with making an abstraction more understandable.

As with short names, the problem is not the length of the name itself: it is what the length usually indicates. With long names, what is indicated is crushing too much meaning into a single name, indicating a confused abstraction.

Consistency and hierarchy

So far, we've talked about the three most important characteristics of a name: *purpose, concept,* and *contract.* One of the easiest ways to bestow these characteristics upon your names is to use consistency and hierarchy to your benefit. Consistency here refers to using the same pattern of naming across many different names within a given area of code. Hierarchy, on the other hand, refers to the way we structure and put together different areas of code to form a holistic architecture. Together, they allow us to give a name a rich context that can be used to make strong inferences about its purpose, concept, and contract.

This is best explained by looking at the JavaScript directory of a fictional app. We have a directory full of files, like so:

```
app/
|-- deepClone.js
|-- deepEquality.js
```

```
|-- getParamsFromURL.js
|-- getURL.js
|-- openModal.js
|-- openModalWithTemplate.js
|-- setupAppWithCustomConfig.js
|-- setupAppWithDefaultConfig.js
|-- setURL.js
|-- ...
```

There is no hierarchy, so we can only discern context from the names themselves and what they appear to relate to. For example, there is a `getURL` and a `setURL` file, which both presumably relate to URLs and could be considered *utilities*. It would, therefore, be helpful to have these occupy the same part of the hierarchy or a shared namespace, such as `app/utils/url`. We can also refactor other parts of our directory structure into a more contextually rich hierarchy:

```
app/
|-- setup/
|   |-- defaultConfig.js
|   |-- setup.js
|-- modal/
|   |-- open.js
|   |-- openWithTemplate.js
|-- utils/
    |-- url/
    |   |-- getParams.js
    |   |-- get.js
    |   |-- set.js
    |-- obj/
        |-- deepEquality.js
        |-- deepClone.js
```

Immediately, things are clearer. The cognitive strain of understanding all of those files and what they do is now lessened by each file having its own rich context. You'll also notice that we've been able to simplify the names at various parts of the hierarchy; for example, we have renamed `openModal.js` to `modal/open.js`. This is an additional benefit of employing hierarchies of names: at each level of naming, we can simplify and shorten the names, lessening comprehension time.

Names within a hierarchy naturally receive a portion of their meaning from the context that they reside in. This means that the name itself does not need to contain all the meaning. Always look for opportunities to provide a common context to similar abstractions so that the burden of comprehension is eased.

Just like we have provided meaning via the hierarchy of a directory structure, we can also provide meaning within the code itself. Within a function, for example, the names within will naturally receive a lot of their context from the function's name itself and its situation within a larger module. Consider how it would be quite unusual to write code like this:

```
function displayModalWithMessage(
  modalDisplayer_Message,
  modalDisplayer_Options
) {
  const modalDisplayer_ModalInstance = new Modal();
  modalDisplayer_ModalInstance.setMessage(modalDisplayerMessage);
  modalDisplayer_ModalInstance.setOptions(modalDisplayerOptions);
  modalDisplayer_ModalInstance.show();
  return modalDisplayer_ModalInstance;
}
```

The names within the function are needlessly prefixed with contextual information (such as `modalDisplayer_...`) that the reader of the code can already get from the function itself. Typically, we write code that takes advantage of where a variable sits and the meaning that it gets from its context. It would be far more normal for the preceding code to appear like so:

```
function showModalWithMessage(message, options) {
  const modalInstance = new Modal();
  modalInstance.setMessage(message);
  modalInstance.setOptions(options);
  modalInstance.show();
  return modalInstance;
}
```

In an previous chapter, we discussed the principle of abstraction and how the implementation of a module should be independent of its interface. We can see that this principle is expressed in this function. The scope of a function (its implementation) should be entirely independent (and even ignorant!) of its interface. So, arguably, it's not the business of the `modalInstance` variable to know which function it resides in and so the former naming technique, which prefixed it with `modalDisplayer_...`, would be in violation of the principle of abstraction.

Thinking about hierarchies in terms of abstraction is key. Hierarchies aren't just useful from an organizational perspective. They should, ideally, be a reflection of the layers of abstraction that reside within our code. Higher-level abstractions are at the top of the hierarchy, and the deeper we go into the hierarchy, the more low-level we will get. This is a good general rule to adopt: **make your hierarchy reflect your abstractions**.

Naming things with consistency complements this rule. Within a single layer of our abstraction, that is, within a single level of the hierarchy, we should adopt common naming patterns so that the reader of our code can easily navigate and understand its concepts. For example, if we are creating an interface that will be used to add and remove items from a data structure, then we should avoid naming similar actions in an inconsistent manner. Consider the following class schematic:

```
class MyDataStructure {
  addItem() {}
  pushItems() {}
  setItemIfNotExists() {}
  // ...
}
```

Very confusingly, this abstraction is offering up three different variations of the concept of *adding* to the data structure: *adding*, *pushing*, and *setting*. These names are all, in fact, referring to the same concept, so we should adopt a common naming pattern, such as the following:

```
class MyDataStructure {
  addItem() {}
  addItems() {}
  addItemIfNotExists() {}
  // ...
}
```

This interface is now far easier to understand. There is less ambiguity and less cognitive burden in using it. As a user of this abstraction, I would no longer need to remember whether I should be using *add*, *set*, or *push*. Consistency is a characteristic that results from the avoidance of needless differences. Inconsistencies are jarring and so they should only be used to demarcate genuine functional or conceptual differences.

Techniques and considerations

JavaScript, due to its ever-changing nature, has gathered a huge variety of conflicting conventions. Many of these conventions garner strong opinions either in support or in disapproval. We have, however, settled on some basic conventions around naming that are more or less globally accepted:

- Constants should be named with underscore-separated capitals; for example, DEFAULT_COMPONENT_COLOR
- Constructors or classes should be camel-cased with an initial uppercase letter; for example, MyComponent

- Everything else should be camel-cased with an initial lower case letter; for example, `myComponentInstance`

Apart from these foundational conventions, the decision of naming is left largely up to the creativity and skill of the programmer. The names you end up employing will be largely defined by what problems you're solving. Most code will inherit naming conventions from the APIs it interfaces with. Using the DOM API, for example, will usually mean that you adopt names such as *element*, *attribute*, and *node*. Many of the popular frameworks available will tend to dictate the names we adopt as well. It is absolutely useful and necessary to adopt such conventional paradigms from the ecosystem that you're working in, but it's also useful to have some foundational techniques and concepts under your belt so that you can craft beautifully named abstractions, even in new and alien problem domains.

Hungarian notation

JavaScript is a dynamically typed language, meaning that the type of a value will be determined at runtime and that the type contained by any variable may be liable to change during runtime. This is in contrast to statically-typed languages, which have compile-time warnings related to your usage of types. The implication of this is that, as JavaScript programmers, we need to be much more careful in the way we employ types and how we name our variables.

As we know, when we name things, we are implying a contract. This contract will define how other programmers make use of that thing. This is part of the reason why, in various languages, something called Hungarian notation has been very popular. It involves including type annotations in a name itself, like so:

- Instead of `button`, we may use `elButton` or `buttonElement`
- Instead of `age`, we may use `nAge` or `ageNumber`
- Instead of `details`, we may use `objDetails` or `detailsObject`

Hungarian notation is useful for the following reasons:

- **Certainty**: It provides more certainty of a name's purpose and contract to the readers of your code
- **Consistency**: It leads to a more consistent naming approach
- **Enforcement**: It may lead to better-enforced typing conventions within your code

However, it also has the following disadvantages:

- **Runtime changes**: If the underlying types are changed by bad code at runtime (for example, if a function mutates nAge into a string), then the name ceases to be useful and may only mislead us.
- **Codebase rigidity**: It may lead to a rigid code base where it's hard to make appropriate changes to types. Refactoring old code may become more burdensome.
- **Lack of meaning**: Knowing only a variable's type does not inform us as to its purpose, concept, or contract as much as a truly descriptive non-typed variable name would.

In the landscape of JavaScript, we see Hungarian notation used in a few places: the most common is when naming a variable that may refer to a DOM element. The notations for these names will usually be in the form elHeader, headerEl, headingElement, or even $header. The latter, with a dollar prefix, is most famously used in the jQuery library. Its fame there led to it being a standard in various other places. **Chromium DevTools**, for example, employs a dollar prefix for element references and methods related to querying the DOM (for example, $$(...) is aliased to document.querySelectorAll(...)).

Hungarian notation is something that can be utilized partially, where you're concerned there may be ambiguity. For example, you can use it where you have both a complex type and a primitive type referring to the same concept within a single scope:

```
function renderArticle(name) {
  const article = Article.getByName(name);
  const title = article.getTitle();
  const strArticle = article.toString();
  // ...
}
```

Here, we have an article variable that refers to an instance of the Article class. In addition to this, we also want to use a string representation of our article. To get around a potential naming conflict, we have used an str prefix to indicate that the variable refers to a string value. In isolated cases like these, Hungarian notation can be useful. You don't need to use it exhaustively, but it's a useful tool to have up your sleeve.

Naming and abstracting functions

Most abstractions you end up crafting in JavaScript will be manifested within functions. Even within grand architectures, it is individual functions and methods that do the work, and it is in their conception that a good abstraction begins to reveal itself. It is, therefore, worth thinking quite deeply about how we should name our functions and what factors we should take into consideration when doing so.

A function's name should typically use what, in grammar, is called the **imperative form**. The imperative form is what we employ when we are giving instructions, such as *walk to the shop, buy bread, stop there!*.

 Although we usually use the *imperative* form when naming functions, there are exceptions. For example, it is also conventional to prefix functions that return Boolean values with *is* or *has*; for example, `isValid(...)`. When creating constructors (which are functions), we name them according to the instance they'll produce; for example, `Route` or `SpecialComponent`.

The direct nature of the imperative form is the most understandable and readable in the context of programming. To find the correct imperative form for your specific problem, it's best to imagine the act of giving a military order, that is, don't mince your words and say exactly what it is that you want to occur:

- If you want a prompt to be displayed, use `displayPrompt()`
- If you want elements to be removed, use `removeElements()`
- If you want a random number between x and y, use `generateRandomNumber(x, y)`

Often, we wish to qualify our instructions. If you were to issue an instruction to a person, such as *find my bicycle*, you would likely further qualify that instruction with information such as *it's blue* and *it's missing its front wheel*. It is important, however, not to let a function's name get bogged down with these qualifications. The following function would be an example of this:

```
findBlueBicycleWithAMissingFrontWheel();
```

As we mentioned earlier, a needlessly long name is a sign of a bad abstraction. When we see this type of over-qualification, we should take a step back and reconsider. Here, it's important to draw a line between what is sensible in spoken language and what is sensible when programming. In programming, functions are ways of abstracting common behavior that can be adjusted or configured, as needed, via arguments.

So, it is via arguments that we should be expressing the qualifications of blue and missing front wheel. And we could, for example, express these as a single object argument like so:

```
findBicycle({
  color: 'blue',
  frontWheel: 'missing'
});
```

By moving the qualifying parts of a function's name into its arguments, we are producing a cleaner and more comprehensible abstraction. This has the added benefit of increasing the configurability of the abstraction, thereby providing the user with more possibilities.

In our case, we may wish to give users the ability to find objects other than bicycles. To cater to this, we would make the name of the function more generic (for example, findObject) and shift the qualifier to the arguments by adding a new option property (for example, type), like so:

```
findObject({
  type: 'bicycle',
  color: 'blue',
  frontWheel: 'missing'
});
```

Something curious happens at this stage of the process. We have, correctly, moved our various qualifiers to the arguments of our function, expanding the usefulness and configuration of our abstraction. But now what we have is an abstraction that is doing many things, so at some point, it may be prudent to take a step back and build higher-level abstractions to encapsulate these different behaviors. In our case, we could achieve this via functional composition, like so:

```
const findBicycle   = config => findObject({ ...config, type: 'bicycle'
});
const findSkateboard = config => findObject({ ...config, type: 'skateboard'
});
const findScooter    = config => findObject({ ...config, type: 'scooter'
});
```

Above all, a function is a unit of behavior. As the SRP tells us, it's important to ensure that they are only doing one discernible thing. When considering these things or units of behavior, it's important to think about what a function does from the perspective of those who'll use it. Technically, it's highly likely that our composed findScooter function does all manner of things beneath the surface. It may be incredibly complex. But at the layer of abstraction where it will be used, it can be said to only do one thing, and that is what's important.

Three bad names

If you're ever stuck for a name, there's a clever approach you can use to unstick yourself. When you have an abstraction or variable that needs a name, look carefully at what it does or what it contains and then come up with at least three bad names that describe it. Don't worry about the abstraction or interface you wish to provide for now; just imagine you were describing the functionality to someone who doesn't know anything about the codebase. Be direct and descriptive.

For example, let's say we're embedded in the part of the code base that deals with setting up new user-names. We need to check that the username does not match a set of specifically forbidden words, such as `admin`, `root`, or `user`. We want to write a function to do this but we're not sure what name to pick. So, we decide to try the three bad names approach. This is what we come up with:

- `matchUsernameAgainstForbiddenWords`
- `checkForForbiddenWordConflicts`
- `isUsernameReservedWord`

Coming up with three less-than-perfect names is a lot easier than spending many minutes trying but failing to come up with the perfect name. It doesn't matter how bad these three names are. What's important is that we can come up with at least three. Now, having seeded the set of possibilities, we're free to compare and contrast the names we've found and mix and match them to find the most descriptive and direct way of describing the purpose of our function. In this case, we may have eventually decided on a name adapted from those three possibilities: `isUsernameForbiddenWord`. We wouldn't have got there if it wasn't for the three bad names approach.

Summary

In this chapter, we have wrestled with the difficult art of naming things. We've discussed the characteristics of a good name, that is, purpose, concept, and contract. We've walked through examples of how to weave these characteristics into our names and what anti-patterns to steer clear of. We've also discussed the importance of hierarchy and consistency in our pursuit of clean abstractions. Finally, we have covered several helpful techniques and conventions that we can utilize when we're having a difficult time naming things.

In the next chapter, we will, at last, begin to delve into the innards of the JavaScript language itself and learn how to wield its constructs and syntax in a way that yields truly clean code.

Section 2: JavaScript and Its Bits

2

In this section, we'll do a deep dive into JavaScript's internals and language constructs. This will give us a really solid foundational understanding of how to use JavaScript's best parts to craft clean code.

This section contains the following chapters:

- Chapter 6, *Primitives and Built-In Types*
- Chapter 7, *Dynamic Typing*
- Chapter 8, *Operators*
- Chapter 9, *Parts of Syntax and Scope*
- Chapter 10, *Control Flow*

Primitive and Built-In Types 6

So far, we have explored the meaning of clean code from several different perspectives. We've explored how the code we write allows our users to wield remarkable complexity by leveraging abstractions. We've gone on to discuss the tenets of clean code, such as reliability and usability, and the various traps and challenges to watch out for when pursuing these goals.

In this chapter, we'll be exploring the JavaScript language itself, in great detail, including both the more common language constructs and the more obscure and confusing aspects. We'll be applying our accrued wealth of knowledge about clean code to all these parts of the language and will build an understanding of JavaScript that's tailored purely to the creation of clean code.

We'll begin by looking at the most atomic part of JavaScript: the primitive values that serve as the building blocks for any program. Then, we'll move on to non-primitive values, known as **objects**. In our exploration of these types, we will, through examples, be exposing the semantics that make each type unique and the pitfalls to avoid in their usage. The crucial knowledge that we'll gain in this chapter will be applied in later chapters as we build up a truly complete knowledge of what it means to write clean code in JavaScript.

By the end of this chapter, you should feel comfortable in the following topic areas:

- Primitive types
- Objects
- Functions
- Arrays and iterables
- Regular expressions

Primitive types

A primitive type in JavaScript is any value that is not an object and thus does not have any methods or properties. There are seven primitive types in JavaScript:

- Number
- String
- Boolean
- Undefined
- Null
- BigInt
- Symbol

In this section, we'll explore the common characteristics among these primitives and delve into each individual type to explore how it works and what potential hazards exist in its usage. We'll gain an appreciation for how the JavaScript language itself is just a set of distinct abstractions that, when wielded masterfully, can make easy work of any problem domain.

Immutability of primitives

All primitive values are immutable, meaning that you cannot mutate their values. This is a core part of their primitiveness. You cannot, for example, change the number value of 3.14 to 42, or change the value of a string to its uppercased variation.

 But I can change the value of a string to its uppercased variation! You may be confused right now if you recall being able to do this. But there is a crucial distinction to be made here between the reassignment of variables to new primitive values, which is fully possible (and likely what you're remembering), and the mutation of primitive values, which is not possible.

When we reassign a variable, giving it a new value, we are not changing the value itself; we are only changing which value the variable refers to, as shown here:

```
let name = 'simon';
let copy = name;

// Assign a new value to `name`:
name = name.toUpperCase();
```

```
// New value referred to by name:
name; // => "SIMON"

// Old value remains un-mutated:
copy; // => "simon"
```

Note how `copy` has remained lowercase. The primitive value `simon` has not been mutated; instead, a new primitive value has been derived from it, via the `toUpperCase` method, and then assigned to the variable that previously held the lowercase variant.

Primitive wrappers

You'll remember that we mentioned that primitive values don't have methods as they are not objects. So, how exactly are we able to call `toUpperCase` on the preceding string? Is that not a method? Yes, it is. And to allow us to access this method, JavaScript wraps primitive values in their respective wrapper objects at the time of property access. This occurs for all primitive values, apart from `null` and `undefined`.

Primitive values, in these moments of being wrapped, remain immutable but, via their wrapped instance, provide access to properties and methods. A string value would be wrapped in a `String` instance, while a number value would be wrapped in a `Number` instance. The same would occur for all other non-null and non-undefined primitives. You are free to instantiate these wrapper objects yourself: you will observe that they no longer behave like primitives, though; they are objects, and, as such, you can add and mutate properties on them:

```
const name = new String('James');

// We can add arbitrary properties, since it is an object:
// (Warning: this is an anti-pattern)
name.surname = 'Padolsey';
name.surname; // => "Padolsey"
```

 If you require an object to add custom properties to, it is best to use a plain object. Using wrapper objects for anything other than wrapping their primitive values is an anti-pattern as it would not be expected by other programmers. Nonetheless, it is useful to observe and remember the differences between primitives and their respective wrapper objects.

Invoking a wrapper constructor (for example, `Number`, `String`, and so on) as a regular function has a unique behavior. Instead of returning a new wrapper instance, it will cast the value to a particular type and return a regular primitive. This is quite useful when you're casting one type to another:

```
// Cast a number to a string:
String(123); // => "123"

// Cast a string to a number
Number("2"); // => 2

// Cast a number to a boolean
Boolean(0); // => false
Boolean(1); // => true
```

Invoking wrapper constructors as functions, as we have done here, is a useful casting technique, though it's not the only one. We'll cover typecasting and coercion in a lot more detail in `Chapter 7`, *Dynamic Typing*.

The falsy primitives

In JavaScript, all the values in Boolean contexts will evaluate to either `true` or `false`. To describe this behavior, we usually refer to values as either truthy or falsy. To determine the truthiness of a value, we can simply pass it to the `Boolean` function:

```
Boolean('hi'); // => true
Boolean(0);    // => false
Boolean(42);   // => true
Boolean(0.1);  // => true
Boolean('');   // => false
Boolean(true); // => true
Boolean(null); // => false
```

There are only eight falsy values in JavaScript, and all of them are primitive types:

- `null`
- `undefined`
- `+0` or `-0` (zero, a number)
- `false` (a Boolean)
- `""` (an empty string)
- `0n` (zero, a `BigInt`)
- `NaN` (not a number)

All values that are not falsy are, therefore, truthy. Throughout this and the next chapter, we will be exploring the implications of these truthy and falsy values. For now, it's only important to know that the preceding falsy values will, when used in conditional or logical contexts, behave as if they were false. A falsy value, when used in an `if` statement, for example, would act the same as if it were false:

```
if (0) {
  // This will not run. 0 is falsy.
}
if (1) {
  // This will run. 1 is truthy.
}
```

The existence of these falsy values means that we must be wary of how we check for certain conditions. It's easy to fall into the trap of testing for the existence of a certain value state by using only its truthiness to determine existence. For example, let's say that we need to be able to check for the age of a person:

```
if (person.age) {
  processIdentity(person);
}
```

This is a contrived example, but we can imagine a system in which the identities of individuals need to be processed somehow, perhaps through a medical application. Checking for the existence of the age property is not going to do what's intended if the age happens to be 0. Perhaps the system needs to cater to the eventuality of a newborn baby being entered into the system, but suddenly it breaks because the age is 0. In such scenarios, it's best to be preemptively explicit, even if you don't expect odd falsy values. In this context, we likely want to check for either `null` or `undefined`, so we should explicitly do that:

```
if (person.age === null || person.age === undefined) {
  processIdentity(person);
}
```

This code is far more resilient to the possible variabilities of the age property. We could also, perhaps, be more in line with our requirements and check only for the specific characteristics that we are interested in, such as that the age property is a number within specific bounds. The point is that it's better to be explicit in Boolean contexts such as `if` statements so that you don't run into an unexpected falsy value.

Number

The number primitive type is used to express numerical data. It stores this data in the double-precision 64-bit floating-point format (IEEE 754). 64 bits here refers to there being 64 binary digits available to store information. The entire 64-bit format that's used in the IEEE 754 standards can be broken down into three chunks:

- **1 bit for the sign of the number being represented**: Whether the number is positive or negative
- **11 bits for the exponent of the number**: This tells us where the radix or decimal dot resides
- **52 bits for what's termed the fraction or significand**: This tells us the integer value

 A side effect of this floating-point formation means that there are technically two zeros: positive zero (+0) and negative zero (−0). Thankfully, in JavaScript, you don't have to be explicit when checking for these values. Both will return true when compared with the strict equality operator (+0 === −0) and both are considered falsy.

Technically, there are 53 bits available (not 52) for the expression of an integer value as the leading bit of the significand field resides within the exponent field. This is an important clarification as it has a direct effect on how much precision we can get from JavaScript numbers. Having 53 bits available to express an integer value means that any numbers greater than 2^{53}-1 are considered unsafe. These safety limits are available as constants on the Number object:

- Integers larger than 2^{53} or 9007199254740991 (Number.MAX_SAFE_INTEGER)
- Integers smaller than -2^{53} or −9007199254740991 (Number.MIN_SAFE_INTEGER)

The loss of precision beyond these bounds can be observed if we try to perform addition on the upper limit:

```
const max = Number.MAX_SAFE_INTEGER;
max + 1; // => 9007199254740992 (correct)
max + 2; // => 9007199254740992 (incorrect)
max + 3; // => 9007199254740994 (correct)
max + 4; // => 9007199254740996 (incorrect)
// ... etc.
```

Here, we can see that the evaluated additions are incorrect. Beyond MAX_SAFE_INTEGER, all mathematical operations will be similarly imprecise.

It is still possible to express values larger than `MAX_SAFE_INTEGER` within JavaScript. Many values up to 2^{1024} (`Number.MAX_VALUE`) can be expressed, but many cannot. Therefore, it is considered very unwise to attempt to express numbers beyond `Number.MAX_SAFE_INTEGER`.

To sum this up, any values between `Number.MIN_SAFE_INTEGER` and `Number.MAX_SAFE_INTEGER` are safe to use and will provide integer precision, while values beyond these bounds should be considered unsafe. If we feel ourselves needing an integer outside of these bounds, then we can use JavaScript's `BigInt` primitive:

```
const max = BigInt(Number.MAX_SAFE_INTEGER)
max + 1n; // => 9007199254740992n (correct)
max + 2n; // => 9007199254740993n (correct)
max + 3n; // => 9007199254740994n (correct)
max + 4n; // => 9007199254740995n (correct)
// ... etc.
```

We'll explore the `BigInt` primitive further in a later part of this section. For now, just remember to always consider the largeness of your numbers and whether they can be fully accommodated by JavaScript's `Number` type. It's also important to consider the precision of decimal values (such as in fractions) as well. When expressing decimals in JavaScript, you'll likely encounter issues like this:

```
0.1 + 0.2; // => 0.30000000000000004
```

This is due to inherent mechanism by which fractions are expressed in the floating-point standard. You can imagine that if we were interested in querying whether a decimal is equal to, greater than, or less than another value, it would be as simple as using the following code:

```
const someValue = 0.1 + 0.2;
if (someValue === 0.3) {
  yay();
}
```

But `yay()` will never run. To get around this problem, there are two options. The first involves something called the epsilon. The epsilon is the margin of error inherent to floating-point math, and JavaScript makes this available to use as `Number.EPSILON`:

```
Number.EPSILON; // => 0.0000000000000002220446049250313
```

This is a very tiny number, but it must be taken into account if we are to have a hope of doing basic mathematical operations on decimals. If we wish to compare two numbers, we can simply subtract them from each other and check that the margin is less than the EPSILON:

```
const someValue = 0.1 + 0.2;
if (Math.abs(someValue - 0.3) < Number.EPSILON) {
  // someValue is (effectively) equal to 0.3
}
```

The other approach we can take is to convert any decimals we're dealing with into integers expressed by either Number or BigInt types. So, if we have a need to represent values from 0 to 1 with a precision of eight decimal places, for example, then we can simply multiply these values by $100,000,000$ (or 10^8):

```
const unwieldyDecimalValue = 0.12345678;

// We can use 1e8 to express Math.pow(10, 8)
unwieldyDecimalValue * 1e8; // => 12345678
```

Now, we are free to conduct integer math on these values and divide them back down into their fractions when done. It's crucial to note that any decimal value longer than 15 digits cannot be expressed in JavaScript's Number type, so you'll need to explore other options. JavaScript currently doesn't have a native BigDecimal type, but there are many third-party libraries available that fulfill a similar purpose (you can easily find these online).

 If you ever find yourself needing to operate on large or very precise numbers in JavaScript, or if your code concerns sensitive matters such as finance, medicine, or science, it's absolutely crucial to take the time to fully understand what levels of precision you require and whether JavaScript can natively support those needs.

There's one more topic to discuss under the Number type, and that is NaN. NaN is a primitive that technically belongs to the Number type. It represents a failure to parse something as a number; for example, Number('wow') evaluates to NaN. Since typeof NaN is a number, we should check for a valid number in the following way:

```
if (typeof myNumber === 'number' && !isNaN(myNumber)) {
  // Do something with your number
}
```

The value NaN can create a headache when its existence is not foreseen. It'll usually crop up in areas where you're attempting to cast strings to numbers or where this happens implicitly (coercion).

We'll be covering the topic of coercion, casting, and detection more in the next chapter. This will include a section where we get into the complexity of NaN and compare isNaN(), the global function, to the slightly different Number.isNaN(). For now, it's only important to appreciate that NaN is its own distinct value and is itself, oddly, considered a number within JavaScript.

There is another value encapsulated by the Number type that is not a normal number: Infinity. You will receive Infinity when you attempt to do mathematical operations such as dividing by 0:

```
100/0; // => Infinity
```

Infinity, like NaN, is a globally available primitive value that you can reference and check for:

```
100/0 === Infinity; // => true
```

There is also -Infinity, which is technically a distinct value:

```
100/-0; // => -Infinity
-Infinity === Infinity; // => false
```

Infinity, like NaN, is of the Number type, so when passed to the typeof operator, it will evaluate to "number":

```
typeof Infinity; // => "number"
```

Outside of Infinity, -Infinity, and NaN, all values that are of the Number type can be considered regular everyday numbers. Overall, and for most use cases, the Number type is very simple to use and operate on. It is, however, vital to know about its limitations, many of which we've covered here so that you can make an informed decision about when it may not be appropriate to use.

String

The String type in JavaScript allows us to express sequences of characters. It is usually used to encapsulate words, sentences, lists, HTML, and many other forms of text-like content.

Strings are expressed by delimiting sequences of characters with either single quotes, double quotes, or backticks:

```
// Single quotes:
const name = 'Titanic';

// Double quotes:
const type = "Ship";

// Template literals (back-ticks):
const report = `
  RMS Titanic was a British passenger liner that sank
  in the North Atlantic Ocean in 1912 after the ship
  struck an iceberg during her maiden voyage.
`;
```

Only backtick-delimited strings, known as **template literals** (or template strings), can occupy multiple lines. Single quote- or double quote-delimited strings can technically be spread along multiple lines as well, but this is only achieved by escaping their invisible newline characters (with a \ character), which effectively removes the newlines:

```
const a = "example of a \
string with escaped newline \
characters";

const b = "example of a string with escaped newline characters";

a === b; // => true
```

Nowadays, template literals are preferred as they retain newlines and allow us to interpolate arbitrary expressions, like so:

```
const nBreadLoaves = 4;
const breadLoafCost = 2.40;

`
  I went to the market and bought ${nBreadLoaves} loaves of
  bread and it cost me ${nBreadLoaves * breadLoafCost} euros.
`
```

Strings come with a number of curious challenges once your usage exceeds the most simple use cases. Under the surface, the humble string is masking a miraculous scale of complexity in the form of Unicode.

Unicode is an industry standard for the encoding, representation, and handling of text that's used in writing systems around the world. The Unicode standard contains over 130,000 characters, including all of your favorite emojis.

To step beneath the veneer of the String abstraction slightly, we can say that Strings in JavaScript are really just an ordered sequence of 16-bit unsigned integers. Each of these integers is interpreted as a UTF-16 code unit. UTF-16 is a type of encoding for the Unicode character set. Using it, we are able to express hundreds of thousands of valid Unicode code points. This means that we can express emojis, many languages, and a myriad of Unicode oddities via our strings:

```
const japan = '日本';
const greece = 'Ελληνική Δημοκρατία';
const smile = '☺';
```

A Unicode code point is a character (such as the letter *B*, a question mark, or a smiling emoji). We can express a code point by using one or more UTF-16 code units. Most code points that we use from day to day only need a single code unit. These are known as **scalars**. There are, however, quite a few Unicode code points that require a pair of code units (known as a **surrogate pair**). The panda emoji is an example of such a surrogate pair:

```
const codeUnits = '🐼'.split('').map(s => s.charCodeAt(0));

[
  55357, // => Leading Surrogate (U+D83D)
  56380  // => Panda Code Unit (U+DC3C)
];
```

Since UTF-16 only has 16 bits to work with, it has to use pairs of 16-bit integers to express some characters. Naturally, if we're using UTF-32 encoding (with 32 bits to play with), then we'd be able to express the panda emoji in a single 32-bit integer.

Here, we've used `charCodeAt()` to determine the individual UTF-16 code units of the Panda emoji and we've found that these are the *55,357th* and *56,380th* decimal code units within Unicode. Since there are so many code units, it is simpler and more convenient to use hexadecimal digits to express them, so we can say that the panda emoji is expressed by code units U+D83D and U+DC3C (Unicode hexadecimal values are conventionally prefixed with U+).

In addition to surrogate pairs, there is another type of combination that's useful to know about. The *Combining Code Point* enables certain traditional *non-combining* code points to be augmented into new characters. Examples of this include traditional Latin characters that can be augmented with accents or other augmentations, such as the combining tilde:

```
const wow = 'w\u0303o\u0303w\u0303'; // => 'w̃õw̃'
```

We've chosen to express this particular combining character via a Unicode escape sequence (\u0303). The format of \uXXXX allows us to express Unicode code units between U+0000 and U+FFFF within JavaScript strings.

 The range of Unicode between U+0000 and U+FFFF is known as the **Basic Multilingual Plane** (**BMP**) and includes the most commonly used everyday characters.

Our panda emoji, as we've already seen, is quite an obscure symbol. It does not exist on the BMP and is thus expressed by a surrogate pair of two UTF-16 code units. We can express these individually in JavaScript strings via two Unicode escape sequences:

```
'\uD83D\uDC3C' === '🐼'; // => true
```

More obscure and ancient symbols are found in the *supplementary* (or *astral*) planes between U+010000 and U+10FFFF. The escaping format of \uXXXX does not have enough slots for us to express these. Symbols within the astral planes require at least five hexadecimal digits to express, so we must use the more recently introduced escape sequence format of \u{X}. This provides up to six hexadecimal slots (\u{XXXXXX}) and can thus express over 1 million different code points. Using this type of escape sequence, we can express our Panda emoji directly via its 32-bit representation (U+1F43C):

```
'\u{1F43C}' === '\uD83D\uDC3C'; // => true
'\u{1F43C}' === '🐼';           // => true
```

The newer \u{X} escape sequence is really convenient and goes some way in making Unicode less burdensome to use than JavaScript. But there is still a little more complexity to explore. Surrogate pairs and combining characters are examples where UTF-16 code units are combined to produce individual symbols. On top of this, there are longer sequences called **grapheme clusters**. These are used to express combinations of code points that can be combined to create an aggregate symbol:

```
const codeUnits = '👨‍👩‍👧‍👦'.split('').map(s => s.charCodeAt(0))

[
  55357, // => leading surrogate
  56425, // => woman (👩)
  8205,  // => zero-width joiner
  55357, // => leading surrogate
  56425, // => woman (👩)
  8205,  // => zero-width joiner
  55357, // => leading surrogate
  56423, // => girl (👧)
  8205,  // => zero-width joiner
  55357, // => leading surrogate
  56422  // => boy (👦)
]
```

Wow! Unicode is a pretty incredible feat of engineering, but it can make things complicated for us. The ability to combine Unicode in all of these ways (combining characters, surrogate pairs, and grapheme clusters) creates a challenge for us. JavaScript strings, as you may know, have a length property. This property returns the number of code units in a given string (that is, the number of 16-bit integers in the entire sequence). For most strings, this is straightforward:

```
'fox'.length;   // => 3
'12345'.length; // => 5
```

However, as we know, we are able to combine code units to create code points and we are also able to combine code points to create grapheme clusters. This means the length property, which is only concerned with the 16-bit code units, can give us unexpected results:

```
'😊'.length; // => 2
```

The smiling-face emoji is composed of two code units, so JavaScript correctly tells us this string has a length of 2. But this may not be what we expect or desire. It's even more challenging when we're dealing with grapheme clusters that may use a dozen different code units to express a single symbol.

 Watch out when attempting to truncate or establish the width of a piece of text within a UI using only its length property. Due to the fact that many Unicode symbols may be expressed by multiple code units, using length alone is not reliable.

Throughout this section, we've explored the tricky domain of Unicode. Va our new understanding of it, we're now far more empowered to cleanly work with strings in JavaScript. Excluding the complexity of Unicode, the behavior of strings in JavaScript is rather intuitive and shouldn't cause many headaches as long as we use them in a way that clearly communicates our intent.

Boolean

The `Boolean` primitive type in JavaScript is used to represent either `true` or `false`. These polar opposites are its only values:

```
const isTrue = true;
const isFalse = false;
```

Semantically, Booleans are used to represent real-life or problem domain values that can be considered on or off (0 or 1), for example, whether a feature is enabled, or whether the user is over a certain age. These are Boolean characteristics and so are appropriate to express via Boolean values. We can use such values to dictate control flow within a program:

```
const age = 100;
const hasLivedTo100 = age >= 100;

if (hasLivedTo100) {
  console.log('Congratulations on living to 100!');
}
```

The `Boolean` primitive, just like `String` and `Number`, can be manually wrapped in a wrapper instance like so:

```
const isTrueObj = new Boolean(true);
```

Note that, once you do this, `Boolean` will behave just like any other object in conditional statements. So, the following conditional statement will succeed, even though the wrapped primitive value is `false`:

```
const isFalseObj = new Boolean(false);

if (isFalseObj) {
  // This will run
}
```

The `Boolean` instance here is not equivalent to its primitive value; it merely contains its primitive value. `isFalseObj` will behave just like any other Object in a `Boolean` context, resolving to `true`. Manually wrapping a `Boolean` like this is not especially useful and should be avoided as an anti-pattern in most programs as it doesn't behave according to Boolean semantics and may produce unexpected results.

> `Boolean` primitives are returned by JavaScript's logical operators such as greater than or equal to (`>=`) or strict equality (`===`). We'll cover these in more detail in `Chapter 8`, *Operators*.

BigInt

The `BigInt` primitive type in JavaScript is used to represent an integer of arbitrary precision. This means that it can be used to represent integers that are not able to be precisely represented by JavaScript's `Number` type (anything larger than ~2^{53}). Literal BigInts are declared by suffixing any sequence of digits with the n character, like so:

```
100007199254740991n
```

`BigInt` is capable of representing integers of arbitrary precision, meaning that you can store integers of unlimited length. This is especially useful in financial applications or any case where high-accuracy integers need to be expressed and operated on.

A `BigInt` can only operate on itself, and is therefore not compatible with many of JavaScript's native `Math` methods:

```
Math.abs(1n); // !! TypeError: Cannot convert a BigInt value to a number
```

All native mathematics operators work with `BigInt` as long as both operands are of the same type:

```
(1n + (2n * 3n)) + 4n; // => 11n
```

However, if one operand is a `BigInt` and the other is a `Number`, then you'll receive a `TypeError`:

```
1n + 1; // !! TypeError: Cannot mix BigInt and other types, use explicit
conversions
```

The semantics of a `BigInt` is similar to `Number`: any value that is intuitively numerical and can be expressed as an integer can be stored in either `BigInt` or `Number`, depending on the extent of precision that it requires.

Symbol

A `Symbol` primitive is used to represent an entirely unique value. Symbols are created via invoking the `Symbol` function, like so:

```
const totallyUniqueKey = Symbol();
```

You can optionally pass an initial argument to this function to annotate your symbol for your own debugging purposes, but this is not necessary:

```
const totallyUniqueKey = Symbol('My Special Key');
```

Symbols are used to act as property keys where uniqueness is required or where you want to store metadata on objects. When you add a property to an object with a `Symbol` key, it will not be iterated over by normal object iteration approaches (such as `for...in`). Symbol keys of an object can only be retrieved via `Object.getOwnPropertySymbols`:

```
const thing = {};
thing.name = 'James';
thing.hobby = 'Kayaking';
thing[Symbol(999)] = 'Something else entirely';

for (let key in thing) console.log(key);
// => "name"
// => "hobby"

const symbols =
  Object.getOwnPropertySymbols(thing); // => [Symbol(999)]

thing[symbols[0]]; // => "Something else entirely"
```

Since `Symbol` keys exist in an explicit but hidden manner, they are useful for storing programmatic information semantically that's unrelated to the core data of the object but useful in fulfilling some programmatic need. For example, you may have a logging library and wish to annotate specific objects with custom-rendering functions that log in a specific way. Such a need could be easily fulfilled with symbols:

```
const log = thing => {
  console.log(
    thing[log.CUSTOM_RENDER] ?
```

```
      thing[log.CUSTOM_RENDER](thing) :
      thing
  );
};
log.CUSTOM_RENDER = Symbol();

class Person {
  constructor(name) {
    this.name = name;
    this[log.CUSTOM_RENDER] = () => {
      return `Person (name = ${this.name})`;
    };
  }
}

log(123); // => Logs "123"
log(new Person('Sarah')); // => Logs: "Person (name = Sarah)"
log(new Person('Wally')); // => Logs: "Person (name = Wally)"
log(new Person('Julie')); // => Logs: "Person (name = Julie)"
```

There are not many everyday situations that would necessitate the creation and usage of new symbols, but there are many instances of prescribing native behavior by such symbols. For example, you can define a custom iterator for your object by using the `Symbol.iterator` property. We will cover this in greater detail in the *Arrays and iterables* section, later in this chapter.

null

The `null` primitive type is used to express the intentional absence of a value. It is a type with only one value: the only null value is `null`.

The semantics of `null` are crucially different from `undefined`. The `undefined` value is used to indicate something that is not declared or defined, while `null` is an explicitly declared absent value. We usually use the `null` value to indicate that a value is either explicitly not yet set or, for whatever reason, unavailable.

For example, let's consider an API where we specify various properties related to a restaurant review:

```
setRestaurantFeatures({
  hasWifi: false,
  hasDisabledAccess: true,
  hasParking: null
});
```

The `null` value, in this context, means that we do not know the value of `hasParking` yet. When we have the necessary information, we can specify `hasParking` as either `true` or `false` (`Boolean`), but to express our ignorance of its true value, we're setting it to `null`. We could also completely leave the value out, meaning that it would effectively be `undefined`. The key difference is that using `null` is always proactively done, while `undefined` is the result of wh something isn't done.

A `null` value, as we mentioned previously, is always falsy, meaning that it will always evaluate to `false` in a `Boolean` context. So, if we attempt to use `null` in a conditional statement, then it would not succeed:

```
function setRestaurantFeatures(features) {
  if (features.hasParking) {
    // This will not run as hasParking is null
  }
}
```

It is important to check for the exact values we want so that we can avoid bugs and communicate effectively to the people reading our code. In this case, we may wish to explicitly check for `undefined` and `null` as we want to execute distinct code for that case versus the case of `false`. We could accomplish this like so:

```
if (features.hasParking !== null && features.hasParking !== undefined) {
  // hasParking is available...
} else {
  // hasParking is not set (undefined) or unavailable (null)
}
```

We can also use the abstract equality operator (==) to compare to `null`, which will helpfully evaluate to `true` if the operand is either `null` or `undefined`:

```
if (features.hasParking != null) {
  // hasParking is available...
} else {
  // hasParking is not set (undefined) or unavailable (null)
}
```

This is, in fact, doing the same as the more explicit comparison, but is far more succinct. Unfortunately, it's not very clear that its intention is to check for both `null` and `undefined`. We should usually prefer being explicit as this allows us to communicate our intent to other programmers in a more efficient way.

A final trap to avoid with null is the `typeof` operator. Due to some legacies of the JavaScript language, `typeof null` will, rather confusingly, return `"object"` and is therefore entirely unreliable.

More information about `typeof` and detection of the `null` type can be found in `Chapter 7`, *Dynamic Typing*, in the *Detection* section.

So, there you have it. Null is a simple enough value and, insofar as clean code is concerned, you won't go wrong if you remember two key points: that it should only be used to express the intentional absence of a value and that it should, ideally, be checked explicitly (prefer `value === null`).

undefined

The `undefined` primitive type expresses that something hasn't been defined yet or remains undefined. Like `null`, it is a type with only one value (`undefined`). Unlike `null`, an `undefined` value should not be explicitly set, but may be returned by the language when something does not have a value:

```
const coffee = {
  type: 'Flat White',
  shots: 2
};

coffee.name; // => undefined
coffee.type; // => "Flat White"
```

Undefined is best thought of as the absence of something. If you ever find yourself wishing to explicitly set something to `undefined`, you should probably reach for `null` instead.

It's important to distinguish between the concepts of undefined and not even declared. In JavaScript, if you try to evaluate an identifier that does not exist within your scope, you will get a `ReferenceError`:

```
thisDoesNotExist; // !! ReferenceError: thisDoesNotExist is not defined
```

However, as you've already seen, if you try to evaluate a property of an object and the property does not exist, you will get no such error. Instead, it will evaluate to `undefined`:

```
const obj = {};
obj.foo; // => undefined
```

However, if you try to access a property under the non-existent `foo` property, you'll receive a `TypeError` complaining that it cannot read a property that has an `undefined` value:

```
obj.foo.baz; // !! TypeError: Cannot read property 'baz' of undefined
```

This behavior is an extension of the fact that seeking to access any property on an `undefined` or `null` value will always throw such a `TypeError`:

```
(undefined).foo;  // !! TypeError: Cannot read property 'foo' of undefined
```

Curiously, the `undefined` value, unlike `null`, is not a literal, but is a globally available value provided by the language. Overwriting this global value is not possible in ECMAScript 2015 onward, but it is still possible to define your own value for the undefined identifier in local (non-global) scopes:

```
undefined; // => undefined

function weird() {
  let undefined = 1;
  undefined; // => 1
}
```

This is an anti-pattern as it can create very awkward and unexpected results. The accidental setting of `undefined` in a scope higher than your scope can mean that, if you were to rely on the value directly, you may end up referring to a value other than `undefined`. This lack of trust in the `undefined` value has historically meant that people have found other ways to forcefully make `undefined` available in their scope. For example, declaring a variable but not assigning it will always result in its value being `undefined`:

```
function scopeWithReliableUndefined() {
  let undefined;
  undefined; // => undefined
}
```

You can also use JavaScript's `void` operator on any value that will always return the *real* undefined value:

```
void 0;         // => undefined
void null;      // => undefined
void undefined; // => undefined
```

Explicitly setting undefined within your scope means that you can safely refer to your undefined value without worrying that it has been compromised. Fortunately, however, you can avoid the pain of having to worry about this risk by using the typeof operator:

```
if (typeof myValue === 'undefined') { ... }
```

This will not throw a ReferenceError even if myValue does not exist. The typeof operator, as we've discovered with null, is a bit of a fair-weather friend as we can't always rely on it, but it is nonetheless very useful when explicitly checking for undefined.

 Another way to avoid the risk of undefined is to enforce its correct usage within your code base by using a linting tool. We'll cover linting tools in Chapter 15, *Tools for Cleaner Code*.

In summary, undefined can be used cleanly if you remember the following two points:

- Avoid directly assigning undefined to a variable; you should use null instead
- Always check for undefined explicitly, preferring the typeof operator

This concludes our exploration of primitive types in JavaScript. Now, we'll move on to non-primitives, that is, objects.

Objects

Everything that is not a primitive value in JavaScript can be considered an object. Even functions are, in fact, specialized objects; their only difference is that they can be invoked. Usually, however, when we use the term Object, we are referring to a plain object that is normally declared as an object literal delimited by curly braces, with a set of key-value pairs within:

```
const animal = {
  name: 'Duck',
  hobby: 'Paddling'
};
```

You can also instantiate an object via the Object constructor and then add properties directly:

```
const animal = new Object();
animal.name = 'Duck';
animal.hobby = 'Paddling';
```

Even though they are equivalent, it's preferable to use an object literal in most situations as it is simpler to declare and to read, especially if there are many properties. It also has the added benefit of allowing you to create and pass an object as an expression without having to prepare it beforehand.

Property names

The keys that are used to add properties to objects (the property names) are internally stored as strings. However, when using the object literal syntax, you can declare the keys as regular identifiers (that is, anything you could use as a variable name), number literals, or string literals:

```
const object = {
  foo: 123,   // Using an identifier as the key
  "baz": 123, // Using a String literal as the key
  123: 123    // Using a Number literal as the key
};
```

It's preferable to use identifiers where possible as this helpfully restricts you to using key names that can easily be accessed as properties. If you use a string literal that is not also a valid identifier, then you'll have to use square-bracket notation to access it, which can be burdensome:

```
const data = {
  hobbies: ['tennis', 'kayaking'],
  'my hobbies': ['tennis', 'kayaking']
};

data.hobbies;        // Easy
data['my hobbies'];  // Burdensome
```

You can also use computed property names (delimited by square brackets) to add dynamically named items to an object literal:

```
const data = {
  ['item' + (1 + 2)]: 'foo'
};

data; // => { item3: "foo" }
data.item3; // => "foo"
```

As we mentioned previously, all non-primitives in JavaScript are technically objects. What else makes something an object, though? Objects allow us to assign arbitrary values to them as properties, which is something primitives are not capable of. Beyond this characteristic, the definition of an object in JavaScript is left invitingly generic. We can wield objects in many different ways to suit the code we're writing. Many languages will provide language constructs for dictionaries or hashmaps. In JavaScript, we can use objects to fulfill most of these needs. When we need to use store a key-value pair where the key is something other than a string, it's common to provide a string representation of that value via the object's `toString` method:

```
const me = {
  name: 'James',
  location: 'England',
  toString() {
    return [this.name, this.location].join(', ')
  }
};

me.toString(); // => "James, England"
String(me); // => "James, England"
```

This will be called internally when the object is put in a context where it is coerced to a string, such as when accessing or assigning via square-bracket notation:

```
const peopleInEurope = {};

peopleInEurope[me] = true;
Object.keys(peopleInEurope); // => ["James, England"]
peopleInEurope[me]; // => true
```

This has historically been used to allow the implementation of data structures where the key is effectively non-primitive (even though objects technically store property names as strings). Nowadays, however, using `Map` or `WeakMap` is preferred.

Property descriptors

When adding properties to objects in the conventional fashion, either via property access or via an object literal, the properties will be given the following implicit traits:

- `configurable`: This means the property can be deleted from the object (and if its property descriptor can be changed)

- `enumerable`: This means the property will be visible to enumerations such as `for...in` and `Object.keys()`
- `writable`: This means the property's value can be changed via an assignment operator (such as `obj.prop = ...`)

JavaScript gives you the power to turn off these traits individually, but be wary that changes to these traits can obscure the behavior of your code. For example, if a property is described as not being writeable but a write is attempted via assignment (for example, `obj.prop = 123`), then the programmer will receive no warning that the write has not occurred. This can create unexpected and hard-to-find bugs. As ever, it's vital to keep in mind the expectations of the programmers who will be consuming your interfaces. So you keep the property descriptors with care and consideration.

You can define your own traits for a given property via the natively provided `Object.defineProperty()`. When setting up a new property descriptor, the default of each trait will be `false`, so if you wish to give the property a trait of either `configurable`, `enumerable`, or `writable`, then you will need to specify these as `true` explicitly:

```
const myObject = {};

Object.defineProperty(myObject, 'name', {
  writeable: false,
  configurable: false,
  enumerable: true,
  value: 'The Unchangeable Name'
});

myObject.name; // => "The Unchangeable Name"
myObject.name = 'something else'; // => (Ineffective)
myObject.name; // => "The Unchangeable Name"

delete myObject.name; // => false (Ineffective)
myObject.name; // => "The Unchangeable Name"
```

You can also use `Object.defineProperties()` to describe many properties at once:

```
const chocolate = Object.defineProperties({
  // Empty object where our described properties
  // will be placed
}, {
 name: { value: 'Chocolate', enumerable: false },
 tastes: { value: ['Bitter', 'Sweet'], enumerable: true }
});
```

```
chocolate.name; // => "Chocolate"
chocolate.tastes; // => ["Bitter", "Sweet"]

Object.keys(chocolate); // => ["tastes"]
```

If you attempt to change the traits of a property that has `configurable` set to `false`, then you will receive a `TypeError`:

```
const obj = {};

Object.defineProperty(
 obj,
 'timestamp',
 { configurable: false, value: Date.now() }
);

Object.defineProperty(
  obj,
  'timestamp',
  { configurable: true }
);
// ! TypeError: Cannot redefine property: timestamp
```

It is also possible to set custom setters and getters. A getter defines what value will be returned when a property is accessed, while a setter will define what occurs when an assignment is attempted on that property (that is, via the assignment operator). Using these can be useful in situations where you wish to have an internal implementation that holds the value in a unique way or somehow filters or processes the value upon assignment, for example:

```
const data = Object.defineProperties({}, {
  name: {
    set(name) { this.normalizedName = name.toLowerCase(); },
    get() { return this.normalizedName; }
  }
});

data.name = 'MoLLy BroWn';
data.name; // => "molly brown"
```

As the `name` property here has been described via `defineProperties`, it will have all of the default traits disabled, which means it is not enumerable, writeable, or configurable. If we try to enumerate it, we'll discover that our internally used `normalizedName` is found:

```
Object.keys(data); // => ["normalizedName"]
```

This is something to keep in mind when working with property descriptors. Make sure you're aware of what traits every property has and watch out for leakage of your internal implementation!

It's worth noting that it is also possible (and often preferable) to define getters and setters for properties directly within an object literal or class definition. For example, we could create a subclass of `Array` with the addition of a `last` property, which acts as a getter for the last element in the array:

```
class SpecialArray extends Array {
  get last() { return this[this.length - 1]; }
}

const myArray = new SpecialArray('a', 'b', 'c', 'd');
myArray.last; // => "d"
myArray.push('e');
myArray.last; // => "e"
```

There are many such creative uses of getters and setters. But, as with the traits of `configurable`, `enumerable`, and `writable`, it's important to be cautious of how your custom behaviors will affect the expectations of your fellow programmers. If the abstraction or data structures you create are not familiar or predictable in their behavior, then you're paving the way for misunderstandings and bugs. The best approach is to align with the natural semantics of the language itself. So, whenever you are about to create a custom setter or describe a property as unwritable, ask yourself whether it would be reasonable for a programmer to expect it to work that way. Follow a helpful rule dubbed as the **Principle of Least Astonishment (POLA)**!

 The POLA (or least surprise) applies to software design and UX design. It broadly means that a given function or component of a system should act as most users would expect it to and should seek not to surprise or astonish too much.

Map and WeakMap

The `Map` and `WeakMap` abstractions are capable of storing key-value pairs where, unlike regular objects, the key can be anything, including non-primitive values:

```
const populationBySpecies = new Map();
const reindeer = { name: 'Reindeer', formalName: 'Rangifer tarandus' };

populationBySpecies.set(reindeer, 2000000);
populationBySpecies.get(reindeer); // => 2,000,000
```

WeakMap is similar to Map, but it only holds a weak reference to the object that's used as a key, meaning that, if the object becomes unavailable due to being garbage-collected elsewhere in your program, then WeakMap will cease to keep a hold of it.

Most of the time, a plain object is all you will need. You should only reach for Map or WeakMap if you need your keys to be non-primitive or if you want to weakly hold your values.

The prototype

JavaScript is a prototypical language where inheritance is achieved via prototypes. This can be a daunting concept, but it is, in fact, beautifully simple. JavaScript's prototypal behavior can be described like this: every time a property is accessed on an object, if it is not available on the object itself, JavaScript will attempt to access it on an internally available property called [[Prototype]]. It will then repeat this process until it either finds the property or gets to the top of the prototype *chain* and returns undefined.

 Understanding what this [[Prototype]] property is capable of will give you great power over the language and will immediately make JavaScript less daunting. It can be difficult to grasp but is worth it in the end.

A [[Prototype]] object, which could feasibly be attached to any other object, is just a regular object itself. We could create one called engineerPrototype and have it contain data and methods related to the role of an engineer, for example:

```
const engineerPrototype = {
  type: 'Engineer',
  sayHello() {
    return `Hello, I'm ${this.name} and I'm an ${this.type}`;
  }
};
```

Then, we could attach this prototype to another object, thus making its properties available there as well. To do this, we use Object.create(), which creates a new object with a hardcoded [[Prototype]]:

```
const pandaTheEngineer = Object.create(engineerPrototype);
```

The internal `[[Prototype]]` property cannot be directly set, so we must use mechanisms such as `Object.create` and `Object.setPrototypeOf`. Note that you may have seen code that uses the non-standard __proto__ property to set `[[Prototype]]`, but this is a legacy feature and should not be relied on.

With this newly created `pandaTheEngineer` object, we are able to access any properties available on its `[[Prototype]]`, such as `engineerPrototype`:

```
pandaTheEngineer.name = 'Panda';
pandaTheEngineer.sayHello(); // => "Hello, I'm Panda and I'm an Engineer"
```

We can illustrate that the objects are now linked by adding a new property to `engineerPrototype` and observe how it is made available on `pandaTheEngineer`:

```
pandaTheEngineer.sayGoodbye; // => TypeError: sayGoodbye is not a function
engineerPrototype.sayGoodbye = () => 'Goodbye!';
pandaTheEngineer.sayGoodbye(); // => 'Goodbye!'
```

As we mentioned previously, the `[[Prototype]]` of an object will only be used to resolve a property if it is not already available on the object itself. The following code shows how we can set our own `sayHello` method on our `pandaTheEngineer` object, and that by doing so we no longer have access to the `sayHello` method defined on `[[Prototype]]`:

```
pandaTheEngineer.sayHello = () => 'Yo!';
pandaTheEngineer.sayHello(); // => "Yo!"
```

However, deleting this newly added `sayHello` method would mean we once again have access to the `[[Prototype]]` `sayHello` method:

```
delete pandaTheEngineer.sayHello;
pandaTheEngineer.sayHello(); // => // => "Hello, I'm Panda and I'm an
Engineer"
```

To understand what's happening and which properties are coming from which object, we are always able to inspect the `[[Prototype]]` of an object using `Object.getPrototypeOf`:

```
// We can inspect its prototype:
Object.getPrototypeOf(pandaTheEngineer) === engineerPrototype; // => true
```

Now, we can inspect its properties via `Object.getOwnPropertyNames`:

```
Object.getOwnPropertyNames(
  Object.getPrototypeOf(pandaTheEngineer)
); // => ["type", "sayHello", "sayGoodbye"]
```

Here, we can see that the `[[Prototype]]` object (that is, `engineerPrototype`) is providing the `type`, `sayHello`, and `sayGoodbye` properties. If we inspect the `pandaTheEngineer` object itself, we can see that it only has a `name` property:

```
Object.getOwnPropertyNames(pandaTheEngineer); // => ["name"]
```

As we observed with our earlier addition of the `sayGoodbye` method, we can modify that prototype at any time and have our changes accessible to any objects that use that prototype. Here's another example of doing this:

```
// Modify the prototype object:
engineerPrototype.type = "Awesome Engineer";

// Call a method on our object (that uses the prototype):
pandaTheEngineer.sayHello(); // => "Hello, I'm Panda and I'm an Awesome
Engineer"
```

Here, you can see how our inherited `sayHello` method is producing a string that includes our mutated type property (that is, `"Awesome Engineer"`).

 Hopefully, you are beginning to see how we could construct a hierarchy of inheritance using prototypes. The very simple mechanism of `[[Prototype]]` allows us to express complex hierarchical relations between problem domains expressed as objects. This is how OOP is achieved in JavaScript.

We could feasibly create another prototype that itself uses `engineerPrototype`, possibly `fullStackEngineerPrototype`, and it would work as expected, with each prototype defining another layer of property resolution.

Below the surface, JavaScript's newer *Class Definition Syntax*, which you may have grown accustomed to, relies on this underlying mechanism of prototypes as well. This can be observed here:

```
class Engineer {
  type = 'Engineer'
  constructor(name) {
    this.name = name;
  }
  sayHello() {
    return `Hello, I'm ${this.name} and I'm an ${this.type}`;
  }
}

const pandaTheEngineer = new Engineer();
```

```
Object.getOwnPropertyNames(pandaTheEngineer); // => ["type", "name"]

Object.getOwnPropertyNames(
  Object.getPrototypeOf(pandaTheEngineer)
); // => ["constructor", "sayHello"]
```

You'll notice that there are some subtle differences here. The most crucial one is that, when declaring classes, there is currently no way to define non-method properties on the prototype object. When we declare the `type` property, we are populating the instance itself so that when we inspect the properties of the instance, we get "type" and "name". However, the methods (such as `sayHello`) will exist on the `[[Prototype]]`. Another difference is that, of course, when using classes, we are able to declare a `constructor`, which itself is a method/property on the `[[Prototype]]`.

 Fundamentally, the *Class Definition Syntax* (introduced in *ECMAScript 2015*), does not make anything possible that was not already possible in the language. It's just utilizing the existing prototypical mechanism. However, the newer syntax does make some things simpler, such as referring to a superclass with the `super` keyword.

Before class definitions existed, we typically wrote class-like abstractions by assigning our intended `[[Prototype]]` object to the `prototype` property of a function, as shown here:

```
function Engineer(name) {
  this.name = name;
}

Engineer.prototype = {
  type: 'Engineer',
  sayHello() {
    return `Hello, I'm ${this.name} and I'm an ${this.type}`;
  }
};
```

When a function is instantiated via the `new` operator, JavaScript will implicitly create a new object with its `[[Prototype]]` set to the function's `prototype` property, if it has one. Let's try instantiating the `Engineer` function:

```
const pandaTheEngineer = new Engineer();
```

Inspecting this yields the same characteristics that we saw in our original `Object.create` approach:

```
Object.getOwnPropertyNames(pandaTheEngineer); // => ["name"]

Object.getOwnPropertyNames(
```

```
  Object.getPrototypeOf(pandaTheEngineer)
); // => ["type", "sayHello"]
```

Broadly, all of these approaches are the same but have some subtle differences around where certain properties reside (that is, whether its properties are on the instance itself or on its [[Prototype]]). The newer *Class Definition Syntax* is useful and succinct and so is preferable nowadays, but it is nonetheless useful to have an underlying knowledge about how prototypes work as it drives the entirety of the language, including all of its native types. We can inspect these native types in the same manner as in the preceding code:

```
const array = ['wow', 'an', 'array'];

Object.getOwnPropertyNames(array); // => ["0", "1", "2", "length"]

Object.getOwnPropertyNames(
  Object.getPrototypeOf(array)
); // => ["constructor", "concat", "find", "findIndex", "lastIndexOf",
"pop", "push", ...]
```

 Mutating native prototypes is an anti-pattern and should be avoided at all costs as it can create unexpected conflicts with other code in your code base. Since a runtime will only have a single set of native types available, when you modify them, you are modifying the capabilities of every single instance of that type that currently exists. Therefore, it is best to abide by a simple rule: **only modify your own prototypes**.

If you ever catch yourself trying to modify a native prototype, it may be better if you created your own subclass of that type and added your functionality there:

```
class HeartArray extends Array {
  join() {
    return super.join(' ❤ ');
  }
}

const yay = new HeartArray('this', 'is', 'lovely');

yay.join(); // => "this ❤ is ❤ lovely"
```

Here, we're creating our own Array subclass called HeartArray so that we can add our own specialized join method.

When and how to use objects

An object of any type, much like our primitive values, should only be used inline with the semantic concept it represents. The preceding case of subclassing `Array` to `HeartArray` makes sense as the data we wish to express via it is indeed array-like, that is, it is a sequential set of words.

When we go about molding objects into abstractions that suit our needs, we should always consider the expectations that other programmers will have about objects and the ramifications of those expectations. We'll go into the subtleties of designing good abstractions in `Chapter 11`, *Design Patterns*, where we will be utilizing objects to craft abstractions in a multitude of ways.

This section has introduced you to the concept of objects in JavaScript—how they are everywhere—and how they operate beneath the surface via prototypes. This fundamental knowledge will make working with JavaScript much easier and will help you write cleaner code.

Functions

Functions in JavaScript are like any other type; they can be passed around just like objects and primitive types. When we talk about most other values, however, we see that there is usually only one way to literally declare them. Object literals are declared using braces. Array literals are delimited square brackets. Functions, however, come in a variety of literal forms.

When outside of an object literal or class definition, you can declare a function in three different ways: as a function declaration, as a function expression, or as a fat-arrow function expression:

```
// Function Declaration
function myFunction() {}

// Function Expression
const myFunction = function () {};

// Named Function Expression
const myFunction = function myFunction() {};

// "Fat"-Arrow Function Expression
const myFunction = () => {};
```

When declaring functions inside object literals, however, there is a more succinct syntax, called a **method definition**:

```
const things = {
  myMethod() {},
  anotherMethod() {}
};
```

We need to separate these method definitions with a comma (just as we'd have to do with any other properties defined in an object literal). Class definitions also allow us to use method definitions, although they don't require separating commas:

```
class Thing {
  myMethod() {}
  anotherMethod() {}
}
```

 Methods are just functions that are *bound* to an object when invoked. This includes functions defined within class definitions and functions that are in any way assigned to a property of an object. When discussing code with other programmers, it's useful to know what people mean when they say *method* versus *function*. Fundamentally, however, the language of JavaScript does not distinguish between these—they are all technically just functions.

All the various ways of defining functions have subtle differences that are worth knowing about because the typical JavaScript code base will use most, if not all, of these styles. The types of differences you'll encounter in how functions are declared include the following:

- Whether the definition style is *hoisted* to the top of its scope; for example, with function declarations
- Whether the definition style creates a function that has its own bindings (for example, `this`); for example, with function expressions
- Whether the definition style creates a function with its own `name` property; for example, with function declarations
- Whether the definition style is contextual to specific areas of code; for example, with method definitions

Now, we can go into more detail about the syntax of the various definition styles.

Syntactic context

There are three syntactic contexts in which a function can exist:

- As a statement
- As an expression
- As a method definition

 Statements can be thought of as the scaffolding. For example, const X = 123 is a *Statement* that contains a const declaration and assignment. **Expressions** can be thought of as the values that you place into the scaffolding; for example, 123 in the latter *statement* is an *expression*. In Chapter 9, *Parts of Syntax and Scope,* we'll talk about this topic in more detail.

The difference between functions as statements and functions as expressions is exemplified by the function expression and the function declaration. The function declaration is quite unique in that it is the only way to declare a function that is technically a statement. To be considered a function declaration, the syntax of function name() {} must reside on its own without being used in the context of an expression. This can be incredibly confusing because you cannot always tell whether a function is a function declaration or function expression based purely on its own syntax; instead, you must look at the context in which it exists:

```
// This is a statement, and a function declaration:
// And will therefore be hoisted:
function wow() {}

// This is a statement containing a function expression:
const wow = function wow() {};
```

As we mentioned previously, a function expression is allowed to have a name, just like a function declaration, but that name may not match the name of the variable that the function is assigned to.

It's easiest to think of expressions as anything that can legally exist to the right-hand side of the assignment operator. All of the following *right-hand sides* are legal expressions:

```
foo = 123;
foo = [1,2,3];
foo = {1:2,3:4};
foo = 1 | 2 | 3;
foo = function() {};
foo = (function(){})();
foo = [function(){}, ()=>{}, function baz(){}];
```

Function expressions are as flexible as all the other values in JavaScript in terms of where they can be placed syntactically. Function declarations, as we will discover, are limited. Method definitions are also limited to exist within the confines of either an object literal or a class definition.

Function bindings and this

A function's bindings refer to a set of additional and implicit values that JavaScript makes available for referencing within the body of the function. These bindings include the following:

- `this`: The `this` keyword refers to the execution context of a function's invocation
- `super`: The `super` keyword in a method or constructor refers to its super-class
- `new.target`: This binding informs you as to whether the function was invoked as a constructor (via the `new` operator)
- `arguments`: This binding provides access to the arguments that are passed to a function when it is invoked

These bindings are available to all functions except those defined with the arrow syntax (`fn = () => {}`). Functions defined in this way will effectively absorb the bindings from the parent scope (if one is available). Each of these bindings has unique behaviors and constraints. We will explore these in the following subsections.

Execution context

The `this` keyword is usually determined at the calltime of the function and will normally resolve to the object that the function is being invoked on. It is sometimes referred to as the execution context of a function or its `thisArg`. This can be unintuitive since it means that the `this` value can technically change between calls. For example, we could assign a method from one object to another, call it on the second, and observe that its `this` is always the object it's been called on:

```
const london = { name: 'London' };
const tokyo = { name: 'Tokyo' };

function sayMyName() {
  console.log(`My name is ${this.name}`);
}

sayMyName(); // => Logs: "My name is undefined"

london.sayMyName = sayMyName;
london.sayMyName(); // => Logs "My name is London"

tokyo.sayMyName = sayMyName;
tokyo.sayMyName(); // => Logs "My name is Tokyo"
```

When called without an object of invocation, as is the case when we directly call `sayMyName`, its presumed execution context is the global environment in which the code resides. On the browser, this global environment is equal to the window object (which provides access to the browser-and-document object models), while in Node.js, this refers to an environment that's unique to each specific module/file, which includes, among other things, that module's exports.

In addition to the case of calling a function globally, there are two cases where the `this` keyword will be something other than the apparent object of invocation:

- If the function being called was defined as an arrow-function, then it will absorb the `this` value from the scope in which it is situated
- If the function being called is a constructor, its `this` value that will be a new object that has its `[[Prototype]]` preset to the prototype property of the function

There are also ways to force the value of `this` when calling or declaring a function. You can use `bind(X)` to create a new function that will have its `this` value set to X:

```
const sayHelloToTokyo = sayMyName.bind(tokyo);
sayHelloToTokyo(); // => Logs "My name is Tokyo"
```

You can also use a function's `call` and `apply` methods to force the `this` value for any given invocation, but note that this will not work if the function is being called as a constructor (that is, with a new keyword) or if it has been defined with the arrow-function syntax:

```
// Forcing the value of `this` via `.call()`:
tokyo.sayMyName.call(london); // => Logs "My name is London"
```

In your everyday function calls, it's best to avoid awkward techniques of invocation like this. Such techniques can make it difficult for the readers of your code to discern what's happening. There are many valid applications of invoking via `call`, `apply`, or `bind`, but these are usually limited to lower-level libraries or utility code. Higher-level logic should avoid them. If you find yourself having to rely on these methods in higher-level abstractions, then you're likely making something more complicated than it needs to be.

super

The super keyword comes in three distinct flavors:

- `super()` as a direct function invocation will call the superclass's constructor (that is, its object's `[[Prototype]]` constructor) and is only valid to call within a constructor. It also must be called before trying to access `this` as it is `super()` itself that'll initiate the execution context.
- `super.property` will access a property on the superclass (that is, the `[[Prototype]]`), and is only valid to reference within a constructor or method defined using the method definition syntax.
- `super.method()` will invoke a method on the superclass (that is, the `[[Prototype]]`), and is only valid to call within a constructor or method defined using the method definition syntax.

The super keyword was introduced to the language at the same time as the class definition and method definition syntax, so it is tied up in those constructs. You are free to use super in class constructors, methods, and also in method definitions within object literals:

```
const Utils {
  constructor() {
    super(); // <= I can use super here
  }
  method() {
    super.method(); // <= And here...
  }
}
```

```
const utils = {
  method() {
    return super.property; // <= And even here...
  }
};
```

The `super` keyword, as its name suggests, is semantically suited to referencing a superclass, so 99% of its valid use cases will be within class definitions, where you're seeking to reference the class being extended, like so:

```
const Banana extends Fruit {
  constructor() {
    super(); // Call the Fruit constructor
  }
}
```

Using `super` in this manner is entirely intuitive, especially to programmers who are used to other OOP languages. For individuals adept with JavaScript's prototype mechanism, however, the implementation of `super` can seem confusing. Unlike the `this` value, `super` is bound at definition time, instead of call time. We've seen how we can manipulate the value of this by calling a method in a specific manner (for example, using `fn.call()`). You cannot similarly manipulate `super`. Hopefully, this will not affect you in any way, but it is useful to remember nonetheless.

new.target

The `new.target` binding will be equal to the current function being called if the function has been called via a `new` operator. We typically use the `new` operator to instantiate classes, and in this case, we will correctly expect `new.target` to be that class:

```
class Foo {
  constructor() {
    console.log(new.target === Foo);
  }
}
new Foo(); // => Logs: true
```

This is useful when we may wish to carry out a certain behavior if a constructor is called directly versus when called via `new`. A common defensive strategy is to make your constructor behave in the same way, regardless of whether it's called with or without `new`. This can be achieved by checking for `new.target`:

```
function Foo() {
  if (new.target !== Foo) {
```

```
      return new Foo();
   }
}

new Foo() instanceof Foo;  // => true
Foo() instanceof Foo;      // => true
```

Alternatively, you may wish to throw an error to check that a constructor has been invoked incorrectly:

```
function Foo() {
   if (new.target !== Foo) {
     throw new Error('Foo is a constructor: please instantiate via new
Foo()');
   }
}

Foo() instanceof Foo; // !! Error: Foo is a constructor: please instantiate
via new Foo()
```

Both of these examples would be considered intuitive use cases of `new.target`. There is, of course, the possibility to use it to deliver entirely different functionality depending on the calling pattern, but in the interest of catering to the reasonable expectations of programmers, it's best to avoid such behavior. Remember the POLA.

arguments

The `arguments` binding is made available as an array-like object and will contain the arguments that a given function was called with.

> When we say that `arguments` is array-like, we are referring to the fact that it has a `length` property and properties indexed from zero (just like a regular `Array`), but it still just a regular `Object` and therefore does not have any of array's built-in methods available, such as `forEach`, `reduce`, and `map`.

Here, we can observe that the arguments are provided within the scope of a given function:

```
function sum() {
  arguments; // => [1, 2, 3, 4, 5] (Array-like object)
  let total = 0;
  for (let n of arguments) total += n;
  return total;
}

sum(1, 2, 3, 4, 5);
```

The `arguments` binding was popularly used to gain access to an arbitrary (that is, non-fixed) amount of arguments, though its usefulness quickly disappeared after the language introduced the *rest parameter* syntax (`...arg`). This newer syntax can be used when defining a function to instruct JavaScript to place remaining arguments into a singular array. This meant that you could achieve all of the utility of the older `arguments` binding, plus you'd have a value that was not merely array-like but actually a genuine array. Here's an example:

```
function sum(...numbers) {
  // We can call reduce() on our array:
  return numbers.reduce((total, n) => total + n, 0);
}

sum(1, 2, 3, 4, 5);
```

Even though the `arguments` object has fallen out of favor, it is still within the language spec and works in older environments, so you may still see it in the wild. Most of the time, its usage can be avoided.

Function names

Confusingly, functions have names, and these names are not the same as the variables or properties that we assign to functions. The name of a function is within its syntax, prior to its parentheses:

```
function nameOfTheFunction() {}
```

You can access a function's name via its `name` property:

```
nameOfTheFunction.name; // => "nameOfTheFunction"
```

When you define a function via the function declaration syntax, it'll assign that function to a local variable of the same name, meaning that we can reference the function as we would expect:

```
function nameOfTheFunction() {}
nameOfTheFunction; // => the function
nameOfTheFunction.name; // => "nameOfTheFunction"
```

Method definitions will also assign the method to a property name that is equal to the function name:

```
function nameOfTheFunction() {}
nameOfTheFunction; // => the function
nameOfTheFunction.name; // => "nameOfTheFunction"
```

You may be thinking this all seems incredibly intuitive. And it is. It makes perfect sense that the names we give our functions and methods are themselves used to dictate what variable or property those things will be assigned to. Oddly, though, it is also possible to have named function expressions, and these names do not cause such an assignment. The following is an example of this:

```
const myFunction = function hullaballoo() {}
```

The `const` name here, `myFunction`, dictates what we will use in subsequent lines to reference the function. However, the function technically has a name of `"hullaballoo"`:

```
myFunction; // => the function
myFunction.name; // => "hullaballoo"
```

If we try to reference the function via its formal name, we will get an error:

```
hullaballoo; // !! ReferenceError: hullaballoo is not defined
```

This can seem odd. Why is it possible to give a function a name if that name itself is not used to refer to the function? This is a mixture of legacy and convenience. One hidden feature of the named function expression is that the name is actually available to you to reference the function, but only inside the scope of the function itself:

```
const myFunction = function hullaballoo() {
  hullaballoo; // => the function
};
```

This can be useful in situations where you want to supply an *anonymous* callback to some other function but still be able to reference your own callback for any repeated or recursive calls, like so:

```
[
  ['chris', 'smith'],
  ['sarah', ['talob', 'peters']],
  ['pam', 'taylor']
].map(function capitalizeNames(item) {
  return Array.isArray(item) ?
    item.map(capitalizeNames) :
    item.slice(0, 1).toUpperCase() + item.slice(1);
});

// => [["Chris","Smith"],["Sarah",["Talob", "Peters"]],["Pam","Taylor"]]
```

So, even though the named function expression is an odd thing, it does have its merits. In usage, however, it's best to take into consideration the clarity of your code for people who might not know of these idiosyncratic behaviors. This does not mean avoiding it altogether, but just being ever more mindful of the readability of your code when using it.

Function declarations

Function declarations are a type of *hoisted declaration*. A hoisted declaration is one that will, at runtime, be effectively hoisted up the top of its execution context, meaning that it will be immediately accessible to preceding lines of code (seemingly *before* it's declared):

```
hoistedDeclaration(); // => Does not throw an error...

function hoistedDeclaration() {}
```

This, of course, is not possible with a function expression that's been assigned to a variable:

```
regularFunctionExpression();
  // => Uncaught ReferenceError:
  // => Cannot access 'regularFunctionExpression' before initialization

const regularFunctionExpression = function() {};
```

The hoisted behavior of function declarations can create unexpected results, so it is typically considered an anti-pattern to rely on the hoist. In general, it's fine to use function declarations, as long as they're used in a way that respects the assumptions that programmers will intuitively make. Hoisting, as a practice, is not very intuitive to most people, and so it's usually best to avoid it.

For more information on scopes and how hoisting occurs in the case of function declarations, please take a look at `Chapter 9`, *Parts of Syntax and Scope*, and go to the *Scopes and Declarations* section.

Function expressions

Function expressions are the easiest and most predictable to use as they are syntactically similar to all the other values within JavaScript. You can use them to *literally* define functions anywhere you would define any other value as they are a type of expression. Observe here, for example, how we're defining an array of functions:

```
const arrayOfFunctions = [
  function(){},
  function(){}
];
```

A common application of the function expression is in passing callbacks to other functions so that they can be called at some later point. Many native `Array` methods, such as `forEach`, accept functions in this manner:

```
[1, 2, 3].forEach(function(value) {
  // do something with each value
});
```

Here, we are passing a function expression to the `forEach` method. We haven't named this function by assigning it to a variable, so it is considered an anonymous function. Anonymous functions are useful as they mean that we don't need to preassign a function to a variable in order to make use of it; we can simply write our function into our code at the exact location of usage.

The function expression is most similar in its expressive manner to the arrow function. The key difference, as we will discover, is that the arrow function does not have access to its own bindings (for example, to `this` or `arguments`). A function expression, however, does have access to these values, and so in some contexts will be more useful to you. It's very common to need a binding to `this` in order to operate successfully with the DOM API, for example, where many native DOM methods will invoke callbacks and event handlers with the relevant element as execution context. Additionally, you'll want to use function expressions when defining methods on objects or prototypes that will need to access the current instance. As illustrated here, using an arrow function would not be appropriate:

```
class FooBear {
  name = 'Foo Bear';
```

```
}

FooBear.prototype.sayHello = () => `Hello I am ${this.name}`;
new FooBear().sayHello(); // => "Hello I am ";

FooBear.prototype.sayHello = function() {
  return `Hello I am ${this.name}`;
};
new FooBear().sayHello(); // => "Hello I am Foo Bear";
```

As you can see, using the arrow function syntax prevents us from accessing the instance via `this`, while the function expression syntax allows us to do this. Therefore, the function expression, although somewhat superseded by the more succinct arrow function, is still a very useful tool.

Arrow functions

The arrow function is, in many ways, just a slightly more succinct version of the function expression, although it does have some practical differences. It comes in two flavors:

```
// Regular Arrow Function
const arrow = (arg1, arg2) => { return 123; };

// Concise Arrow Function
const arrow = (arg1, arg2) => 123;
```

As you can see, the *concise* variant includes an implicit return, while the *regular* variant, much like other function definition styles, requires you to define a regular function body delimited by curly braces in which you must explicitly return a value with a `return` statement.

Additionally, arrow functions allow you to avoid using parentheses when declaring a function with only one argument. In these cases, you can just place the identifier of the argument by itself prior to the arrow, like so:

```
const addOne = n => n + 1;
```

The succinctness of the arrow function can be very useful in situations where you need to pass functions around quite a lot. This is common, for example, when operating on arrays via native methods such as `map`:

```
[1, 2, 3]
  .map(n => n*2)
  .map(n => `Number ${n}`);

// => ["Number 2", "Number 4", "Number 6"]
```

Despite its superhero status as the succinct variant of otherwise verbose function definitions, the arrow function comes with its own challenges. The fact that the language must accommodate both *concise* and *regular* variants of syntax means that there is some ambiguity when attempting to return an object literal from the concise arrow function:

```
const giveMeAnObjectPlease = () => { name: 'Gandalf', age: 2019 };
// !! Uncaught SyntaxError: Unexpected token `:`
```

This syntax will confuse the JavaScript parser as the opening curly brace implies that a regular function body resides within. Due to this, the parser gives us an error about an unexpected token as it is not expecting the body of an object literal. If we want to return an object literal from the concise form of the arrow function, then we must awkwardly wrap it in parentheses to disambiguate the syntax:

```
const giveMeAnObjectPlease = () => ({ name: 'Gandalf', age: 2019 });
```

Functionally, the arrow function differs from the function expression in two ways:

- It does not provide access to bindings such as `this` or `arguments`
- It does not have a `prototype` property, so it cannot be used as a constructor

These differences mean that, on the whole, arrow functions are typically unsuitable to use as methods or constructors. They are best used in contexts where you wish to pass a callback or handler to another function, and especially in cases where you wish to retain your `this` binding. For example, if we were to bind event handlers within the context of a `UIComponent` abstraction, we may wish to retain the `this` value in order to carry out certain instance-specific functionality:

```
class MyUIComponent extends UIComponent {
  constructor() {
    this.bindEvents({
      onClick: () => {
        this; // <= usefully refers to the MyUIComponent instance
      }
    });
```

```
  }
}
```

The arrow function feels most at home in scenarios like this. Its succinctness, however, means that there can be a risk of confusion when reading overly dense lines of code, such as the following:

```
process(
  n=>n.filter((nCallback, compute)=>compute(()=>nCallback())
)
```

For this reason, it is best to employ the arrow function with the same consideration and practicality with which you would employ any other construct: ensure that you always put the usability and readability of your code first, above the very enticing niftiness of *cool* or succinct syntax.

Immediately Invoked Function Expressions

Function expressions and arrow functions are the only function definition styles that are, technically, expressions. As we have seen, this quality makes them useful when we need to pass them as values to other functions without having to go through the process of assignment.

As we mentioned previously, a function without an assignment, and thus without a reference to its value, is typically called an *anonymous function* and will look like this:

```
(function() {
  // I am an anonymous function
})
```

The idea of an *anonymous function* is extended further by the concept of an **Immediately Invoked Function Expression** (**IIFE**). An IIFE is just a regular *anonymous function* that is invoked immediately, like so:

```
(function() {
  // I am immediately invoked
}());
```

Note the invocation parentheses (that is, . . . ()) after the closing curly brace. This will call the function and thus makes the preceding syntactic construct an IIEE.

An IIFE is not a distinct concept within the language itself. It is just a useful term that the community has come up with to describe the common pattern of *immediately* invoking a function. It's a useful pattern because it allows us to create an ad hoc scope, meaning that any variables defined within it are constrained to that scope and will not leak outside, just as we'd expect from any function. This immediate scope is useful to quickly do self-contained work without affecting the parent scope.

 IIFEs were popularized in the browser era when it was preferable to avoid polluting the global namespace. Nowadays, with pre-compilation being so popular, the IIFE is less useful.

The exact syntax of an IIFE can vary. For example, if we use an arrow function, then the calling parenthesis must be placed after the wrapped function expression:

```
(() => {
  // I am immediately invoked
})(); // <- () actually calls the function
```

The mechanism remains essentially the same, regardless of whether we use a function expression or an arrow function.

If the concept of an IIFE is confusing, it's simpler to understand what's going on if we replace the actual function with an identifier, fn, and imagine that we have previously assigned a function to this identifier. Here, we can call fn like so:

```
fn();
```

Now, we could choose to wrap the fn reference in parentheses. This would make no difference to the invocation, although it may look bizarre:

```
(fn)();
```

It's useful to remember that parentheses are just syntactic vessels that are sometimes needed to avoid syntactic ambiguity. So, all of these are technically equivalent:

```
fn();
(fn)();
((fn))();
```

If we replace the `fn` reference here with an inline anonymous function, nothing groundbreaking occurs. Instead of referencing an existing function, we are just expressing an inline function, on the spot, and then invoking it:

```
(function() {
  // Called immediately...
})();
```

 We call the pattern of an inline function expression an IIFE, but it really isn't anything special. Consider that the invocation parentheses, that is, `...()`, don't really care what they're attached to, as long as it's a function. The expression prior to the invocation could be literally *anything* as long as it evaluates to a function.

IIFEs are useful because they provide scope isolation without the burden of having to define a function with a name and then later reference and invoke it, as we're doing here:

```
const initializeApp = () => {
  // Initializing...
};

initializeApp();
```

Within the browser, prior to complex builds involving compilation and bundling, IIFEs were useful because they provided scope isolation while not leaking any names into the global scope. Nowadays, however, the IIFE is rarely necessary.

Interestingly, the `initializeApp` function in the preceding code is, arguably, more readable and understandable with an explicit name. This is why, even if necessary, IIFEs are sometimes considered needlessly confusing and fancy. A named function usefully provides a clue as to its purpose and the intent of the author. Without a name, the reader of our code is left with the cognitive burden of having to read through the function itself to discover its broad purpose. For this reason, it is usually preferable to avoid IIFEs and similar anonymous constructs unless you have a very specific need.

Method definitions

Method definitions were added to the language at the same time as class definitions to allow you to easily declare methods bound to a specific object. They are not limited to class definitions, though. You can use them freely in object literals as well:

```
const things = {
  myFunction() {
    // ...
```

```
    }
};
```

In classes, you can also declare methods in this manner:

```
class Things {
  myFunction() {
    // ...
  }
}
```

You can also use traditional styles of function definition to declare your methods, such as a function expression assigned to an identifier:

```
class Things {
  myFunction = function() {
    // ...
  };
}
```

There is, however, a crucial difference between method definitions and other styles of function definition. A method definition will always be bound to the object in which it was first defined. This is known internally as its [[HomeObject]]. This home object will determine what super binding is available to the method when it is called. Only method definitions are allowed to make reference to super, and the super they reference will always be the [[Prototype]] of their [[HomeObject]]. This means that if you try to *borrow* methods from other objects, you may be surprised to discover that super is not what you intended:

```
class Dog {
  greet() { return 'Bark!'; }
}

class Cat {
  greet() { return 'Meow!'; }
}

class JessieTheDog extends Dog {
  greet() { return `${super.greet()} I am Jessie!`; }
}

class JessieTheCat extends Cat {
  greet() { return `${super.greet()} I am Jessie!`; }
}
```

Here, we can observe that both `JessieTheCat` and `JessieTheDog` have `greet` methods:

```
new JessieTheDog().greet(); // => "Bark! I am Jessie!"
new JessieTheCat().greet(); // => "Meow! I am Jessie!"
```

We can also observe that their greet methods are implemented in identical ways. They both return the interpolated string `` `${super.greet()} I am Jessie!` ``. Due to this, it might seem logical to be able to let `JessieTheCat` borrow the method from `JessieTheDog`. After all, they're exactly the same:

```
class JessieTheCat extends Cat {
  greet = JessieTheDog.prototype.greet
}
```

We might intuitively expect `super` in the greet method to refer to the superclass of the current instance, which in the case of `JessieTheCat` will be `Cat`. But curiously, when we call this borrowed method, we experience something different:

```
new JessieTheCat().greet(); // => "Bark! I am Jessie!"
```

It barks! The borrowed method has annoyingly retained its binding to its original `[[HomeObject]]`.

In summary, method definitions are simpler and more succinct variants of their more verbose cousins, the function declaration and function expression. However, they come with an implicit mechanic that sets them apart and can create confusion. 99% of the time, method definitions won't bite you; they'll behave as expected. The other 1% of the time, it's useful at the very least to know why your code is misbehaving so that you can explore other options. As always, knowledge about the idiosyncrasies of JavaScript can only help us in our pursuit of a cleaner and more reliable code base.

Async functions

Asynchronous (async) functions are specified with an `async` keyword preceding the function keyword. All function definition styles can be prefixed with it:

```
// Async Function Declaration:
async function foo() {}

// Async Function Expression:
const foo = async function() {};

// Async Arrow-Function:
const foo = async () => {};
```

```
// Async Method Definition:
const obj = {
  async foo() {}
};
```

An async function allows you to easily conduct asynchronous operations by providing you with two key features:

- You can use `await` within your async function to await the completion of Promises
- Your function will always return a Promise, which can, itself, be awaited

The Promise is a natively supplied abstraction for dealing with asynchronous operations. It can seem complicated, but it's best to think of a Promise as an object that will either resolve or reject at a time later than *now* (that is, asynchronously).

Traditionally, in JavaScript, we'd have to pass around callbacks to ensure that we're able to respond to such asynchronous activity:

```
getUserDetails('user1', function(userDetails) {
  // This callback is called asynchronously
});
```

However, with an async function and `await`, we can achieve this more succinctly:

```
const userDetails = await getUserDetails('user1');
```

The `await` clause here will halt current execution until `getUserDetails` completes and resolves to a value. Note that we can only use await within functions that are themselves async.

 Asynchronous execution is a complex topic, so there is a whole chapter dedicated to it, that is, `Chapter 10`, *Control Flow*. For now, it's useful to know that async functions are a distinct type of a function that will always return a Promise.

Other than allowing `await` clauses and returning Promises, async functions carry the same features and characteristics as the respective function definition style that's used. An async arrow function, just like a regular arrow function, does not have its own bindings to this or arguments. An async function declaration is hoisted just like its non-async cousin. Essentially, async should be thought of as a layer atop all of the learnings you've already picked up concerning the different function definition styles.

Generator functions

The very last type of function definition style we will cover is the very powerful *generator function*. Broadly, generators are used to supply and control the iteration behavior for a sequence of one or more, or even infinite, items.

Generator functions in JavaScript are specified with an asterisk following the function keyword:

```
function* myGenerator() {...}
```

When called, they will return a generator object, which uniquely conforms to both the iterable protocol and the iterator protocol, meaning that they can be iterated over themselves or can serve as an object's iteration logic.

 Feel free to skip ahead to the section on the iterable protocol. The generator function makes far more sense when you think of it as a convenient way to create an iterator or iterable.

A generator function will halt and return a value at the point of a `yield` statement, and this can occur multiple times. After a `yield`, the function is effectively stalled while it waits for a consumer to need its next value. This is best illustrated with an example:

```
function* threeLittlePiggies() {
  yield 'This little piggy went to market.';
  yield 'This little piggy stayed home.';
  yield 'This little piggy had roast beef.';
}

const piggies = threeLittlePiggies();

piggies.next().value; // => 'This little piggy went to market.'
piggies.next().value; // => 'This little piggy stayed home.'
piggies.next().value; // => 'This little piggy had roast beef.'

piggies.next(); // => {value: undefined, done: true}
```

As you can see, the generator object that's returned from the function has a `next` method, which, when called, will return an object with a `value` (indicating the current value of the iteration) and a `done` property (indicating whether the iteration/generation is complete). This is the *iterator protocol* and is the contract you can expect all generators to fulfill.

A generator fulfills not only the iterator protocol but also the iterable protocol, which means it can be iterated over by language constructs that accept iterables (such as for...of or the ...spread operator):

```
for (let piggy of threeLittlePiggies()) console.log(piggy);
// => Logs: "This little piggy went to market."
// => Logs: This little piggy stayed home."
// => Logs: This little piggy had roast beef."

[...threeLittlePiggies()];
// => ["This little piggy went to market", "This little piggy stayed...",
"..."]
```

Async generator functions can also be specified. They usefully combine the async and generator formats into a hybrid that allows for custom asynchronous generation logic, like so:

```
async function* pages(n) {
  for (let i = 1; i <= n; i++) {
    yield fetch(`/page/${i}`);
  }
};

// Fetch five pages (/page/1, /page/2, /page/3)
for await (let page of pages(3)) {
  page; // => Each of the 3 pages
};
```

You'll notice how we're using the for await iteration construct to iterate through our asynchronous generator. This will ensure that each iteration will await its result before continuing.

Generator functions are very powerful, but it's important to be aware of the underlying mechanics at play. They are not regular functions and are not guaranteed to run to completion. Their implementation should take into account the context in which they will be run. If your generator is intended to be used as an iterator, then it should respect the implied expectations of iteration: that it is a read-only operation of an underlying piece of data or generation logic. While it is possible to mutate underlying data within a generator, this should be avoided.

Arrays and iterables

An array in JavaScript is a type of object that is specialized in that it contains a set of ordered elements.

You can express an array using its literal syntax, which is a comma-separated list of expressions delimited by square brackets:

```
const friends = ['Rachel', 'Monica', 'Ross', 'Joe', 'Phoebe', 'Chandler'];
```

These comma-separated expressions can be as complex or simple as we desire:

```
[
  [1, 2, 3],
  function() {},
  Symbol(),
  {
    title: 'wow',
    foo: function() {}
  }
]
```

An array is capable of containing all manner of values. There are very few constraints on how we can use arrays. Technically, an array's limited to a `length` of around 4 billion, due to its `length` being stored as a 32-bit integer. For most purposes, of course, this should be absolutely fine.

Arrays have a numeric property for every indexed element within them and a `length` property to describe how many elements there are. They also have a set of useful methods for reading from and operating on the data within them:

```
friends[0]; // => "Rachel"
friends[5]; // => "Chandler"
friends.length; // => 6

friends.map(name => name.toUpperCase());
// => ["RACHEL", "MONICA", "ROSS", "JOE", "PHOEBE", "CHANDLER"]

friends.join(' and ');
// => "Rachel and Monica and Ross and Joe and Phoebe and Chandler"
```

Historically, arrays were iterated over using conventional `for(...)` and `while(...)` loops that increment a counter toward the `length` so that, upon each iteration, the current element could be accessed via `array[counter]`, like so:

```
for (let i = 0; i < friends.length; i++) {
  // Do something with `friends[i]`
}
```

Nowadays, however, it's preferable to use other methods of iteration, such as `forEach` or `for...of`:

```
for (let friend of friends) {
  // Do something with `friend`
}

friends.forEach((friend, index) => {
  // Do something with `friend`
});
```

`for...of` has the benefit of being breakable, meaning you can use `break` and `continue` statements within them and easily escape from the iteration. It will also work on any object that is iterable, whereas `forEach` is only an `Array` method. The `forEach` style, however, is useful in that it provides you with the current index of the iteration via the second argument to your callback.

 Which style of iteration you use should be determined by the value you are iterating over and what you wish to do on each iteration. Nowadays, it is quite rare to need to use traditional styles of array iteration such as `for(...)` and `while(...)`.

Array-like objects

Most native Array methods are generic, meaning that they can be used on any object that *looks like* an array. All we need to achieve the appearance of an array is use a `length` property and individual properties for each index (indexed from zero):

```
const arrayLikeThing = {
  length: 3,
  0: 'Suspiciously',
  1: 'similar to',
  2: 'an array...'
};

// We can "borrow" an array's join method by assigning
```

```
// it to our object:
arrayLikeThing.join = [].join;

arrayLikeThing.join(' ');
// => "Suspiciously similar to an array..."
```

Here, we've constructed an array-like object and then provided it with a `join` method of its own by borrowing the `join` method of an array (that is, from `Array.prototype`). The native array `join` method is so generically implemented that it doesn't mind operating on an object as long as that object fulfills the contract of an array by providing a `length` property and corresponding indexes (0, 1, 2, and so on). Most native array methods are similarly generic.

One example of an array-like object within the language itself is the `arguments` binding that we explored earlier in this chapter. Another example is `NodeList`, which is a type of object that is returned from various DOM selection methods. If necessary, we can derive proper arrays from these objects by borrowing and calling the array `slice` method, like so:

```
const arrayLikeObject = { length: 2, 0: 'foo', 1: 'bar' };

// "Borrowing" a method from an array and forcing its
// execution context via call():
[].slice.call(arrayLikeObject);

// "Borrowing" a method explicitly from the Array.prototype
// and forcing its execution context via call():
Array.prototype.slice.call(arrayLikeObject);
```

However, in the case of `arguments` or the `NodeList` object, we can also rely on them being iterable, meaning that we can use the spread syntax to derive a true array:

```
// "spread" a NodeList into an Array:
[...document.querySelectorAll('div span a')];

// "spread" an arguments object into an Array:
[...arguments];
```

If you find yourself needing to create an array-like object, consider having it implement the iterable protocol (which we're about to explore) so that the spread syntax can be used in this way.

Set and WeakSet

Set and WeakSet are native abstractions that allow us to store sequences of unique objects. This is in contrast to arrays, which give you no assurances as to the uniqueness of your values. Here's an illustration:

```
const foundNumbersArray = [1, 2, 3, 4, 3, 2, 1];
const foundNumbersSet = new Set([1, 2, 3, 4, 3, 2, 1]);

foundNumbersArray; // => [1, 2, 3, 4, 3, 2, 1]
foundNumbersSet;   // => Set{ 1, 2, 3, 4 }
```

As you can see, values given to a Set will always be ignored if they already exist in the Set.

Sets can be initialized by passing an iterable value to the constructor; for example, a string:

```
new Set('wooooow'); // => Set{ 'w', 'o' }
```

If you need to convert a Set into an array, you can most simply do this with the spread syntax (as sets are, themselves, iterable):

```
[...foundNumbersSet]; // => [1, 2, 3, 4]
```

WeakSets are similar to the previously covered WeakMaps. They are for *weakly* holding values in a way that allows that value to be garbage-collected in another part of the program. The semantics and best practices around using sets are similar to those concerning arrays. It's advisable to only use sets if you need to store unique sequences of values; otherwise, just use a simple array.

Iterable protocol

The iterable protocol allows values containing sequences to share a common set of characteristics, allowing them to all be iterated over or treated in a similar way.

 We can say that an object that implements the iterable protocol is iterable. Iterable objects within JavaScript include Array, Map, Set, and String.

Any object can define its own iterable protocol by simply supplying an iterator function under the property name's Symbol.iterator (which maps to the internal @@iterator property).

This iterator function must fulfill the iterator protocol by returning an object with a `next` function. This `next` function, when called, must return an object with `done` and `value` keys indicating what the current value of the iteration is and whether the iteration is completed:

```
const validIteratorFunction = () => {
  return {
    next: () => {
      return {
        value: null, // Current value of the iteration
        done: true // Whether the iteration is completed
      };
    }
  }
};
```

So, to be utterly clear about this, there are two distinct protocols:

- **The iterable protocol**: Any object that implements an `@@iterator` via `[Symbol.iterator]` fulfills this protocol. Native examples include `Array`, `String`, `Set`, and `Map`.
- **The iterator protocol**: Any function that returns an object of the form `{ ... next: Function}` and whose `next` method, when called, returns an object in the following form: `{value: Boolean, done: ...}`.

For an object to fulfill the iterable protocol, it must implement `[Symbol.iterator]`, like so:

```
const zeroToTen = {};
zeroToTen[Symbol.iterator] = function() {
  let current = 0;
  return {
    next: function() {
      if (current > 10) return { done: true };
      return {
        done: false,
        value: current++
      };
    }
  }
};

// We can see the effect of the iterable via the spread operator:
[...zeroToTen]; // => [0, 1, 2, 3, 4, 5, 6, 7, 8, 9, 10]
```

Providing custom methods of iteration via the iterable protocol can be useful when you want to control the order of iteration or if you want to somehow process, filter, or generate values during iteration. Here, for example, we are specifying an iterator function as a generator function, which, as you may recall, returns a generator that fulfills both the *iterator* and iterable protocols. This generator function will yield two variants for every word stored – one uppercase and one lowercase:

```
const words = {
  values: ['CoFfee', 'ApPLE', 'Tea'],
  [Symbol.iterator]: function*() {
    for (let word of this.values) {
      yield word.toUpperCase();
      yield word.toLowerCase();
    }
  }
};

[...words]
// => ["COFFEE", "coffee", "APPLE", "apple", "TEA", "tea"]
```

Specifying iterator functions as generator functions like this is far simpler than having to manually implement the iterator protocol. Generators naturally fulfill this contract, so they can be used far more seamlessly. Generators also tend to be more readable and succinct and have the dual benefit of implementing both the iterator and iterable protocols, meaning that they can be used to decorate an object with iteration capabilities:

```
const someObject = {
  [Symbol.iterator]: function*() { yield 123; }
};

[...someObject]; // => [123]
```

They can, themselves, also provide that iteration capability:

```
function* someGenerator() {
  yield 123;
}

[...someGenerator()]; // => [123]
```

It's important to keep in mind that any work that's done within a custom iterable should be in line with the expectations of consumers. Iteration is usually considered a read-only operation, so you should steer clear of mutations of the underlying value-set during iteration. Implementing your own iterables can be incredibly powerful, but can also lead to unexpected behavior by the consumers of your code who aren't aware of your custom iteration logic.

It's vital to balance the convenience of custom iteration for those people who are *in the know* with those people who might only be experiencing your interface or abstraction for the first time.

RegExp

JavaScript natively supports regular expressions via the object type `RegExp`, allowing them to be expressed via the literal syntax `/foo/` or directly via the constructor (`RegExp('foo')`). Regular expressions are used to define patterns of characters that can be matched or executed against strings.

Here is an example in which we extract only the long words (>=10 characters) from a corpus of text:

```
const string = 'Lorem ipsum dolor sit amet, consectetur adipiscing elit.
Etiam sit amet odio ultrices nunc efficitur venenatis laoreet nec leo.';

string.match(/\w{10,}/g); // => ["consectetur", "adipiscing"]
```

The grammar and syntax of regular expressions can be complex. It is technically an entire language unto itself, requiring many days of study. We won't be able to explore all of its complexity here. We will, however, be covering the ways in which we typically operate on regular expressions within JavaScript and explore some of the challenges in doing so. It is suggested that you conduct further study into regular expressions yourself.

Regular expression 101

Regular expressions allow us to describe a pattern of characters. They are used for matching and extracting values from strings. For example, if we had a string that contained digits (`1`, `2`, `3`) at various positions, a regular expression would allow us to easily retrieve them:

```
const string = 'some 1 content 2 with 3 digits';
string.match(/1|2|3/g); // => ["1", "2", "3"]
```

A regular expression is written as a pattern delimited by forward slashes, with optional flags following the final forward slash:

```
/[PATTERN]/[FLAGS]
```

The pattern you write can contain both literal and special characters that together inform the regular expression engine of what to look for. The regular expression we're using in our example contains literal characters (that is, 1, 2, 3) and the pipe (that is, |) special character:

```
/1|2|3/g
```

The pipe special character tells the regular expression engine that the characters on the left or the right of the pipe may match. The g, following the final forward slash, is a *global* flag that directs the engine to search globally within the string and not to give up after the first match is found. For us, this means that our regular expression will match either "1", "2", or "3", wherever they appear within a subject string.

There are specific special characters we can use within regular expressions that act as shortcuts. The notation [0-9] is an example of this. It is a *character class* that will match all the digits from 0 to 9 so that we don't have to list all of these digits individually. There is also a *shorthand character class*, \d, that allows us to express this even more succinctly. Thus, we can shorten our regular expression to the following:

```
/\d/g
```

For a more realistic application, we may imagine a scenario in which we wish to match sequences of digits, such as phone numbers. Perhaps we wish to match only those phone numbers beginning with 0800 and containing a further 4 to 6 digits. We could do this with the following regular expression:

```
/0800\d{4,6}/g
```

Here, we are using the {n, n} syntax, which allows us to express a quantity for the preceding special character, \d. We can confirm that our pattern works by passing it to a test string's match method:

```
`
  This is a test in which exist some phone
  numbers like 0800182372 and 08009991.
`.match(
  /0800\d{4,6}/g
);
// => ["0800182372", "08009991"]
```

This brief introduction only touches on the very surface of what regular expressions can do. The syntax of regular expressions allows us to express significant complexity, allowing us to validate that specific text exists within a string or to extract specific text for use within our programs.

RegExp flags

The literal syntax of regular expressions allows for specific *flags*, such as i (*ignore-case*), to be specified after the final delimiting forward slash. These flags will affect the way the regular expression is executed:

```
/hello/.test('hELlO');  // => false
/hello/i.test('hELlO'); // => true
```

When using the RegExp constructor, you can pass your flags as the second argument:

```
RegExp('hello').test('hELlO');      // => false
RegExp('hello', 'i').test('hELlO'); // => true
```

There are six available flags in JavaScript's flavor of regular expression:

- i: The *ignore-case* flag will ignore the case of the string when matching letters (that is, /a/i would match both 'a' andor 'A' in a string).
- g: The *global-match* flag will make the regular expression find *all* matches instead of stopping after the first match.
- m: The *multiline* flag will make beginning and end anchors (that is, ^ and $) mark the beginnings and ends of individual lines instead of entire strings.
- s: The *dotAll* flag will cause the dot character in your regular expression (which usually only matches non-newline characters) to match newline characters.
- u: The *Unicode* flag will treat the sequence of characters in your regular expression as individual Unicode code points instead of code units. This broadly means you can painlessly match and test for rare or exotic symbols such as emojis (see the section within this chapter on the String type to get a more thorough understanding of Unicode).
- y: The *sticky* flag will cause all RegExp operations to attempt a match at the exact index detailed by the lastIndex property and then mutate lastIndex upon matches.

As we've seen, regular expressions can also be constructed via the RegExp constructor. This can usefully be invoked as both a constructor or a regular function: either way, you'll receive a RegExp object equivalent to what was derived from the literal syntax:

```
new RegExp('[a-z]', 'i'); // => /[a-z]/i
RegExp('[a-z]', 'i');     // => /[a-z]/i
```

This is quite a unique behavior. In fact, the `RegExp` constructor is the only natively provided constructor that can be invoked as both a constructor and a regular function and, in both cases, returns a new instance. You'll recall that the primitive constructors (such as `String` and `Number`) can be invoked as regular functions but will behave differently when invoked as constructors.

Methods accepting RegExp

There are seven methods provided by JavaScript that are capable of utilizing regular expressions:

- `RegExp.prototype.test(String)`: Runs the regular expression against the passed string and return true if it finds at least one match. It will return false if no matches are found.

- `RegExp.prototype.exec(String)`: If the regular expression has a global (`g`), flag then `exec()` will return the next match from the current `lastIndex` (and will update the regular expression's `lastIndex` after doing so); otherwise, it will return the first match of the regular expression (similar to `String.prototype.match`).

- `String.prototype.match(RegExp)`: This `String` method will return a match (or if the global flag is set, all matches) of the passed regular expression made against the string.

- `String.prototype.replace(RegExp, Function)`: This `String` method will execute the passed function on every single match and will, for each match, replace the matched text with whatever the function returns.

- `String.prototype.matchAll(RegExp)`: This `String` method will return an iterator of all results and their individual groups. This is useful when you have a global regular expression with individual matching groups.

- `String.prototype.search(RegExp)`: This `String` method will return the index of the first match or -1 if there are no matches found.

- `String.prototype.split(RegExp)`: This `String` method will return an array containing parts of the string split by the provided separator (which can be a regular expression).

There are many methods to choose from, but for most situations, you'll likely find that the RegExp method, `test()`, and the String methods, `match()` and `replace()`, are the most useful.

Here's a rundown of some examples of these methods. This should give you an idea of the situations in which each method may be used:

```
// RegExp.prototype.test
/@/.test('a@b.com'); // => true
/@/.test('aaa.com'); // => false

// RegExp.prototype.exec
const regexp = /\d+/g;
const string = '123 456 789';
regex.exec(string); // => ["123"]
regex.exec(string); // => ["456"]
regex.exec(string); // => ["789"]
regex.exec(string); // => null

// String.prototype.match
'Orders: #92838 #02812 #92833'.match(/\d+/);  // => ["92838"]
'Orders: #92838 #02812 #92833'.match(/wo+w/g); // => ["92838", "02812",
"92833"]

// String.prototype.matchAll
const string = 'Orders: #92333 <fulfilled> #92835 <pending>';
const matches = [
  ...string.matchAll(/#(\d+) <(\w+)>/g)
];
matches[0][1]; // => 92333
matches[0][2]; // => fulfilled

// String.prototype.replace
'1 2 3 4'.replace(/\d/, n => `<${n}>`); // => "<1> 2 3 4'
'1 2 3 4'.replace(/\d/g, n => `<${n}>`); // => "<1> <2> <3> <4>'

// String.prototype.search
'abcdefghhijklmnop'.search(/k/); // => 11

// String.prototype.split
'time_in____a__tree'.split(/_+/); // ["time", "in", "a", "tree"]
```

Most of these methods, as you can see, behave intuitively. However, there is some complexity surrounding *stickiness* and the `lastIndex` property, which we will now go over.

RegExp methods and lastIndex

By default, if your RegExp is global (that is, uses the g flag), the RegExp methods (that is, test() and exec()) will mutate the lastIndex property of the RegExp object upon each execution. These methods will attempt to match the subject string from the index specified by the current lastIndex property, which is 0 by default, and will then update the lastIndex upon every subsequent call.

This can lead to unexpected behavior if you expect exec() or test() to always return the same result for a given global regular expression and string:

```
const alphaRegex = /[a-z]+/g;

alphaRegex.exec('aaa bbb ccc'); // => ["aaa"]
alphaRegex.exec('aaa bbb ccc'); // => ["bbb"]
alphaRegex.exec('aaa bbb ccc'); // => ["ccc"]
alphaRegex.exec('aaa bbb ccc'); // => null
```

It will also lead to confusion if you attempt to execute a global regular expression on more than one string without resetting the lastIndex yourself:

```
const alphaRegex = /[a-z]+/g;

alphaRegex.exec('monkeys laughing'); // => ["monkeys"]
alphaRegex.lastIndex; // => 7
alphaRegex.exec('birds flying'); // => ["lying"]
```

As you can see, following the match with the "monkeys" substring, the lastIndex is updated to the next index (7), which means, when executed on a different string, the regular expression will continue where it left off and attempt to match everything beyond that index, which in the case of the second string, "birds flying", is the substring "lying".

As a rule, to avoid these confusions, it's important to always have ownership over your regular expressions. Don't accept regular expressions from elsewhere in a program if you're using RegExp methods. Also, don't attempt to use exec() or test() on different strings without resetting the lastIndex before each execution:

```
const petRegex = /\b(?:dog|cat|hamster)\b/g;

// Testing multiple strings without resetting lastIndex:
petRegex.exec('lion tiger cat'); // => ["cat"]
petRegex.exec('lion tiger dog'); // => null

// Testing multiple strings with resetting lastIndex:
```

```
petRegex.exec('lion tiger cat'); // => ["cat"]
petRegex.lastIndex = 0;
petRegex.exec('lion tiger dog'); // => ["dog"]
```

Here, you can see that, if we don't reset the lastIndex, our regular expression fails to match on subsequent strings that are passed to the exec() method. If, however, we reset the lastIndex prior to each subsequent exec() call, we'll observe a match.

Stickiness

Stickiness means that a regular expression will try to match at the exact lastIndex and that, if a match is not available at that exact index, it will fail (that is, return null or false, depending on the method used). The sticky flag (y) will force RegExp to read and mutate lastIndex with each match. Traditionally sticky methods such as exec() and test(), as we mentioned previously, will always do this, but the y flag will *force* stickiness even when using non-sticky methods, such as match():

```
const regexp = /cat|hat/y; // match 'cat' or 'hat'
const string = 'cat in a hat';

// lastIndex is always zero by default, so will
// match from the start of the string:
regexp.lastIndex; // => 0
regexp.test(string); // => ["cat"]

// lastIndex has been modified following the last
// match but will not match anything as there is
// no cat or hat at index 3:
regexp.lastIndex; // => 3
string.match(regexp); // => null

// Set lastIndex to 9 (index of "hat"):
regexp.lastIndex = 9;
string.match(regexp); // => ["hat"]
```

Stickiness can be useful if you're looking for a match at a specific index in a string or series of strings. However, its behavior can be unexpected if you're not in full control of lastIndex. As we mentioned previously, a good general rule is to always have ownership over your own RegExp objects so that any mutations to lastIndex are only made by your code.

Summary

In this chapter, we have begun to delve into JavaScript by looking at the built-in types that the language provides. The point of our exploration has been to look at these language constructs through the lens of clean code. By doing so, we've highlighted the importance of caution when dealing with some of the more obscure areas of the language.

We've discovered many of the nasty edge cases and challenges involved in using JavaScript types, such as the lack of precision in the floating-point `Number` type and the complexity of Unicode in the `String` type. Exploring these more difficult parts of the language allows us not only to avoid specific traps but instills a fluency within us that will hugely boost our ability to wield JavaScript in the service of clean code.

In the next chapter, we will continue to enhance this fluency. We will learn more about JavaScript's type system and begin to operate on and manipulate these types to suit our needs.

7
Dynamic Typing

In the previous chapter, we explored JavaScript's built-in values and types and covered some of the challenges involved when using them. The next natural step is for us to explore how JavaScript's dynamic system plays out in the real world. Since JavaScript is a dynamically typed language, the variables in your code are not constrained in terms of the type of values they refer to. This introduces a huge challenge for the clean coder. Without certainty regarding our types, our code can break in unexpected ways and can become incredibly fragile. This fragility can be explained quite simply by imagining a numeric value embedded within a string:

```
const possiblyNumeric = '203.45';
```

Here, we can see that the value is numeric but that it has been wrapped in a string literal and so, as far as JavaScript is concerned, is just a regular string. But because JavaScript is dynamic, we can freely pass this value around to any function—even a function that is expecting a number:

```
setWidth('203.45');

function setWidth(width) {
  width += 20;        // Add margins
  applyWidth(width); // Apply the width
}
```

The function adds a margin value to the number via the += operator. This operator, as we will learn later in this chapter, is an alias for the operation a = a + b, and the + operator here will, in the case of either operand being a String type, simply concatenate the two strings together. What's funny is that this simple and innocent-looking implementation detail is the crux of millions of exhausting debugging sessions that have occurred around the world at various times. Thankfully, knowing about this operator and its exact behavior will save you countless hours of pain and exhaustion, and will cement in your mind the importance of writing code that avoids the very trap we've fallen into with our possiblyNumeric value.

In this chapter, we will cover the following topics:

- Detection
- Conversion, coercion, and casting

The first crucial step in being able to wrangle our types with more ease is to learn about detection, which is the skill of being able to discern what type or types you're dealing with in the least complex way.

Detection

Detection refers to the practice of determining a value's type. Usually, this will be done with the intention of using that determined type to carry out specific behavior such as falling back to a default value or throwing an error in the case of misuse.

Due to JavaScript's dynamic nature, detecting types is an important practice that can often be a great aid to other programmers. If you can usefully throw errors or warnings when someone is using an interface incorrectly, it can mean a much more fluid and speedy flow of development for them. And if you can helpfully populate undefined, null, or empty values with smart defaults, then it'll allow you to provide a more seamless and intuitive interface.

Unfortunately, due to legacies within JavaScript, and some choices made in its design, detecting types can be challenging. A number of different approaches are used, some of which are not considered best practice. We will be going over all of these practices within this section. First, however, it's worth discussing one fundamental question regarding detection: **what exactly are you trying to detect?**

We often think we require a specific type in order to carry out certain actions, but due to JavaScript's dynamic nature, we may not need to do so. In fact, doing so can lead us to create needlessly restrictive or rigid code.

Consider a function that accepts an array of people objects, like so:

```
registerPeopleForMarathon([
  new Person({ id: 1, name: 'Marcus Wu' }),
  new Person({ id: 2, name: 'Susan Smith' }),
  new Person({ id: 3, name: 'Sofia Polat' })
]);
```

In our `registerPeopleForMarathon`, we may be tempted to implement some kind of check to ensure that the passed argument is of the expected type and structure:

```
function registerPeopleForMarathon(people) {
  if (Array.isArray(people)) {
    throw new Error('People is not an array');
  }
  for (let person in people) {
    if (!(person instanceof Person)) {
      throw new Error('Each person should be an instance of Person');
    }
    registerForMarathon(person.id, person.name);
  }
}
```

Are these checks necessary? You may be inclined to say yes as they're ensuring our code is resilient (or defensive) toward potential error cases and is thus more reliable. But if we think about it, none of these checks are necessary to ensure the kind of reliability we're seeking. The intention of our checks, presumably, is to prevent downstream errors in the case that the wrong types or structures are passed to our function, but if we look closely at the preceding code, there are no risks of downstream errors of the types we're worried about.

The first check we conduct is `Array.isArray(people)` to determine whether the `people` value is indeed an array. We are doing this, ostensibly, so that we can safely loop through the array. But, as we discovered in the previous chapter, the `for...of` iteration style is not dependent on its `of {...}` value being an array. All it cares about is that the value is iterable. An example of this is as follows:

```
function* marathonPeopleGenerator() {
  yield new Person({ id: 1, name: 'Marcus Wu' });
  yield new Person({ id: 2, name: 'Susan Smith' });
  yield new Person({ id: 3, name: 'Sofia Polat' });
}

for (let person of marathonPeopleGenerator()) {
 console.log(person.name);
}

// Logged => "Marcus Wu"
// Logged => "Susan Smith"
// Logged => "Sofia Polat"
```

Here, we've used a generator as our iterable. This will work just an array would when being iterated over in `for...of`, so, technically, we could argue that our `registerPeopleForMarathon` function should accept such values:

```
// Should we allow this?
registerPeopleForMarathon(
  marathonPeopleGenerator()
);
```

The checks we've made thus far would reject this value as it is not an array. Is there any sense in that? Do you remember the principle of abstraction and how we should be concerned with interface, not implementation? Seen this way, arguably, our `registerPeopleForMarathon` function does not need to know about the implementation detail of the passed value's type. It only cares that the value performs according to its needs. In this case, it needs to loop through the value via `for...of`, so any iterable is suitable. To check for an iterable, we might employ a helper such as this:

```
function isIterable(obj) {
  return obj != null &&
 typeof obj[Symbol.iterator] === 'function';
}

isIterable([1, 2, 3]); // => true
isIterable(marathonPeopleGenerator()); // => true
```

Also, consider that we are currently checking that all of our `person` values are instances of the `Person` constructor:

```
// ...
if (!(person instanceof Person)) {
  throw new Error('Each person should be an instance of Person');
}
```

Is it necessary for us to explicitly check the instance in this way? Could we, instead, simply check for the properties that we wish to access? Perhaps all we need to assert is that the properties are non-falsy (empty strings, null, undefined, zero, and so on):

```
// ...
if (!person || !person.name || !person.id) {
  throw new Error('Each person should have a name and id');
}
```

This check is arguably more specific to our true needs. Checks like these are often called **duck-typing**, that is, *If it walks like a duck and it quacks like a duck, then it must be a duck*. We don't always need to check for specific types; we can check for the properties, methods, and characteristics that we're truly dependent on. By doing so, we are creating code that is more flexible.

Our new checks, when integrated into our function, would look something like this:

```
function registerPeopleForMarathon(people) {
  if (isIterable(people)) {
    throw new Error('People is not iterable');
  }
  for (let person in people) {
    if (!person || !person.name || !person.id) {
      throw new Error('Each person should have a name and id');
    }
    registerForMarathon(person.id, person.name);
  }
}
```

By using a more flexible `isIterable` check and employing *duck-typing* on our `person` objects, our `registerPeopleForMarathon` function can now be passed; for example, here, we have a generator that yields plain objects:

```
function* marathonPeopleGenerator() {
  yield { id: 1, name: 'Marcus Wu' };
  yield { id: 2, name: 'Susan Smith' };
  yield { id: 3, name: 'Sofia Polat' };
}

registerPeopleForMarathon(
  marathonPeopleGenerator()
);
```

This level of flexibility wouldn't have been possible if we had kept our strict type-checking in place. Stricter checks usually create more rigid code and needlessly limit flexibility. There is a balance to strike here, however. We cannot be endlessly flexible. It may even be the case that the rigidity and certainty provided by stricter type-checks enable us to ensure cleaner code in the long run. But the opposite may also be true. The balancing act of flexibility versus rigidity is one you should be constantly considering.

Generally, an interface's expectations should attempt to be as close as possible to the demands of the implementation. That is, we should not be performing detection or other checks unless the checks genuinely prevent errors within our implementation. Over-zealous checking may seem safer but may only mean that future requirements and use cases are more awkward to accommodate.

Now that we've covered the question of why we detect things and exposed some use cases, we can begin to cover the techniques of detection that JavaScript provides us with. We'll begin with the `typeof` operator.

The typeof operator

The first thing you'll often be exposed to when you first try to detect a type in JavaScript is the `typeof` operator:

```
typeof 1; // => number
```

The `typeof` operator accepts a single operand, to its right-hand-side, and will evaluate to one of eight possible string values, depending on the value that's passed:

```
typeof 1; // => "number"
typeof ''; // => "string"
typeof {}; // => "object"
typeof function(){}; // => "function"
typeof undefined; // => "undefined"
typeof Symbol(); // => "symbol"
typeof 0n; // => "bigint"
typeof true; // => boolean
```

If your operand is an identifier without a binding, that is, an undeclared variable, then `typeof` will usefully return `"undefined"` instead of throwing a `ReferenceError` like any other reference to that variable would do:

```
typeof somethingNotYetDeclared; // => "undefined"
```

`typeof` is the only operator in the JavaScript language that does this. Every other operator and every other way of referencing a value will throw an error if that value is not yet declared.

Outside of detecting undeclared variables, `typeof` is really only useful when determining primitive types—and even that's too generous since not all primitive types are detectable. A `null` value, for example, when passed to `typeof`, will evaluate to a rather useless `"object"`:

```
typeof null; // => "object"
```

This is an unfortunate and unfixable legacy of the JavaScript language. It will likely never be fixed. To check for `null`, it is preferred to explicitly check for the value itself:

```
let someValue = null;
someValue === null; // => true
```

The `typeof` operator does not differentiate between different types of objects, except for functions. All non-function objects in JavaScript will return, plainly, `"object"`:

```
typeof [];          // => "object"
typeof RegExp('');  // => "object"
typeof {};          // => "object"
```

All functions, whether declared via class definitions, method definitions, or plain function expressions, will evaluate to `"function"`:

```
typeof () => {};          // => "function"
typeof function() {};     // => "function"
typeof class {};          // => "function"
typeof ({ foo(){} }).foo; // => "function"
```

If `typeof class {}` evaluating to `"function"` is confusing, consider that, as we've learned, all classes are just constructor functions with a prepared prototype (which will later determine the `[[Prototype]]` of any produced instances). There's nothing special about them. Classes are not a unique type or entity within JavaScript.

When it comes to comparing the result of `typeof` to a given string, we can use either the strict equality (===) or abstract equality (==) operator. Since `typeof` always returns a string, we don't have to worry about any discrepancies here, so whether you adopt a strict versus abstract equality check is up to you. These would both be fine, technically:

```
if (typeof 123 == 'number') {...}
if (typeof 123 === 'number') {...}
```

 The strict and abstract equality operators (double-equals and triple-equals) behave slightly differently, although when the values on both sides of the operator are of the same type, they act identically. Skip ahead to the *Operator* section to get the lowdown on how they differ. In general, it's best to prefer === over ==.

In conclusion, the `typeof` operator is only a fair-weather friend. We cannot rely on it in all circumstances. Sometimes, we'll need to use other type detection techniques.

Type-detecting techniques

Given the unsuitability of the `typeof` operator for detecting a number of types, especially objects, we have to rely on a number of different approaches, depending on the exact thing we want to check. Sometimes, we may want to detect a characteristic instead of a type, for example, whether an object is an instance of a constructor or whether it's just a plain object. In this section, we'll be exploring a number of common detection needs and their solutions.

Detecting Booleans

Booleans are thankfully very simple to check. The `typeof` operator correctly evaluates to `"boolean"` for values of `true` and `false`:

```
typeof true;  // => "boolean"
typeof false; // => "boolean"
```

It's rare that we'll want to do this, though. Usually, when you are receiving a `Boolean` value, you are most interested in checking its truthiness rather than its type.

When placing a Boolean value in a Boolean context, such as a conditional statement, we are implicitly relying on its truthiness or falsiness. For example, take the following check:

```
function process(isEnabled) {
  if (isEnabled) {
    // ... do things
  }
}
```

This check does not determine whether the `isEnabled` value is truly Boolean. It just checks that it evaluates to something truthy. What are all the possible values that `isEnabled` could be? Is there a list of all these truthy values? These values are virtually infinite, so there is no list. All we can say about truthy values is that they are not falsy. And as we know, there are only seven falsy values. If we wish to observe the truthiness or falsiness of specific values, we can always cast to a `Boolean` via the `Boolean` constructor invoked as a function:

```
Boolean(true); // => true
Boolean(1); // => true
Boolean(42); // => true
Boolean([]); // => true
Boolean('False'); // => true
Boolean(0.0001); // => true
```

In most situations, the implicit coercion to a `Boolean` is sufficient and won't end up biting us, but if we ever wish to absolutely determine that a value is both `Boolean` and specifically `true` or `false`, we can use the strict equality operator to compare them, like so:

```
if (isEnabled === true) {...}
if (isEnabled === false) {...}
```

Due to the dynamic nature of JavaScript, some people prefer this level of certainty but usually, it isn't necessary. If the value we are checking is obviously intended as a `Boolean` value, then we can use it as so. Checking for its type via `typeof` or strict equality is usually unnecessary unless there is a possibility that the value may be non-`Boolean`.

Detecting numbers

In the case of a `Number`, we can rely on the `typeof` operator to correctly evaluate to `"number"`:

```
typeof 555; // => "number"
```

However, it will also evaluate to `"number"` in the case of `NaN`, `Infinity`, and `-Infinity`:

```
typeof Infinity;  // => "number"
typeof -Infinity; // => "number"
typeof NaN;       // => "number"
```

Because of this, we may wish to carry out additional checks to determine whether a number is not any of those values. Thankfully, JavaScript provides native helpers for just this scenario:

- `isFinite(n)`: Returns `true` if `Number(n)` is not `Infinity`, `-Infinity`, or `NaN`
- `isNaN(n)`: Returns `true` if `Number(n)` is not `NaN`
- `Number.isNaN(n)`: Returns `true` if `n` is not `NaN`
- `Number.isFinite(n)`: Returns `true` if `n` is not `Infinity`, `-Infinity`, or `NaN`

Both of the global variants are older parts of the language and, as you can see, are slightly different than their `Number.*` equivalents. Global `isFinite` and `isNaN` cast their values to a number via `Number(n)`, while the equivalent `Number.*` methods do not do this. The reason for this difference is mostly one of legacy.

The more recently added `Number.isNaN` and `Number.isFinite` were introduced to enable more explicit checks without relying on casting:

```
isNaN(NaN)    // => true
isNaN('foo')  // => true

Number.isNaN(NaN);    // => true
Number.isNaN('foo');  // => false
```

As you can see, `Number.isNaN` is more restrictive as it won't cast the value to a `Number` before checking for `NaN`. With the `'foo'` string, we would need to cast it to `Number` (and thus evaluate to `NaN`) before we passed it:

```
const string = 'foo';
const nan = Number(string);
Number.isNaN(nan); // => true
```

The global `isFinite` function works in the same way, that is, it casts its value to a number before checking for finiteness, while the `Number.isFinite` method will do no casting whatsoever:

```
isFinite(42)    // => true
isFinite('42')  // => true

Number.isFinite(42);    // => true
Number.isFinite('42');  // => false
```

If you are confident that your value is already a number, then you may as well use the more succinct `isNaN` and `isFinite` as their implicit casting will have no effect on you. And if you'd like for JavaScript to attempt to cast your non-`Number` value to `Number`, then you should, once again, use `isNaN` and `isFinite`. If, however, you require an explicit check for whatever reason, then you should use `Number.isNaN` and `Number.isFinite`.

Combining all of these discussed checks, we are able to confidently detect a number that is neither `NaN` nor `Infinity` by using `typeof` in combination with the global `isFinite`. As we mentioned previously, `isFinite` will check for `NaN` itself, so we needn't bother with an additional `isNaN` check:

```
function isNormalNumber(n) {
  return typeof n === 'number' && isFinite(n);
}
```

When it comes to detection, your needs should be driven by the context of your code. For example, it may not be necessary to check for finite numbers if you're embedded in a piece of code where you can safely assume the number is finite. But if you're building a more public API, then you may want to conduct such checks before sending those values down into your internal interfaces, both to reduce the possibilities of bugs and to provide your users with helpful and sensible errors or warnings.

Detecting strings

Detecting strings is pleasantly simple. The `typeof` operator is all we need:

```
typeof 'hello'; // => "string"
```

In order to check for the length of a given `String`, we can simply use the `length` property:

```
'hello'.length; // => 5
```

If we need to check whether a `String` has a length greater than 0, we can either explicitly do so via `length` or rely on the falsiness of a 0 length, or even rely on the falsiness of the empty `string` itself:

```
const string = '';

Boolean(string);          // => false
Boolean(string.length);   // => false
Boolean(string.length > 0); // => false

// Since an empty String is falsy we can just check `string` directly:
if (string) { }

// Or we can be more explicit:
if (string.length) { }

// Or we can be maximally explicit:
if (string.length > 0) { }
```

If we're only checking for the truthiness of a value, then we are also potentially detecting all potential truthy values, including non-zero numbers and objects. To be completely sure that you have a `String` and that it is not empty, the most succinct technique is as follows:

```
if (typeof myString === 'string' && myString) {
  // ...
}
```

Emptiness by itself, however, may not be all we're interested in. We may wish to detect whether a string has actual content in it. In most cases, *actual content* starts at the beginning of the String and ends at the end of the String, but in some cases, it may be embedded within whitespace on either side. To account for this, we can trim the String and then confirm its emptiness:

```
function isNonEmptyString(string) {
  return typeof string === 'string' && string.trim().length > 0;
}

isNonEmptyString('hi');  // => true
isNonEmptyString('');    // => false
isNonEmptyString(' ');   // => false
isNonEmptyString(' \n'); // => false
```

Notice that our function, `isNonEmptyString`, is using a `length > 0` check on the trimmed string instead of just relying on its falsiness as an empty string. This is so that we can safely and confidently know that our `isNonEmptyString` function will always return a Boolean value. Even though, 99% of the time, it will be used in a Boolean context such as `if (isNonEmptyString(...))`, we should still ensure that our function has an intuitive and consistent contract.

> The logical AND operator (`a && b`) will, if its left-hand side is truthy, return its right-hand side. Therefore, expressions such as `typeof str === "string" && str` are not always guaranteed to return a Boolean. Go to the *Operator – Logical Operators – Logical AND Operator* section of `Chapter 8`, *Operators* for more information.

Strings are simple to detect, but as we mentioned in the previous chapter, working with them can be a challenge due to Unicode. Therefore, it's vital to remember that while the detection of a string may provide us some certainty, it does not tell us what is inside the string and whether it is the value we're expecting. If your detections have the intention of providing a guide or warning to those who are using your interface, you might be better served by explicitly checking the contents of the value.

Detecting undefined

The `undefined` type can be checked directly by referring to its globally available value via the strict equality operator:

```
if (value === undefined) {
  // ...
}
```

Unfortunately, however, since undefined can be overridden within non-global scopes (depending on your precise setup and environment), this approach can be troublesome. Historically, undefined could be overridden globally. This meant that things like this were possible:

```
let value = void 0;  // <- actually undefined
let undefined = 123; // <- cheeky override

if (value === undefined) {
  // Does not occur
}
```

The void operator, as we will explore later, takes one operand to its right-hand side (void foo) and will always evaluate to undefined. As such, void 0 has become a synonym for undefined and is useful as a substitute. So, if you have low confidence in the undefined value, then you can simply check for void 0 like so:

```
if (value === void 0) {
  // value is undefined
}
```

Various other approaches emerged to ensure a reliable undefined value. One, for example, would simply declare an unassigned variable (which will always default to undefined) and then use that within the scope:

```
function myModule() {
  // My local `undefined`:
  const undef;

  void 0 === undef; // => true

  if (someValue === undef) {
    // Instead of `VALUE === undefined` I can
    // use `VALUE === undef` within this scope
  }
}
```

Over time, the mutability of the undefined value has been locked down. *ECMAScript 2015* forbade global modification, but curiously still allowed local modification.

Thankfully, it has always remained possible to check for undefined via the simple typeof operator:

```
typeof undefined; // => "undefined"
```

Using `typeof` in this way is far less risky than relying on `undefined` as a literal value, though with the advent of linting tools, it is generally safe to directly check for `undefined`.

 We'll explore ESLint, a popular JavaScript linting tool, in `Chapter 15`, *Tools For Cleaner Code*. In the case of overwriting `undefined` in a local scope, which is unquestionably a bad thing to do, it'll helpfully give us a warning. Such warnings can provide us with a level of confidence, allowing us to safely use previously risky aspects of the language.

Detecting null

As we've seen, `typeof null` evaluates to `"object"`. This is an odd legacy of the language. Unfortunately, it means that we cannot rely on `typeof` for the detection of `null`. Instead, we must compare to the literal `null` value directly using a strict quality operator, as shown here:

```
if (someValue === null) {
  // someValue is null...
}
```

Unlike `undefined`, `null` cannot be overwritten in any version of the language, nor in any environment, and so it doesn't come with any headaches around its usage.

Detecting null or undefined

So far, we've covered how to independently check for both `undefined` and `null`, but we may want to check for both at the same time. It's quite common, for example, to have a function signature that has an optional argument. And if that argument is not passed or is explicitly set to `null`, it's normal to fall back to some default value. This can be achieved by explicitly checking for both `null` and `undefined`, like so:

```
function printHello(name, message) {
  if (message === null || message === undefined) {
    // Default to a hello message:
    message = 'Hello!';
  }
  console.log(`${name} says: ${message}`);
}
```

Often, since both `null` and `undefined` are falsy values, it is quite normal to imply their presence by checking the falsiness of a given value:

```
if (!value) {
  // Value is definitely not null and definitely not undefined
}
```

This, however, will also check whether the value is any of the other falsy values (including, `false`, `NaN`, 0, and so on). So, if we want to confirm that a value is specifically `null` or `undefined`, and no other falsy value, then we should stick to the explicit variation:

```
if (value === null || value === undefined) //...
```

Even more succinctly, however, we can adopt the abstract (non-strict) equality operator to check for either `null` or `undefined` since it considers these values to be equal:

```
if (value == null) {
  // value is either null or undefined
}
```

Although this utilizes the generally frowned-upon abstract equality operator (which we'll explore later in this chapter), it is still a popular way to check for both `undefined` and `null`. This is due to its succinct nature. However, adopting this more succinct check makes the code less obvious. It may even leave the impression that the author meant to check solely for `null`. This ambiguity of intent should leave us doubting its cleanliness. Therefore, in most situations, we should opt for the more explicit and strict check.

Detecting arrays

Detecting arrays in JavaScript is thankfully very straightforward due to the `Array.isArray` method:

```
if (Array.isArray(value)) {
 // ...
}
```

What this method tells us is that the passed value was constructed via the array constructor or an array literal. However, it does not check the `[[Prototype]]` of the value, so it is entirely possible (although unlikely) that the value, although appearing like an array, may not have the characteristics you desire.

When we believe that we need to check whether a value is an array, it's important to ask ourselves what we're really trying to detect. It may be the case that we can check for the characteristics we desire instead of the type itself. It's crucial to consider what we will be doing with the value. If we are intending to loop over it via `for...of`, then it may be more suitable for us to check for its iterable-ness instead of its array-ness. As we mentioned earlier, we can employ a helper like this to do so:

```
function isIterable(obj) {
  return obj != null &&
    typeof obj[Symbol.iterator] === 'function';
}

const foo = [1,2,3];
if (isIterable(foo)) {
  for (let f in foo) {
    console.log(f);
  }
}

// Logs: 1, 2, 3
```

If, alternatively, we are looking to use specific array methods such as `forEach` or `map`, then it's best to check via `isArray` as this will give us as a reasonable level of confidence that these methods exist:

```
if (Array.isArray(someValue)) {
  // Using Array methods
  someValue.forEach(v => {/*...*/});
  someValue.sort((a, b) => {/*...*/});
}
```

If we were inclined to be really thorough, we could also individually check for specific methods, or we could even force the value into an array of our own so that we could operate on it freely while knowing that the value is truly an array:

```
const myArrayCopy = [...myArray];
```

Note that copying an array-like value via the spread syntax (`[...value]`) will only work if the value is iterable. An example of when using `[...value]` is appropriate is when operating on `NodeList`s that have been returned from the DOM API:

```
const arrayOfParagraphElements = [...document.querySelectorAll('p')];
```

A `NodeList` is not a true `Array`, so it does not give us access to native array methods. Due to this, it is useful to create and use a copy of it that is a true `Array`.

On the whole, it is safe to adopt and rely on `Array.isArray`, but it's important to consider whether you even need to check for `Array`, whether it's more appropriate to check for whether the value is iterable, or even whether it has a specific method or property. As with all other checks, we should seek to make it obvious what our intent is. If we're employing checks that are more obscure than `Array.isArray`, then it may be prudent to add a comment or abstract the operation away with a descriptively named function.

Detecting instances

To detect whether an object is an instance of a constructor, we can simply use the `instanceof` operator:

```
const component = new Component();
component instanceof Component;
```

 The `instanceof` operator will be covered in more detail in `Chapter 8`, *Operators*.

Detecting plain objects

When we say *plain* objects, we are typically referring to those that are constructed as either `Object` literals or via the `Object` constructor:

```
const plainObject = {
  name: 'Pikachu',
  species: 'Pokémon'
};

const anotherPlainObject = new Object();
anotherPlainObject.name = 'Pikachu';
anotherPlainObject.species = 'Pokémon';
```

This is in contrast to other objects, such as those provided natively by the language (for example, arrays) and those that we construct ourselves via instantiating constructors (for example, `new Pokemon()`):

```
function Pokemon() {}
new Pokemon(); // => A non-plain object
```

The simplest way to detect a plain object is to inquire as to its `[[Prototype]]`. If it has a `[[Prototype]]` equal to `Object.prototype`, then we can say it is plain:

```
function isPlainObject(object) {
  return Object.getPrototypeOf(object) === Object.prototype;
}

isPlainObject([]);              // => false
isPlainObject(123);             // => false
isPlainObject(new String);      // => false
isPlainObject(new Pokemon());   // => false

isPlainObject(new Object());    // => true
isPlainObject({});              // => true
```

Why would we need to know whether a value is a plain object? It may, for example, be useful to discern plain from non-plain objects when creating an interface or function that accepts configuration objects in addition to more complex object types.

In most situations, we will need to detect a plain object explicitly. Instead, we should rely only on the interface or data that it provides us. If a user of our abstraction wishes to pass us a non-plain object but it still has the properties that we require, then who are we to complain?

Conversion, coercion, and casting

So far, we have learned how to tell the difference between various types and characteristics within JavaScript using detection. As we have seen, detection is useful when needing to provide alternative values or warnings in the case of unexpected or incompatible values. There is an additional mechanism for dealing with such values, however: we can convert them from the values we don't desire into the values we do desire.

In order to convert a value, we use a mechanism known as **casting**. Casting is the intentional and explicit derivation of one type from another type. In contrast to casting, there is also **coercion**. Coercion is the implicit and internal process of conversion employed by JavaScript when we use operators or language constructs that require specific types. An example of this would be when passing `String` values to a multiplication operator. The operator will naturally coerce its `String` operands to numbers so that it can attempt to multiply them:

```
'5' * '2'; // => 10 (Number)
```

The underlying mechanisms in both *casting* and *coercion* are identical. They are both mechanisms of conversion. But how we access these low-level behaviors is key. If we do so explicitly, clearly communicating our intent, then the readers of our code will have a far nicer time.

Consider the following code, which contains two different mechanisms for converting a String into a Number:

```
Number('123'); // => 123
+'123'; // => 123
```

Here, we are using two different techniques to force the conversion of a value from a String into a Number. The Number() constructor, when called as a function, will internally convert the passed value into a Number primitive. The unary + operator will do the same, although it is arguably less clear. Coercion is even less clear as it often appears to occur as a side effect of some other operation. Here are some examples of this:

```
1 + '123'; // => "1234"
[2] * [3]; // => 6
'22' / 2; // => 11
```

The + operator, when either operand is a string, will coerce the opposite operand to a string and then concatenate them both together. The * operator, when given arrays, will call toString() on them and then coerce the resulting String into Number, effectively meaning that [2] * [3] is equal to 2 * 3. Also, the division operator will coerce its operands to numbers before operating on them. All of these coercive behaviors are happening implicitly.

 The line between *coercion* and *casting* is not set in stone. It is possible, for example, to explicitly and intentionally convert a type via a coercive side effect. Consider the expression someString * 1, which could be used to *cast* a string to a number, using coercion to do so. In our conversions, what's crucial is that we **clearly communicate our intent**.

Coercion, since it happens implicitly, can be the cause of many bugs and unexpected behaviors. To avoid this trap, we should always have a strong level of confidence in the types of our operands. Casting, however, is entirely intentional and can help create a more reliable code base. It's common, on the more public or exposed sides of your interfaces, to preemptively cast to the types you desire, just in case the types you've received are not correct.

Observe here how we are explicitly casting both `haystack` and `needle` values to the `String` type:

```
function countOccurrences(haystack, needle) {

  haystack = String(haystack);
  needle = String(needle);

  let count = 0;

  for (let i = 0; i < haystack.length; count++, i += needle.length) {
    i = haystack.indexOf(needle, i);
    if (i === -1) break;
  }

  return count;
}

countOccurrences('What apple is the best type of apple?', 'apple'); // => 2
countOccurrences('ABC ABC ABC', 'A'); // => 3
```

Since we're relying on the `indexOf()` method on the `haystack` string, it makes sense, depending on our desired level of defensiveness, to cast the `haystack` to a string so that we can ensure it has the method available. Casting `needle` to a string also encodes a higher level of certainty so that we, and fellow programmers, can feel at ease.

 The defensive approach of preemptively casting values to protect against undesirable types is best when we're crafting reusable utilities, public-facing APIs, or any interfaces that'll be consumed in a way that reduces your confidence in the types you'll be receiving.

Dynamically typed languages such as JavaScript are seen by many as an invitation to chaos. Such people may be used to the comfort and certainty provided by strictly typed languages. In truth, if wielded fully and carefully, a dynamic language can allow our code to be more thoughtfully composed and more resilient to the changing needs of users. In the remainder of this section, we'll be discussing the conversion to individual types, including the explicit casting mechanisms we can utilize and the various coercive behaviors the language adopts internally. We'll begin by looking at Boolean conversion.

Converting into a Boolean

All values in JavaScript when converted into a Boolean will return `true` unless they are one of the seven falsy primitives (`false`, `null`, `undefined`, `On`, `0`, `""`, and `NaN`), in which case they will return `false`.

To cast a value to a Boolean, we can simply pass the value to the Boolean constructor, invoking it as a function:

```
Boolean(0); // => false
Boolean(1); // => true
```

The language will coerce values to Booleans when the values exist in a Boolean context. Here are some examples of such contexts (each marked with `HERE`):

- `if ( HERE ) {...}`
- `do {...} while (HERE)`
- `while (HERE) {...}`
- `for (...; HERE; ...) {...}`
- `[...].filter(function() { return HERE })`
- `[...].some(function() { return HERE })`

This list is not exhaustive. There are quite a few other situations in which our values will be coerced to Booleans. It's usually quite easy to tell. If a language construct or natively-provided function or method allows you to specify one of two possible pathways (that is, *if X then do THIS otherwise do THAT*), then you can bet that it will be internally coercing whatever value you've expressed to a Boolean.

A common idiom for casting to a Boolean, in addition to the more explicit call to `Boolean()`, is the *double-bang*, that is, the unary logical NOT operator (`!`) repeated twice:

```
!!1;  // => true
!![]; // => true
!!0;  // => false
!!""; // => false
```

Repeating the logical NOT operator twice will invert the Boolean representation of the value twice. It's easier to understand the semantics of the *double-bang* by seeing it parenthesized:

```
!( !( value ) )
```

This is effectively doing four things:

- Casting the value to a Boolean (`Boolean(value)`).
- If the value is `true`, then make it `false`. If the value is `false`, then return `true`.
- Cast the resulting value to a Boolean (`Boolean(value)`).
- If the value is `true`, then make it `false`. If the value is false, then return `true`.

In other words: this does one logical NOT, followed by another, resulting in the Boolean representation of the original value itself.

Explicitly casting values to Booleans is especially useful when you're creating a function or method that must return a Boolean value but deals with values that are not Boolean. For example, I may wish to create an `isNamePopulated` function that returns `false` if the name variable is not a populated string or is `null` or `undefined`:

```
function isNamePopulated(name) {
  return !!name;
}
```

This will helpfully return `false` if name is an empty `String`, `null`, or `undefined`:

```
isNamePopulated('');         // => false
isNamePopulated(null);       // => false
isNamePopulated(undefined);  // => false

isNamePopulated('Sandra');   // => true
```

It will incidentally also return `false` if name were any other falsy value (such as 0) and it would return `true` if name were any truthy value:

```
isNamePopulated(0); // => false
isNamePopulated(1); // => true
```

This may seem entirely undesirable but, in this context, it may be okay since we're already operating under the assumption that name is a `String`, `null`, or `undefined`, and so we only care about the function's fulfillment of its contract in regards to those values. How comfortable you are with this would depend entirely on your specific implementation and the interface it provides.

Converting into a String

Casting a value to a String can be achieved by invoking the String constructor as a regular function (that is, not as a constructor):

```
String(456); // => "456"
String(true); // => "true"
String(null); // => "null"
String(NaN); // => NaN
String([1, 2, 3]); // => "1,2,3"
String({ foo: 1 }); // => "[object Object]"
String(function(){ return 'wow' }); // => "function(){ return 'wow' }"
```

Calling String() with your value is the most explicit and clear way of casting to a String, although there are more succinct patterns that are sometimes used:

```
'' + 1234; // => "1234"
`${1234}`; // => "1234"
```

These two expressions may appear equivalent, and for many values, they are. But, internally, they work differently. As we'll see later, the + operator will discern whether a given operand is a String by calling its internal ToPrimitive mechanism in such a way that the operand's valueOf (if it has one) will be queried before its toString implementation. However, when using template literals (such as `${value}`), any interpolated values will be converted directly to strings (without going via ToPrimitive). There is always the possibility that a value's valueOf and toString methods will provide different values. Take a look at the following example, which shows how we can manipulate the return values of the two seemingly equivalent expressions by defining our own toString and valueOf implementations:

```
const myFavoriteNumber = {
  name: 'Forty Two',
  number: 42,
  valueOf() { return number; },
  toString() { return name; }
};

`${myFavoriteNumber}`; // => "Forty Two"
'' + myFavoriteNumber; // => 42
```

This would be a rare situation to encounter but is still worth thinking about. Often, we presume that we can reliably cast *any* value to a string quite easily, but that may not always be the case.

Traditionally, it's quite common to rely on a value's `toString()` method and call it directly:

```
(123).toString(); // => 123
```

However, if the value is `null` or `undefined`, then you'll receive a `TypeError`:

```
null.toString();      // ! TypeError: Cannot read property 'toString' of
null
undefined.toString(); // ! TypeError: Cannot read property 'toString' of
undefined
```

Additionally, the `toString` method is not guaranteed to return `string`. Observe here how we can implement our own `toString` method that returns `Array`:

```
({
  toString() { return ['not', 'a', 'string'] }
}).toString(); // => ["not", "a", "string"]
```

Therefore, it is always advisable to cast to a `string` via the very explicit and clear `String(...)`. Using indirect forms of coercion, side effects, or blindly relying on `toString` can create unexpected results. Remember that even if you have a good knowledge of these mechanisms and feel comfortable using them, it doesn't mean other programmers will.

Converting into a Number

Casting a value to a `Number` can be achieved by invoking the `Number` constructor as a regular function:

```
Number('10e3');      // => 10000
Number(' 4.6');      // => 4.6
Number('Infinity');  // => Infinity
Number('wat');       // => NaN
Number(false);       // => 0
Number('');          // => 0
```

Additionally, there is the unary plus + operator, which does essentially the same thing:

```
+'Infinity'; // => Infinity
+'55.66';    // => 55.66
+'foo';      // => NaN
```

These are the only two approaches available for casting a non-Number to a Number type, but JavaScript also provides other techniques for extracting numerical values from strings. One such technique is parseInt, a globally available native function that accepts both a String and an optional radix argument (which defaults to *base 10*, that is, decimal). It will, naturally, coerce its first argument to a String if it is not already a String and then attempt to extract the first integer of the specified radix from the String. By doing this, you can achieve the following outcomes:

```
parseInt('1000');    // => 1000
parseInt('100', 8);  // => 64 (i.e. octal to decimal)
parseInt('AA', 12);  // => 130 (i.e. hexadecimal to decimal)
```

If the string has a prefix of 0x or 0X, then parseInt will assume the radix to be 16 (*hexadecimal*):

```
parseInt('0x10'); // => 16
```

Some browsers and other environments may also treat a prefix of 0 as an indicator of an octal radix:

```
// (In *some* environments)
parseInt('023'); // => 19 (assumed octal -> decimal)
```

parseInt() will also effectively trim the String, ignoring any initial whitespace, and will ignore all the content of the String beyond the first found integer:

```
parseInt(' 111 222 333'); // => 111
parseInt('\t\n0xFF');     // => 255
```

 parseInt is usually frowned upon due to its obscure mechanism of extracting an integer from String and the fact that it may dynamically pick its own radix if none is provided. If you must use parseInt, use it with caution and full awareness of how it operates. And always provide a radix argument.

In a similar spirit to parseInt there is also a native parseFloat function, which will attempt to extract a *float* (that is, *a floating-point number*) from a given String:

```
parseFloat('42.01');  // => 42.01
parseFloat('\n1e-3'); // => 0.001
```

`parseFloat` will trim the string and then look for the longest set of characters from the 0th character that can be naturally parsed by the language in the same way a numeric literal may be parsed. As such, it works fine with Strings that include non-numeric characters beyond a parseable numeric sequence:

```
parseFloat('   123 ... rubbish here...'); // => 123
```

Such a string would cause `NaN` to be evaluated if we passed it to `Number(...)`. So, in some rare cases, `parseFloat` may be more useful to you.

Both `parseFloat` and `parseInt` will convert their initial argument into a `String` before attempting extraction. As such, if your first argument is an object, you should be wary of how it may naturally coerce to a string. If your object implements distinct `toString` and `valueOf` methods, then you should expect `parseInt` and `parseFloat` to only use `toString` (unless `[Symbol.toPrimitive]()` is also implemented). This is in contrast to `Number(...)`, which will attempt to convert its argument into a `Number` directly (without first converting it into a `String`) and will thus prioritize `valueOf` over `toString`:

```
const rareSituation = {
  valueOf() { return "111"; },
  toString() { return "999"; }
};

Number(rareSituation); // => 111
parseFloat(rareSituation); // => 999
parseFloat(rareSituation); // => 999
```

In most situations, converting any value into a `Number` should be attempted via `Number` or the unary plus + operator. You should only use `parseFloat` or `parseInt` if you have a specific need for their numerical extraction algorithms.

Converting into a primitive

Converting a value into its primitive representation is not something we can do directly, but is done implicitly (that is, *coercively*) by the language in a number of different situations, such as when you try to use the abstract equality operator, ==, to compare a `String`, `Number`, or `Symbol` to a value that is an `Object`. The `Object`, in that scenario, will be converted into its primitive representation via an internal procedure called `ToPrimitive`, which in summary does the following:

1. If `object[Symbol.toPrimitive]` exists, and when called it returns a primitive value, use that

2. If `object.valueOf` exists, and it returns a primitive (non-`Object`), use its return value

3. If `object.toString` exists, use its return value

We can see `ToPrimitive` in action if we attempt a comparison with `==`:

```
function toPrimitive() { return 1; }
function valueOf() { return 2; }
function toString() { return 3; }

const one = { [Symbol.toPrimitive]: toPrimitive, valueOf, toString };
const two = { valueOf, toString };
const three = { toString };

1 == one; // => true
2 == two; // => true
3 == three; // => true
```

As you can see, if an object has all three methods (`[Symbol.toPrimitive]`, `valueOf`, and `toString`), then `[Symbol.toPrimitive]` will be used. If it has just `valueOf` and `toString`, then `valueOf` will be used. And, of course, if there is only `toString`, then it will be used.

There is the possibility that *2* and *3* in that procedure will swap if `ToPrimitive` is called with a hint of `String` (meaning that it has been instructed to attempt to coerce to a `String` instead of any primitive). An example of such a case would be when you use a computed member access operator (`object[something]`), where if `something` is an object, it would be converted into a `String` via `ToPrimitive` with a hint of `String`, meaning `toString()` will be attempted before `valueOf()`. We can see this in action here:

```
const object = { foo: 123 };
const something = {
  valueOf() { return 'baz'; },
  toString() { return 'foo'; }
};

object[something]; // => 123
```

We have both `toString` and `valueOf` defined on `something`, but only `toString` is used to determine which property to access on `object`.

If we do not define our own methods, such as `valueOf` and `toString`, then the default methods available on the `[[Prototype]]` of whatever object we're using will be used instead. The primitive representation of an array, for example, is defined by `Array.prototype.toString`, which will simply join its elements together with a comma as a separator:

```
[1, 2, 3].toString(); // => "1,2,3"
```

All types have their own natively provided `valueOf` and `toString` methods, so if we wish to force the `ToPrimitive` internal procedure to use our own methods, then we'll need to override the native ones by supplying our object with its own methods directly or by inheriting from the `[[Prototype]]`. For example, if you wished to provide a custom array abstraction that had its own primitive conversion behavior, then you could implement it by extending the `Array` constructor:

```
class CustomArray extends Array {
  toString() {
    return this.join('|');
  }
}
```

Then, you'd be able to rely on your `CustomArray` instances being handled in their own unique way by the `ToPrimitive` procedure:

```
String(new CustomArray(1, 2, 3));    // => 1|2|3
new CustomArray(1, 2, 3) == '1|2|3'; // => true
```

The coercive behaviors of all operators and native language constructs will vary. Any time you pass a value to a language construct or operator that is expecting a primitive (typically either a string or a number), it will likely be passed through `ToPrimitive`. As such, it's useful to know about this internal procedure. We'll refer to this section as well as we start to explore all of JavaScript's operators in detail.

Summary

In this chapter, we have continued to explore the innards of JavaScript, covering the dynamic nature of the language. We've seen how we can go about detecting various types and the nuanced intricacies of coercion and casting. These topics are difficult to pick up, but they will be useful. Many anti-patterns that appear in JavaScript code come down to fundamental misunderstandings of language constructs and mechanisms, so having a deep understanding of these topics will aid our ambition of writing clean code tremendously.

In the next chapter, we will continue our exploration of types by exploring JavaScript's operators. It's likely that you will already have a very good knowledge of many of these, but thanks to JavaScript's dynamic nature, their usage can sometimes yield unexpected results. For this reason, the next chapter dedicates itself fully to the careful exploration of the language's operators.

8
Operators

In the previous chapter on *dynamic typing*, we explored topics such as type-coercion and detection; we also covered several operators. In this chapter, we'll continue this exploration by delving into every single operator that the JavaScript language makes available. Having a rich understanding of JavaScript's operators will make us feel utterly empowered in a language that can, at times, appear confusing. There is, unfortunately, no shortcut to understanding JavaScript, but as you begin to explore its operators, you will see patterns emerge. For example, many of the multiplicative operators work in a similar manner, as do the logical operators. Once you are comfortable with the main operators, you will begin to see that there is a grace underlying the complexity.

 It may be useful to treat this chapter as more of a reference if you're pressed for time. Do not feel like you need to exhaustively retain every detail of every operator's behavior.

In this chapter, we will cover the following topics:

- What is an operator?
- Arithmetic and numeric operators
- Logical operators
- Comparative operators
- Assignment operators
- Property access operators
- Other operators and syntax
- Bitwise operators

Now that we're ready to dive in, the very first question we need to ask ourselves is: what even *is* an operator?

What is an operator?

An operator in JavaScript is a standalone piece of syntax that forms an *expression* and is typically used to derive something or compute a logical or mathematical output from a set of inputs (called **operands**).

Here, we can see an expression containing an operator (+) with two operands (3 and 5):

```
3 + 5
```

Any operator can be said to have four characteristics:

- **Its arity**: how many operands the operator accepts
- **Its function**: what the operator does with its operands and what it evaluates to
- **Its precedence**: how the operator will be grouped when used in combination with other operators
- **Its associativity**: how the operator will behave when neighbored with operators of the same precedence

It's important to understand these foundational characteristics as it will vastly aid your usage of operators in JavaScript.

Operator arity

Arity refers to how many operands (or inputs) an operator can receive. An *operand* is a formal term for the value(s) that you can give or pass to an operator.

If we consider the greater-than operator (>), it receives two operands:

```
a > b
```

In this example, a is its first operand (or left-side operand). And b is its second (or right-side operand). Since it receives two operands, the greater-than operator is considered a binary operator. In JavaScript, we have unary, binary, and ternary operators:

```
// Unary operator examples (one operand)
-a
!a

// Binary operator examples (two operands)
a == b
a >= b
```

```
// Ternary operator examples (three operands)
a ? b : c
```

 There is only one ternary operator in JavaScript, the conditional operator (a ? b : c). Since it is the only ternary operator, it is sometimes simply referred to as the ternary operator instead of its formal name.

Knowing about the arity of a given operator is vital—just as it would be vital to know how many arguments to pass a function. It's also important to consider how we are communicating our intent when we compose operations. Since operations can appear in series, it can sometimes be unclear which operator refers to which operand. Consider this confusing expression:

```
foo + + baz - - bar
```

To avoid confusion in understanding operations like this, it is conventional to move unary operators closer to their operands and even to employ parentheses to make it absolutely crystal clear what the intent is:

```
foo + (+baz) - (-bar)
```

As with all of the parts of code, operators must be wielded with care and concern for the individual or individuals (including your future self) who'll have to encounter, understand, and maintain the code going forward.

Operator function

An operator's function is simply what it does and what it evaluates to. We'll be going over each operator individually, so there's not a lot to say here beyond a few basic assumptions you can carry with you when working with operators.

In JavaScript, every operator is its own entity and is not tied to the type of operands it is operated on. This is in contrast to some other languages where operators are mapped to overridable functions or are somehow attached to the operands themselves. In JavaScript, operators are their own syntactic entity and have non-overridable functionality. Their functionality is, however, extensible in certain situations.

When using any of the following types of operators, the language will internally attempt coercion:

- Arithmetic operators (namely, +, *, /, -, and so on)
- Increment operators (namely, ++ and --)

- Bitwise operators (namely, ~, <<, |, and so on)
- Computed member access operator (that is, ... [...])
- Non-strict comparative operators (namely, >, <, >=, <=, and ==)

And to specifically override these mechanisms of coercion, you can supply `valueOf()`, `toString()`, or `[Symbol.toPrimitive]()` methods to any objects you intend to use as operands:

```
const a = { valueOf() { return 3; } };
const b = { valueOf() { return 5; } };

a + b; // => 8
a * b; // => 15
```

As we covered in the previous chapter's *Conversion to a primitive* section, these methods will be called in a specific order depending on the exact operator or language construct used. In the case of all arithmetic operators, for example, `valueOf` will be attempted before `toString`.

Operator precedence and associativity

The order of operation when multiple operators are used in combination is defined by two mechanisms: *precedence* and *associativity*. An operator's precedence is a number from 1 to 20, and defines the order in which a series of operators will run. Some operators share the same precedence. Associativity defines the order in which operators of the same precedence will be operated on (either left-to-right or right-to-left).

Consider the following operation:

```
1 + 2 * 3 / 4 - 5;
```

In JavaScript, these specific mathematic operators have the following precedences:

- The addition operator (+) has a precedence of 13
- The multiplication operator (*) has a precedence of 14
- The division operator (/) has a precedence of 14
- The subtraction operator (–) has a precedence of 13

And all of them have *left-to-right* associativity. Since operators of higher precedence occur first and operators of the same precedence will occur according to their associativity, we can say that our example operation occurs in the following order:

1. Multiplication (left most amongst operators with a precedence of 14)
2. Division (next on the left amongst operators with a precedence of 14)
3. Addition (left most amongst operators with a precedence of 13)
4. Subtraction (next on the left amongst operators with a precedence of 13)

If we were to group our operation explicitly using parentheses, it would, therefore, look like this:

```
(
  1 +
  (
    (2 * 3)
    / 4
  )
) - 5;
```

Every operator, even non-mathematical ones, have specific precedences and associativities. The `typeof` operator, for example, has a precedence of 16. This can cause a headache if you use it in combination with a lower-precedence operator:

```
typeof 1 + 2; // => "number2"
```

Due to the + operator having a lower precedence than `typeof`, JavaScript would internally run this operation like so:

```
(typeof 1) + 2;
```

This, therefore, results in `typeof 1` (that is, `"number"`) being concatenated with 2 (producing `"number2"`). To avoid this, we must force the order using our own parentheses:

```
typeof (1 + 2); // => "number"
```

Incidentally, this is why you may often see `typeof` with parentheses (`typeof(...)`), which can make it look like a function being invoked. It is, however, an operator, and the parentheses are only there to force a specific order of operation.

You can discover the exact precedences of every operator by reading the ECMAScript specification or searching online for `JavaScript operator precedences`. Note that the numbers used to indicate precedence between 1 and 20 are not from the ECMAScript specification itself but are rather just a useful way of understanding precedence.

Knowing the precedences and associativities of every operator is not something we should expect of our colleagues. It may be reasonable to assume that they know the precedences of some basic mathematical operators, but knowledge beyond that should not be considered guaranteed. Therefore, it is often necessary to provide clarity by employing parentheses even in situations where they may not be strictly necessary. This is especially crucial in complex operations where there are a large number of consecutive operators, as in this example:

```
function calculateRenderedWidth(width, horizontalPadding, scale) {
  return (width + (2 * horizontalPadding)) * scale;
}
```

Here, the parentheses wrapping `(2 * horizontalPadding)` is technically unnecessary as the multiplication operator naturally has a higher precedence than the addition operator. However, it is useful to provide extra clarity. Programmers reading this code will be grateful to spend less cognitive energy discerning the exact order of operations. As with many well-intended things, however, this can be taken too far. Parentheses that provide neither clarity nor a different forced order of operation should not be included. An example of such redundancy might be wrapping the entire `return` expression in additional parentheses:

```
function calculateRenderedWidth(width, horizontalPadding, scale) {
  return ((width + (2 * horizontalPadding)) * scale);
}
```

This should ideally be avoided, as if it's taken too far, it can introduce additional cognitive load for the reader of the code. A good guide for such situations is if you're inclined to add additional parentheses for clarity, you should probably split the operation into multiple lines:

```
function calculateRenderedWidth(width, horizontalPadding, scale) {
  const leftAndRightPadding = 2 * horizontalPadding;
  const widthWithPadding = width + leftAndRightPadding;
  const scaledWidth = widthWithPadding * scale;
  return scaledWidth;
}
```

These added lines provide not only clarity around the order of operations but also the purpose of each individual operation by usefully assigning each operation to a descriptive variable.

Knowing every single operator's precedence and associativity is not necessarily vital, but knowing how these mechanisms underly every operation is very useful. Most of the time, as you've seen, it's preferable to split operations into self-contained lines or groups for clarity, even when the internal precedence or associativity of our operators does not demand it. Above all, we must always consider whether we are clearly communicating our intent to the readers of our code.

The average JavaScript programmer will not have an encyclopedic knowledge of the ECMAScript specification, and as such, we should not demand such knowledge to comprehend the code we have written.

Knowledge of the mechanisms underlying operators paves the way for us to now explore individual operators within JavaScript. We'll begin by exploring arithmetic and numeric operators.

Arithmetic and numeric operators

There are eight arithmetic or numeric operators in JavaScript:

- **Addition**: `a + b`
- **Subtraction**: `a - b`
- **Division**: `a / b`
- **Multiplication**: `a * b`
- **Remainder**: `a % b`
- **Exponentiation**: `a ** b`
- **Unary plus**: `+a`
- **Unary minus**: `-a`

Arithmetic and numeric operators will typically coerce their operands to numbers. The only exception is the + addition operator, which will, if passed a non-numerical operand, assume the function of string concatenation instead of addition.

There is one guaranteed outcome of all of these operations that is worth knowing about beforehand. An input of NaN guarantees an output of NaN:

```
1 + NaN; // => NaN
1 / NaN; // => NaN
1 * NaN; // => NaN
-NaN;    // => NaN
+NaN;    // => NaN
// etc.
```

Beyond that basic assumption, each of these operators behaves in a slightly different way, so it's worth going over each of them individually.

The addition operator

The addition operator is a dual-purpose operator:

- If either operand is String, then it'll concatenate both operands together
- If neither operand is String, then it'll add both operands as numbers

To accomplish its dual purpose, the + operator first needs to discern whether the operands you've passed can be considered strings. Obviously, a primitive String value is clearly a string, but for non-primitives, the + operator will attempt to convert your operands into their primitive representations by relying on the internal ToPrimitive procedure that we detailed in the last chapter, in the *Conversion to a primitive* section. If the output of ToPrimitive for either of our + operands is a string, then it will concatenate both operands as strings. Otherwise, it'll add them as numbers.

The fact that the + operator caters to both numeric addition and concatenation can make it quite complicated to understand, so it's helpful for us to walk through a few examples.

Both operands are numbers

Explanation: When both operands are primitive numbers, the + operator very simply adds them together:

```
1 + 2; // => 3
```

Both operands are strings

Explanation: When both operands are primitive strings, the + operator very simply concatenates them together:

```
'a' + 'b'; // => "ab"
```

One operand is a string

Explanation: When only one operand is a primitive string, the + operator will coerce the other into String and will then concatenate both resulting strings together:

```
123 + 'abc'; => "123abc"
'abc' + 123; => "abc123"
```

One operand is a non-primitive

Explanation: When either operand is a non-primitive, the + operator will convert it into a primitive, and then act as it usually would with that new primitive representation. Here's an example:

```
[123] + 123; // => "123123"
```

In this case, JavaScript will convert [123] into its primitive value by using the return value of [123].toString() (that is, "123"). Since the primitive representation of an array is its String representation, the + operator will operate as if we were simply doing "123" + 123, which, as we know, evaluates to "123123".

Conclusion – know your operands!

When using the + operator, it's especially vital to know what operands you're dealing with. If you don't, then the outcome of your operation may be unexpected. The + operator is probably one of the more complex operators since it has a dual purpose. Most operators aren't as complex. The subtraction operator, which we'll explore next, is thankfully far simpler.

The subtraction operator

The subtraction operator (–) does what it says on the tin. It takes two operands, subtracting the right-side operand from the left-side operand:

```
555 - 100; // => 455
```

If either operand is not a number, it will be coerced into one:

```
'5' - '3'; // => 2
'5' - 3;   // => 2
5 - '3';   // => 2
```

This includes non-primitive types too:

```
[5] - [3]; // => 2
```

Here, we're seeing two arrays, each with a single element, being subtracted from each other. This seemingly makes no sense until we recall that the primitive representation of an array is its joined elements as a string, that is, `"5"` and `"3"` respectively:

```
String([5]); // => "5"
String([3]); // => "3"
```

These will then be converted into their numerical representations, 5 and 3, via an operation that is equivalent to the following:

```
Number("5"); // => 5
Number("3"); // => 3
```

Therefore, we are left with the intuitive operation of 5 minus 3, which we know is 2.

The division operator

The division operator, much like the subtraction operator, accepts two operands that it will coerce to numbers. It will divide its left-side operand by its right-side operand:

```
10 / 2; // => 5
```

The two operands are formally called the dividend and the divisor (`DIVIDEND / DIVISOR`) and will always evaluate according to floating-point math. Integer division does not exist in JavaScript, which means, effectively, that the results of your divisions may always include decimal points, and may hence be liable to the error margin of `Number.EPSILON`.

Watch out when dividing by zero, as you may end up with either NaN (when dividing zero by zero) or Infinity (when dividing a non-zero number by zero):

```
10 / 0;   // => Infinity
10 / -0;  // => -Infinity
0 / 0;    // => NaN
```

If your divisor is Infinity, your division will always evaluate to zero (0 or -0), unless your dividend is also Infinity, in which case, you'll receive NaN:

```
1000 / Infinity;    // => 0
-1000 / Infinity;   // => -0
Infinity / Infinity; // => NaN
```

In circumstances where you expect a divisor or dividend of zero, NaN or Infinity, it is best to be defensive and either check for those values explicitly beforehand or following the operation, like so:

```
function safeDivision(a, b) {
  const result = a / b;
  if (!isFinite(result)) {
    throw Error(`Division of ${a} by ${b} is unsafe`);
  }
  return result;
}

safeDivision(1, 0); // ! Throws "Division of 1 by 0 is unsafe"
safeDivision(6, 2); // => 3
```

The edge cases of division may seem scary but they're not frequently encountered in everyday applications. If we were, however, authoring a medical or financial program, then it'd be absolutely vital to carefully consider our operations' potential error states.

The multiplication operator

The multiplication operator behaves similarly to the division operator, apart from the obvious fact that it performs multiplication:

```
5 * 25; // => 125
```

It is necessary to watch out for effects of coercion and situations where either operand is NaN or Infinity. Rather intuitively, multiplying any non-zero finite value by Infinity will always result in Infinity (with the appropriate sign):

```
100 * Infinity; // => Infinity
-100 * Infinity; // => -Infinity
```

However, multiplying zero by Infinity will always result in NaN:

```
0 * Infinity; // => NaN
-Infinity * -0; // => NaN
```

Outside of these cases, most usages of the multiplication operator are fairly intuitive.

The remainder operator

The remainder operator (%), also known as the **modulo operator**, is similar to the division operator. It accepts two operands: a dividend, on the left side, and a divisor on the right side. It will return the remainder following an implied division operation:

```
10 % 5; // => 0
10 % 4; // => 2
10 % 3; // => 1
10 % 2; // => 0
```

If the divisor is zero, the dividend is Infinity, or either operand is NaN, then the operation will evaluate to NaN:

```
Infinity % Infinity; // => NaN
Infinity % 2; // => NaN
NaN % 1; // => NaN
1000 % 0; // => NaN
```

And if the divisor is Infinity, then the result will be equal to the dividend:

```
1000 % Infinity; // => 1000
0.03 % Infinity; // => 0.03
```

The modulo operator is useful in situations where you wish to know whether a number *goes into* another number squarely, such as when wishing to establish the *evenness* or *oddness* of an integer:

```
function isEvenNumber(number) {
  return number % 2 === 0;
}
```

```
isEvenNumber(0); // => true
isEvenNumber(1); // => false
isEvenNumber(2); // => true
isEvenNumber(3); // => false
```

As with all other arithmetic operators, it's useful to be aware of how your operands will be coerced. Most usages of the remainder operator are straightforward, so outside of its coercive behaviors and its treatment of NaN and Infinity, you should find its behavior intuitive.

The exponentiation operator

The exponentiation operator (**) takes two operands, a base on the left side and an exponent on the right side. It will evaluate to the base raised to the power of the exponent:

```
10 ** 2; // => 100
10 ** 3; // => 1,000
10 ** 4; // => 10,000
```

It is functionally identical to using the Math.pow(a, b) operation, although is more succinct. As with other arithmetic operations, it will internally coerce its operands to the Number type, and passing in any operands of NaN, Infinity, or zero will result in possibly unexpected outcomes, so you should try to avoid such cases.

One curious case worth mentioning is that, if the exponent is zero, then the result will always be 1, regardless of what the base is. So, the base could even be Infinity, NaN, or anything else, and the result would still be 1:

```
1000 ** 0;    // => 1
0 ** 0;       // => 1
Infinity ** 0; // => 1
NaN ** 0;     // => 1
```

All other arithmetic operators will evaluate to NaN if one of their operands is NaN, so the behavior of ** here is quite unique. Another unique behavior is that it will throw SyntaxError if your first operand is itself a unary operation:

```
+2 ** 2;
// SyntaxError: Unary operator used immediately
// before exponentiation expression. Parenthesis
// must be used to disambiguate operator precedence
```

This is to prevent ambiguity for the programmer. Depending on their previous exposure to other languages (or strict mathematical notation), they may expect cases such as `-2 **  2` to be either 4 or −4. As such, JavaScript will throw in such cases, hence forcing you to be more explicit with either `(-2) **  2` or `- (2 ** 2)`.

Apart from these unique characteristics, the exponentiation operator can be considered similar to other binary (two-operand) arithmetic operators. As always: be aware of your operands' types and how they may be coerced!

The unary plus operator

The unary plus operator (`+...`) will convert its operand into `Number` as if it were passed to `Number(...)`:

```
+'42'; // => 42
+({ valueOf() { return 42; } });
```

To do this, our cherished internal `ToPrimitive` procedure will be utilized, as discussed in the last chapter, in the *Conversion to a primitive* section. Its result will then be re-coerced into `Number` if it is not already `Number`. So, if `ToPrimitive` were to return `String`, that `String` would be converted into `Number`, meaning that non-numeric strings will result in `NaN`:

```
+({ toString() { return 'not a number'; } }); // => NaN
```

And naturally, if `String` from `ToPrimitive` can be converted into `Number`, then that is what the unary + operator will evaluate to:

```
+({ toString() { return '12345'; } }); // => 12345
```

This is more realistically observed when coercing an array via +:

```
+['5e3']; // => 5000

// Equivalent to:
Number(String(['5e3'])); // => 5000
```

The unary + operator is usually used in places where a programmer wishes to cast a number-like object to `Number` so that they can then use it with other numeric operations. Usually, however, it is preferable to explicitly use `Number(...)` as it is much clearer what the intention is.

The unary + operator can sometimes be confused with other operations. Consider this scenario:

```
number + +someObject
```

To someone unfamiliar with the unary plus or someone not attuned to seeing it regularly, this code may look like it contains a typo. We could potentially wrap the entire unary operation in its own parentheses to make it clearer:

```
number + (+someObject)
```

Or we could instead use the much clearer `Number(...)` function:

```
number + Number(someObject)
```

In summary, the unary + operator is a convenient shortcut to `Number(...)`. It's useful and quick, though in most cases, we should prefer to communicate our intent more clearly.

The unary minus operator

The unary minus operator (`-...`) will first convert its operand into `Number` in the same way as the unary + operator, detailed in the last section, and will then negate it:

```
-55;     // => -55
-(-55);  // => 55
-'55';   // => -55
```

Its usage is fairly straightforward and intuitive, although, as with unary +, it's useful to disambiguate cases where you have a unary operator next to its binary operator counterpart. Cases like these can be confusing:

```
number - -otherNumber
```

It is best, in these situations, to lend clarity with parentheses:

```
number - (-otherNumber)
```

The unary minus operator is usually only used directly with a literal number operand to specify a negative value. As with all other arithmetic operators, we should ensure that our intent is clear and that we are not confusing people with long or confusing expressions.

Now that we've explored arithmetic operators, we can begin to look into logical operators.

Logical operators

Logical operators are typically used to build logical expressions where the result of the expression informs some action or inaction. There are three logical operators in JavaScript:

- The NOT operator (`!a`)
- The AND operator (`a && b`)
- The OR operator (`a || b`)

As with most other operators, they can accept a variety of types and will coerce as necessary. The AND and OR operators, unusually, do not always evaluate to a `Boolean` value, and both utilize a mechanism called **short-circuit evaluation** to only execute both operands if some condition is met. We'll learn more about this as we explore each individual logical operator.

The logical NOT operator

The NOT operator is a unary operator. It accepts only a single operand and converts that operand into its Boolean representation, then inverts it, so that truthy items become `false` and falsy items become `true`:

```
!1;    // => false
!true; // => false
!'hi;  // => false

!0;    // => true
!'';   // => true
!true; // => false
```

Internally, the NOT operator will perform the following:

1. Cast the operand to a Boolean (`Boolean(operand)`)
2. If the resulting value is `true`, then return `false`; otherwise, return `true`

As discussed in the *Conversion to a Boolean* section in the last chapter, a typical idiom for converting a value to its Boolean representation is the double NOT (that is, `!!value`) as this effectively reverses the truthiness or falsiness of the value twice and evaluates to a Boolean. The more explicit and slightly more preferred idiom is to use `Boolean(value)`, as the intention is far clearer than with `!!`.

As a result of there being only seven falsy values in JavaScript, the NOT operator can only evaluate to `true` in these seven scenarios:

```
!false;      // => true
!'';         // => true
!null;       // => true
!undefined;  // => true
!NaN;        // => true
!0n;         // => true
!0;          // => true
```

JavaScript's rigid definition of falsiness and truthiness is reassuring. It means that even if someone constructs an object with all manner of primitive representations (imagine an object with `valueOf()` that returns a falsy value), all internal Boolean coercions will still only ever return `false` for the seven falsy values and nothing else. That means we only need to worry about those seven (*it could be much worse...*).

On the whole, usage of the logical NOT operator is very straightforward. It's a well-understood syntax across programming languages with clear semantics. As such, there is not a lot in the way of *best practices* concerning it. At the very least, it's best to avoid too many double negatives in your code. A double negative is when an already negatively-named variable is applied to the NOT operator, like so:

```
if (!isNotEnabled) {
  // ...
}
```

This is cognitively expensive for those who read your code and is therefore liable to misunderstanding. It's best to use positively-named Boolean variable names so that any logical operations using them are straightforward to comprehend. In this situation, we would simply rename our variable and reverse the operation, like so:

```
if (isEnabled) {
  // ...
}
```

The logical NOT operator, in summary, is most useful in Boolean contexts such as `if()` and `while()`, though is also idiomatically found in the double-NOT `!!` operation. And it is technically the only operator in JavaScript that is guaranteed to return a `Boolean` value regardless of its operand's type. Next, we'll explore the AND operator.

The logical AND operator

The logical AND operator (`&&`) in JavaScript accepts two operands. If its *left-side* operand is truthy, then it will evaluate and return the *right-side* operand; otherwise, it will return the *left-side* operand:

```
0 && 1; // => 0
1 && 2; // => 2
```

It can be a confusing operator for many people because they wrongfully assume that it is equivalent to the question *Are both A and B true?* when, in fact, it is more akin to *If A is truthy then give me B; otherwise, I'll settle for A*. People may have an assumption that JavaScript will evaluate both operands, but it in fact will only evaluate the right-side operand if the left-side operand is truthy. This is known as **short-circuit evaluation**. And JavaScript will not cast the resulting value of the operation to `Boolean`: instead, it'll just give us that value back, unchanged. If we were to implement the operation ourselves, it might look something like this:

```
function and(a, b) {
  if (a) return b;
  return a;
}
```

Given a simple operation, such as making an `if(...)` statement conditional upon two values being truthy, the `&&` operator will behave in an entirely unsurprising and expected way:

```
if (true && 1) {
  // Both `true` and `1` are truthy!
}
```

However, the `&&` operator can be used in more interesting ways too, such as when needing to return a value but only if some prior condition is met:

```
function getFavoriteDrink(user) {
  return user && user.favoriteDrink;
}
```

Here, the `&&` operator is being used in a non-Boolean context, where there is no coercion of its result occurring. In this case, if its left-side operand is falsy (that is, if `user` is falsy), then it will return that; otherwise, it will return the right-side operand (that is, `user.favoriteDrink`):

```
getFavoriteDrink({ favoriteDrink: 'Coffee' }); // => 'Coffee'
getFavoriteDrink({ favoriteDrink: null }); // => null
getFavoriteDrink(null); // => null
```

The `getFavoriteDrink` function behaves in a way that fulfills a basic contract, returning `favoriteDrink` if the `user` object is available and if the `favoriteDrink` property appears on that object, although its actual functionality is a little more chaotic:

```
getFavoriteDrink({ favoriteDrink: 0 }); // => 0
getFavoriteDrink(0); // => 0
getFavoriteDrink(NaN); // => NaN
```

Our `getFavoriteDrink` function is not making any deliberations about the specific nature of the user or `favoriteDrink` values; it is just blindly yielding to the `&&` operator, returning either its left-side or its right-side operand. If we are confident in the potential values of our operands, then this approach may be fine.

It's important to take the time to consider the possible ways that `&&` will evaluate the operands you provide it with. Take into consideration the fact that it is not guaranteed to return `Boolean` and is not guaranteed to even evaluate the right-side operand.

The `&&` operator, thanks to its short-circuiting nature, can also be used to express control flow. Let's consider a scenario in which we wish to call `renderFeature()` if the `isFeatureEnabled` Boolean is truthy. Conventionally, we may employ an `if` statement to do this:

```
if (isFeatureEnabled) {
  renderFeature();
}
```

But we could also employ `&&`:

```
isFeatureEnabled && renderFeature();
```

This and other unconventional usages of `&&` are typically frowned upon because they can obscure the intention of the programmer and create confusion for readers of your code who may not have such a thorough understanding of how `&&` operates in JavaScript. Nonetheless, the `&&` operator is truly powerful and should be used when well-suited to the task at hand. You should feel empowered to use it as you wish but always be aware of how the typical reader of your code may see the operation and always consider the prospective values that the operation may produce.

The logical OR operator

The logical OR operator (`||`) in JavaScript accepts two operands. If its left-side operand is truthy, then it will return that immediately; otherwise, it will evaluate and return the right-side operand:

```
0 || 1; // => 1
2 || 0; // => 2
3 || 4; // => 3
```

Much like the `&&` operator, the `||` operator is flexible in that it does not cast what it returns to `Boolean`, and it evaluates in a short-circuited manner, meaning that it only evaluates the right-hand side operand if the left-side operand meets a condition—in this case, if the right-side operand is falsy:

```
true || thisWillNotExecute();
false || thisWillExecute();
```

Conventionally, a programmer may assume that the logical OR operator is akin to the question *Are either A or B true?* but in JavaScript, it is more akin to: *If A is falsy, then give me B; otherwise, I'll settle for A.* If we were to implement this operation ourselves, it might look something like this:

```
function or(a, b) {
  if (a) return a;
  return b;
}
```

Just as with `&&`, this means that `||` can be used flexibly to provide control flow or to evaluate specific expressions conditionally:

```
const nameOfUser = user.getName() || user.getSurname() || "Unknown";
```

As such, it should be used cautiously in a way that considers what readers of the code are familiar with, and in a way that considers all prospective operands and the resulting values from the operation.

Comparative operators

Comparative operators are a collection of binary operators that always return `Boolean` derived from a comparison between the two operands:

- Abstract equality (`a == b`)
- Abstract inequality (`a != b`)
- Strict equality (`a === b`)
- Strict inequality (`a !== b`)
- Greater than (`a > b`)
- Greater than or equal to (`a >= b`)
- Less than (`a < b`)
- Less than or equal to (`a <= b`)
- Instance of (`a instanceof b`)
- In (`a in b`)

Each of these operators has slightly different functions and coercive behavior so it's useful to go through each of them individually.

Abstract equality and inequality

The abstract equality (`==`) and inequality (`!=`) operators rely on the same algorithm internally, which is responsible for determining whether two values can be considered equal. In this section, our examples will only explore `==`, but rest assured that `!=` will always simply be the opposite of whatever `==` is.

In the vast majority of cases, it is not advisable to rely on abstract equality because its mechanism can create unexpected results. Most of the time, you'll want to opt for strict equality (that is, `===` or `!==`).

Where both operands, the left-side and the right-side, are of the same type, then the mechanism is quite simple—the operator will check whether the two operands are identical values:

```
100 == 100;      // => true
null == null;    // => true
'abc' == 'abc';  // => true
123n == 123n;    // => true
```

When both operands are of the same type, abstract equality (==) is exactly identical to strict equality (===).

Since all non-primitives in JavaScript are of the same type (Object), abstract equality (==) will always return false if you try to compare two non-primitives (two objects) that don't refer to the exact same object:

```
[123] == [123]; // => false
/123/ == /123/; // => false
({}) == ({});   // => false
```

However, where both operands are of different types, for example, where you are comparing a Number type to a String type or an Object type to a Boolean type, the exact behavior of abstract equality will depend on the operands themselves.

If either operand is Number, and the other is String, then the a == b operation is equivalent to the following:

```
Number(a) === Number(b)
```

Here are some examples of this in action:

```
123 == '123';   // => true
'123' == 123;   // => true
'1e3' == 1000;  // => true
```

Note how, as discussed in the *Conversion to a number* section in the last chapter, the "1e3" string will be internally converted to the number 1000.

Continuing down the rabbit hole—if only one operand to the == operator is `Boolean`, then the operation is, once again, equivalent to `Number(a) === Number(b)`:

```
false == ''; // => true
// Explanation: Number(false) is `0` and Number('') is `0`

true == '1'; // => true
// Explanation: Number(true) is `1` and Number('1') is `1`

true == 'hello'; // => false
// Explanation: Number(true) is `1` and Number('hello') is `NaN`

false == 'hello'; // => false
// Explanation: Number(false) is `0` and Number('hello') is `NaN`
```

Finally, if previous conditions are not met, and if either operand is `Object` (not a primitive), then it will compare the primitive representation of that object to the other operand. As discussed in the last chapter, in the *Conversion to a primitive* section, this will attempt to call the `[Symbol.toPrimitive]()`, `valueOf()`, and then `toString()` methods to establish the primitive. We can see this in action here:

```
new Number(1) == 1; // => true
new Number().valueOf(); // => 1
({ valueOf() { return 555; }) == 555; // => true
```

Due to their complicated coercive behaviors, the *abstract equality* and *inequality* operators are best avoided. Anyone reading code littered with these operators won't be able to have a good level of confidence in the conditions and control flow of the program because there are simply too many odd edge cases where abstract equality can bite.

If you find yourself wanting to use abstract equality, for example, when one operand is a number and another is a string, consider whether it might be clearer and less error-prone to use a combination of stricter checks or to explicitly cast your values for clarity; for example, instead of `aNumber == aNumericString`, you could do `aNumber === Number(aNumericString)`.

Strict equality and inequality

The *strict equality* (===) and *strict inequality* (!==) operators in JavaScript are a staple of clean code. Unlike their abstract equality cousins, they provide certainty and simplicity in how they treat their operands.

The === operator will only ever return `true` if both of its operands are identical:

```
1 === 1;         // => true
null === null;   // => true
'hi' === 'hi';   // => true
```

The only exception to this rule is when either operand is `NaN`, in which case, it'll return `false`:

```
NaN === NaN; // => false
```

No internal coercion will ever occur with strict equality, so even if you have two primitives that could be coerced to the same number, for example, they will still be considered inequal:

```
'123' === 123; // => false
```

In the case of non-primitives, both operands must refer to the exact same object:

```
const me = { name: 'James' };
me === me; // => true
me !== me; // => false
```

Even if the object is of the equivalent structure or shares other characteristics, if it is not a reference to the same exact object, it'll return `false`. We can illustrate this by attempting to compare a wrapped `Number` instance with a value of 3 to the numeric literal, 3:

```
new Number(3) === 3; // => false
```

The abstract equality operator (==) would evaluate to true in such a case. You may consider the coercion of `new Number(3)` to 3 to be preferable, but it's far better to explicitly set up your operands so that they are of the desired types before comparison. So, in the example of `String` that contains a numerical value that we wish to compare to `Number`, it would be best to first explicitly cast it via `Number()`:

```
Number('123') === 123; // => true
```

It is always advisable to use strict equality instead of abstract equality. It provides far more certainty and reliability in the outcome of every operation and allows you to free your mind from the myriad coercive behaviors that abstract equality entails.

Greater than and less than

The *greater-than* (>), *less-than* (<), *greater-than-or-equal-to* (>=), and *less-than-or-equal-to* (<=) operators all operate in a similar manner. They follow an algorithm similar to abstract equality, although how values are coerced is slightly different.

The first thing to note is that all operands to these operators will first be coerced to their primitive representation. Following that, if their primitive representations are both strings, then they'll be compared lexicographically. If their primitive representations are not both strings, then they'll be coerced from whatever they are to numbers and then compared. This means that even if only one of your operands is a string, they'll both be compared numerically.

Lexicographic comparison

Lexicographic comparison occurs when both operands are strings, and involves the character-by-character comparison of each string. Broadly, strings that are *greater* are those that would appear later in a dictionary. Therefore, *banana* would be lexicographically greater than *apple*.

As we discovered in `Chapter 6`, *Primitive and Built-In Types*, JavaScript uses UTF-16 to encode strings and therefore each codeunit is a 16-bit integer. The UTF-16 codeunits from `65` (U+0041) to `122` (U+007A) are as follows:

```
ABCDEFGHIJKLMNOPQRSTUVWXYZ[\]^_`abcdefghijklmnopqrstuvwxyz
```

Those characters appearing later are represented by larger UTF-16 integers. To compare any two given codeunits, JavaScript will simply compare their integer values. For the case of comparing B to A, this might look something like this:

```
const intA = 'A'.charCodeAt(0); // => 65
const intB = 'B'.charCodeAt(0); // => 66
intB > intA; // => true
```

Every character in each operand string must be compared. To do this, JavaScript will go codeunit-by-codeunit. At each index of each string, if codeunits differ, the larger codeunit will be considered greater, and that string will, therefore, be considered greater than the other:

```
"AAA" > "AAB"
"AAB" > "AAC"
```

And if one operand is equal to the prefix of the other, then it will always be considered *less than*, as shown here:

```
'coff' < 'coffee'; // => true
```

As you may have spotted, the lowercase English letters occupy higher UTF-16 integers than uppercase letters. This has the effect of meaning that uppercase is considered less than lowercase and would, therefore, appear before it in a lexicographic ordering:

```
'A' < 'a'; // => true
'Z' < 'z'; // => true
'Adam' < 'adam'; // => true
```

You'll also notice that the codeunits from `91` to `96` include the punctuation characters, `[\]^_``. This will also affect our lexicographic comparisons:

```
'[' < ']'; // => true
'_' < 'a'; // => true
```

Unicode tends to be arranged in a way that any given language's characters will be naturally sorted lexicographically so that the first symbols in a language's alphabet are expressed by lower 16-bit integers than the later symbols. Here, we see, for example, the word for chicken ("ไก่") in Thai is lexicographically less than the word for egg ("ไข่") since the ก character appears before ข in the Thai alphabet:

```
'ไก่' < 'ไข่'; // => true ("chicken" comes before "egg")
'ก'.charCodeAt(0); // => 3585
'ข'.charCodeAt(0); // => 3586
```

The natural order of Unicode may not always yield a sensible lexicographic order. As we learned in the previous chapter, complex symbols can be expressed by combining together multiple codeunits into combining character pairs, surrogate pairs (creating *code points*), or even grapheme clusters. This can create various difficulties. One example would be the following case where a given symbol, in this case, *LATIN CAPITAL LETTER A WITH CIRCUMFLEX*, can be expressed either via the lone Unicode code-point `U+00C2` or via combining the capital letter "A" (`U+0041`) with the *COMBINING CHARACTER ACCENT* (`U+0302`). Symbolically and semantically, these are identical:

```
'Â'; // => Â
'A\u0302'; // => Â
```

However, since U+00C2 (decimal: 194) is technically larger than U+0041 (decimal: 65), it will be considered *greater than* in a lexicographic comparison, even though they are symbolically and semantically identical:

```
'Â' > 'A\u0302'; // => true
```

There are thousands of these potential discrepancies to watch out for, so if you ever find yourself needing to compare lexicographically, be mindful that JavaScript's *greater-than* and *less-than* operators will be limited by Unicode's inherent ordering.

Numeric comparison

Numeric comparison using JavaScript's greater-than and less-than operators is fairly intuitive. As mentioned, your operands will be coerced first to their primitive representations, and then coerced a second time, explicitly, to a number. For cases where both operands are numbers, the result is entirely intuitive:

```
123 < 456; // => true
```

And for NaN and Infinity, the following assertions can be made:

```
Infinity > 123; // => true
Infinity >= Infinity; // => true
Infinity > Infinity; // => false

NaN >= NaN; // => false
NaN > 3; // => false
NaN < 3; // => false
```

If one operand has a primitive representation that is not Number, then it will be coerced to Number before comparison. If you were to accidentally pass Array as an operand to >, then it would first coerce it to its primitive representation, which for arrays, is String with all individual coerced elements joined with a comma, and then attempt to coerce that to Number:

```
// Therefore this:
[123] < 456;

// Is equivalent to this:
Number(String([123])) < 456
```

Due to the potentially complicated coercions that may occur, it is always best to pass operands of the same type to >, <, >=, and <=.

The instanceof operator

The `instanceof` operator in JavaScript allows you to detect whether an object is an instance of a constructor:

```
const component = new Component();
component instanceof Component;
```

This operation will climb the `[[Prototype]]` chain of its left-side operand looking for a specific `constructor` function. It will then check whether this constructor is equal to the right-side operand.

Since it climbs the `[[Prototype]]` chain, it can work safely with multiple inheritances:

```
class Super {}
class Child extends Super {}

new Super() instanceof Super; // => true
new Child() instanceof Child; // => true
new Child() instanceof Super; // => true
```

If the *right-side* operand is not a function (that is, is not callable as a constructor), then `TypeError` will be thrown:

```
1 instanceof {}; // => TypeError: Right-hand side of 'instanceof' is not
callable
```

The `instanceof` operator is sometimes useful in discerning native types such as whether an object is an array:

```
[1, 2, 3] instanceof Array; // => true
```

This usage, however, has been largely replaced by `Array.isArray()`, which is generally more trustworthy as it will work correctly in rare cases where `Array` has been passed to you from another native context such as a frame (within the browser).

The in operator

The `in` operator will return `true` if a property can be found in an object:

```
'foo' in { foo: 123 }; // => true
```

The *left-side* operand will be coerced to its primitive representation, which, if not `Symbol`, will be coerced to `String`. Here, we can see how a left-side operand that is `Array` will be coerced into a comma-separated serialization of its contents (the native and default way that arrays are coerced to primitives, thanks to `Array.prototype.toString`):

```
const object = {
  'Array,coerced,into,String': 123
};

['Array', 'coerced', 'into', 'String'] in object; // => true
```

All seemingly numeric property names in JavaScript are stored as strings, so accessing `someArray[0]` is equal to `someArray["0"]`, and therefore enquiring as to whether an object has a numeric property with `in` will also consider both `0` and `"0"` equally:

```
'0' in [1]; // => true
0 in { '0': 'foo' }; // => true
```

When establishing whether a property is in a given object, the `in` operator will traverse the entire `[[Prototype]]` chain, hence returning `true` for all accessible methods and properties at all levels of the chain:

```
'map' in [];     // => true
'forEach' in []; // => true
'concat' in [];  // => true
```

This means that if you're looking to distinguish between the concepts of *having a property* and *having a property on itself*, you should instead use `hasOwnProperty`, a method inherited from `Object.prototype` that will only check the object itself:

```
['wow'].hasOwnProperty('map'); // => false
['wow'].hasOwnProperty(0);     // => true
['wow'].hasOwnProperty('0');   // => true
```

On the whole, it is best to only use `in` if you're confident that there are no collisions with the property names you expect to use and properties provided by the object's `[[Prototype]]` chain. Even if you're just using plain objects, you still need to worry about the native prototype. If it's been modified in any way (by a utility library, for example), then you can no longer have a high level of trust in the results of your `in` operations and should hence use `hasOwnProperty`.

In older library code, you may even find code that chooses not to rely on `hasOwnProperty` on the object of inquiry, fearing that it may have been overridden. Instead, it'll opt for using the `Object.prototype.hasOwnProperty` method directly and calls it with that object as its execution context:

```
function cautiousHasOwnProperty(object, property) {
  return Object.prototype.hasOwnProperty.call(object, property);
}
```

This is likely overly-cautious though. It's safe enough in most code bases and environments to trust and use the inherited `hasOwnProperty`. The `in` operator as well, if you've considered the risks, is usually safe enough to use.

Assignment operators

An assignment operator will assign the value of its right-side operand to its left-side operand and will return the newly assigned value. The left-side operand of an assignment operation must always be an assignable and valid identifier or property. Examples of this would include the following:

```
value = 1;
value.property = 1;
value['property'] = 1;
```

You can additionally use *destructuring assignment,* which enables you to declare your *left-side* operand as either an object-literal-like or array-like structure that designates the identifiers you wish to assign and the values you wish to be assigned:

```
[name, hobby] = ['Pikachu', 'Eating Ketchup'];
name; // => "Pikachu"
hobby: // => "Eating Ketchup"
```

We will explore *destructuring assignment* further in a little bit. For now, it's only important to know that it, along with regular identifiers (`foo=...`) and property accessors (`foo.baz = ..., foo[baz] = ...`), can be used as the left-side operand to an assignment operator.

There are technically a large number of assignment operators because JavaScript combines regular operators with the basic assignment operator to create more succinct assignment operations in the common case of needing to mutate the value referred to by an existing variable or property. The assignment operators in JavaScript are as follows:

- **Direct assignment**: =
- **Additive assignment**: +=
- **Subtractive assignment**: -=
- **Multiplicative assignment**: *=
- **Divisive assignment**: /=
- **Remainder assignment**: %=
- **Bitwise left-shift assignment**: <<=
- **Bitwise right-shift assignment**: >>=
- **Bitwise unsigned right-shift assignment**: >>>=
- **Bitwise AND assignment**: &=
- **Bitwise XOR assignment**: ^=
- **Bitwise OR assignment**: |=

All assignment operators, apart from the direct assignment = operator, will conduct the operation that is indicated by the operator preceding =. So, in the case of +=, the + operator will be applied to the left-and right-side operands, the result of which will then be assigned to the left-side operand. So, consider the following statement:

```
value += 5
```

It would be equivalent to:

```
value = value + 5
```

The same follows for all other assignment operators that are of the combined type. The addition operator, as we know, will concatenate its operands if either is a string. And the exponentiation operator (**) will always evaluate to 1 if the exponent operand is zero (2 ** 0 === 1). We can rely on this and other existing knowledge to know how such operators will work when combined with assignment. We, therefore, don't need to individually explore all of these assignment operator variants.

Assignment conventionally occurs in the context of a singular line. It's typical to see an assignment statement on its own terminated by a semicolon:

```
someValue = someOtherValue;
```

But there's nothing implicit in the assignment operator that requires this. In fact, you can embed an assignment anywhere where you would be able to embed any expression within the language. The following syntax would be entirely legal, for example:

```
processStep(nextValue += currentValue);
```

This is carrying out an addition combined with an assignment, and then passing the resulting value to the `processStep` function. It is exactly equivalent to the following code:

```
nextValue += currentValue;
processStep(nextValue);
```

Note here how it is `nextValue` that is passed to `processStep`. The result of an assignment operation expression is always the value being assigned:

```
let a;
(a = 1); // => 1
(a += 2); // => 3
(a *= 2); // => 6
```

It is common to see assignment in contexts of `for` and `while` loops:

```
for (let i = 0, l = arr.length; i < l; i += 1) { }
//           \___/ _____/          \___/
//             |          |                  |
//        Assignment  Assignment      Additive Assignment
```

This and other patterns of assignment are totally fine as they are so widely used they have become idiomatic of JavaScript. But in most other situations, it is preferable not to embed assignment within other language constructs. Code such as `fn(a += b)` is potentially unintuitive to some, as it may not be clear what value is actually passed to `fn()`.

 In regard to clean code, the only question we need to ask ourselves when assigning values is whether the reader of our code (*including us!*) will find it obvious that assignment is occurring and whether they'll understand *what* is being assigned.

Increment and decrement (prefix and postfix) operators

These four operators technically fall under the umbrella of assignment but they are unique enough to warrant their own section:

- The postfix increment operator (`value++`)
- The postfix decrement operator (`value--`)
- The prefix increment operator (`++value`)
- The prefix decrement operator (`--value`)

These will simply increment or decrement the value by 1. They're usually found in iteration contexts such as `for` or `while` loops. They are best thought of as succinct alternatives to additive and subtractive assignment (that is, `value += 1` or `value -= 1`). However, they have a couple of unique characteristics that are worth covering.

Prefix increment/decrement

The prefix increment and decrement operators allow you to increment or decrement any given value and will evaluate to the newly incremented value:

```
let n = 0;

++n; // => 1 (the newly incremented value)
n;   // => 1 (the newly incremented value)

--n; // => 0 (the newly decremented value)
n;   // => 0 (the newly decremented value)
```

`++n` would technically be equivalent to the following additive assignment:

```
n += Number(n);
```

Note how the current value of n is first converted into `Number`. This is the nature of both the increment and decrement operators: they operate strictly on numbers. So, if n were `String`, that could not be coerced successfully, then the new incremented or decremented value of n would be `NaN`:

```
let n = 'foo';
++n; // => NaN
n;   // => NaN
```

Here, we can observe how, since the coercion of `foo` to a `Number` fails, the attempted incrementation of it also fails, returning `NaN`.

Postfix increment/decrement

The postfix variants of the increment and decrement operators are identical to the prefix variants, except for one fact: the postfix variants will evaluate to the old value, not the newly incremented/decremented value:

```
let n = 0;

n++; // => 0 (the old value)
n;   // => 1 (the newly incremented value)

n--; // => 1 (the old value)
n;   // => 0 (the newly decremented value)
```

This is crucial and can, if not used intentionally, lead to undesirable bugs. Increment and decrement operators are usually used in contexts where this difference is irrelevant. For example, when used in the last expression of a `for  (_;_;_)` statement, the return value is not used anywhere, so we'd see no difference between the two following approaches:

```
for (let i = 0; i < array.length; i++) { ...}
for (let i = 0; i < array.length; ++i) { ...}
```

However, in other circumstances, the evaluated value is absolutely key. In the following `while` loop, for example, the `++i < array.length` expression is evaluated on every iteration, meaning that the newly incremented value is compared to `array.length`. If we swapped this for `i++ < array.length`, then you'd be comparing the value before incrementing, meaning that it'd be one less and hence we'd get an additional (unwanted!) iteration. You can observe the difference here:

```
const array = ['a', 'b', 'c'];

let i = -1;
while (++i < array.length) { console.log(i); } Logs: 0, 1, 2

let x = -1;
while (x++ < array.length) { console.log(x); } // Logs: 0, 1, 2, 3
```

This is quite a rare occurrence, especially with more modern iteration techniques available in the language. But the increment and decrement operators are still very popular in other contexts, so it's useful to appreciate the difference between their prefix and postfix variants.

777777777777777

77777

Destructuring assignment

As briefly mentioned, the left-side operand of an assignment operator (. . . =) can be specified as a destructuring object or array pattern, like so:

```
let position = { x: 123, y: 456 };
let { x, y } = position;
x; // => 123
y; // => 456
```

These patterns typically look like `Object` or `Array` literals as they start and end with `{}` and `[]` respectively. They are, however, slightly different.

With the destructuring object pattern, where you want to declare the identifier or property you wish to assign to, you must place it as if it were a value in an object literal. That is, where `{ foo: bar }` usually means assign `bar` *to* `foo`, in a *destructuring pattern*, it means *assign the value of* `foo` *to the identifier*, `bar`. It is reversed. Where the name of the property of the value you wish to access matches the name that you wish to be assigned in the local scope, you can use a shorter syntax of simply `{ foo }`, as shown here:

```
let message = { body: 'Dear Customer...' };

// Accessing `body` and assigning to a different name (`theBody`):
const { body: theBody } = message;
theBody; // => "Dear Customer..."

// Accessing `body` and assigning to the same name (`body`):
const { body } = message;
body; // => "Dear Customer..."
```

For arrays, the slots of syntax where you would usually designate the values (that is, `[here, here, and here]`) are used to designate the identifiers to which you wish to assign your values, so each identifier in a sequence relates to the same index elements in the array:

```
let [a, b, c] = [1, 2, 3];
a; // => 1
b; // => 2
c; // => 3
```

You can also use the rest operator (. . . foo) to instruct JavaScript to assign the *rest* of the properties to a given identifier. Here's an example of using it within the *destructuring array pattern*:

```
let [a, b, c, ...others] = [1, 2, 3, 4, 5, 6, 7];
others; // => [4, 5, 6, 7];
```

And here's an example of using it within the *destructuring object pattern*:

```
let { name, ...otherThings } = {
 name: 'James', hobby: 'JS', location: 'Europe'
};
name; // => "James"
otherThings; // => { hobby: "JS", location: "Europe" }
```

 Only destructure your assignments when it provides *genuine* increased readability and simplicity.

Destructuring can also occur for object structures that involve multiple levels of hierarchy:

```
let city = {
  suburb: {
    inhabitants: ['alice', 'steve', 'claire']
  }
};
```

If we wish to extract the inhabitants array and assign it to a variable of the same name, then we can do the following:

```
let { suburb: { inhabitants } } = city;
inhabitants; // => ["alice", ...]
```

And a *destructuring array pattern* can be embedded in a *destructuring object pattern* and vice versa:

```
let {
  suburb: {
    inhabitants: [firstInhabitant, ...otherInhabitants]
  }
} = city;

firstInhabitant; // => "alice"
otherInhabitants: // => ["steve", "claire"]
```

Destructuring assignment is very useful in avoiding otherwise length, assignments like this:

```
let firstInhabitant = city.suburb.inhabitants[0];
```

However, it should be used with reservation as it can sometimes overcomplicate things for those who have to read your code. While it may appear intuitive when writing it for the first time, *destructuring assignments* are notoriously difficult to untangle. Consider the following statement:

```
const [{someProperty:{someOtherProperty:[{foo:baz}]}}] = X;
```

This is cognitively expensive to untangle. It would, perhaps, be more intuitive to express this logic traditionally:

```
const baz = X[0].someProperty.someOtherProperty[0].foo;
```

On the whole, *destructuring assignment* is an exciting and useful feature of the JavaScript language, but it should be used in a guarded way with consideration of the possibility of the confusion it can cause.

Property access operators

Accessing properties in JavaScript is achieved by using one of two operators:

- **Direct property access**: `obj.property`
- **Computed property access**: `obj[property]`

Direct property access

The syntax for directly accessing a property is a single period character, with a *left-side* operand that is the object you wish to access, and with a *right-side* operand that is the property name you wish to access:

```
const street = {
  name: 'Marshal St.'
};

street.name; // => "Marshal St."
```

The *right-side* operand must be a valid JavaScript identifier, and as such, cannot start with a number, cannot contain whitespace, and in general, cannot contain any punctuation characters that exist elsewhere within the JavaScript specification. You can, however, have properties that are named with so-termed exotic Unicode characters such as π (PI):

```
const myMathConstants = { π: Math.PI };
myMathConstants.π; // => 3.14...
```

This is an unconventional practice and is usually only used in novelty settings. It may, however, be genuinely useful in code that is embedded in problem domains where there are legitimate exotic symbols with existing meanings (*mathematics*, *physics*, and so on).

Computed property access

In cases where you cannot directly access a property via *direct property access*, it is possible to compute the property name you wish to access, delimiting it with square brackets:

```
someObject["somePropertyName"]
```

It's a *right-side* operand of any expression, meaning that you can freely compute some value that'll then be coerced to a string (if it is not already a string) and used as the property name to access the object:

```
someObject[ computeSomethingHere() ]
```

Typically this is used to access property names that contain characters that make them invalid identifiers, and hence illegal to use with the *direct property access* operator. This would include numeric property names (such as those found in an array), names with whitespace, or names with punctuation or keywords that exist elsewhere in the language:

```
object[1];
object['a property name with whitespace'];
object['{[property.name.with.odd.punctuation]}'];
```

It is best to only rely on computed property access in scenarios when you have no other choice. If there is the possibility of just accessing the property directly (that is, `object.property`), then you should prefer that. Likewise, if you're deciding what properties an object might contain, it's best to use names that are valid identifiers within the language so they can be directly accessed with ease.

Other operators and syntax

There are a few remaining operators and pieces of syntax that we have yet to explore and that don't fall into any other operator category:

- **The delete operator**: `delete VALUE`
- **The void operator**: `void VALUE`
- **The new operator**: `new VALUE`
- **Spread syntax**: `... VALUE`
- **Grouping**: `(VALUE)`
- **The comma operator**: `VALUE, VALUE, ...`

The delete operator

The `delete` operator can be used to remove properties from objects, as such its only operand usually takes the form of a property accessor, like so:

```
delete object.property;
delete object[property];
```

Only properties that are deemed configurable can be deleted in this manner. All properties added conventionally are, by default, configurable and can, therefore, be deleted:

```
const foo = { baz: 123; };

foo.baz;          // => 123
delete foo.baz;   // => true
foo.baz;          // => undefined
'baz' in foo;     // => undefined
```

However, if the property has been added via `defineProperty` with `configurable` set to `false`, then it'll not be deletable:

```
const foo = {};
Object.defineProperty(foo, 'baz', {
  value: 123,
  configurable: false
});

foo.baz; // => 123
delete foo.baz; // => false
foo.baz; // => 123
'baz' in foo; // => true
```

As you can see, the `delete` operator evaluates to `true` or `false` depending on whether the property has been successfully deleted. Following successful deletion, the property is not merely set to `undefined` or `null` but is entirely removed from the object so that checking its existence via `in` will return `false`.

The `delete` operator can technically be used to delete any variable (or so-termed *environment record binding* internally), but attempting to do so is considered a deprecated behavior and will produce `SyntaxError` in strict mode:

```
'use strict';
let foo = 1;
delete foo; // ! SyntaxError
```

The `delete` operator has historically been the subject of many inconsistencies between JavaScript implementations, most especially between different browsers. Because of this, only its conventional usage of deleting properties on objects is advisable.

The void operator

The `void` operator will evaluate to `undefined` regardless of its operand. Its operand can be any valid reference or expression:

```
void 1; // => undefined
void null; // => undefined
void [1, 2, 3]; // => undefined
```

It doesn't have many uses nowadays, although `void 0` is sometimes used as an idiom for `undefined` either for succinctness or to avoid issues in legacy environments where `undefined` was an untrusted mutable value.

The new operator

The `new` operator is used to form an instance from a constructor. Its *right-side* operand must be a valid constructor, either provided by the language (for example, `new String()`) or by ourselves:

```
function Thing() {}
new Thing(); // => Instance of Thing
```

By *instance,* what we truly mean is an object that has a `[[Prototype]]` equal to the
constructor's `prototype` property, and that has been passed to the constructor as
its `this` binding so that the constructor can fully prepare it for its purpose. Observe here
how, whether we define our constructor via a class definition or conventional syntax, we
can make the same assertions about the produced instances:

```
// Conventional Constructor Definition:
function Example1() {
  this.value = 123;
}

Example1.prototype.constructor === Example1; // => true
Object.getPrototypeOf(new Example1()) === Example1.prototype; // => true
new Example1().value === 123; // => true

// Class Definition:
class Example2 {
  constructor() { this.value = 123; }
}

Example2.prototype.constructor === Example2; // => true
Object.getPrototypeOf(new Example2()) === Example2.prototype; // => true
new Example2().value === 123; // => true
```

The `new` operator only cares that its *right-side* operand is constructible. This means it cannot
be a function formed by an arrow function, as in this example:

```
const Thing = () => {};
new Thing(); // ! TypeError: Thing is not a constructor
```

As long as you've defined your constructor using a function expression or declaration, it'll
work fine. You can even instantiate an anonymous inline constructor if you want:

```
const thing = new (function() {
  this.name = 'Anonymous';
});

thing.name; // => "Anonymous"
```

The `new` operator does not formally require the calling parentheses. They only need to be
included if you are passing arguments to the constructor:

```
// Both equivalent:
new Thing;
new Thing();
```

When you wish to instantiate something and then immediately access a property or method, however, you'd need to disambiguate by providing the calling parentheses and *then* accessing the property following that; otherwise, you'd receive `TypeError`:

```
function Component() {
  this.width = 200;
  this.height = 200;
}

new Component().width; // => 200
new Component.width; // => ! TypeError: Component.width is not a
constructor
(new Component).width; // => 200
```

The usage of the `new` operator is usually very straightforward. Semantically, it is understood to relate to the construction of an instance and should therefore ideally only be used to do that. It's also, therefore, assumed that anything being referenced by the *right-side* operand of `new` is identified with a name beginning with a capital letter and is a noun. These naming conventions indicate that it is a constructor, providing a useful hint to any programmers who may wish to use it. Here are some examples of both good and bad constructor names:

```
// Bad (non-idiomatic) names for Constructors:
new dropdownComponent;
new the_dropdown_component;
new componentDropdown;
new CreateDropdownComponent;

// Good (idiomatic) names for Constructors:
new Dropdown;
new DropdownComponent;
```

The correct naming of a constructor is crucial. It makes our fellow programmers immediately aware of what *contract* a specific abstraction fulfills. If we name a constructor so that it appears like a regular function, then our colleagues may try to invoke it incorrectly and suffer possible errors as a result. It, therefore, makes perfect sense to take advantage of a name's ability to communicate *contract*, as discussed in the earlier chapter on naming (`Chapter 5`, *Naming Things is Hard*).

The spread syntax

The *spread syntax* (also known as *rest syntax*) is composed of three dots followed by an operand expression (`...expression`). It allows the expression to be expanded in places where either multiple arguments or multiple array elements are expected. It technically exists in five distinct areas of the language:

- In *array literals*, of the form `array = [a, b, c, ...otherArray]`
- In *object literals*, of the form `object = {a, b, c, ...otherObject}`
- In *function parameter lists*, in the form `function(a, b, c, ...otherArguments) {}`
- In *destructuring array patterns*, in the form `[a, b, c, ...others] = array`
- In *destructuring object patterns*, in the form `{a, b, c, ,,,otherProps} = object`

In the context of a *function parameter list*, the *spread syntax* must be the very last parameter and would indicate that you wish for all arguments passed to the function from that point onward to be collected into a singular array by the name indicated:

```
function addPersonWithHobbies(name, ...hobbies) {
  name; // => "Kirk"
  hobbies; // => ["Collecting Antiques", "Playing Chess", "Drinking"]
}

addPersonWithHobbies(
  'Kirk',
  'Collecting Antiques',
  'Playing Chess',
  'Drinking'
);
```

If you attempt to use it amid other parameters, then you will receive `SyntaxError`:

```
function doThings(a, ...things, c, d, e) {}
// ! SyntaxError: Rest parameter must be last formal parameter
```

In the context of an *array literal* or a *destructuring array pattern*, the *spread syntax* is similarly used to indicate that the values referred to should be spread out. It's best to see these as two opposites, *deconstruction* and *reconstruction*:

```
// Deconstruction:
let [a, b, c, ...otherLetters] = ['a', 'b', 'c', 'd', 'e', 'f'];
a; // => "a"
b; // => "b"
c; // => "c"
otherLetters; // => ["d", "e", "f"]

// Reconstruction:
let reconstructedArray = [a, b, c, ...otherLetters];
reconstructedArray; // => ["a", "b", "c", "d", "e", "f"]
```

When used in the context of an *array literal* or a *destructuring array pattern*, the *spread syntax* must refer to an iterable value. This doesn't necessarily have to be an array. Strings, as an example, are iterable, so the following also works:

```
let [...characters] = 'Hello';
characters; // => ["H", "e", "l", "l", "o"]
```

In the context of an *object literal* or a *destructuring object pattern*, the *spread syntax* is similarly used to spread out all properties of any given object into the receiving object. Once again, we can see this as processes of *deconstruction* and *reconstruction*:

```
// Deconstruction:
const {name, ...attributes} = {
  name: 'Nissan Skyline',
  engineSize: '2500cc',
  year: 2009
};
name; // => "Nissan Skyline"
attributes; // => { engineSize: "2500cc", year: 2009 }

// Reconstruction:
const skyline = {name, ...attributes};
skyline; // => { name: "Nissan Skyline", engineSize: "2500cc", year: 2009 }
```

When used in this context, the value of the right side of the *spread syntax* must be either an object or a primitive that can be wrapped as an object (for example, `Number` or `String`). This means that all values in JavaScript are permissible except `null` and `undefined`, both of which, as we know, cannot be wrapped as objects:

```
let {...stuff} = null; // => TypeError
```

It's, therefore, best to only use the *spread syntax* in an object context when you're confident that the value is an object.

In conclusion, the *spread syntax*, as we've seen, is remarkably useful in a variety of different situations. Its main advantage is that it reduces the amount of syntax required to extract and designate values.

The comma operator

The comma operator (a, b) accepts a left-side and right-side operand and will always evaluate to its right-side operand. It is sometimes not considered an operator since it does not technically operate on its operands. It's also quite rare.

The comma operator should not be confused with the comma we use to separate arguments when declaring or invoking a function (for example fn(a,b,c)), the comma used when creating array literals and object literals (for example [a, b, c]), or the comma used when declaring variables (for example let a, b, c;). The comma operator is distinct from all of these.

It's most commonly seen in the iteration statement portion of a for(;;) loop:

```
for (let i = 0; i < length; i++, x++, y++) {
  // ...
}
```

Note how three increment operations are occurring in the third statement (which occurs at the end of each iteration in a conventional for(;;) statement), and that they are each separated by a comma. In this context, the comma is used merely to ensure that all of these individual operations will occur, regardless of each other, within the context of a singular statement. In regular code outside a for(;;) statement, you would likely just have these each dedicated to their own line and statement, like so:

```
i++;
x++;
y++;
```

However, due to the constraints of the for(;;) syntax, they must all exist within a singular statement and so the comma operator becomes necessary.

The fact that the comma operator evaluates to its *right-side* operand is not important in this context, but in other contexts, it may be important:

```
const processThings = () => (firstThing(), secondThing());
```

Here, `processThings`, when invoked, will first call `firstThing` and
then `secondThing` and will return whatever `secondThing` returns. It is therefore
equivalent to the following:

```
const processThings = () => {
  firstThing();
  return secondThing();
};
```

It is rare to see the comma operator used, even in scenarios like this, as it tends to
unnecessarily obscure code that could be more clearly expressed. It's useful to know that it
exists and how it behaves, but we shouldn't expect it to be an everyday operator.

Grouping

Grouping, or parenthesizing, is achieved by using regular brackets (`(...)`). This should
not be mistaken for other pieces of syntax that use parentheses, such as function invocation
(`fn(...)`).

The grouping parentheses can be considered an operator just like all of the others we've
learned about. They accept one operand—an expression of any form—and will evaluate to
whatever resides within them:

```
(1);                // => 1
([1, 2, 3]);        // => [1, 2, 3]
(false && true);    // => false
((1 + 2) * 3);      // => 9
(()=>{});           // => (A function)
```

As it simply evaluates its contents, you may wonder what the purpose of a group is.
Earlier, we covered the concepts of operator precedence and associativity. Sometimes, if
you're using a series of operators and wish to force a specific order of operations, then the
only way to do that is by wrapping them in a group, which, when used in combination
with other operators, has the highest precedence of all:

```
// The order of operations is dictated
// by each operator's precedence:
1 + 2 * 3 - 5;

// Here, we are forcing the order:
(1 + 2) * (3 - 5);
```

It's wise to use a group when the order of operations is either not what you desire or has the potential to be unclear to readers of the code. For example, it is sometimes common to wrap items being returned from a function in a group to provide aesthetic containment and clarity:

```
function getComponentWidth(component) {
  return (
    component.getInnerWidth() +
    component.getLeftPadding() +
    component.getRightPadding()
  );
}
```

Another obvious solution to this may be to merely indent the items you wish to contain, but the issue with this is that the JavaScript return statement will not know to look beyond its own line for the start of the expression or value it must return:

```
// WARNING: this won't work
return
  component.getInnerWidth() +
  component.getLeftPadding() +
  component.getRightPadding();
```

The return statement in the preceding code effectively terminates itself with a semicolon when the parser observes that there is no value or expression on the same line. This is known as **Automatic Semicolon Insertion** (**ASI**) and its existence means we often have to use groups to make it obvious to the parser what our intentions are:

```
// Clear to humans; clear to the parser:
return (
  component.getInnerWidth() +
  component.getLeftPadding() +
  component.getRightPadding()
);
```

In summary, *grouping* is a useful tool for containment and re-ordering operations, and it is a cheap and easy way to increase the clarity and readability of an expression.

Bitwise operators

JavaScript has seven bitwise operators. The term *bitwise* here means *to operate on binary numbers*. These operators are rarely utilized but are useful to know about nonetheless:

- **Bitwise unsigned right-shift operator**: >>>
- **Bitwise left-shift operator**: <<
- **Bitwise right-shift operator**: >>
- **Bitwise OR**: |
- **Bitwise AND**: &
- **Bitwise XOR**: ^
- **Bitwise NOT**: ~ (a unary operator)

 Bitwise operations are incredibly rare in JavaScript since you're usually dealing with higher-level sequences of bits like strings or numbers. However, it's worth having at least a cursory understanding of bitwise operations so that if you encounter the need, you can cope.

All bitwise operators in JavaScript will first coerce their operands (or a singular operand, in the case of bitwise NOT ~) to a 32-bit integer representation. This means that, internally, a number such as 250 would be manifested as follows:

```
00000000 00000000 00000000 11111010
```

The last eight bits, in this case of 250, contain all of the information regarding the number:

```
1 1 1 1 1 0 1 0
+ + + + + + + +
| | | | | | | | +---> 0 * 001 = 000
| | | | | | | +-----> 1 * 002 = 002
| | | | | | +-------> 0 * 004 = 000
| | | | | +---------> 1 * 008 = 008
| | | | +-----------> 1 * 016 = 016
| | | +-------------> 1 * 032 = 032
| | +---------------> 1 * 064 = 064
| +-----------------> 1 * 128 = 128
+-------------------> 1 * 128 = 128
===================================
                      SUM = 250
```

Adding together all of the bits will get us a decimal integer value of 250.

Every bitwise operator available will operate on these bits and derive a new value. A bitwise AND operation, for example, will yield a bit value of 1 for every pair of bits that are both *on*:

```
const a = 250;  // 11111010
const b = 20;   // 00010100
a & b; // => 16 // 00010000
```

We can see that only the fifth bit from the right (that is, 16) is *on* in both 250 and 20, therefore the AND operation will result in only that bit being left on.

Bitwise operators should only be utilized when you are carrying out binary mathematics. Outside of that, any usage of bitwise operators (for example, for side-effects) should be avoided because it drastically limits the clarity and comprehensibility of our code.

It was not uncommon, for a time, to see bitwise operators such as ~ and | being used in JavaScript because they were popular for succinctly deriving the integer floor of a number (for example, ~34.6789 === 34). It goes without saying that this approach, while clever and ego-boosting, created unreadable and unfamiliar code. It remains preferable to use more explicit techniques. In the case of flooring, using Math.floor() is ideal.

Summary

In this chapter, we have exhaustively covered the operators available in JavaScript. Collectively, the last past three chapters have given us an incredibly strong foundational understanding of JavaScript syntax, enabling us to feel utterly comfortable when constructing expressions.

In the next chapter, we'll continue to explore the language by applying our existing knowledge of types and operators to the landscapes of declaration and control flow. We'll be exploring how to use larger language constructs to craft clean code and will be discussing many of the traps and idiosyncrasies present in those constructs.

Parts of Syntax and Scope 9

In this chapter, we will continue to explore JavaScript's syntax and constructs. We'll be delving into the fundamentals of expressions, statements, blocks, scopes, and closures. These are the less visible parts of the language. Most programmers assume that they already have a good grasp of how things such as expressions and scopes work, but, as we've seen, our intuitions of how things should work may not always align with how they truly do work. The constructs we'll be learning about in this chapter are the crucial larger building blocks of our programs, so it is of vital importance to understand them fully before we explore more abstract concepts such as control flow and design patterns.

 Why are we learning this now? We've now got a solid grasp of what types are available in JavaScript and how to manipulate them via operators. The next logical step is to study *syntactic scaffolding* components, where we can place these types and operations, and how these scaffolding components behave. The end goal here is a high level of fluency in JavaScript so that we are better able to write clean code.

In this chapter we're going to cover the following topics:

- Expressions, statements, and blocks
- Scopes and declarations

Expressions, statements, and blocks

There are broadly three types of syntactic **container** that exist within JavaScript: expressions, statements, and blocks. They are all containers in that they all hold other pieces of syntax and all have distinct behaviors that are worth distinguishing.

There are additional constructs that you can call containers, such as functions or modules, but for now we're only interested in the types of syntax that you would find *within* these. As we continue to explore the language, we are slowly *zooming out* all the way from granular operators and expressions to the much larger and more complex functions and programs in which they reside.

It's best to visualize the individual syntactic parts of a program as a hierarchy:

```
const numbers =  [ 1 ,  2 ,  3 ,  4 ] ;

if ( numbers.length )
  {

      numbers =   numbers.map(  n =>   n  *  2   )   ;

  }

    = Block Statement   |  = Regular Statement    = Expression
```

Here, we can see that individual **expressions** (with a lower border) are wrapped in **statements**, either of the **regular** or **block** variety. It's useful to always have this hierarchical view of the language in our mind as this is how our code will be parsed and understood by the machine. We don't need to see our code as a parser would, of course, but it's indisputably useful to know how our code will be parsed.

This hierarchical view of the language will also help us write programs that communicate their intent well to our fellow programmers. Hierarchy is not only a syntactic concern but a human one. When we write a program, we will typically model problems at different layers of abstraction: each part of a program goes within another part, and from all these individual parts, we can build a program that contains many different layers of complexity.

As we explore the syntactic parts of JavaScript, it's worth remembering how individual elements of a program's syntax, its expressions and statements, will have a natural symmetry with the individual elements and layers of the problem domain.

Expressions

An expression is the most granular type of syntactic container. We've already been working a lot with expressions. Even expressing a literal value, like the number 1, will produce an expression:

```
1 // <= An expression containing the literal value 1
```

Using an operator also forms an expression:

```
'hi ' + 'there'
```

In fact, we can consider an operator as something that is itself applied to expressions. So the addition operator's syntax can be understood like so:

```
EXPRESSION + EXPRESSION
```

An expression can be as simple as a literal value or a variable reference, but may also be complex. The following expression encompasses a series of operations and is spread over a few lines:

```
(
  'this is part of' +
  ' ' +
  ['a', 'very', 'long', 'expression'].join(' ')
)
```

Expressions are not limited to primitive types or simple literal values.
Class definitions, function expressions, array literals, and object literals are all things that can appear in the context of an expression. The easy way to know whether something is an expression is the question of whether or not it can go within a group operator (that is, parentheses) without causing a SyntaxError:

```
(class Foo {});    // Legal Expression
(function() {});   // Legal Expression
([1, 2, 3]);       // Legal Expression
({ a: 1, b: 2 });  // Legal Expression

(if (a) {});       // ! SyntaxError (Not an Expression!)
(while (x) {});    // ! SyntaxError (Not an Expression!)
```

The syntactic building blocks of any program involve various different layers of syntactic structures. We have individual values and references: if we zoom out a little bit, we have expressions, and if we zoom out even further we have statements, which we will now explore.

Statements

A **statement** contains an expression, and is, therefore, another type of syntactic container. Knowing how JavaScript sees expressions as distinct from statements is hugely helpful in avoiding the various traps and idiosyncrasies of the language.

A statement is formed in a variety of situations. These include the following:

- When you terminate an expression with a semicolon (`1 + 2;`)
- When you use any of the `for`, `while`, `switch`, `do..while`, or `if` constructs
- When you create a function via a function declaration (`function Something() {}`)
- They are automatically formed by the language's natural **automatic semicolon insertion** (**ASI**)

 The syntax of a function declaration (`function name() {}`) will always form a statement unless it appears in the context of an expression, in which case it'll naturally be a *named function expression*. For the nuanced differences between these, please revisit `Chapter 6`, *Primitive and Built-In Types*.

Forming statements with semicolons

When we place one expression after another, we tend to terminate each individual one with a semicolon. By doing this, we are forming a statement. Explicitly terminating a statement ensures that the JavaScript parser will not have to do so automatically. If you don't use semicolons, then the parser will guess where to insert them via a process called ASI. This process relies on our placement of new lines (that is, `\n`).

As ASI is automatic, it won't always provide the outcomes you desire. For example, consider the following case where there is a function expression followed by a syntax that is intended as a group (that is, an expression delimited by parentheses):

```
(function() {})
(
 [1, 2, 3]
).join(' ')
```

This will cause a mysterious `TypeError` that says: `Cannot read property join of undefined`. This is because, from the parser's point of view, the following is what we're doing:

```
(function() {})([1, 2, 3]).join(' ')
```

Here, we're creating an inline anonymous function and then immediately calling it, passing the `[1, 2, 3]` array as our sole argument, and then we're attempting to invoke the `join` method on whatever's returned. But as our function returns `undefined`, there is no `join` method there, and so we receive an error. This is a rare situation, but variations of this issue do crop up from time to time. The best way to avoid them is to consistently use semicolons to terminate lines that are intended as statements, as shown in the following code:

```
(function() {});
(
  [1, 2, 3]
).join(' ');
```

ASI can bite you in other ways as well. A common example is when you attempt to use a `return` statement within a function, with its intended return value on the next line. In such cases, you'll get a nasty surprise:

```
function sum(a, b) {
  return
    a + b;
}
sum(a, b); // => undefined (odd!)
```

JavaScript's ASI mechanism will presume that the `return` statement is terminated if there is nothing else present on the same line, and so the following is closer to what the JavaScript engine will see when running the code:

```
function sum(a, b) {
  return;
  a + b;
}
```

To fix this, we can either place `a + b` on the same line as our `return` statement or we can use a group operator to contain our indented expression:

```
function sum(a, b) {
  return (
    a + b
  );
}
```

It's not necessary to know every ASI rule, but it is very useful to know that it exists. The best way of working with ASI is to avoid it wherever possible. If you're explicit about the termination of your statements, then you won't need to rely on obscure ASI rules, and you won't be relying on your fellow programmers knowing these rules either.

Blocks

If we consider statements as containers of expressions, then we can consider blocks as containers of statements. In other languages, they are sometimes called **compound statements** as they allow several statements to exist together.

Strictly speaking, blocks are statements. From a language-design perspective, this is a useful thing because it allows statements that form part of other constructs to be expressed as either single-line statements or entire blocks containing several statements—for example, following `if(...)` or `for(...)` constructs.

Blocks are formed by delimiting zero or more statements with curly braces:

```
{
    // I am inside a block
    let foo = 123;
}
```

Blocks are very rarely used as completely isolated units of code (there's very limited benefit from doing so). You'll usually find them within `if`, `while`, `for` and `switch` statements, as follows:

```
while (somethingIsTrue()) {
    // This is a block
    doSomething();
}
```

The `{ ... }` part of the `while` loop here is a block. It is not an inherent part of the `while` syntax. If we wish to, we can entirely exclude the block and in its place just have a regular single-line statement:

```
while (somethingIsTrue()) doSomething();
```

That would be identical to the version in which we use a block, but obviously this would be limiting if we intend to add more iteration logic. As a result, it's usually preferable to preemptively use a block in such scenarios. Doing so has the added benefit of legitimizing indentation and the containment of the iteration logic.

Blocks are not only syntactic containers. They affect the runtime of our code as well by providing their own scope, which means that we can declare variables within via `const` and `let` statements. Observe here how we declare a variable within an `if` block and how it is not available outside that block:

```
if (true) {
  let me = 'here';
  me; // => "here"
}

me; // ! ReferenceError
```

Scoping is a topic that we should not take lightly. It can be quite difficult to understand, and so what follows is an entire section in which we explore its nature and nuances.

Scopes and declarations

The scope of a given variable can be thought of as the areas within the program where that variable can be accessed.

When we declare a variable at the beginning of a module (outside all functions), we think that it's only natural that this variable should then be accessible to all functions within the module:

```
var hello = 'hi';

function a() {
  hello; // a() can "see" the hello variable
}

function b() {
  hello; // b() can "see" the hello variable
}
```

And if we define a variable within a function, then we expect all inner functions to have access to it:

```
var value = 'I exist';

function doSomething() {
  value; // => "I exist"
}
```

The fact that we can access `value` in the `doSomething` function here is thanks to its scope. The scope of a given variable will depend on how it is declared. When you declare a variable via a `var` declaration, it will have a different potential scope to a variable created via a `let` declaration. We will cover these differences soon, but first, it's useful to have a clearer idea of how scopes operate internally.

Internally, when you declare variables, JavaScript will create and store that variable within a lexical environment, which contains the mappings of identifiers to values. A typical JavaScript program can be thought of as having four types of lexical environments, as shown in the following list:

- **The global environment**: There is only one of these, and it is considered the outer scope of all other scopes. It is the global context in which all other environments (that is, scopes) exist. The global environment mirrors a global object that can be referred to by `window` or `self` in the browser and `global` in Node.js.
- **A module environment**: This environment will be created for each distinct JavaScript module that is run as part of a singular Node.js process or for each `<script type="module">` in the browser.
- **A function environment**: This environment will be in effect for every running function, however it is declared or invoked.
- **A block environment**: This environment will be in effect for every block (`{ ... }`) in your program, whether following another language construct, such as `if(...)` or `while(...)`, or situated independently.

As you know, both functions and blocks can exist within other functions and blocks. Consider the following piece of code that expresses various environments (scopes):

```
function setupApp(config) {
  return {
    setupUserProfileMenu() {

      if (config.isUserProfileEnabled) {

        const onDoneRendering = () => {
          console.log('Done Rendering!');
        };

        // (Do some rendering here...)
        onDoneRendering();

      }

    }
```

```
    };

}

    setupApp({ isUserProfileEnabled: true }).setupUserProfileMenu();
```

At the point where `Done Rendering!` is logged, we may expect the hierarchy of environments to look something like this:

```
Browser Global Environment
\--> Function Environment (setupApp)
     \--> Block Environment (if block)
          \--> Function Environment (onDoneRendering)
```

This hierarchy of environments will change throughout the runtime of a given program. If a function is run to completion and its internal scope is no longer used in any exposed internal functions (known as **closures**), then the lexical environment will be destroyed. Essentially, when a scope is guaranteed to no longer be needed, then JavaScript is free to get rid of it.

Variable declarations

A variable declaration occurs via a `var` keyword followed by a valid identifier or an assignment of the form `a = b`:

```
var foo;
var baz = 123;
```

 We call things declared via `var` keyword variable declarations, but it's important to note that, in popular terminology, declarations made by both `let` and `const` are also considered variables.

Variables declared via `var` are scoped to the nearest function, module, or global environment—that is, they are not block-scoped. At parse time, variable declarations within a given scope will be collected and then, at the point of execution, those declared variables will be hoisted to the top of their execution context and initialized with the `undefined` value. This means that, within a given scope, technically you can access a variable prior to its assignment, but it'll be `undefined`:

```
foo; // => undefined
var foo = 123;
foo; // => 123
```

The **execution context** is a name given to the top of the call stack, meaning the currently running function, script, or module. It is a concept that is only seen when code is run, and will change as the program progresses. You can usually think of it as simply the currently-running function (or outer module or <script>). var declarations are always hoisted to the top of their execution context and initialized to undefined.

The hoisting behavior of var is in contrast to variables declared via let and const, which will produce an ReferenceError if you attempt to access them prior to their declaration:

```
thing; // ! ReferenceError: Cannot access 'thing' before initialization
let thing = 123;
```

If you're not careful, the hoisting behavior of var can lead to some unexpected results. For example, there may be a situation where you're attempting to refer to a variable that exists within the outer scope but you are unable to do so because of a variable declaration in your current scope being hoisted:

```
var config = {};

function setupUI() {
  config; // => undefined
  var config;
}

setupUI();
```

Here, the inner scope's variable declaration of config will be hoisted to the top of its scope, meaning that, from the very first line of setupUI, config is undefined.

Since variable declarations are hoisted to the very top of their execution context, even those within a block will be hoisted as if they were first initialized outside of it:

```
// This:
// (VariableDeclaration inside a Block)
if (true) {
  var value = 123;
}

// ... Is equivalent to:
// (VariableDeclaration preceding a Block)
var value;
if (true) {
  value = 123
};
```

In summary, variable declarations create a variable that is scoped to the nearest function, module, or global environment. In the browser, there are no module environments, so it'll either be scoped to its function or the global scope. A variable declaration will be hoisted, before execution, to the top of its respective execution context. This may be the function, the module (in Node.js), or the `<script>` (in the browser). Variable declarations have fallen out of favor because of the more recently introduced `const` and `let` declarations, which are both block-scoped and do not have any odd hoisting behavior.

Let declarations

Let declarations are thankfully far simpler than `var` declarations. They will be scoped to their nearest environment (whether it is a block, a function, a module, or the global environment) and have no complicated hoisting behaviors.

Their ability to be scoped to a block means that a let declaration inside a block will not have an effect on the `outer` function scope. In the following code, we can see three different environments (scopes) with a respective `place` variable in each:

```
let place = 'outer';

function foo() {
  let place = 'function';

  {
    let place = 'block';
    place; // => "block"
  }

  place; // => "function"
}

foo();
place; // => "outer"
```

This demonstrates two things to us:

- Declaring via `let` will not overwrite or mutate a variable by the same name in an `outer` scope
- Declaring via `let` will allow each scope to have its own variable, invisible to `outer` scopes

When you use `let` in either `for(;;)`, `for...in`, or `for...of` constructs, even outside of the following block, then that `let` declaration will be scoped as if it were inside the block. This makes sense intuitively: when we initialize a `for` loop with let declarations, we naturally expect those to be scoped to the `for` loop itself and not outside of it:

```
for (let i = 0; i < 5; i++) {
  console.log(i); // Logs: 0, 1, 2, 3, 4
}
console.log(i); // ! ReferenceError: i is not defined
```

We should only use `let` if we expect the variable to be reassigned at some later point. If no new assignment will occur, then we should prefer `const`, as it gives us a little bit of extra peace of mind.

Const declarations

A `const` declaration has the same characteristics as `let`, except for one crucial difference: variables declared via `const` are immutable, meaning that the variable cannot be reassigned to a different value:

```
const pluto = 'a planet';
pluto = 'a dwarf planet'; // ! TypeError: Assignment to constant variable.
```

It's important to note that this does not affect the mutability of the value itself. So if the value is any type of object, then all of its properties will retain their mutability:

```
const pluto = { designation: 'a planet' };

// Assignment to a property:
pluto.designation = 'a dwarf planet';

// It worked! (I.e. the object is mutable)
pluto.designation; // => "a dwarf planet"
```

Even though `const` does not protect values from all mutability, it does protect us from some common mistakes and bad practices, such as reusing a variable to refer to several different concepts, or accidentally reassigning a variable because of a typo. The `const` code phrase is generally safer to use than `let`, and is now considered the best practice for the declaration of all variables, unless you have an explicit need to reassign a variable after its declaration.

You should also feel free to use `const` when declaring variables in `for...of` and `for...in` iteration constructs, such as in the following case:

```
for (const n of [4, 5, 6]) console.log(n);
// Logs 4, 5, 6
```

People often mistakenly opt for using `let` here because they believe that the looping construct will effectively reassign the variable, making `const` unsuitable. But in fact, the declaration within `for(...)` will be tied to a new block scope on each iteration, and thus the `const` variable will be newly initialized on each iteration within this fresh scope.

Function declarations

In terms of scoping, function declarations behave similarly to variable declarations (that is, `var`). They will be scoped to their closest function, module, or global environment, and will be hoisted to the top of their respective execution context.

Unlike variable declarations, however, a function declaration will cause the actual assignment of the `Function` to its identifier to be hoisted as well, meaning that the `Function` is effectively available before it is declared:

```
myFunction(); // => "This works!"
function myFunction() { return 'This works!' }
```

This behavior is quite obscure and as such is inadvisable unless it is very obvious where the definition for `myFunction` comes from upon invocation. A programmer will typically expect a definition for a function to exist above the place where it is called (or imported as a dependency at some prior point in time), so it can be confusing.

There is further complexity if we consider the possibility of a function declaration residing within a block that is conditionally activated (**warning: don't do this!**):

```
giveMeTheBestNumber; // => (Varies depending on implementation!)
if (something) {
  function giveMeTheBestNumber() { return 76; }
} else {
  function giveMeTheBestNumber() { return 42; }
}
```

Unfortunately, previous versions of ECMAScript did not prescribe the behavior of function declarations within blocks. This led to various browser implementations choosing their own unique way of handling such situations. Over time, implementations have begun to align. The ECMAScript 2015 specification sensibly forbids either of the `giveMeTheBestNumber` functions from having their values hoisted. The declaration itself can, however, still be hoisted, meaning that `giveMeTheBestNumber` would be `undefined` on lines prior to its declarations (similar to `var`), as mentioned. This is, at the time of writing, the prevalent behavior of most (but not all) implementations.

Because of the obscurity and the remaining inconsistencies across implementations, it is strongly suggested that you *don't use function declarations within blocks*. And ideally, it's best not to rely on their hoisting behavior (by referencing function declarations) unless you're confident that doing so would not be misunderstood by those who must read your code.

For more information on how functions produced by function declarations differ from other ways of creating functions (for example, function expressions or arrow functions), please revisit the *Functions* section in `Chapter 6`, *Primitive and Built-In Types*.

Closures

Inner scopes, as we've seen, have access to the variables of outer scopes:

```
function outer() {
  let thing = 123;
  function inner() {
    // I can access `thing` within here!
    thing; // => 123
  }
  inner();
}
outer();
```

What naturally follows from this is the concept of a closure. A closure is how JavaScript enables you to continue to access the scope of an `inner` function regardless of where or when it is called.

It's simplest to think of a closure as simply a retained scope. A closure is a wrapped-up or enclosed scope that is passed around alongside the function, invisibly. When you call the function, it has implicit access to its scope provided by this closure.

Consider the following function (`fn`), which returns another function. It has its own scope, in which we declare the `coolNumber` variable:

```
function fn() {
  let coolNumber = 1;
  return function() {
    console.log(`
      I have access to ${coolNumber}
      wherever and whenever I am called
    `);
  };
}
```

The inner function, which we return, has access to the `coolNumber` variable, as we would expect. When we call `fn()`, its scope is effectively kept alive so that, when we eventually call the `inner` function, it is still able to access `coolNumber`.

The following is another example, where we're making use of the continued access to the retained scope (that is, the closure) by reassigning and returning the local variable whenever our inner function is called:

```
function valueIncrementer() {
  let currentValue = 0;
  return function() {
    return currentValue++;
  };
}

const increment = valueIncrementer();
increment(); // => 0
increment(); // => 1
increment(); // => 2
```

The concept of closures is often over-complicated, so at the risk of doing that, I'll state things quite simply. A closure is not an odd thing, really: it is a natural extension of how we should expect a scope to work. All functions have access to a given scope, so it shouldn't matter how we then pass around these functions after their initial definition. They will continue to have access to that same scope, and are free to access or mutate variables within that scope as they see fit. A function is always anchored to the place it was originally defined and so whether it is called immediately or in a thousand minutes' time, it will have access to the same scope (that is, the same set of lexical environments).

Summary

In this chapter, we continued to explore the JavaScript language, zooming out from previous chapters to consider larger pieces of syntax, such as expressions, statements, and blocks. These are programmatic scaffolding components in which we can place the types and operations we've previously learned about. We also covered the complicated mechanisms of scopes, hoisting, and closures. Understanding how these concepts all work together is vital to understanding other people's JavaScript programs and constructing your own.

In the next chapter, we explore how to control flow within JavaScript. This'll allow us to weave together expressions and statements into larger bodies of logic in a clean way. We will then explore the art of abstraction design by learning about design patterns. Though the process of learning these topics individually may appear arduous, by the end of the book you'll have a thorough and powerful understanding of JavaScript that'll enable you to pay less attention to the oddities of the language and more attention to the cleanliness of your code.

10
Control Flow

This is the final chapter of our exploration into the syntax of JavaScript. We have so far covered its more atomic components its many types, operators, declarations, and statements. Gaining fluency in these is crucial to working effectively with the language at a foundational level and allows us now to take a step back and consider a larger concern: controlling a program's flow. We'll combine all of the syntax we've picked up into clean and understandable programs.

In this chapter, we will cover the following topics:

- What is control flow?
- Imperative versus declarative programming
- The movement of control
- Statements of control flow
- Handling cyclomatic complexity
- Asynchronous control flow

What is control flow?

Control flow refers to the order in which expressions and statements (and entire blocks of code) will run. Programming is, in part, the *art of controlling flow*. By writing code, we are specifying where control resides at any single moment.

At a granular level, the order of execution is dictated by the individual operators we use in our expressions. We explored the precedence and associativity of operators in the last chapter, discovering that, even if you have a series of operators, one after another, the exact order of their execution is defined by the individual operators' precedence and associativities so that, in the expression, `1 + 2 * 3`, the `2 * 3` operation will occur before the addition.

Outside expressions, on the statement level, we control flow in the following ways:

- We can do so by ordering our statements in the order we wish them to occur.
- We can do so by using conditional or iterative language constructs, including the following:
  - `switch()` statements
  - `if()` statements
  - `for()` statements
  - `while()` statements
  - `do{...} while()` statements
- We can do so by invoking and then returning or yielding from functions or generators (*yielding* and *returning* are both ways of *giving back control* to the caller).

It's easiest to imagine the control flow globally as a type of *cursor* or *finger* that is always pointing to a specific expression or statement of code. When a program is executing, the control flow will go down, line by line, until it encounters a piece of syntax that will redirect control to another piece of code. If it encounters an invocation of a function, then that function will be executed in the same manner; the control will be with each consecutive line within the function until it is returned to the caller of the function via a `return` statement. As *control* traverses down through a program, each language construct it encounters will be given control over the execution until they each complete. Consider the following simple piece of code:

```
let basket = [];
for (let i = 0; i < 3; i++) {
  basket.push(
    makeEgg()
  );
}
```

The flow of control that is taken in the preceding code is as follows:

1. We start with `let basket = [];`
2. The `for` loop begins: `let i = 0`
3. Check `i < 3` (`true`!):
   1. Run `makeEgg()`
   2. Push result via `basket.push(...)`
   3. `i++` (`i` is now 1)

1. Check i < 3 (true!):
   1. Run makeEgg()
   2. Push the result via basket.push(...)
   3. i++ (i is now 2)
2. Check i < 3 (true!):
   1. Run makeEgg()
   2. Push result via basket.push(...)
   3. i++ (i is now 3)
3. Check i < 3 (false!).
4. End of Program

Even for quite a simple program such as this, the flow can be quite complicated and lengthy. For the benefit of our fellow programmers, it makes sense to try to reduce this complexity whenever possible. The way to accomplish this is via abstraction. Abstracting something won't eliminate that complexity, but it will hide it so that programmers don't need to concern themselves with it. Therefore, before delving into the specific language constructs of control flow in JavaScript, we'll be exploring how these concepts of control flow and abstraction interrelate via the two opposing approaches of imperative and declarative programming.

Imperative versus declarative programming

Imperative programming concerns itself with **how** something is accomplished, while declarative programming concerns itself with **what** we want accomplished. It's difficult to see the difference between these so it's best to illustrate them with a simple program:

```
function getUnpaidInvoices(invoiceProvider) {
  const unpaidInvoices = [];
  const invoices = invoiceProvider.getInvoices();
  for (var i = 0; i < invoices.length; i++) {
    if (!invoices[i].isPaid) {
      unpaidInvoices.push(invoices[i]);
    }
  }
  return unpaidInvoices;
}
```

This function's problem domain would be: *getting unpaid invoices*. That is the task the function has and it is *what* we want to achieve within the function. This particular function, however, concerns itself a lot with *how* to achieve its task:

- It initializes an empty array
- It initializes a counter
- It checks that counter (*multiple times*)
- It increments that counter (*multiple times*)

These and other elements of our function are not at all related to the problem domain of *getting unpaid invoices*. Instead, they are the rather annoying implementation details that we must go through to get our desired output. Functions like this are called **imperative** because they are mostly concerned with *how*.

While the *imperative* form of programming busies itself with procedural low-level steps involved in a task, the *declarative* form of programming uses abstractions to avoid the use of direct control flow, preferring to express things only in terms of the problem domain itself. The following is a more declarative version of our `getUnpaidInvoices` function:

```
function getUnpaidInvoices(invoiceProvider) {
  return invoiceProvider.getInvoices().filter(invoice => {
    return !invoice.isPaid;
  });
}
```

Here, we are delegating to `Array#filter` so it handles the specifics of initializing a new array, iteration, and conditional checking. We have freed ourselves from the complexity of conventional control flow by using an abstraction.

Declarative patterns such as this have become the staple of modern JavaScript. They allow you to express the logic you desire at the level of your problem domain, instead of having to worry about lower layers of abstraction such as *how to iterate*. It's important to see that both declarative and imperative approaches are not completely distinct. They are at either end of a spectrum. On the declarative side of the spectrum, you are operating at a higher level of abstraction, and are hence not exposed to the implementation details that you would be without such abstraction. On the imperative side of the spectrum, you are operating at a lower level of abstraction, utilizing lower-level imperative constructs to tell the machine what you want to accomplish:

Imperative Approach	Declarative Approach

```
const output = [];
for (let i = 0, l = input.length; i < l; i++) {
  if (input[i].isTrue) {
    output.push(input[i].specificValue);
  }
}
```

```
output = (
  input
    .filter(item => item.isTrue)
    .map(item => item.specificValue)
);
```

◄ Less Abstraction (low level)
More Implementation Details

More Abstraction (high level) ►
Less Implementation Details

Both of these approaches have implications for our control flow. The more imperative approach directly states that it will iterate once through the array and then conditionally push to the output array. The more declarative approach does not make any demands about how the array is iterated through. Naturally, of course, we know that the native Array#filter and Array#map methods will independently iterate through their input arrays, but that is not something we are specifying. All we are specifying is the condition on which our data should be filtered and mapped. How the data is iterated through is completely the concern of the Array#filter and Array#map abstractions.

The benefit of a more declarative approach is that it can increase clarity for the human reader and enable you to more efficiently model complex problem domains. Since you're not having to worry about *how* things are occurring, your mind is left free to purely concern itself with *what* you wish to achieve.

Imagine we're given of task of conditionally executing a specific piece of code but only if a certain feature is enabled. In our mind, this is how it should work:

```
if (feature.isEnabled) {
  // Do the task.
}
```

This is the code we want to write, but we later find out that things are not so simple. For starters, there is no isEnabled property for us to use on the feature object. There is, however, a flags array property, which when fully disabled will include Feature.DISABLED_FLAG:

```
// A feature that is disabled:
feature.flags; // => [Feature.DISABLED_FLAG]
```

That seems simple enough. But then we discover that, even if the feature does not have this flag and so seems enabled, we also need to check that the time right now aligns with a set of times stored in `feature.enabledTimeSlots`. If the current time is not in one of the enabled time slots, then we must conclude that the feature is disabled, regardless of whether it has the flag.

This is starting to become quite complicated. In addition to checking for the *disabled* flag, we'll need to go through these time slots to discover whether the feature is currently enabled based on the current time. So, our simple `if` statement has very quickly become an unwieldy mess, with several layers of control flow:

```
let featureIsEnabled = true;

for (let i = 0; i < feature.flags.length; i++) {
  if (feature.flags[i] === Feature.DISABLED_FLAG) {
    featureIsEnabled = false;
    break;
  }
}

if (!featureIsEnabled) {
  for (let i = 0; i < feature.enabledTimeSlots.length; i++) {
    if (feature.enabledTimeSlots[i].isNow()) {
      featureIsEnabled = true;
      break;
    }
  }
}

if (featureIsEnabled) {
  // Do the task.
}
```

This is undesirably complex code. It's very far away from the original declarative code we wanted to write. To understand this code, a fellow programmer will have to maintain the state of `featureIsEnabled` in their head while scanning through each of the individual constructs. This is a mentally burdensome piece of code to navigate through and is, therefore, more liable to misunderstandings, bugs, and general unreliability.

The key question we must now ask ourselves is the following: what would it take for us to abstract away all of these nested layers of control flow away so that we can have our simple `if` statement back?

We eventually decide to place all of this logic in a newly created `isEnabled` method within the `Feature` class—but not only that! We decide to abstract the logic further, by delegating to two internal methods, `_hasDisabledFlag` and `_isEnabledTimeSlotNow`. And these methods themselves delegate their iteration logic to array methods, `includes(...)` and `filter(...)`:

```
class Feature {
  // (Other methods of the Feature class here,..)

  _hasDisabledFlag() {
    return this.flags.includes(Feature.DISABLED_FLAG);
  }

  _isEnabledTimeSlotNow() {
    return this.enabledTimeSlots.filter(ts => ts.isNow()).length;
  }

  isEnabled() {
    return !this._isDisabledFlag() && this._isEnabledTimeSlotNow();
  }
}
```

These very small declarative additions to the `Feature` class enable us to write the declarative code we were originally aiming for:

```
if (feature.isEnabled()) {
  // Do the task.
}
```

This has not only been an exercise in simple abstraction. This has been an exercise in reducing the layers of control flow. We've avoided the need to use nested layers of for `if` and `for` blocks, reducing the cognitive burden faced by ourselves and our fellow programmers, and fulfilling the task we originally set out to accomplish in the cleanest way possible.

By carefully refactoring and abstracting our original mess of control flow we have, quite oddly, ended up with a set of code that includes very few traditional control flow statements (`if`, `for`, `switch`, and so on). This doesn't mean our code is without control flow; rather, it means that the control flow is either minimized or hidden away under layers of abstractions. When using the native control flow constructs of the JavaScript language, it is important to remember that they are not your only tool with which to express the flow of a program; you can redirect and split complicated logic into abstractions that each handle a very specific part of your program's flow.

Now that we've got a solid foundational understanding of what control flow is and how it melds with what we know about abstractions, we can go through each of JavaScript's individual control flow mechanisms, highlighting challenges and potential gotchas.

The movement of control

In JavaScript, there are several ways that control can be moved from one piece of code to another. Generally, code will be evaluated from *left-to-right* and *top-to-bottom* until it reaches any of the following situations:

- **Invoking** (invocation of a function by `fn()`, `fn`` `` or `new fn()`)
- **Returning** (returning from a function via either implicit or explicit `return`)
- **Yielding** (yielding from a generator via `yield`)
- **Breaking** (breaking from a loop or switch via `break`)
- **Continuing** (continuing an iteration via `continue`)
- **Throwing** (throwing an exception via `throw`)

Invocation

Invocation occurs, in its most simple form, by explicitly calling a function. We do this by attaching calling parentheses (`(...)`) to a value we know to be a function. This value on the left side of `(...)` can be a direct reference to a variable or property that holds a function or any expression that evaluates to a function:

```
someFunction();
(function(){})();
someObject.someMethod();
[function(){}][0]();
```

To construct instances, as we've explored, you can use the `new` operator. This is also a type of invocation although, in the case of zero arguments, it doesn't technically require calling parentheses:

```
function MyConstructor() {}

// Both equivalent:
new MyConstructor();
new MyConstructor;
```

The exact syntax of evaluation before the calling parentheses (on the left side of `(...)`) is not important as long as it evaluates to a function. If it does not, then you will receive `TypeError`:

```
1();     // ! TypeError: 1 is not a function
[]();    // ! TypeError: [] is not a function
'wat'(); // ! TypeError: "wat" is not a function
```

When a function is called, JavaScript will create a new **Lexical Environment** (a scope) in which that function will be evaluated, and the function will become the current *execution context*, shifting control from the current area of code to the function's code. This should not be too unintuitive. It makes sense that, in the code, `foo();`, `baz();`, and `foo()` will be given control and will run to completion before `baz()` is then given control.

A function will return control to you in the following ways:

- By *returning* (implicitly or via an explicit `return` statement)
- By *throwing* (implicitly due to `SyntaxError`, `TypeError`, and so on or via an explicit `throw` statement)
- By *yielding* (in the case of a generator)

Invocation can also occur indirectly, via JavaScript's internal mechanisms. For example, in the case of coercion, as explored in the last chapter, methods such as `valueOf`, `toString`, or `Symbol.toPrimitive` may be called in various scenarios. Additionally, JavaScript enables you to define *setters* and *getters* so that your custom functionality is activated whenever a given property is accessed or assigned to:

```
const person = {
  set name(name) {
    console.log('You are trying to set the name to', name);
  }
};

person.name = 'Leo';
// Logs: "You are trying to set the name to Leo"
```

By assigning to the `name` property here, we are effectively invoking a function, which itself may then do all manner of things, potentially invoking other functions itself. You can imagine how the control flow of a given program can become potentially incomprehensible when there are many implicit means of invocation such as this. Such implicit mechanisms do have their advantages, but if too much of our problem domain's logic is embedded within such places, then it's less plainly visible to our fellow programmers and hence more likely to cause confusion.

Returning

Returning is a shift of control from a function to its caller. It is achieved either via an explicit `return` statement within the function itself or implicitly when the function runs to completion:

```
function sayHiToMe(name) {

  if (name) {
    return `Hi ${name}`;
  }

  // In the case of a truthy `name` this code is never arrived at
  // because `return` exists on a previous line:
  throw 'You do not have a name! :(';

}

sayHiToMe('James'); // => "Hi James"
```

Here, you'll notice that we don't bother placing the implied `else` condition of a falsy name in its own else block (`else {...}`) as this would be unnecessary. Because we return when the name is truthy, any code following that return statement will therefore only run in the implied `else` condition. It's quite common to see such patterns in functions that carry out preemptive input checks:

```
function findHighestMountain(mountains) {

  if (!mountains || !mountains.length) {
    return null;
  }

  if (mountains.length === 1) {
    return mountains[0];
  }

  // Do the actual work of finding the
  // highest mountain here...
}
```

As we see here, returning is not only used to return control to the caller but also for its side-effect: avoiding work that exists on lines below itself in its function. This is often termed *returning early* and can significantly help to reduce the overall complexity of a function.

Yielding

Yielding is a shift of control between a generator and its caller. It is achieved by the `yield` expression, which can optionally designate a value to its right side (the yielded value). It is only valid to use a `yield` statement within a generator function:

```
function* makeSomeNumbers() {
  yield 645;
  yield 422;
  yield 789;
}

const iterable = makeSomeNumbers();
iterable.next(); // => {value: 645, done: false}
iterable.next(); // => {value: 422, done: false}
iterable.next(); // => {value: 789, done: false}
```

If you yield without a value (`yield;`) then the result will be the same as yielding `undefined`.

Yielding will force any subsequent calls to the generator function to continue evaluation from the point of yield (as if the yield hadn't occurred). Yielding can be thought of as *pausing* a function with the prospect of coming back to it later. We can see this in action if we log which part of our generator runs during consecutive calls:

```
function* myGenerator() {
  console.log('Chunk A');
  yield;
  console.log('Chunk B');
  yield;
}

const iterable = myGenerator();

console.log('Calling first time');
iterable.next();
console.log('Done calling first time');

console.log('Calling second time');
iterable.next();
console.log('Done calling second time');
```

This will log the following:

- `"Calling first time"`
- `"Chunk A"`

- "Done calling first time"
- "Calling second time"
- "Chunk B"
- "Done calling second time"

It is also possible to return from a generator function with a regular return; statement. This is the same as yielding for the final time. That is, no further code will ever be run within that generator.

Yielding to a yield

Yielding is not necessarily a shift of control in just one direction. You can use a generator as a *data consumer* or *observer*. In such scenarios, when a caller requests the next yielded value by calling iterable.next(), it can optionally pass an argument to this next() method. Whatever value is passed will then cause the yield expression within the generator to evaluate to that value.

This is more easily explained with an example. Here, we have created a generator that consumes numbers and yields the sum of all numbers previously consumed:

```
function* createAdder() {
  let n = 0;
  while (true) n += yield n;
}

const adder = createAdder();
adder.next(); // Initialize (kick things off!)

adder.next(100).value; // => 100
adder.next(100).value; // => 200
adder.next(150).value; // => 350
```

Here, we are using the return value of our yield expression (yield n) and then adding it to the existing value of n on each run of the generator. We need to call next() once initially to kick things off as, before this, the n += yield n expression has not been run and is hence is not *waiting for* a next() call yet.

Using generators as consumers does not have many use cases and can be quite an awkward pattern to employ since we must use the designated next() method to pass in data. It is, however, useful to know about the flexibility of the yield expression since you may encounter it in the wild.

Complexity of yielding

For fellow programmers, comprehending the flow of control within generators can be complicated and counter-intuitive since it involves a lot of *back-and-forth* between the caller and the generator. Knowing what exact code is running at any specific point may be difficult to determine and so it is advisable to keep your generators short and ensure that they yield consistently—in other words, don't have too many different pathways of yielding within your generators and generally attempt to keep *cyclomatic complexity* quite low (you can read more about this if you skip ahead to the *Handling cyclomatic complexity* section).

Breaking

Breaking is a shift of control from within the current `for`, `while`, `switch`, or labeled statement to the code following the statement. It effectively terminates the statement, preventing any following code from being executed.

In the context of iteration, whether or not to continue or break from iteration is usually determined by `ConditionExpression` within the construct itself (for example, `counter < array.length`), or by the length of the data structure in the case of `for..in` and `for..of`. However, it may still be necessary, at times, to *break out* of the iteration early.

For example, if you are looking for a specific item within a data structure (a *needle-in-a-haystack* situation), then it would make sense to stop looking once the item is found. We achieve that by breaking:

```
for (let i = 0; i < array.length; i++) {
  if (myCriteriaIsMet(array[i]) {
    happyPath();
    break;
  }
}
```

Breaking from an iteration will immediately halt and exit the iteration, meaning any remaining code within the containing `IterationBody` will not be run. The code immediately following `IterationBody` will then run.

The `break` statement is also used to break out from `switch` statements, typically when you have executed the relevant `case` statement. As we will discuss later in this chapter, the `switch` statement will transfer control to the `case` statement that is considered strictly equal (`===`) to the value passed to `switch(...)`, and will then run all code following that `case` statement until an explicit `break;` (or `return;`, `yield;`, or `throw;`) occurs:

```
switch (2) {
  case 1: console.log(1);
  case 2: console.log(2);
  case 3: console.log(3);
  case 4: console.log(4); break;
  case 5: console.log(5);
}

// Logs: 2, 3, 4
```

Here, we see that a value of 2 shifts control to the matching `case` 2, and then all of the following code within the switch's body will run naturally until a `break;` statement is encountered. Hence, we only see logs for 2, 3, and 4. A log for 1 is avoided as `case` 1 does not match the value, 2, and a log for 5 is avoided as `break;` occurs before it.

When `case` within `switch` does not break, it is called **fallthrough**. This common technique used in `switch` statements is useful when you want to carry out a single action or cascade of actions based on more than one matching condition (we will cover this concept more in the *The switch statement se*).

To the right side of the `break` keyword there may be a label that refers to the `switch`, `for`, or `while` statement. If you don't supply a label, then JavaScript will assume you are referring to the current containing iteration or `switch` construct. This is only useful when you have two or more breakable constructs within each other, for example, an iteration within an iteration. Observe here how we've labeled our outer `for` loop with the `outerLoop` label, enabling us to break out of it from within the inner `for` loop:

```
outerLoop: for (let obj in objects) {
  for (let key in obj) {
    if (/* some condition */) {
      break outerLoop;
    }
  }
}
```

You can, in fact, break out of any labeled statement (even if it is outside of an iteration or `switch` construct) but you must explicitly provide the label:

```
specificWork: {
  doSomeSpecificWork();
  if (weAreFinished) {
    break specificWork;
      // immediately exits the `specificWork: {...}` block
  }
  doOtherWork();
}
```

This is very rarely applicable but is nonetheless worth knowing about in case you ever run into such code.

One last thing to note on *breaking out* of iterations or `switch` statements is that, although we typically do so by using an explicit `break;` statement, it is something that can also effectively occur via other mechanisms of moving control such as *yielding, returning,* or *throwing*. It's quite common, for example, to see an iteration that uses `return;` to *break out* not only of itself but also of the containing function.

Continuing

Continuing is a shift of control from the current statement to the potential start of the next iteration. It is achieved via a `continue` statement.

> The `continue` statement is valid in all iteration constructs, including `for, while, do...while, for...in,` and `for...of.`

Here is an example of continuing conditionally, so that the body of the iteration does not execute for a specific item but the iteration still continues to progress:

```
const numbers = [1, 2, 3];

for (const n of numbers) {
  if (n === 2) continue;
  console.log(n);
}

// Logs: 1, 3
```

Continuing skips all of the code following `continue` in the current iteration and then moves onto whatever would naturally occur next.

Similar to the `break` statement, to the right side of the `continue` keyword can optionally be a label that indicates which iteration construct should be continued. If you don't supply it, then JavaScript will assume you are referring to the current iteration construct. If you have two or more iteration constructs nested within each other, then it may be necessary to use an explicit label:

```
objectsIteration: for (let obj in objects) {
  for (let key in obj) {
    if (/* some condition */) {
      continue objectsIteration;
    }
  }
}
```

 The `continue` statement will only work in our native looping constructs. If we wish to continue in an abstracted looping construct such as `Array#forEach`, then we'll typically want to use a `return` statement instead (to return from the callback and hence continue the iteration).

Since *continuing* is a movement of control, we want to remain cautious about how clearly we are communicating our intent. If we have several layers of loops or several `continue` or `break` statements, it can burden the reader with an unnecessary level of complexity.

Throwing

Throwing is a shift of control from the current statement to the nearest containing `try...catch` statement on the call stack. If no such `try...catch` statement exists, then the execution of the program will terminate entirely. Throwing is conventionally used to raise exceptions when specific requirements or expectations are not met:

```
function nameToUpperCase(name) {
  if (typeof name !== 'string') {
    throw new TypeError('Name should be a string');
  }
  return name.toUpperCase();
}
```

To catch this error, we would need to have a `try...catch` block somewhere on the call-stack, wrapping the call to the `nameToUpperCase` function or the call to the function that calls it (and so on):

```
let theUpperCaseName;
try {
  theUpperCaseName = nameToUpperCase(null);
} catch(e) {
  e.message; // => "Name should be a string"
}
```

It is a best practice to throw objects that are instances of the natively provided generic `Error` constructor. There are several native sub-classed constructors of `Error`:

- `SyntaxError`: This indicates that a parsing error has occurred
- `TypeError`: This indicates an unsuccessful operation when none of the other `Error` objects are appropriate
- `ReferenceError`: This indicates that an invalid reference value has been detected
- `RangeError`: This indicates a value that is not in the set or range of allowable values
- `URIError`: This indicates that a URI handling function was used in a way that is incompatible with its definition

JavaScript will naturally raise such exceptions to you if you misuse native APIs or produce invalid syntax, but you can also use these constructors yourself to provide more semantically meaningful errors to your fellow programmers. If none of the preceding are suitable, then you can directly use `Error` or extend from it to produce your own specialized instance, as follows:

```
class NetworkError extends Error {}

async function makeDataRequest() {
  try {
    const response = await fetch('/data');
  } catch(e) {
    throw NetworkError('Cannot fetch data');
  }
  // ... (process response) ...
}
```

All `Error` instances will contain a `name` and `message` property. Depending on the JavaScript implementation, there may also be additional properties related to the stack trace of the error. In both the V8 JavaScript engine (used in Chromium and Node.js) and in SpiderMonkey (Mozilla), there is a stack property that gives us serialized call stack information:

```
try {
  throw new Error;
} catch(e) {
  e.stack; // => "Error\n at filename.js:2:9"
}
```

There may be unique situations where you wish to throw a value that is not an `Error` instance, and technically, this is perfectly legal, but it is rarely useful to do so. It's best to only throw in the case of an actual error, and in that case, it is best to use an appropriate `Error` object to represent the error.

Statements of control flow

Now that we've cemented our understanding of how *control* is moved at a high level, we can delve further into the specific statements and mechanisms that JavaScript gives us to control flow. We'll combine an exploration of the syntax of each statement with some best practices and pitfalls to avoid.

The if statement

The `if` statement is composed of the `if` keyword followed by a parenthesized expression and then an additional statement:

```
if (ConditionExpression) Statement
```

`ConditionExpression` can be of limitless complexity as long as it is truly an expression:

```
if (true) {}
if (1 || 2 || 3) {}
if ([1, 2, 3].filter(n => n > 2).length > 0) {}
```

The statement following the parenthesized expression can be a single-line statement or a block and designates the code that should be run if the `ConditionExpression` evaluates to a truthy value:

```
// These are equivalent
if (true) { doBaz(); }
if (true) doBaz();
```

The value you pass as `ConditionExpression` is compared to a Boolean to determine its truthiness. We've already been aptly introduced to the concepts of truthiness and falsiness in Chapter 6, *Primitive and Built-In Types*, but just in case you're rusty: there are only seven falsy values in JavaScript, and as such, only seven possible values that you can pass to an `if` statement that won't satisfy it:

```
if (false) {}
if (null) {}
if (undefined) {}
if (0n) {}
if (0) {}
if ('') {}
if (NaN) {}
```

When an `if` statement is not satisfied, it will run an optional `else` statement, which you may specify immediately following your `if` statement. Just as with `if`, you may use a block here as well:

```
if (isLegalDrinkingAge) drink(); else leave();

// Equivalent, with Blocks:
if (isLegalDrinkingAge) {
  drink();
} else {
  leave();
}
```

You can effectively *chain* together `if`/`else` statements as follows:

```
if (number > 5) {
  // For numbers larger than five
} else if (number < 3) {
  // For numbers less than three
} else {
  // For everything else
}
```

Syntactically, it's important to understand that this isn't a construct of its own (there is no such thing as an if/else/if/else construct); it is merely a regular if statement, followed by an else statement that itself contains its own if/else duo. Therefore, it is more accurate, perhaps, to see it as follows:

```
if (number > 5) {
  // For numbers larger than five
} else {
  if (number < 3) {
    // For numbers less than three
  } else {
    // For everything else
  }
}
```

An if statement is best suited for when there are one or two possible outcomes of a condition. If there are more possible outcomes, then you may be better off using a switch statement. Long if/else chains can get unwieldy. See the *Handling cyclomatic complexity* section later in this chapter to explore other novel ways of handling complex conditional logic.

The for statement

The for statement is used to iterate through a set, typically, an array or any iterable structure. It comes in four broad varieties:

- **Conventional for**: This includes the following:
  - **Syntax**: for (initializer; condition; incrementer) {...}
  - **Usage**: Typically used to iterate in a custom fashion through an indexed structure
- **For...in**: This includes the following:
  - **Syntax**: for (let item in object) {...}
  - **Usage**: Used to iterate through the keys of any object (typically used on *plain objects*)
- **For...of**: This includes the following:
  - **Syntax**: for (let item of iterable) {...}
  - **Usage**: Used to iterate over an iterable (typically array-like) structure

The type of `for` construct you'll employ will depend on what exactly you wish to iterate over. For straightforward indexed and array-like structures, for example, the `for...of` construct will be most useful. We'll go over each of these constructs to explore use cases and potential challenges.

Conventional for

The conventional `for` statement is used to iterate over all manner of data structures or conceptual looping scenarios. It includes three expressions, parenthesized and separated by semicolons, and a statement at the end, which is considered the body of the iteration:

```
for (
  InitializerExpression;
  ConditionExpression;
  UpdateExpression
) IterationBody
```

The purpose of each part is as follows:

- The `InitializerExpression` initializes the iteration; this will be evaluated first and only once. This can be any statement (it usually includes a `let` or `var` assignment, but doesn't need to).
- The `ConditionExpression` checks whether the iteration may continue; this will be evaluated and coerced to a Boolean (as if via `Boolean(...)`) before each iteration to determine whether the next iteration will occur. This can be any expression, though it is usually used to check whether the current index is less than some upper bound (usually the length of the data structure that you are iterating through).
- The `UpdateExpression` finalizes each iteration, ready for the next iteration. This will be evaluated at the end of each iteration. This can be any statement though is most idiomatically used to increment or decrement the current index.
- The `IterationBody` contains the actual iteration logic—the code that will be evaluated on every iteration. This is typically a *block* but can be a single-line statement.

Using the conventional `for` statement to loop over an array would look like this:

```
for (let i = 0; i < array.length; i++) {
  array[i]; // => (Each `array` item)
}
```

It is preferable to use `for...of` if you're just iterating over a regular array or iterable structure. However, if you need to iterate over a structure indexed unconventionally, then it may be appropriate to use the conventional `for` loop.

An example of an unconventionally indexed structure is the pixel data of a `<canvas>` element, which forms an array containing the RGBA (*Red, Green, Blue,* and *Alpha*) values of every pixel consecutively, like so:

```
[r, g, b, a, r, g, b, a, ...]
```

Since each individual pixel occupies four elements of the array, we would need to iterate over it four indexes at a time. The conventional `for` loop is perfectly suited to this:

```
const pixelData = canvas.getContext('2d').getImageData(0, 0, 100,
100).data;

for (let i = 0; i < pixelData.length; i += 4) {
  let red = pixelData[i];
  let blue = pixelData[i + 1];
  let green = pixelData[i + 2];
  let alpha = pixelData[i + 3];
  // (do something with RGBA)
}
```

The conventional `for` statement is a well understood and idiomatic piece of syntax. It is best to ensure that you use each of its parts for its purpose. It is entirely possible (though unadvisable) to exploit its syntax by including the actual logic of your iteration in the parenthesized portion of the construct, but this and other misuses can be quite hard to parse for humans:

```
var copy = [];
for (
  let i = 0;
  i < array.length;
  copy[i] = array[i++]
);
```

`UpdateExpression` here includes the `copy[i] = array[i++]` expression, which will copy across the element of the array at the current index and will then increment the index. The postfix ++ operator ensures that the previous value of its operand will be returned, guaranteeing that the index accessed on `copy[i]` is always equal to `array[i++]`. This is a clever but rather obscure syntax. It would have been far clearer to use the idiomatic `for` structure, which places the iteration logic in its own statement after `for(...)`:

```
for (
  let i = 0;
```

```
    i < array.length;
    i++
) {
    copy[i] = array[i];
}
```

This is a more familiar and comprehensible piece of code for most programmers. It is more verbose, and perhaps not as fun to write, but in the end, as explored in the initial chapters of this book, we are most interested in writing code that communicates its intent clearly.

 Naturally, this fictional scenario, copying the contents of one array to another array, would be better solved by using the `Array#slice` method (`array.slice()`) but we used it here as an illustration.

for...in

The `for...in` construct is used to iterate over an object's set of enumerable property names. It has the following syntax:

```
for (LeftSideAssignment in Object) IterationBody
```

The various parts have the following constraints:

- `LeftSideAssignment` can be anything that would be valid on the left side of an assignment expression and is evaluated within the scope of `IterationBody` on every new iteration
- `Object` can be any expression that evaluates to (or can be coerced to) an object—in other words, anything except `null` or `undefined`
- `IterationBody` is any single-line or block statement

The `for...in` construct is usually used to iterate through a plain object's properties:

```
const city = { name: 'London', population: 8136000 };
for (const key in city) {
    console.log(key);
}
// Logs: "name", "population"
```

You can see that we're using `const key` here to initialize our `key` variable on each iteration. This is the preferred declaration to use unless you have a specific need for the mutable behavior of `let` or the different scoping behavior of `var`. Naturally, all of these declarations are perfectly valid to use, in addition to using no declaration whatsoever:

```
for (let key in obj) {}
for (var key in obj) {}
for (const key in obj) {}
for (key in obj) {}
```

A new block scope is created for each iteration. When you use either a `let` or `const` declaration, it will be scoped to that iteration, while a variable declared via `var` will, as we know, be scoped to the nearest execution context's scope (*function scope*). Using no declaration whatsoever is fine, but you should ensure that you have already initialized that identifier beforehand:

```
let key;
for (key in obj) {}
```

Since anything that would be valid on the left side of an assignment expression is valid on the left side of `in`, we can also place a property reference here, as in the following example:

```
let foo = {};
for (foo.key in obj) {}
```

This would result in `foo.key` being assigned each key of `obj` as the iteration progresses. This would be quite an odd thing to do, but will nonetheless work correctly.

Now that we have the syntax out of the way, we can discuss the behavior and use cases of `for..in`. It is, as mentioned, useful in iterating through the properties of an object. By default, this will include all properties inherited from the object's `[[Prototype]]` chain as well, but only if they are *enumerable*:

```
const objectA = { isFromObjectA: true };
const objectB = { isFromObjectB: true };

Object.setPrototypeOf(objectB, objectA);

for (const prop in objectB) {
 console.log(prop);
}

// Logs: "isFromObjectB", "isFromObjectA"
```

As you can see, properties on the object itself are iterated over before those from inherited objects. The order of iteration, however, should not be depended upon as this may differ between implementations. If you're looking to iterate through a set of keys in a specific order, it may be better instead to gather the keys via `Object.keys(obj)` and then iterate over that as an array.

Since `for...in` will naturally iterate over inherited properties, it's conventional to place an additional check within the iteration body to avoid these properties:

```
for (const key in obj) {
  if (obj.hasOwnProperty(key)) {
    // `key` is a non-inherited (direct) property of `obj`
  }
}
```

Where you have an iterable object (such as an array), it is advisable to use `for...of` instead, which is more performant and idiomatic for such situations.

for...of

The `for...of` construct is used to iterate over an iterable object. Natively provided iterable objects include `String`, `Array`, `TypedArray`, `Map`, and `Set`. Syntactically, `for...of` shares the characteristics of `for...in`:

```
for (LeftSideAssignment in IterableObject) IterationBody
```

The purpose of each part is as follows:

- `LeftSideAssignment` can be anything that would be valid on the left side of an assignment expression and is evaluated within the scope of `IterationBody` on every new iteration
- `IterableObject` can be any expression that evaluates to an *iterable* object—in other words, anything that implements `[Symbol.iterator]` as a method
- `IterationBody` is any single-line or block statement

An idiomatic `for...of` usage may look like this:

```
const array = [1, 2, 3];

for (const i of array) {
  console.log(i);
}

// Logs: 1, 2, 3
```

Since its introduction into the language, `for...of` has become the most idiomatic way to loop over arrays, replacing the previously idiomatic `for (var i = 0; i < array.length; i++) {...}` pattern.

The scoping behavior of `let`, `var`, and `const` is identical to that described in the last section on `for...in`. It is advisable to use `const` as it will initialize a fresh and immutable variable for each iteration. Using `let` is not awful but, unless you have a specific reason to need to mutate the variable yourself within `IterationBody`, you'll be better off using `const`.

The while statement

The `while` statement is used to run a piece of code until some condition stops being met. It has the following syntax:

```
while (ConditionExpression) IterationBody
```

The purpose of each part is as follows:

- `ConditionExpression` is evaluated to determine whether `IterationBody` should run. If it evaluates to `true`, then the `IterationBody` portion will run. `ConditionExpression` will then be re-evaluated and so on. The cycle only stops when `ConditionExpression` evaluates to `false`.
- `IterationBody` can be either a single-line or block statement and will be run as many times as `ConditionExpression` evaluates to `true`.

It is rare to use `while` for straightforward iteration because there are more suitable constructs for this (for example, `for...of`), but if we wanted to, it might look something like the following:

```
const array = ['a', 'b', 'c'];

let i = -1;
while (++i < array.length) {
  console.log(array[i]);
}

// Logs: 'a', 'b', 'c'
```

Since we are initializing i to −1 and are using the prefix increment operator (++i), ConditionExpression will evaluate to 0 < array.length, 1 < array.length, 2 < array.length, and 3 < array.length. Naturally, the last check will fail as 3 is not less than array.length, meaning that the while statement will stop running its IterationBody. This means Body will only 3 times in total.

It's common to use while when the limit of iteration is, as yet, unknown or computed in a complex fashion. In such instances, it is common to see true directly passed as ConditionExpression to while(...) and then a manual break; statement within the iteration to force it to end:

```
while (true) {
  if (/* some custom condition */) {
    break;
  }
}
```

The while statement is also used in the context of generator functions if those generators are intended to produce infinite outputs. For example, you may wish to create a generator that always produces the *next* letter in an alphabet, and then loops round to the start of the alphabet when it gets to z:

```
function *loopingAlphabet() {
  let i = 0;
  while (true) {
    yield String.fromCharCode(
      97 + (i >= 26 ? i = 0 : i++)
    );
  }
}

const alphabet = loopingAlphabet();

alphabet.next(); // => { value: "a" }
alphabet.next(); // => { value: "b" }
alphabet.next(); // => { value: "c" }
// ...
alphabet.next(); // => { value: "z" }
alphabet.next(); // => { value: "a" }
alphabet.next(); // => { value: "b" }
// ...
```

Such infinite applications of generators are rare but they do exist and are a perfect place to use `while(...)`. Most other applications of `while` have been replaced with more succinct and contained methods of iteration such as `for...in` and `for...of`. Nonetheless, it is useful to know how to cleanly wield it.

The do...while statement

The `do...while` statement is similar to while it although guarantees an iteration before the check is carried out. Its syntax is formed of the `do` keyword followed by its body and then a typical parenthesized `while` expression:

```
do IterationBody while (ConditionExpression)
```

The purpose of each part is as follows:

- `IterationBody` can be either a single-line or block statement and will be run once initially and then as many times as `ConditionExpression` evaluates to `true`.
- `ConditionExpression` is evaluated to determine whether `IterationBody` should run more than once. If it evaluates to `true`, then the `Body` portion will run. `ConditionExpression` will then be re-evaluated and so on. The cycle only stops when `ConditionExpression` evaluates to `false`.

Although the behavior of the `do...while` statement is different from regular `while` statement, its semantics and broad applications remain the same. It is most useful in contexts where you need to always complete at least one step of an iteration before either checking whether to continue or changing the subject of the iteration. An example of this would be upward DOM traversal. If you have a DOM element and wish to run certain code on it and each of its DOM ancestors, then you may wish to use a `do...while` statement as follows:

```
do {
  // Do something with `element`
} while (element = element.parentNode);
```

A loop like this will execute its body once for the `element` value, whatever `element` is, and then will evaluate the assignment expression, `element = element.parentNode`. This assignment expression will evaluate to its newly assigned value, meaning that, in the case of `element.parentNode` being falsy (for example, `null`) the `do...while` will halt its iteration.

Assigning values in the `ConditionExpression` portion of a `while` or `do...while` statement is relatively common although it can be obscure to fellow programmers, so it's best to only do so if it's plainly obvious what the intent of the code is. If the preceding code was wrapped in a function called `traverseDOMAncestors`, then that would provide a helpful clue.

The switch statement

The `switch` statement is used to move control to a specific inner `case` clause that specifies a value that matches the value passed to `switch(...)`. It has the following syntax:

```
switch (SwitchExpression) SwitchBody
```

`SwitchExpression` will be evaluated once and its value compared via strict-equality to case statements within `SwitchBody`. Within `SwitchBody` there may be one or more `case` clauses and/or a `default` clause. The `case` clauses designate `CaseExpression`, whose value will be compared to that of `SwitchExpression`, and their syntax is as follows:

```
case CaseExpression:
  [other JavaScript statements or additional clauses]
```

The `switch` statement is usually used to specify a selection of two or more mutually exclusive outcomes based on a specific value. With fewer conditions, it'd be conventional to use an `if...else` construct, but to accommodate more potential conditions, it's simpler to use `switch`:

```
function generateWelcomeMessage(language) {

  let welcomeMessage;

  switch (language) {
    case 'DE':
      welcomeMessage = 'Willkommen!';
      break;
    case 'FR':
      welcomeMessage = 'Bienvenue!';
      break;
    default:
      welcomeMessage = 'Welcome!';
  }

  return welcomeMessage;
}
```

```
generateWelcomeMessage('DE'); // => "Willkommen!"
generateWelcomeMessage('FR'); // => "Bienvenue!"
generateWelcomeMessage('EN'); // => "Welcome!"
generateWelcomeMessage(null); // => "Welcome!"
```

Once the `switch` mechanism finds the appropriate `case`, it will execute all code following that `case` statement until the very end of the `switch` statement or until it encounters a `break` statement. A `break` statement is used to *break out* of `SwitchBody` when the desired work is accomplished.

Breaking and fallthrough

Given that `switch` statements are usually used to execute specific and mutually exclusive pieces of code depending on the value, it is conventional to use `break` between every `case` statement to ensure that only the appropriate code runs for any given value. Sometimes, however, it is desirable to avoid breaking between cases and let the `SwitchBody` code continue to run through multiple `case` statements and beyond. Doing this is known as **fallthrough**:

```
switch (language) {

  case 'German':
  case 'Deutsche':
  case 'DE':
    welcomeMessage = 'Willkommen!';
    break;

  case 'French':
  case: 'Francais':
  case 'FR':
    welcomeMessage = 'Bienvenue!';
    break;

  default:
    welcomeMessage = 'Welcome!';
}
```

Here, you can see that we are employing fallthrough so that a language of either `'German'`, `'Deutsche'`, or `'DE'` will result in the same code running `welcomeMessage = 'Willkommen!'`. And following that, we immediately break to prevent any more of `SwitchBody` from running.

It's unfortunately quite easy to accidentally forget the odd `break;` statement, resulting in accidental fallthrough and a very confused programmer. To avoid this, I'd recommend using a linter that has a rule that warns or gives an error in such cases unless given a specific directive. (We will cover linters in more detail in `Chapter 15`, *Tools for Cleaner Code*.)

Returning from a switch directly

When you have a `switch` statement residing in a function, it is sometimes best to simply `return` the intended values instead of having to rely on `break` statements. For example, in `generateWelcomeMessage`, we can simply return the welcome string. There's no need to go through the rigamarole of initializing a variable, assigning it, and breaking between cases:

```
function generateWelcomeMessage(language) {
  switch (language) {
    case 'DE':
      return 'Willkommen!';
    case 'FR':
      return 'Bienvenue!';
    default:
      return 'Welcome!';
  }
}
```

Returning directly, in this way, is arguably clearer than breaking within each case, especially if each case's logic is fairly simple.

Case blocks

Usually, the code following a `case` or `default` clause will not only occupy a single line. As such, it has become conventional to wrap these statements with a block, so that there is a sense of containment:

```
switch (speed) {
  case 'slow': {
    console.log('Initiating slow speed');
    car.changeSpeedTo(speed);
    car.enableUrbanCollisionControl();
  }
  case 'fast': {
    console.log('Initiating fast speed');
```

```
      car.changeSpeedTo(speed);
      car.enableSpeedLimitWarnings();
      car.enableCruiseControlOption();
    }
    case 'regular':
    default: {
      console.log('Initiating regular speed');
      car.changeSpeedTo(speed);
    }
}
```

This isn't strictly necessary and doesn't change any functionality, but it does offer more clarity to the reader of our code. It also paves the way for any block-level variables, should we wish to introduce these later. As we know, within a block (delimited with { and }), we can use `const` and `let` to declare variables that will be scoped only to that block:

```
switch (month) {
  case 'December':
  case 'January':
  case 'February': {
    const message = 'In the UK, Spring is coming soon!';
    // ...
  }
  //...
}
```

Here, we're able to declare specific variables that are scoped to the `February` case only. This is useful if we have a large amount of logic that we'd like to isolate. At this point, however, we should consider abstracting that logic in some other way. Lengthy `switch` statements can be incredibly hard to understand.

Multivariant conditions

Often, there's a need to express more complex conditions in each `case`, instead of just matching a singular value. If we pass `true` as `SwitchExpression`, then we are free to express custom conditional logic within each `CaseExpression`, as long as each `CaseExpression` evaluates to `true` when successful:

```
switch (true) {
  case user.role === 'admin' || user.role === 'root': {
    // ...
    break;
  }
  case user.role === 'member' && user.isActive: {
    // ...
```

```
      break;
   }
   case user.role === 'member' && user.isRecentlyInactive: {
      // ...
      break;
   }
}
```

This pattern allows us to express more multivariate and hybrid conditions. You may usually feel inclined toward multiple `if/else/if/else` statements, but if your logic can be expressed in a `switch` statement, then it may be best to opt for that. As always, you should consider the nature of your problem domain and its logic, and seek to make an informed decision about how you wish to implement your control flow. In some cases, a `switch` statement will only end up being more confusing.

In the next section, we will cover some other approaches you can use to handle complex and lengthy logic that doesn't suit native constructs such as `switch`.

Handling cyclomatic complexity

Cyclomatic complexity is a measure of how many *linearly independent paths* there are through a program's code.

Consider a simple program that contains several conditional checks and function invocations:

```
if (a) {
  alpha();
  if (b) bravo();
  if (c) charlie();
}
if (d) delta();
```

Even in this misleadingly simple piece of code, nine distinct paths can be taken. So, depending on the values of a, b, c, and d, there are nine possible sequences of `alpha`, `bravo`, `charlie`, and `delta` that will run:

- `alpha()`
- `alpha()` and `bravo()`
- `alpha()`, `bravo()`, and `charlie()`
- `alpha()`, `bravo()`, `charlie()`, and `delta()`
- `alpha()`, `bravo()`, and `delta()`

- `alpha()` and `charlie()`
- `alpha()`, `charlie()`, and `delta()`
- `alpha()` and `delta()`
- `delta()`

A high level of cyclomatic complexity is undesirable. It can lead to the following:

- **Cognitive burden**: Cyclomatically complex code can be difficult for programmers to understand. Code with many branches is difficult to internalize and hold in our minds and therefore harder to maintain or change.
- **Unpredictability**: Cyclomatically complex code can be unpredictable, especially if rare situations occur where there is, for example, an unforeseen state transition or underlying change of data.
- **Fragility**: Cyclomatically complex code can be fragile in the face of change. Changing one line can have a disproportionate effect on the functionality of many other lines.
- **Bugginess**: Cyclomatically complex code can cause obscure bugs. If there are a dozen or more code paths within a singular function, then it's possible for a maintainer to not see all of them, leading to regressions.

 There are tools that can quantify a code base's cyclomatic complexity. We will cover these in `Chapter 15`, *Tools for Cleaner Code*. Knowing areas of high cyclomatic complexity can help us to focus on those areas for maintenance and testing.

It's frustratingly easy to end up in a situation where there are so many different conditions and branches within a singular module that nobody can understand what's happening. In addition to using tools to help us to identify areas of high complexity, we can use our own judgment and intuitions. The following are some examples of complexity that we can easily identify and avoid:

- A function that has more than one `if`/`else`/`if` combination
- An `if` statement that has many sub-conditions (many `if` statements within `if` statements)
- A `switch` statement that has many sub-conditions following each `case` clause
- Many `case` clauses within a `switch` block (for example, over 20 would be alarming!)

These are not precise cautions but they should give you an idea of what you should watch out for. When we find such complexity, the first thing we should do is to sit back and re-consider our problem domain. Can we describe our logic differently? Can we form new or different abstractions?

Let's explore an example of a piece of code with high cyclomatic complexity and consider how we might simplify it with these questions in mind.

Simplifying conditional spaghetti

To illustrate too much cyclomatic complexity and how we should approach simplifying it, we're going to be refactoring a piece of code that is responsible for deriving a set of ID numbers and types from a set of licenses:

```
function getIDsFromLicenses(licenses) {
  const ids = [];
  for (let i = 0; i < licenses.length; i++) {
    let license = licenses[i];
    if (license.id != null) {
      if (license.id.indexOf('c') === 0) {
        let nID = Number(license.id.slice(1));
        if (nID >= 1000000) {
          ids.push({ type: 'car', digits: nID });
        } else {
          ids.push({ type: 'car_old', digits: nID });
        }
      } else if (license.id.indexOf('h') === 0) {
        ids.push({
          type: 'hgv',
          digits: Number(license.id.slice(1))
        });
      } else if (license.id.indexOf('m') === 0) {
        ids.push({
          type: 'motorcycle',
          digits: Number(license.id.slice(1))
        });
      }
    }
  }
  return ids;
}
```

This function accepts an array of licenses and then extracts the ID numbers of those licenses (avoiding cases of `null` or `undefined` IDs). We determine the type of license based on characters found within its ID. There are four types of licenses that need to be identified and extracted:

- `car`: These are of the `c{digits}` form, where digits form a number greater than or equal to 1,000,000
- `car_old`: These are of the `c{digits}` form, where digits form a number less than 1,000,000
- `hgv`: These are of the `h{digits}`
- `motorcycle`: These are of the `m{digits}`

The following is an example of the input and the derived output of the `getIDsFromLicenses` function:

```
getIDsFromLicenses([
    { name: 'Jon Smith', id: 'c32948' },
    { name: 'Marsha Brown' },
    { name: 'Leah Oak', id: 'h109' },
    { name: 'Jim Royle', id: 'c29283928' }
]);
// Outputs:
[
  {type: "car_old", digits: 32948}
  {type: "hgv", digits: 109}
  {type: "car", digits: 29283928}
]
```

As you may have observed, the code we've used to extract the IDs is quite cyclomatically complex. You may consider it perfectly reasonable code, and it arguably is, but it could be simpler still. Our function achieves its results imperatively, using up a lot of syntax to explain *how* it wants to accomplish its task instead of *what* it wants to accomplish.

To simplify our code, it's first useful to take a fresh look at the problem domain. The task we want to accomplish is to take an input array and, from it, derive a set of license ID types and values. The output array will be an almost **1:1** mapping from the input array, except for cases where licenses have a falsy `id` property (`null`, in this case). The following is an illustration of our I/O flow:

```
[INPUT LICENSES] ==> (DERIVATION LOGIC) ==> [OUTPUT ID TYPES AND DIGITS]
```

Looked at abstractly in this way, this seems like the perfect opportunity to use `Array#map`. The `map` method allows us to run a function on every element within an array to derive a new array containing mapped values.

The first thing we'll want to map is the license to its `id`:

```
ids = licenses.map(license => license.id)
```

We'll want to handle cases where there is no `id`. To do this, we can apply a filter on the derived IDs:

```
ids = ids.filter(id => id != null)
```

And, in fact, because we know that all valid IDs are truthy, we can simply do a Boolean check by directly passing `Boolean` as our filter function:

```
ids = ids.filter(Boolean)
```

From this, we'll receive an array of our licenses but only those with a truthy `id` property. Following this, we can consider the next transformation we wish to apply to the data. We'd like to split the `id` value into its constituent parts: we need the initial character of the ID (`id.charAt(0)`), and then we want to extract the remaining characters (the digits) and cast them to the `Number` type (`Number(id.slice(1))`). We can then pass these parts to another function, which will be responsible for extracting the correct ID fields (`type` and `digits`) from this information:

```
ids = ids.map(id => getIDFields(
  id.charAt(0),
  Number(id.slice(1))
));
```

The `getIDFields` function will need to determine the type from the individual character and digits for the ID, returning an object of the `{ type, digits }` form:

```
function getIDFields(idType, digits) {
  switch (idType) {
    case 'c': return {
      type: digits >= 1000000 ? 'car' : 'car_old',
      digits
    };
    case 'h': return { type: 'hgv', digits };
    case 'm': return { type: 'motorcycle', digits };
  }
}
```

Since we've abstracted this part our logic away to an individual function, we can independently observe and test its behavior:

```
getIDFields('c', 1000); // => { type: "car_old", digits: 1000 }
getIDFields('c', 2000000); // => { type: "car", digits: 1000 }
getIDFields('h', 1000); // => { type: "hgv", digits: 1000 }
getIDFields('i', 1000); // => { type: "motorcycle", digits: 1000 }
```

Tying everything together, we end up with a new implementation of getIDsFromLicenses that looks like this:

```
function getIDsFromLicenses(licenses) {
  return licenses
    .map(license => license.id)
    .filter(Boolean)
    .map(id => getIDFields(
      id.charAt(0),
      Number(id.slice(1))
    ))
}
```

What we have achieved here is a significant reduction in the amount of cyclomatic complexity that our fellow programmers will need to contend with. We are utilizing Array#map and Array#filter to abstract away both decision-making and iteration logic. This means we end up with an implementation that is far more *declarative*.

You may notice, as well, that we have extracted repeated logic and generalized it. For example, in our initial implementation, we were implementing many calls to discover the first character of the ID (for example, license.id.indexOf('m') === 0). Our new implementation generalizes this by mapping to a data structure that already includes the first character as a distinct value that we can then pass through to getIDFields to get the relevant type and digits for that ID.

To summarize, our general refactoring approach has involved the following considerations:

- We've considered the problem domain with a fresh perspective
- We've considered whether there is a common functional or declarative idiom for our I/O
- We've considered whether individual logic can be abstracted away or separated

Our code is now easier to comprehend, and hence easier to maintain and debug. It'll likely also be more reliable and stable since its individual units can be more simply tested and can hence avoid regressions in the future. There is, naturally, the potential for a slight performance decrease due to the increased usage of higher abstracted declarative idioms and functions over imperative code, but this is an incredibly marginal difference and, in the vast majority of situations, is worth implementing for the significant benefits that the refactoring produces in terms of maintainability and reliability.

Asynchronous control flow

Most of the constructs we've looked at so far are used for synchronous code, where statements are evaluated sequentially, with each line completing before the next one begins:

```
const someValue = getSomeValue();
doSomethingWithTheValue(someValue);
```

Code like this is straightforward. We intuitively understand that these two lines of code will run one after the other. There is also an assumption that neither of these lines will take very long to execute, probably taking no more than a few micro- or milliseconds.

But what happens if we wish to bind to a user Event or fetch some remote data? These are things that take time and will only complete when some future Event occurs. In a less kind universe, there would be no way to deal with such scenarios other than simply waiting for them to complete and then continuing the execution of our program:

```
fetchSomeData();
processFetchedData();
```

In this unkind universe, fetchSomeData() would be a *blocking* function call, so named because it would block the execution of all other code until it finally completes. This means that we wouldn't be able to carry out any other vital tasks, and our application would essentially be at a standstill state until the task is completed, negatively affecting the user experience.

Thankfully, JavaScript gives us a nicer universe than this—one in which we can initialize a task, such as fetching data, and then continue on with the rest of our program while that task is running. Such tasks are named *asynchronous* because they occur and complete non-synchronously, at a later time than *now*. When they do finally complete, JavaScript can helpfully notify us of this fact, calling whatever code depends upon the completion of that task.

The Event Loop

To accomplish this, JavaScript maintains a single-threaded *Event Loop*. When the *Event Loop* kicks off, it'll run our program. Following the execution of a piece of code (such as that which initiates our program), the *Event Loop* will await messages (or Events) indicating that something has occurred (for example, a network request has completed or a browser UI event has occurred). When it receives a message, it will then execute any code that is depending upon or listening for that Event. The *Event Loop* will, again, run that code to completion before continuing to await other messages. This process repeats infinitely until the JavaScript program is halted (for example, by closing a tab in a browser).

The fact that the *Event Loop* will always run a given piece of code to its completion means that any long-running or *blocking* code will prevent any other code from executing until it has completed. Some older browser API methods such as `alert()` and `prompt()` are examples of blocking functions that you may encounter. Calling these will effectively block any further execution of your JavaScript program:

```
alert('Hello!');
console.log('The alert has been dismissed by the user');
```

Here, `console.log()` will not be evaluated until the alert dialog is dismissed by the user. This could be milliseconds, minutes, or even hours. During this period, our JavaScript program is halted, unable to continue. Its *Event Loop* may be receiving Events but it will not run the code associated with those Events until `alert()` finally completes.

Native asynchronous APIs

Nowadays, it's normal to expect APIs within a browser and server to provide non-blocking asynchronous ways to call native mechanisms. Common examples of such APIs include the following:

- The DOM Event API, enabling code such as `window.addEventListener('click', callback)`
- The Node.js file API, enabling code such as `fs.readFile(path, callback)`
- The Browser Fetch API, enabling code such as `fetch().then(callback)`

All such interfaces share something in common: they all provide a way to somehow listen for their completion. Usually, this is achieved via a provided callback (a function). This callback will be called at some later point when the task has completed. Similarly, some native APIs return promises, which enable a richer mechanism of asynchronous control flow, but fundamentally still rely on passing callbacks via the Promise API. Additionally, ECMAScript 2017 introduced the concept of asynchronous functions (`async function() {}`) and the `await` keyword, which finally provided language support for promises, meaning that the completion of asynchronous work no longer requires callbacks.

Let's explore each of these asynchronous of control flow mechanisms individually.

Callbacks

A callback is a conventional approach to providing a way to hook into asynchronous tasks. A callback is simply a function that is passed to another function and is expected to be called at some later point, possibly immediately, possibility soon, and possibly never. Consider the following `requestData` function:

```
function requestData(path, callback) {
  // (Implementation of requestData)
}
```

As you can see, it accepts a callback as its second argument. When calling `requestData`, the callback will typically be anonymously passed inline, like so:

```
requestData('/data/123', (response) => { /* ... */ });
```

It is, of course, totally fine to have previously declared the callback, and doing so can aid comprehensibility as now the reader of your code will have an inkling as to when a callback might be invoked. Observe here how we're calling our `onResponse` callback to make clear that it is expected to be called upon the response becoming available (when it completes):

```
function onResponse(response) {
  // Do something with the response...
}

requestData('/data/123', onResponse);
```

Similarly, in complex APIs with multiple asynchronous state changes, it's common to see named callbacks registered in bulk, via an *object literal*:

```
createDropdownComponent({
  onOpen() {},
  onSelect() {},
  onClose() {},
  onHover() {} // etc.
});
```

A callback will typically be passed arguments that indicate some important state that has been determined from the asynchronous work. For example, the Node.js `readFile` function invokes its callback with two arguments, a (possibly null) error and the (possibly null) data from the file itself:

```
fs.readFile('/path/to/file', (error, data) => {
  if (error) {
    // Handle the error!
  } else {
    // Handle the data! (No error has occurred!)
  }
});
```

The function you pass a callback to is entirely in control of when your callback is invoked, how it is invoked, and what data is passed along with that invocation. This is why sometimes callbacks are spoken about as an *inversion of control*. Normally, you are in control of what functions you call, but when using callbacks, the control is inverted so that you are relying on another function or abstraction to (at some point) call your callback in the expected manner.

Callback hell is the name given to the undesirable proliferation of multiple nested callbacks within a piece of code, usually done to carry out a series of asynchronous tasks that each rely on another previous asynchronous task. Here is an example of such a situation:

```
requestData('/data/current-user', (userData) => {
  if (userData.preferences.twitterEnabled) {
    requestData(userData.twitterFeedURL, (twitterFeedData) => {
      renderTwitterFeed(twitterFeedData, {
        onRendered() {
          logEvent('twitterFeedRender', { userId: userData.id });
        }
      });
    });
  }
});
```

Here, you can see we have three different callbacks, all appearing in one hierarchy of scopes. We await the response of `/data/current-user`, then we optionally make a request to `twitterFeedURL`, and then, upon the rendering of the twitter feed (`renderTwitterFeed()`), we finally log a `"twitterFeedRender"` Event. That final log depends on two previous asynchronous tasks completing and so is (seemingly unavoidably) nested quite deeply.

We can observe that this deeply nested piece of code is at the peak of a kind of *horizontal pyramid* of indentation. This is a common trait of *callback hell*, and as such, you can use the existence of these *horizontal pyramids* as something to watch out for. Not all deep indentations will be due to callbacks, of course, but it's usually high on the list of suspects:

```
asyncTask(data => {
    asyncTask(data => {
        asyncTask(data => {
            asyncTask(data => {
                asyncTask(data => {
                    asyncTask(data => {
                        // ... Callback Hell
                    });
                });
            });
        });
    });
});
```

The Deadly Horizontal Pyramid.

To avoid the *callback hell* indicated by the *horizontal pyramid*, we should consider re-thinking and potentially re-abstracting our code. In the preceding case, logging a Twitter feed render Event, we could, for example, have a generalized function for *getting and rendering Twitter feed data*. This would simplify the top-level of our program:

```
requestData('/data/current-user', (userData) => {
  if (userData.preferences.twitterEnabled) {
    renderTwitterForUser(userData);
  }
});
```

Observe how we have shortened our *horizontal pyramid* here. We are now free to implement `renderTwitterForUser` as we wish and import it as a dependency. Even though its implementation may involve its own callbacks, it is still a reduction in overall complexity for the programmer as it abstracts away half of the *pyramid* to a neatly separated abstraction. Most *callback hell* scenarios can be solved with a similar approach to re-designing and abstraction. This was a simple scenario, though. With more intertwined asynchronous tasks, it may be useful to use other mechanisms of asynchronous control flow.

Event subscribing/emitting

JavaScript is a language that feels right at home when subscribing to and emitting Events. Events are incredibly common in most JavaScript programs, whether dealing with user-derived Events within the browser or server-side Events in Node.js.

There are various names used for operations relating to Events in JavaScript, so it's useful to know all of these names upfront so we're not confused when encountering them. An event is an occurrence in time that will result in the invocation of any callbacks that have been subscribed for that Event. Subscribing to an Event has many names, which all effectively mean the same thing: *subscribing, registering, listening, binding,* and so on. When the Event occurs, the subscribed callback is invoked. This, as well, has many names: *invoking, calling, emitting, firing,* or *triggering.* The actual function that is called can also have various names: *function, callback, listener,* or *handler.*

At its core, any abstraction that supports Events will usually do so by storing callbacks to be called later, keyed with specific Event names. We can imagine that a DOM element might store its Event listeners in a structure like the following:

```
{
  "click": [Function, Function, Function],
  "mouseover": [Function, Function],
  "mouseout": [Function]
}
```

Any Event-supporting abstraction will simply store a series of callbacks to be called later. As such, when subscribing to an Event, you will need to provide both the callback you wish it to call and the Event name that it will be tied to. In the DOM, we would do this like so:

```
document,body.addEventListener('mousemove', e => {
  e; // => the Event object
});
```

Here, we see that an `Event` object is passed to the callback. This is idiomatically named `e` or `evt` for succinctness. Most abstractions that provide an Events API will pass specific Event-related information to the callback. This may be in the form of a singular `Event` object or several arguments.

It's important to note that there truly is no single standard for Events although there are conventions that have emerged. Typically there will always be a method used to register or subscribe to an Event and then another to remove that subscription. The following is an example of using the Node.js Event-Emitter API, which is supported by the native HTTP module:

```
const server = http.createServer(...);

function onConnect(req, cltSocket, head) {
  // Connect to an origin server...
}

// Subscribe
server.on('connect', onConnect);

// Unsubscribe
server.off('connect', onConnect);
```

Here, you can see that the `on()` method is used to subscribe to Events, and the `off()` method is used to unsubscribe. Most Events APIs have similar event registration and de-registration methods although they may implement them in different ways. If you're crafting your own *Events* implementation, then it's advisable to ensure that you're providing a familiar set of methods and abstractions. To do this, take inspiration from either the native DOM Events interface or the Node.js **Event Emitter**. This will ensure that your Events implementation does not surprise or horrify other programmers too much.

Even though an Events API is essentially just a series of callbacks stored and invoked at specific times, there are still challenges in crafting it well. Amongst them are the following:

- Ensuring the order of invocation when a singular Event fires
- Handling cases where Events are emitted while other Events are mid-emission
- Handling cases where Events can be entirely canceled or removed per callback
- Handling cases where Events can be bubbled, propagated, or delegated (this is usually a DOM challenge)

Propagation, bubbling, and *delegation* are terms related to firing Events within a hierarchical structure. In the DOM, since <div> may exist within <body>, the Events API has prescribed that, if the user clicks on <div>, the emitted Event will propagate or *bubble* upward, first triggering any click listeners on <div> and then <body>. Delegation is intentional listening at a higher level of hierarchy, for example, listening at the <body> level and then reacting in a certain way, depending on what the Event object tells you about the Event's target node.

Events provide more possibilities than a simple callback. Since they allow several different Events to be listened for, and the same Event to be listened for several times, any consuming code has far more flexibility in how it constructs its asynchronous control flow. An object that has an Events interface can be passed around throughout a code base and may be subscribed to many times, potentially. The nature of distinct Events, as well, means that different asynchronous concepts or occurrences are usefully kept separated so that a fellow programmer can easily tell which action will be taken in specific circumstances:

```
const dropdown = new DropDown();
dropdown.on('select', () => { /*...*/ });
dropdown.on('deselect', () => { /*...*/ });
dropdown.on('hover', () => { /*...*/ });
```

This type of transparent separation helps to encode expectations within the mind of the programmer. It's simple to discern which function will be called in each case. Compare this to a generalized *something happened* event with an internal switch statement:

```
// Less transparent & more burdensome:
dropdown.on('action', event => {
  switch (event.action) {
    case 'select': /*...*/; break;
    case 'deselect': /*...*/; break;
    // ...
  }
});
```

Well-implemented Events provide a good semantic separation between conceptually different Events and, therefore, provide the programmer with a predictable series of asynchronous actions that they can reason about easily.

Promises

A *Promise* is an abstraction that surrounds the concept of an eventual value. It's easiest to think of a *Promise* as a simple object that will, at some point, contain a value. A Promise provides an interface via which you can pass callbacks to wait for either the eventually-fulfilled value or an error.

At any given time a *Promise* will have a certain state:

- **Pending**: The *Promise* is awaiting its resolution (the asynchronous task has not yet completed).
- **Settled**: The *Promise* is no longer pending and has either been fulfilled or rejected:
  - **Fulfilled**: The *Promise* has been successful and now has a value
  - **Rejected**: The *Promise* has failed with an error

Promises can be constructed via the *Promise* constructor, by passing a singular function argument (called an *executor*) that calls either a `resolve` or `reject` function to indicate either a settled value or an error, respectively:

```
const answerToEverything = new Promise((resolve, reject) => {
  setTimeout(() => {
    resolve(42);
  }, 1000);
});
```

The instantiated `Promise` has the following methods available so that we can access its changed state (when it moves from *pending* to either *fulfilled* or *rejected):*

- `then(onFulfilled[, onRejected])`: This will append a fulfillment callback to the *Promise* and optionally a *rejection* callback. It will return a new *Promise* object, which will resolve to the return value of the called fulfillment or rejection handler, or will resolve as per the original *Promise* if there is no handler.
- `catch(onRejected)`: This will append a *rejection* callback to the *Promise* and will return a new *Promise* that will resolve to either the return value of the callback or (if the original *Promise* succeeds) its fulfillment value.
- `finally(onFinally)`: This will append a handler to the *Promise*, which will be called when the *Promise* is resolved, regardless of whether the resolution is a fulfillment or a rejection.

We can access the eventually resolved value of `answerToEverything` by passing a callback to its `then` method:

```
answerToEverything.then(answer => {
  answer; // => 42
});
```

We can illustrate the exact nature of a *Promise* by exploring the native Fetch API, supported by most modern browsers:

```
const promiseOfData = fetch('/some/data?foo=bar');
```

The `fetch` function returns a *Promise* that we assign to our variable, `promiseOfData`. We can then hook into the request's eventual success (or failure) like so:

```
const promiseOfData = fetch('/some/data');

promiseOfData.then(
  response => {
    response; // The "fulfilled" Response
  },
  error => {
    error; // The "rejected" Error
  }
);
```

It may appear as though promises are just a slightly more verbose abstraction than callbacks. Indeed, in the simplest case, you might just pass a *fulfillment* callback and a *rejection* callback. This, arguably, does not provide us with anything more useful than the original callback approach. But promises can be so much more than this.

Since a *Promise* is just a regular object, it can be passed around your program just like any other value, meaning that the eventual resolution of a task no longer needs to be tied to code at the call site of the original task. Additionally, the fact that each `then`, `catch`, or `finally` call returns a *Promise* of its own, we can chain together any number of either synchronous or asynchronous tasks that rely on some original fulfillment.

In the case of `fetch()`, for example, the fulfilled `Response` object provides a `json()` method, which itself completes asynchronously and returns a *Promise*. Hence, to get the actual JSON data from a given resource, you would have to do the following:

```
fetch('/data/users')
  .then(response => response.json())
  .then(jsonDataOfUsers => {
    jsonDataOfUsers; // the JSON data that we got from response.json()
  });
```

Chaining together `then` calls is a popular pattern used to derive a new value from some prior value. Given the response, we wish to compute the JSON, and given the JSON, we may wish to compute something else:

```
fetch('/data/users')
  .then(response => response.json())
  .then(users => users.map(user => user.forename))
  .then(userForenames => userForenames.sort());
```

Here, we are using multiple `then` calls to compute the sorted forenames of our users. There are, in fact, four distinct promises being created here, as foll:

```
const promiseA = fetch('/data/users');
const promiseB = promiseA.then(response => response.json());
const promiseC = promiseB.then(users => users.map(user => user.forename))
const promiseD = promiseC.then(userForenames => userForenames.sort());

promiseA === promiseB; // => false
promiseB === promiseC; // => false
promiseC === promiseD; // => false
```

Each *Promise* will only ever resolve to a single value. Once it's been either *fulfilled* or *rejected*, no other value can take its place. But as we see here, we can freely derive a new *Promise* from an original *Promise* by simply registering a callback via `then`, `catch`, or `finally`. The nature of only resolving once and of returning new derived promises means that we can compose promises together in a number of useful ways. In our example, we could derive two promises from our `users` data *Promise*: one that collects the forenames of users and another that collects their surnames:

```
const users = fetch('/data/users').then(r => r.json());
const forenames = users.then(users => users.map(user => user.forename));
const surnames = users.then(users => users.map(user => user.surname));
```

We can then freely pass around these `forenames` and `surnames` promises, and any consuming code can do what it wants with them. For example, we may have a DOM element that we'd like to populate with the forenames when they are eventually available:

```
function createForenamesComponent(forenamesPromise) {

  const div = document.createElement('div');

  function render(forenames) {
    div.textContent = forenames ? forenames.join(', ') : 'Loading...';
  }

  render(null); // Initial render
```

```
    forenamesPromise.then(forenames => {
      // When we receive the forenames we want to render them:
      render(forenames);
    });

    return div;
  }
```

This `createForenamesComponent` function accepts the `forenames` *Promise* as an argument and then returns a `<div>` element. As you can see, we have called `render()` initially with `null`, which populates the DIV element with the `"loading..."` text. Once the *Promise* is fulfilled, we then re-render with the newly populated forenames.

The ability to pass around promises in this manner makes them far more flexible than callbacks, and similar in spirit to an object that implements an Events API. However, with all of these mechanisms, it is necessary to create and pass around functions so that you can listen for future Events and then act on them. If you have a significant amount of asynchronous logic to express, this can be a real struggle. The control flow of a program littered with callbacks, Events, and promises can be unclear, even to those well accustomed to a particular code base. Even a small number of independently asynchronous Events can create a large variety of *states* throughout your application. A programmer can become very confused, as a result; the confusion relates to *what* is happening *when*.

 The *state* of your program is determined at runtime. When a value or piece of data changes, no matter how small, it will be considered a *change of state*. *State* is typically expressed in terms of outputs from the program, such as a GUI or a CLI can be also be held internally and manifest in a later observed output.

To avoid confusion, it's best to implement any timing-related code as transparently as possible, so that there is no room for misunderstanding. The following is an example of code that may lead to misunderstanding:

```
    userInfoLoader.init();

    appStartup().then(() => {
      const userID = userInfoLoader.data.id;
      const userName = userInfoLoader.data.name;
      renderApplication(userID, userName);
    });
```

This code seems to assume that the *Promise* returned by `appStartup()` will always fulfill after `userInfoLoader` has completed its work. Perhaps the author of this code happens to know that the `appStartup()` logic will always complete after `userInfoLoader`. Perhaps that is a certainty. But for us, reading this code for the first time, we have no confidence that `userInfoLoader.data` will be populated by the time `appStartup()` is fulfilled. It would be better to make the timing more transparent by, for example, returning a *Promise* from `userInfoLoader.init()` and then carrying out `appStartup()` on the explicit fulfillment of that *Promise:*

```
userInfoLoader.init()
  .then(() => appStartup())
  .then(() => {
    const userID = userInfoLoader.data.id;
    const userName = userInfoLoader.data.name;
    renderApplication(userID, userName);
  });
```

Here, we are arranging our code so that it is obvious what actions are dependent on what other actions and in what order the actions will occur. Using promises by themselves, just like any other asynchronous control flow abstraction, does not guarantee that your code will be easily comprehensible. It's important to always consider the perspective of your fellow programmers and the temporal assumptions that they'll make. Next, we will explore a newer addition to JavaScript that gives us native linguistic support for asynchronous code: you'll see how these additions enable us to write asynchronous code that is clearer in terms of *what* is happening *when*.

async and await

The ECMAScript 2017 specification introduced new concepts to the JavaScript language in the form of the `async` and `await` keywords. The `async` keyword is used to designate a function as asynchronous:

```
async function getNumber() {
  return 42;
}
```

Doing this, effectively, wraps whatever the function returns in `Promise` (if it is not already `Promise`). So, if we attempt to call this function we will receive `Promise`:

```
getNumber() instanceof Promise; // => true
```

As we've learned, we can subscribe to the fulfillment of `Promise` by using its `then` method:

```
getNumber().then(number => {
  number; // => 42
});
```

In concert with async functions that return *Promises,* we also have an `await` keyword. This enables us to wait for the fulfillment (or rejection) of the `Promise` simply by passing it to the right side of `await`. This may, for example, be a `Promise` returned from an `async` function call:

```
await someAsyncFunction();
```

Or it may be a *Promise* designated inline, like so:

```
const n = await new Promise(fulfill => fulfill(123));
n; // => 123
```

As you can see, the `await` keyword will wait for its *Promise* to resolve and thereby prevents any following lines from executing until that occurs.

The following is another example—a `setupFeed` async function that awaits both `fetch()` and `response.json()`:

```
async function setupFeed() {
  const response = await fetch('/data');
  const json = await response.json();
  console.log(json);
}
```

It's important to note that the `await` keyword does not block like `alert()` or `prompt()`. Instead, it simply pauses the execution of the asynchronous function, freeing up the *Event Loop* to continue with other work, and then, when its *Promise* resolves, it will continue execution where it left off. Remember, `await` is only syntactic *sugar* over functionality that we can already achieve. If we wanted to implement our `setupFeed` function without `async`/`await`, we could easily do that by reverting to our old pattern of passing callbacks to `Promise#then`:

```
function setupFeed() {
  fetch('/data').then(response => {
    return response.json()
  }).then(json => {
    console.log(json);
  });
}
```

Observe how the code is slightly clunkier and more congested when we don't use `await`. Using `await` in concert with asynchronous functions gives us the same satisfyingly linear and procedural appearance as regular synchronous code. This can vastly simplify an otherwise complicated asynchronous control flow, making it clearer to our fellow programmer *what* is happening *when*.

The await keyword is also available for use within the `for...of` iteration construct. Doing so will await each value iterated over. If, during iteration, any encountered value is a *Promise*, the iteration will not continue until that *Promise* has been resolved:

```
const allData = [
  fetch('/data/1').then(r => r.json()),
  fetch('/data/2').then(r => r.json()),
  fetch('/data/3').then(r => r.json())
];

for await (const data of allData) {
  console.log(data);
}

// Logs data from /data/1, /data/2 and /data/3
```

Without *Promises* or `await` and `async`, expressing this kind of asynchronous process would require not only also more code but also more time to understand. The beauty of these constructs and abstractions is that they allow us to ignore the implementation details of asynchronous operations, enabling us to focus purely on expressing our problem domain. As we move forward in this book, we will further explore this spirit of abstraction as we tackle some larger and more unwieldy problem domains.

Summary

In this chapter, we have finalized our exploration of the JavaScript language, discussing the difference between imperative and declarative syntax, exploring how to cleanly control flow, and learning how to handle cases of cyclomatic complexity in both synchronous and asynchronous contexts. This has involved an in-depth study of all iteration and conditional constructs within the language, guidance on their usage, and cautions against anti-patterns.

In the next chapter, we will take all of the knowledge we've accrued about the JavaScript language and combine it with some explorations into real-world design patterns and paradigms that'll help us to build clean abstractions and architectures.

Section 3: Crafting Abstractions 3

In this section, we'll take what we've learned about clean code and JavaScript's language constructs and apply this in order to build clean and coherent JavaScript abstractions. By doing this, we'll learn how to design intuitive abstractions using well-known patterns, how to think about common JavaScript problem domains, how to deal with error states, and how to work effectively with the sometimes awkward DOM API.

This section contains the following chapters:

- Chapter 11, *Design Patterns*
- Chapter 12, *Real-World Challenges*

11
Design Patterns

Most problems we encounter are not new. Many programmers that have come before us have tackled similar problems and, via their struggles, various patterns of programming have emerged. We call these design patterns.

Design patterns are the useful structures, styles, and stencils that our code sits within. A design pattern may prescribe anything from the overall scaffolding of a code base to the individual syntactic pieces used to build expressions, functions, and modules. By building software, we are constantly, and often unknowingly, in the process of *designing*. It is through this process of designing that we are defining the experience that users and maintainers will go through when exposed to our code.

To attune us to this perspective of the designer instead of programmer, for a moment, let's consider the design of a simple software abstraction.

In this chapter, we will cover the following topics:

- The perspective of a designer
- Architectural design patterns
- JavaScript modules
- Modular design patterns
- Planning and harmony

The perspective of a designer

To bestow us with the perspective of a designer, let's explore a simple problem. We must construct an abstraction that allows users to give us two strings, a subject string and a query string. We must then calculate a count of the query strings found within the subject string.

So, consider the following query string:

```
"the"
```

And have a look at the following subject string:

```
"the fox jumped over the lazy brown dog"
```

We should receive a result of 2.

For our purposes as a designer, we care about the experience of those who must use our code. For now, we won't worry about our implementation; we will instead only consider the interface, as it is primarily the interface to our code that will drive our fellow programmers' experiences.

The very first thing we may do as a designer is to define a function with a carefully chosen name and a specific set of named arguments:

```
function countNeedlesInHaystack(needle, haystack) { }
```

This function accepts `needle` and `haystack` and will return `Number`, indicating the count of `needle` within `haystack`. The consumer of our code would make use of it like so:

```
countNeedlesInHaystack('abc', 'abc abc abc'); // => 3
```

 We are using the popular idiom of needle-in-a-haystack to describe the problem of looking for a substring within another string. Considering popular idioms is a crucial part of designing code, but we must be wary of idioms being misunderstood.

The design of a piece of code should be defined by the problem domain we wish to solve and the user experience we wish to reveal. Another programmer, given the same problem domain, may have chosen a different solution. For example, they may have employed partial application to allow the following calling syntax:

```
needleCounter('app')('apple apple'); // => 2
```

Or perhaps they may have designed a more verbose syntax that involves invoking a `Haystack` constructor and calling its `count()` method like so:

```
new Haystack('apple apple'),count('app'); // => 2
```

This *classical* approach arguably has a nice semantic relationship between the object (`Haystack`) and the `count` method. It meshes well with the OOP concepts we've explored in previous chapters. That said, some programmers may find it to be overly verbose.

There's also the possibility of a more descriptive API where the arguments are defined within a configuration object (that is, a plain object literal passed as the sole argument):

```
countOccurancesOfNeedleInHaystack({
  haystack: 'abc abc abc',
  needle: 'abc'
}); // => 3
```

There's also the possibility that this counting functionality may form the part of a larger set of string-related utilities and, hence, can be incorporated into a larger custom-named module:

```
str('omg omg omg').count('omg'); // => 3
```

We may even consider it okay to modify the native `String.prototype`, even though it is inadvisable, so that we have a `count` method available on all strings:

```
'omg omg omg'.count('omg'); // => 3
```

In terms of our naming conventions as well, we may wish to avoid the needle-in-a-haystack idiom and, instead, use more descriptive names where perhaps there is less risk of misunderstanding, like the following:

- `searchableString` and `subString`
- `query` and `content`
- `search` and `corpus`

The choices available to us, even within this very narrow problem domain, are overwhelming. You'll likely have many of your own strong opinions about which approach and naming conventions would have been superior here.

The fact that we can solve a seemingly simple problem with so many different approaches shows us how there is a need for a decision process. And this process is software design. Effective software design employs design patterns to encapsulate problem domains and provide familiarity and ease of comprehension to fellow programmers.

 The intent with our exploration of the needle-in-a-haystack problem was not to find a solution, but rather to highlight the difficulty of software design, and to expose our minds to a more user-oriented perspective. It also reminds us that there is very rarely one ideal design.

A well-chosen design pattern, given any problem domain, can be said to have two basic characteristics:

- **It solves the problem well**: A well-chosen design pattern will be well-suited to the problem domain so that we can fluidly express the nature of the problem and its solution easily.
- **It is familiar and usable**: A well-chosen design pattern will be familiar to our fellow programmers. It'll be immediately obvious how can they can use it or make changes to the code.

Design patterns are useful in a variety of contexts and scales. We use them when we write individual operations and functions, but we also use them when structuring our entire code base. Design patterns, as such, are hierarchical. They exist on the macro and micro scale of a code base. A singular code base can easily contain many design pattern within.

In Chapter 2, *Tenets of Clean Code,* we spoke about familiarity as a crucial characteristic. A car mechanic opening the hood of a car will hope to see many familiar patterns: from the individual pieces of wiring and welding of Components to the larger construction of the cylinders, valves, and pistons. There is a certain layout they would expect to find and if it is not there, then they would be left scratching their heads, wondering how to approach whatever problem they're trying to solve.

Familiarity increases the maintainability and usability of our solutions. Consider the following directory structure and the displayed `logger.js` source code:

What design patterns can we observe here? Let's take a look at some examples:

- The use of a top-level `app/` directory to contain all the source code
- The existence of **Models, Views, and Controllers (MVC)**

- The separation of utilities into its own directory (`utils/`)
- The camel case naming of files (for example,`binarySearch.js`)
- The use of a Conventional Module pattern in `logger.js` (that is, exporting a plain object of methods)
- The use of `...` `&& msgs.length` to confirm a nonzero (that is, truthy) length
- Declaring constants at the top of a file (that is, `const ALL_LOGS_LEVEL`)
- (Possibly others...)

Design patterns are not just large, lofty architectural structures. They can exist in every part of our code base: the directory structure, the naming of files, and the individual expressions of our code. At every level, our usage of common patterns can increase our ability to express the problem domain, and increase the familiarity of our code to newcomers. Patterns exist within patterns.

Using design patterns well can have beneficial effects on all of the tenets of clean code we covered previously—reliability, efficiency, maintainability, and usability:

- **Reliability**: A good design pattern will suit the problem domain and allow you to easily express your desired logic and data structures without too much complexity. The familiarity of your adopted design patterns will also enable other programmers to easily understand and improve upon the reliability of your code over time.
- **Efficiency**: A good design pattern will enable you to fuss less about how to structure your code base or your individual modules. It'll enable you to spend more time worrying about the problem domain. Well-selected design patterns will also aid in making the interfaces between different pieces of code streamlined and understandable.
- **Maintainability**: A good design pattern allows for easy adaptation. If there is a change of specification or a bug that needs to be fixed, the programmer can easily find the desired area of change/insertion and make the change without hassle.
- **Usability**: A good design pattern is easy to understand due to its familiarity. A fellow programmer can easily comprehend the flow of the code and quickly make correct assertions about how it works and how they can make use of it. A good design pattern will also create a pleasant user experience, whether expressed via a programmatic API or a GUI.

You can see that a lot of what makes design patterns useful is only actualized if we pick the right one. We'll be exploring a selection of popular design patterns and, for each, we'll discuss the types of situations they're suited to. This exploration should hopefully give you a good idea of what it means to select a good design pattern.

Be warned: just as good design proliferates via convention, so does bad design. We discussed the phenomenon of cargo culting in `Chapter 3`, *The Enemies of Clean Code*, and so we are not strangers to how such types of bad designs may spread, but it's important to remain mindful of these traps when employing design patterns.

Architectural design patterns

Architectural design patterns are the ways in which we tie our code together. If we have a dozen different modules, it is how those modules talk to each other that defines our architecture.

The architectural design patterns utilized in JavaScript code bases have changed massively over recent years. With the steady proliferation of popular frameworks such as React and Angular, we've seen code bases take on new conventions. The landscape is still very much shifting, so we shouldn't expect any specific standard to emerge any time soon. Nonetheless, most frameworks tend to follow the same broad architectural patterns.

An example of a popular architectural pattern is the separation of data logic and rendering logic. This is famously adopted by many different UI frameworks, albeit with different styles. This is likely due to the heritage of software UI and the early established pattern of MVC that eventually became the de facto approach.

In this section, we'll be covering two famous architectural design patterns, MVC and its offshoot, **Model-View-ViewModel** (**MVVM**). Together, these should give us an awareness of the types of concerns that are typically separated and will hopefully inspire us to seek a similar level of clarity in the architectures we create.

MVC

MVC is characterized by a separation between these three concepts. An MVC architecture may involve many individual Models, Views, and Controllers that all work in concert to solve a given problem. Each of these parts can be described as follows:

- **The Model**: This describes the data and how business logic mutates that data. Changes in the data will manifest in changes to the View.
- **The View**: This describes how the Model is rendered (its format, layout, and appearance) and will invoke the Controller whenever there is an action that needs to occur, possibly in response to a user event.

- **The Controller**: This accepts instructions from the View and informs the Model what actions or changes to carry out, which will go on to affect whatever is rendered to the user via the View.

We can observe the flow of control in the following diagram:

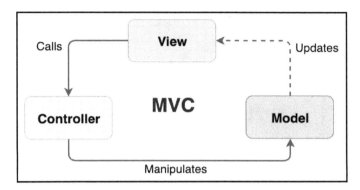

The MVC pattern provides us with a way to separate our various concerns. It prescribes where we should put logic about business decisions (that is, in Models) and where we should put logic about displaying things to the user (that is, Views). Additionally, it gives us the Controller, which enables these two concerns to talk to each other. The separation that MVC fosters is hugely beneficial as it means our fellow programmers can easily discern where to make required changes or fixes.

 MVC was originally posed in 1978 by Trygve Reenskaug while working at Xerox PARC. Its original purpose was to support the user's illusion of seeing and manipulating the domain information directly. At the time, this was quite revolutionary, but we now, as end users, take such UIs (and their transparent relation to their data) for granted.

A working example of MVC

To illustrate how an implementation of MVC might look in JavaScript, let's build a very simple program. It will be a basic mutable number application that renders a simple UI where the user can see the current number and choose to update it via either incrementing or decrementing its value.

First, we can implement the logic and containment of our data using a Model:

```
class MutableNumberModel {
  constructor(value) {
    this.value = value;
  }
  increment() {
    this.value++;
    this.onChangeCallback();
  }
  decrement() {
    this.value--;
    this.onChangeCallback();
  }
  registerChangeCallback(onChangeCallback) {
    this.onChangeCallback = onChangeCallback;
  }
}
```

In addition to storing the value itself, this class also accepts and relies upon a callback function called `onChangeCallback`. This callback function will be provided by the Controller and will be called whenever the value changes. This is necessary so that we can kick off a re-render of the View if the Model changes.

Next, we need to build the Controller, which will act as a very simple bridge (or glue) between `view` and `model`. It registers the necessary callbacks to know when either the user requests a change via `view` or the underlying data of the `model` changes:

```
class MutableNumberController {
  constructor(model, view) {
    this.model = model;
    this.view = view;
    this.model.registerChangeCallback(
      () => this.view.renderUpdate()
    );
    this.view.registerIncrementCallback(
      () => this.model.increment()
    );
    this.view.registerDecrementCallback(
      () => this.model.decrement()
    );
  }
}
```

Our `view` is responsible for retrieving data from `model` and rendering it to the user. To do this, it creates a DOM hierarchy in which the data will sit. It also listens for and escalates user events to `controller` when either the `increment` or `decrement` button is clicked:

```
class MutableNumberView {
  constructor(model, controller) {
    this.model = model;
    this.controller = controller;
  }
  registerIncrementCallback(onIncrementCallback) {
    this.onIncrementCallback = onIncrementCallback;
  }
  registerDecrementCallback(onDecrementCallback) {
    this.onDecrementCallback = onDecrementCallback;
  }
  renderUpdate() {
    this.numberSpan.textContent = this.model.value;
  }
  renderInitial() {
    this.container = document.createElement('div');
    this.numberSpan = document.createElement('span');
    this.incrementButton = document.createElement('button');
    this.decrementButton = document.createElement('button');
    this.incrementButton.textContent = '+';
    this.decrementButton.textContent = '-';
    this.incrementButton.onclick =
       () => this.onIncrementCallback();
    this.decrementButton.onclick =
       () => this.onDecrementCallback();
    this.container.appendChild(this.numberSpan);
    this.container.appendChild(this.incrementButton);
    this.container.appendChild(this.decrementButton);
    this.renderUpdate();
    return this.container;
  }
}
```

This is quite a lengthy View as we're having to create its DOM representation manually. Many modern frameworks (React, Angular, Svelte, and so on) allow you to declaratively express your hierarchy using either plain HTML or a hybrid syntax such as JSX (a syntax extension to JavaScript itself that permits XML-like tags within JavaScript code).

This *View* has two rendering methods: `renderInitial` will carry out the initial render, which sets up the DOM elements, and then the `renderUpdate` method is responsible for updating the number whenever it changes.

Tying this all together, our simple program would be initialized like so:

```
const model = new MutableNumberModel(5);
const view = new MutableNumberView(model);
const controller = new MutableNumberController(model, view);

document.body.appendChild(view.renderInitial());
```

`view` is given access to `model` so that it can retrieve the data to render. `controller` is given to both `model` and `view` so that it can glue them together by setting up the appropriate callbacks.

In the case of a user clicking the + (increment) button, the following process would kick off:

1. The DOM click event from `incrementButton` is received by the View
2. The View fires its `onIncrementCallback()`, listened to by the Controller
3. The Controller instructs the Model to `increment()`
4. The Model calls its mutation callback, that is, `onChangeCallback`, listened to by the Controller
5. The Controller instructs the View to re-render

You may be wondering why we bother with the separation between the Controller and the Model. Why can't the *View* just communicate with the Model directly and vice versa? Well, it can! But if we did that, we'd be polluting both our *View* and our *Model* with more logic and hence more complexity. We could equally just place everything in the *View* and have no Model, but you can imagine how unwieldy that would get. Fundamentally, the degree and quantity of separation will vary with every project you pursue. At its core, MVC teaches us about the general idea of how to separate the problem domain from its presentation. How we wield this separation is up to us.

Since 1978, when MVC was first coined, many adaptations of it have surfaced, but its central theme of separation between *Model* and *View* has persisted through the decades. Consider the architectural design of a React application. It includes Components, which contain the logic for rendering state, and typically will include several domain-specific reducers, which take actions (for example, *user has clicked something!*) and derive state from those actions.

This architecture looks surprisingly similar to traditional MVC:

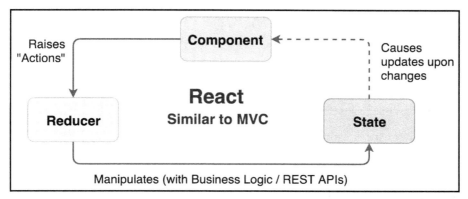

MVC, as a general guiding pattern, has impacted the design of countless frameworks and code bases throughout the last few decades, and it will continue to do so. Not every adaptation, reproduction, or MVC will abide by the original description posed in 1978 but, usually, these adaptations will stay true to the centrally important theme of separating a Model from its View and of having a View be a reflection (or even, a derivation) of a Model.

MVVM

MVVM is similar in spirit to its ancestor, MVC. It prescribes a strict separation between the underlying business logic and data that drives a program and the rendering of that data:

- **The Model**: This describes the data and how business logic mutates that data. Changes in the data will manifest in changes to the **View**.
- **The View**: This describes how the **Model** is rendered (its structure, layout, and appearance) and will invoke the **Data Binding** mechanism of the **ViewModel** whenever there is an action that needs to occur, possibly in response to a user event.
- **The ViewModel**: This is the glue between the **Model** and the **View** and enables them to talk to each other via a **Data Binding** mechanism. This mechanism tends to vary a lot between implementations.

The relationship between these parts is illustrated in the following diagram:

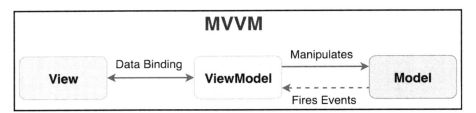

The MVVM architecture is more popular in frontend JavaScript as it suits the need of having a constantly updated **View**, while traditional MVC is more popular on the backend as it caters well to the simple render-once nature of most HTTP responses.

Within MVVM, the data binding between the **ViewModel** and the **View** usually uses DOM events to track user intent and then mutates data on the **Model**, which then emits mutation events of its own that can be listened for by the **ViewModel**, resulting in the **View** being constantly kept up to date with changing data.

Many frameworks will have their own adaptation of data-binding. Angular, for example, allows you to specify in your HTML templates a custom attribute called `ng-model`, which will tie a user input element such as `<input>` to a given data model, allowing data to flow in both directions. If the Model is updated, `<input>` will be updated to reflect that and vice versa.

MV* and the nature of software

Throughout your time as a JavaScript programmer, you will encounter variations of both MVC and MVVM. As patterns, they are infinitely applicable as they are concerned with the very basic tenets of a software system: the input of data into a system, the processing of that data, and the subsequent output of that processed data. There are a few other ways we could choose to architect these tenets into a code base, but it's likely that, in the end, almost every time, we'll end up with a system that delineates these concerns in a spirit similar to MVC (or MVVM).

Now that we have a firm idea of how we might architect a code base and the types of delineations that characterize a well-designed architecture, we can explore the individual pieces of that code base: the modules themselves.

JavaScript modules

In JavaScript, the word module has changed over the years. A module used to be any piece of code that was distinct and self-contained. A few years ago, you might have expressed several modules within the same file like so:

```
// main.js

// The Dropdown Module
var dropdown = /* ... definition ... */;

// The Data Fetcher Module
var dataFetcher = /* ... definition ...*/;
```

Nowadays, however, the word *module* tends to refer to Modules (capital *M*) as prescribed by the ECMAScript specification. These Modules are distinct files imported and exported across a code base via `import` and `export` statements. Using such Modules, we might have a `DropdownComponent.js` file that looks like this:

```
// DropdownComponent.js
class DropdownComponent {}
export default DropdownComponent;
```

As you can see, it uses the `export` statement to export its class. If we wish to use this class as a dependency, we would import it like so:

```
// app.js
import DropdownComponent from './DropdownComponent.js';
```

ECMAScript Modules are slowly gaining more support across various environments. To make use of them within the browser, you can provide an *entry* script tag with a type of *module*, that is, `<script type="module" />`. Within Node.js, at the time of writing, ES Modules are still an experimental feature, so you can either rely on the old style of importing (`const thing = require('./thing')`) or you can enable *experimental modules* by using the `--experimental-modules` flag and using the `.mjs` extension on all of your JavaScript files.

Both the `import` and `export` statements permit a variety of syntaxes. These allow you to define the names of what you're exporting or importing. In a scenario where a Module is only exporting one item, it is conventional to use `export default [item]` as we have done in `DropdownComponent.js`. This ensures that any dependents of the Module can import it and name it as they wish, as shown in this example:

```
import MyLocallyDifferentNameForDropdown from './DropdownComponent.js';
```

In contrast to this, you can specifically name your exports by declaring them within curly braces and using the `as` keyword:

```
export { DropdownComponent as TheDropdown };
```

This will mean that any importers will need to specifically specify the name of `TheDropdown`, like so:

```
import { TheDropdown } from './DropdownComponent.js';
```

Alternatively, you can export named items by having specific declarations inline with your `export` statements, such as `var`, `const`, `let`, function declarations, or class definitions:

```
// things.js
export let x = 1;
export const y = 2;
export var z = 3;
export function myFunction() {}
export class MyClass {}
```

On the importing side, such named exports can be imported by, again, using curly braces:

```
import { x, y, z, myFunction, MyClass } from './things.js';
```

When importing, you can also optionally designate the local name of that import with the `as` keyword to have its local name be different to its exported named (this is especially useful in cases of naming conflicts):

```
import { MyClass as TheClass } from './things.js';
TheClass; // => The class
MyClass; // ! ReferenceError
```

It's conventional to aggregate exports in areas of your code that provide several related abstractions. For example, if you have composed a small Component library, where each Component exports itself as `default`, then you could have `index.js` that exposes all of the Components together:

```
// components/index.js
export {default as DropdownComponent} from './DropdownComponent.js';
export {default as AccordianComponent} from './AccordianComponent.js';
export {default as NavigationComponent} from './NavigationComponent.js';
```

> In Node.js, an `index.js/index.mjs` file is imported by default if you try to import an entire directory. That is, if you import `'./components/'`, it would first look for the index file and, if available, would import it. In the browser, no such convention currently exists. All imports must be fully qualified filenames.

We can, very conveniently, now import our entire set of Components by using the asterisk with our `import` statement:

```
// app.js
import * from 'components/index.js';

// Make use of the imported components:
new DropdownComponent();
new AccordianComponent();
new NavigationComponent();
```

There are some additional nuances and complexities around modules in JavaScript, especially when considering the legacies of Node.js, that we, unfortunately, don't have time to go into, but what we've covered so far should give you a good enough coverage of the topic to be productive and nicely paves the way for us to explore the topic of modular design patterns.

Modular design patterns

Modular design patterns are the structures and syntactic conventions we use to craft individual modules. We would usually employ these patterns within distinct JavaScript Modules. Each distinct file should offer up and export a specific abstraction.

> If you find yourself using these patterns several times within the same file, then it may be worth splitting them out. The directory and file structure of a given code base should ideally reflect its landscape of abstractions. You shouldn't have several abstractions crammed into a single file.

Constructor patterns

The Constructor pattern uses a singular constructor and then manually fills its `prototype` with methods and properties. This was the traditional approach for creating classical OOP-like classes in JavaScript before the class definition syntax existed.

Typically, it begins with the definition of a constructor as a function declaration:

```
function Book(title) {
  // Initialization Logic
  this.title = title;
}
```

This would then be followed by assigning individual methods to the prototype:

```
Book.prototype.getNumberOfPages = function() { /* ... */ };
Book.prototype.renderFrontCover: function() { /* ... */ };
Book.prototype.renderBackCover: function () { /* ... */ };
```

Or it would be followed by replacing the entire `prototype` with an object literal:

```
Book.prototype = {
  getNumberOfPages: function() { /* ... */ },
  renderFrontCover: function() { /* ... */ },
  renderBackCover: function () { /* ... */ }
};
```

The latter approach tends to be preferred as it's more encapsulated and succinct. Nowadays, of course, if you wished to use the Constructor pattern, you would likely opt for method definitions as they take up less space than individual key-value pairs:

```
Book.prototype = {
  getNumberOfPages() { /* ... */ },
  renderFrontCover() { /* ... */ },
  renderBackCover () { /* ... */ }
};
```

The instantiation of a constructor would be via the `new` keyword:

```
const myBook = new Book();
```

This creates a new object that has an internal `[[Prototype]]` of the constructor's `prototype` (that is, our object, which contains `getNumberOfPages`, `renderFrontCover`, and `renderBackCover`).

If you're struggling to recall the prototypal mechanisms that underlie constructors and instantiation, then please revisit `Chapter 6`, *Primitives and Built-in Types*, and, specifically, the section called *The prototype*.

When to use the Constructor pattern

The Constructor pattern is useful in scenarios where you wish to have an abstraction that encapsulates the concept of a noun, that is, a thing that would make sense to have an instance of. Examples may include `NavigationComponent` or `StorageDevice`. The Constructor pattern allows you to create abstractions akin to traditional OOP classes. So, if you're coming from a classical OOP language, then you can feel free to use the Constructor pattern where you may have previously used classes.

If you're not sure whether the Constructor pattern is applicable, consider whether the following questions are true:

- Is the concept expressible as a noun?
- Does the concept require construction?
- Will the concept vary between instances?

If the concept you're abstracting does not fulfill any of the preceding criteria, then you may want to consider another modular design pattern. An example of this may be a utility module that has various helper methods. Such a module may not require construction since it is essentially a collection of methods, and these methods and their behaviors would not vary between instances.

The Constructor pattern has largely fallen out of favor since the introduction of class definitions into JavaScript, which allow you to declare classes in a fashion much more akin to classical OOP languages (that is, `class X extends Y {...}`). Skip ahead to *The Class pattern* section to see this in action!

Inheritance with the Constructor pattern

To achieve inheritance with the Constructor pattern, you need to manually make your `prototype` objects inherit from your parent constructor's `prototype`.

At the risk of over simplifying, we'll illustrate this with the classic example of an `Animal` super-class and a `Monkey` subclass. Here is our definition of `Animal`:

```
function Animal() {}
Animal.prototype = {
  isAnimal: true,
  grow() {}
};
```

Technically, to achieve inheritance, we want to create an object that has `[[Prototype]]` of `Animal.prototype` prototype and then use that newly-created object as our sub-class `prototype` subclass. The end goal is a prototypal tree that looks like this:

```
Object.prototype
    └── Animal.prototype
          └── Monkey.prototype
```

The easiest way to create an object with a given `[[Prototype]]` is with `Object.create(ThePrototype)`. Here, we can use it to extend `Animal.prototype` and assign the result to `Monkey.prototype`:

```
function Monkey() {}
Monkey.prototype = Object.create(Animal.prototype);
```

We can then freely assign methods and properties to this new object:

```
Monkey.prototype.isMonkey = true;
Monkey.prototype.screech = function() {};
```

If we now try to instantiate `Monkey`, then we should be able to access not only its own methods and properties but also those we inherited from `Animal.prototype`:

```
new Monkey().isAnimal; // => true
new Monkey().isMonkey; // => true
typeof new Monkey().grow; // => "function"
typeof new Monkey().screech; // => "function"
```

 Remember, this only works because `Monkey.prototype` (that is, `[[Prototype]]` of every `Monkey` instance) does itself have `[[Prototype]]` of `Animal.prototype`. And, as we know, if a property cannot be found on a given object, then it'll be looked for on its `[[Prototype]]` (*if available*).

It can be quite cumbersome to individually set a prototype's properties and methods one at a time, as shown in this example:

```
Monkey.prototype.method1 = ...;
Monkey.prototype.method2 = ...;
Monkey.prototype.method3 = ...;
Monkey.prototype.method4 = ...;
```

Due to this, another pattern has emerged to make things easier: using `Object.assign()`. This allows us to set properties and methods in bulk as object literals, and it means we can make use of the method definition syntax as well:

```
function Monkey() {}
Monkey.prototype = Object.assign(Object.create(Animal.prototype), {
  isMonkey: true,
  screech() {},
  groom() {}
});
```

`Object.assign` here will assign any properties from its second (and third, fourth, and so on) arguments to the object passed as the first argument. This provides us with a more succinct syntax for adding properties to our child `prototype` object.

The Constructor pattern and its inheritance conventions have largely lost favor due to the newer class definition syntax, which allows a more succinct and simpler way to harness prototypal inheritance in JavaScript. As such, the very next thing we will explore is the Class pattern, which uses this newer syntax.

 Reminder: For a more thorough refresher on `[[Prototype]]` (which is vital to understanding constructors and classes in JavaScript), you should re visit the section on *The prototype* in `Chapter 6`, *Primitives and Built-in Types*. A lot of the design patterns in this chapter make use of the prototype mechanism, so it's useful to have it fresh in your mind.

The Class pattern

The Class pattern, which relies on the newer class definition syntax, has largely replaced the Constructor pattern. It involves the creation of classes, analogous to classical OOP languages, although behind the scenes it uses the same prototypal mechanism that the Constructor pattern uses. So, it can be said that it's just a bit of extra syntactic *sugar* to make the language a bit more expressive.

Here is an example of a basic class that abstracts the concept of a name:

```
class Name {
  constructor(forename, surname) {
    this.forename = forename;
    this.surname = surname;
  }
  sayHello() {
   return `My name is ${this.forename} ${this.surname}`;
  }
}
```

The creation of a class via this syntax is effectively the creation of a constructor with an attached prototype, hence the following code is exactly equivalent:

```
function Name(forename, surname) {
  this.forename = forename;
  this.surname = surname;
}

Name.prototype.sayHello = function() {
  return `My name is ${this.forename} ${this.surname}`;
};
```

Using the Class pattern is certainly aesthetically preferable to the clunky and older Constructor pattern, but do not be misled! Behind the scenes, exactly the same mechanisms are at play.

When to use the Class pattern

The Class pattern, much like the Constructor pattern, is useful when you have a self-contained concept that fulfills the following criteria:

- The concept is expressible as a noun
- The concept requires construction
- The concept will vary between instances of itself

Here are some examples of concepts that abide by these criteria and are hence reasonable to express via the Class pattern:

- A database record (represents a piece of data and allows inquiry and manipulation)
- A todo item component (represents a todo item and allows it to be rendered)
- A binary tree (represents a binary-tree data structure)

Typically such cases will stick out quite obviously to you. If you're having trouble, consider the use cases of your abstraction and try to write some consumer code, that is, pseudo code that utilizes your abstraction. If it seems sensible and doesn't feel too awkward to use, then you've probably landed on a good pattern.

Static methods

Static methods and properties can be declared by using the `static` keyword:

```
class Accounts {
  static allAccounts = [];
  static tallyAllAccounts() {
    // ...
  }
}

Accounts.tallyAllAccounts();
Accounts.allAccounts; // => []
```

These properties and methods could also easily be added after the initial class definition:

```
Accounts.countAccounts = () => {
  return Accounts.allAccounts.length;
};
```

Static methods are useful when you have a method or property whose functionality and existence are semantically related to the entire class as opposed to a singular instance.

Public and private fields

To declare a public field (that is, a property) on your instance, you can simply declare this within the class definition syntax in line:

```
class Rectangle {
  width = 100;
  height = 100;
}
```

These fields are initialized for each instance and are, therefore, mutable on the instance itself. They're most useful when you need to define some sensible default for a given property. This can then be easily overridden within the constructor:

```
class Rectangle {
  width = 100;
  height = 100;

  constructor(width, height) {
    if (width && !isNaN(width)) {
      this.width = width;
    }
    if (height && !isNaN(height)) {
      this.height = height;
    }
  }
}
```

You can also define private fields by prefixing their identifier with a # symbol:

```
class Rectangle {
  #width = 100;
  #height = 100;

  constructor(width, height) {
    if (width && !isNaN(width)) {
      this.#width = width;
    }
    if (height && !isNaN(height)) {
      this.#height = height;
    }
  }
}
```

 Traditionally, JavaScript had no concept of private fields, so programmers opted instead to prefix properties intended as private with one or more underscores (for example, __somePropertyName). This was understood as a social contract where other programmers would not mess with these properties (knowing that doing so might break things in unexpected ways).

Private fields are only accessible by the class itself. Sub-classes do not have access:

```
class Super { #private = 123; }
class Sub { getPrivate() { return this.#private; } }

// !SyntaxError: Undefined private field #private:
// must be declared in an enclosing class
```

Private fields should be used with extreme caution as they can severely limit the extensibility of your code, hence increasing its rigidity and lack of flexibility. If you use a private field, you should ensure that you have considered the consequences. It may be the case that what you need is, in fact, just a pseudo-private field, prefixed with an underscore (for example, `_private`) or another obscure piece of punctuation (for example, `$_private`). Doing this will, by convention, ensure that fellow programmers making use of your interface will (hopefully) understand that they should not make use of the field publicly. If they do so, then the implication is that they may break things. If they wish to extend your class with their own implementation, then they can make use of your private field freely.

Extending classes

Inheritance within the Class pattern can very simply be achieved by using the `class` ... `extends` syntax like so:

```
class Animal {}
class Tiger extends Animal {}
```

This will ensure that any instance of `Tiger` will have `[[Prototype]]`, which itself has `[[Prototype]]` of `Animal.prototype`:

```
Object.getPrototypeOf(new Tiger()) === Tiger.prototype;
Object.getPrototypeOf(Tiger.prototype) === Animal.prototype;
```

Here, we have confirmed that each new instance of `Tiger` has `[[Prototype]]` of `Tiger.prototype` and that `Tiger.prototype` inherits from `Animal.prototype`.

Mixing-in classes

Conventionally, an extension is used not only to create semantic sub-classes but also to provide mixins of methods. JavaScript provides no native mixing-in mechanism so to achieve it you, either need to augment the prototype after the definition or effectively inherit from your mixins (as if they are superclasses).

Augmenting a `prototype` with your mixins is the simplest approach. We can achieve this by specifying mixins as objects and then adding them to `prototype` of a class via a convenient method such as `Object.assign`:

```
const fooMixin = { foo() {} };
const bazMixin = { baz() {} };

class MyClass {}
Object.assign(MyClass.prototype, fooMixin, bazMixin);
```

This approach, however, does not allow `MyClass` to override its own mixin methods:

```
// Specify MyClass with its own foo() method:
class MyClass { foo() {} }

// Apply Mixins:
Object.assign(MyClass.prototype, fooMixin, bazMixin);

// Observe that the mixins have overwritten MyClass's foo():
new MyClass().foo === fooMixin.foo; // true (not ideal)
```

This is expected behavior but creates a headache for us in some cases. Therefore, to achieve a more generalized mixin approach, we can explore a different mechanism. Instead of directly *mixing-in* methods to an existing `prototype` object, we can use inheritance. This can most easily be achieved by so-called *Subclass Factories*. These are essentially just functions that themselves return a class that extends a specified super-class:

```
const fooSubclassFactory = SuperClass => {
  return class extends SuperClass {
    fooMethod1() {}
    fooMethod2() {}
  };
};
```

Here's an example of how it might work in reality:

```
const greetingsMixin = Super => class extends Super {
  hello() { return 'hello'; }
  hi() { return 'hi'; }
  heya() { return 'heya'; }
};

class Human {}
class Programmer extends greetingsMixin(Human) {}

new Programmer().hi(); // => "hi"
```

We can additionally implement a helper to combine any number of these *Subclass Factories*. It can do so by constructing a chain (or tree) of `[[Prototype]]` links that is as long as the list of `mixins` we provide:

```
function mixin(...mixins) {
  return mixins.reduce((base, mixin) => {
    return mixin(base);
  }, Object);
}
```

 Note how we have the default `base` class of our mixin reduction as `Object`. This is to ensure that `Object` is always at the top of our inheritance tree (and that we're not creating pointless intermediary classes).

And here's how we would make use of our `mixin` helper: first, we'd define our sub-class factories (that is, the actual mixins):

```
const alpha = Super => class extends Super { alphaMethod() {} };
const bravo = Super => class extends Super { braveMethod() {} };
```

Then, we can construct a class definition using both of these mixins via the `mixin` helper:

```
class MyClass extends mixin(alpha, bravo) {
  myMethod() {}
};
```

This means that the result's `MyClass` instances will have access to its own prototype (containing `myMethod`), alpha's prototype (containing `alphaMethod`), and bravo's prototype (containing `bravoMethod`):

```
typeof new MyClass().myMethod;    // => "function"
typeof new MyClass().alphaMethod; // => "function"
typeof new MyClass().braveMethod; // => "function"
```

Mixins can be awkward to get right, so it helps to utilize a library or proven piece of code to take care of this for you. The mixin mechanism you should use will probably depend on the exact characteristics you're seeking. In this section, we've seen two examples: one where we compose methods into a singular `[[Prototype]]` via `Object.assign()`, and another where we create a tree of inheritance (that is, a chain of `[[Prototypes]]`) to represent our mixin hierarchy. Hopefully, you are now in a better position to select which one of these (or indeed, all of the others available online) are best suited to your needs.

Accessing a super-class

All functions within a class defined using the method definition syntax have the `super` binding available, which provides access to the super-class and its properties. The `super()` function is available to invoke directly (which will call the constructor of the super-class) and can provide access to specific methods (`super.methodName()`).

If you are extending another class and you are defining your own constructor, you must call `super()` and you must do so before any other code within your constructor that modifies the instance (that is, `this`) in any way:

```
class Tiger extends Animal {
  constructor() {
    super(); // I.e. Call Animal's constructor
  }
}
```

If your constructor attempts to call `super()` after modifying the instance, or if it attempts to avoid calling `super()`, then you will receive `ReferenceError`:

```
class Tiger extends Animal {
  constructor() {
    this.someProperty = 123;
    super();
  }
}

new Tiger();
// ! ReferenceError: You must call the super constructor in a derived class
// before accessing 'this' or returning from the derived constructor
```

The `super` binding and its oddities are described in greater detail in Chapter 6, *Primitives and Built-in Types* (see the section on *Function bindings*).

The Prototype pattern

The Prototype pattern involves using plain objects to act as templates for other objects. The Prototype pattern extends this template object directly without fussing with instantiation via `new` or `Constructor.prototype` objects. You can think of it as similar to conventional constructor or Class patterns minus the constructor.

Typically, you'll first create an object to act as your template. This will have all of the methods and properties associated with your abstraction. In the case of an `inputComponent` abstraction, it may look like this:

```
const inputComponent = {
  name: 'Input Component',
  render() {
    return document.createElement('input');
  }
};
```

 Note how `inputComponent` starts with a lowercase character. By convention, only constructor functions should be named with an initial capital letter.

Using our `inputComponent` template, we can then create (or instantiate) specific instances using `Object.create`:

```
const inputA = Object.create(inputComponent);
const inputB = Object.create(inputComponent);
```

As we've learned, `Object.create(thePrototype)` simply creates a new object and sets its internal `[[Prototype]]` property to `thePrototype`, meaning that any properties accessed on the new object will be looked for on `thePrototype` if they are not available on the object itself. As such, we can treat the resulting object just like any other classical instance, accessing properties as we would on instances resulting from the more conventional Constructor or Class patterns:

```
inputA.render();
```

For convenience, we could also introduce a method on `inputComponent` itself designed to do the object creation work:

```
inputComponent.extend = function() {
  return Object.create(this);
};
```

This means that we can create individual instances with slightly less code:

```
const inputA = inputComponent.extend();
const inputB = inputComponent.extend();
```

And if we wish to create other types of inputs, then we can easily extend `inputComponent`, as we already have; add some methods to our the resulting object; and then offer that new object up for others to extend:

```
const numericalInputComponent = Object.assign(inputComponent.extend(), {
  render() {
    const input = InputComponent.render.call(this);
    input.type = 'number';
    return input;
  }
});
```

To override a particular method and access its parent, as you can see, we need to reference and call it directly (`InputComponent.render.call()`). You may expect that we should be able to use `super.render()` but, unfortunately, `super` only refers to `[[Prototype]]` of the object (the home) on which the containing method is defined. And because `Object.assign()` effectively steals these methods off their home objects, `super` would refer to the wrong thing.

> The Prototype pattern is rather confusingly named. As we've seen, both the conventional Constructor pattern and the newer Class pattern involve the prototype, so you may want to instead refer to this pattern as the *Object Extension Pattern* or even the *No-Constructor Approach to Prototypal Inheritance*. Whatever you decide, it's quite a rare pattern. The classical OOP patterns are usually favored.

When to use the Prototype pattern

The Prototype pattern is most useful in scenarios where you have an abstraction that will have varying characteristics between instances (or extensions) but does not require construction. At its core, the Prototype pattern really only refers to the extension mechanism (that is, via `Object.create`), so it can equally be used in any scenario where you have objects that may semantically relate to other objects via inheritance.

Imagine a scenario in which we need to represent sandwich data. Every sandwich has a name, a bread type, and three slots for ingredients. For example, here is the representation of a BLT:

```
const theBLT = {
  name: 'The BLT',
  breadType: 'Granary',
  slotA: 'Bacon',
  slotB: 'Lettuce',
  slotC: 'Tomato'
};
```

We may wish to create an adaptation of the BLT, reusing most of its characteristics except the Tomato ingredient, which will be replaced with Avocado. We could simply clone the object wholesale, by using Object.assign to copy all the properties from theBLT to a fresh object and then specifically copying over (that is, overwriting) slotC:

```
const theBLA = Object.assign({}, theBLT, {
  slotC: 'Avocado'
});
```

But what if the BLT's breadType was changed? Let's take a look:

```
theBLT.breadType = 'Sourdough';
theBLA.breadType; // => 'Granary'
```

Now, theBLA is out of sync with theBLT. We have realized that what we actually want here is an inheritance Model so that breadType of theBLA will always match breadType of its parent sandwich. To achieve this, we can simply change our creation of theBLA so that it inherits from theBLT (using the Prototype pattern):

```
const theBLA = Object.assign(Object.create(theBLT), {
  slotC: 'Avocado'
});
```

If we later change a characteristic of theBLT, it will helpfully be reflected in theBLA via inheritance:

```
theBLT.breadType = 'Sourdough';
theBLA.breadType; // => 'Sourdough'
```

This constructor-less Model of inheritance, as you can see, can be useful in some scenarios. We could equally represent this data using straightforward classes but with such basic data that may be overkill. The Prototype pattern is useful in that it provides a simple and explicit mechanism of inheritance that *can* result in less clunky code (although, equally, if misapplied, can lead to more complexity).

The Revealing Module pattern

The Revealing Module pattern is a pattern used to encapsulate some private logic and then expose a public API. There are a few adaptations of this pattern, but usually it is expressed via an **Immediately Invoked Function Expression (IIFE)** that returns an object literal containing the public methods and properties:

```
const myModule = (() => {
  const privateFoo = 1;
  const privateBaz = 2;

  // (Private Initialization Logic goes here)

  return {
    publicFoo() {},
    publicBaz() {}
  };
})();
```

Any functions returned by the IIFE will form a closure around their respective scopes, meaning that they will continue to have access to the *private* scope.

An example of a real-world Revealing Module would be this simple DOM Component that contains logic for rendering a notification to users:

```
const notification = (() => {

  const d = document;
  const container = d.body.appendChild(d.createElement('div'));
  const message = container.appendChild(d.createElement('p'));
  const dismissBtn = container.appendChild(d.createElement('button'));
  container.className = 'notification';

  dismissBtn.textContent = 'Dismiss!';
  dismissBtn.onclick = () => {
    container.style.display = 'none';
  };

  return {
    display(msg) {
      message.textContent = msg;
      container.style.display = 'block';
    }
  };
})();
```

The notification variable in the outer scope will refer to the object returned by the IIFE, meaning we have access to its public API:

```
notification.display('Hello user! Something happened!');
```

The Revealing Module pattern is especially useful in scenarios where you need to have a delineation between private and public, where you have specific initialization logic, and where, for whatever reason, your abstraction does not suit more object-oriented patterns (Class or Constructor patterns).

Before the existence of class definitions and `#private` fields, the Revealing Module pattern was the only easy way to emulate real privacy. As such, it has somewhat fallen out of favor. Some programmers still make use of it but, usually, only due to aesthetic preferences.

The Conventional Module pattern

The Conventional Module pattern is usually expressed as a plain object literal with a set of methods:

```
const timeDiffUtility = {
  minutesBetween(dateA, dateB) {},
  hoursBetween(dateA, dataB) {},
  daysBetween(dateA, dateB) {}
};
```

It's quite typical for such a module to also reveal specific initialization methods such as `initialize`, `init`, or `setup`. Alternatively, we may want to provide methods that change the state or configuration of the entire module (such as `setConfig`):

```
const timeDiffUtility = {
  setConfig(config) {
    this.config = config;
  },
  minutesBetween(dateA, dateB) {},
  hoursBetween(dateA, dataB) {},
  daysBetween(dateA, dateB) {}
};
```

The Conventional Module pattern is incredibly flexible since it is just a plain object. JavaScript's treatment of functions as first-class citizens (that is, they're just like any other value) means that you can easily compose the objects of methods from functions defined elsewhere, as well:

```
const log = () => console.log(this);

const library = {
  books: [],
  addBook() {},
  log // add log method
};
```

Conventionally, you may have considered using an inheritance or mixin pattern to include this `log` method in our library module, but here we're simply composing it ourselves by referencing and inserting it directly into our object. This pattern gives us a lot of flexibility in terms of how we reuse code in JavaScript.

When to use the Conventional Module pattern

The Conventional Module pattern is useful in any scenario where you simply wish to wrap up a set of related methods or properties into something with a common name. They are often used for collections of common methods that somehow relate to each other, such as logging utilities:

```
const logger = {
  log(message) { /* ... */ },
  warn(message) { /* ... */ },
  error(message) { /* ... */ }
};
```

The Conventional Module pattern is just an object, so it's arguably unnecessary to even mention it at all. But, technically, it is an alternative to other techniques of abstraction definition, so it's useful to designate it as a pattern of its own.

The Singleton Class pattern

The Class pattern is quite quickly become the de facto pattern for creating abstractions of all types, including singletons and utility objects as well, so it may not always be the case that your class will need to be utilized as a conventionally OOP class with inheritance and instantiation. For example, we may wish to set up a utility object with a class definition so that we can define any initialization logic within the constructor and provide a semblance of encapsulation within its methods:

```
const utils = new class {
  constructor() {
    this.#privateThing = 123;
    // Other initialization logic here...
  }
  utilityA() {}
  utilityB() {}
  utilityC() {}
};

utils.utilityA();
```

Here, we're creating and immediately instantiating a class. This is similar in spirit to the Revealing Module pattern where we utilize an IIFE to encapsulate initialization logic and the public API. Here, instead of achieving that encapsulation via a scope (and the resulting closure around private variables), we are using the straightforward constructor to define our initialization. We then are using the regular instance properties and methods to define both our private variables and our public interface.

When to use the Singleton Class pattern

Singletons are useful when only one instance of a class is required. The singular instance produced is similar in nature to the Conventional or Revealing Module pattern. It enables you to wrap up an abstraction with the option of private variables and implicit construction logic. Common use cases of singletons include *Utilities, Logging, Caching, Global Event Buses*, and so on.

Planning and harmony

Deciding on which architectural and modular design patterns to use can be a tricky process, as usually at the time of deciding, it may not be immediately obvious what all of the requirements of the project are. Also, we as programmers are not omniscient. We are flawed, egoistic, and usually passionate individuals. This combination, if not kept in check, can yield chaotic code bases with designs that block the very productivity, reliability, and maintainability that we are trying to foster. To be wary of these pitfalls, remember the following:

- **Expect change and adaptation**: Every software project will involve change at some point. If we are forward-thinking in our architectural and modular designs, then we will be able to limit this future pain, but never begin a project thinking that you will create the *One True Solution*. Instead, iterate, question your judgment, and then iterate again.
- **Consult with other programmers**: Talk to the stakeholders who will have to make use of your code. That may be fellow programmers on your team or other programmers who'll be making use of the interfaces that you're providing. Field opinions and data and then make an informed decision.
- **Avoid cargo culting and ego**: Be aware of cargo culting and your ego and how, if we're not careful, we can blindly inherit ways of doing things without crucially considering their suitability, or we can be trapped by our egos: thinking that one specific design or methodology is perfect just because it's the one we personally know and love.
- **Bias toward harmony and consistency**: When designing an architecture, above all, seek harmony. There is always the possibility of many individually tailored parts of a code base, but too many internal differences can confuse maintainers and lead to a code base of splintered quality and reliability.

Summary

In this chapter, we have explored the purpose and application of design patterns in JavaScript. This has spanned a foundational introspection on what it even means for something to be a design pattern and an exploration of some common modular and architectural design patterns. We have explored the various ways we can declare abstractions using JavaScript's native mechanisms such as classes and prototypes, and some more novel mechanisms such as the Revealing Module pattern. Our deep coverage of these patterns will ensure that, in the future, we have ample options available to us when crafting our abstractions.

In the next chapter, we will be exploring real-world challenges encountered by JavaScript programmers, such as state management and network communication, and applying our knowledge of new perspectives to them.

Real-World Challenges **12**

Many challenges a JavaScript programmer faces may not be with the language itself but with the ecosystems that their code must exist within and interface with. JavaScript is usually used in the context of the web, on either a browser or server, and so the problem domains encountered are usually characterized by topics such as HTTP and the DOM. We often have to wrestle with frameworks, APIs, and mechanisms that can sometimes seem awkward, unintuitive, and complicated. In this chapter, we're going to familiarize ourselves with some of the most common challenges and the approaches and abstractions we can use to surmount them.

We will begin by exploring the DOM and the challenges inherent in building ambitious **Single-Page Applications (SPAs)** in JavaScript. We'll then explore the topics of **dependency management** and **security** as these are both increasingly vital competencies in today's landscape. This chapter is not intended as an exhaustive coverage of topics, but rather a quick whirlwind of deep-dives that you may find relevant to the weighty task of crafting clean JavaScript on today's web platform.

In this chapter, we will cover the following topics:

- The DOM and single-page applications
- Dependency management
- Security (XSS, CSRF, and so on)

The DOM and single-page applications

The **Document Object Model (DOM)** API is provided within browsers to allow developers to read from and dynamically mutate web documents. Upon its initial introduction in 1997, it was very limited in scope but has expanded greatly in the last two decades, allowing us to now have programmatic access to a wide variety of browser functionality.

The DOM itself presents us with a hierarchy of elements that are derived from the parsed HTML of a given page. This hierarchy is made accessible to JavaScript via an API. This API allows us to select elements, traverse trees of elements, and inspect element properties and characteristics. Here is an example of a DOM tree with the corresponding JavaScript used to access it:

```
<div id="topics">                          const topics = document.querySelector('#topics');

    <ul>                                    const list = topics.children[0];

        <li> JavaScript </li>               list.children[0]
            TEXT NODE                    ▶  list.children[0].firstChild.data; // => "JavaScript"

        <li> CSS </li>                      list.children[1]
            TEXT NODE                    ▶  list.children[1].firstChild.data; // => "CSS"

        <li> HTML </li>                     list.children[2]
            TEXT NODE                    ▶  list.children[2].firstChild.data; // => "HTML"

    </ul>

</div>
```

The way we access specific DOM nodes has changed over the years but its fundamental tree-like structure has remained the same. Via access to this structure, we can read from the elements, mutate them, or indeed add to the tree of elements ourselves.

Alongside the DOM API is a collection of other natively provided browser APIs that make it possible to do things such as reading cookies, mutating local storage, setting up background tasks (*workers*), and operating on the **CSS Object Model** (**CSSOM**).

As recently as the year 2012, it was quite typical for web developers to only use JavaScript to enhance experiences already manifested in the markup of a page. For example, they might've simply added a rollover state to a button or validation to a form field. Such additions were considered a type of *progressive enhancement*, where the user could experience the website without JavaScript if they wanted but having JavaScript enabled would enhance their experience in some small way.

Progressive enhancement is a principle that espouses the importance of functionality that is resilient to environmental constraints. It tells us that we should try to provide all users with as much functionality as their environment allows. It is often conceptually paired with **graceful degradation**, which is the ability for a piece of software to maintain limited functionality even when its dependencies are unmet or only partially met (for example, a client-side validated `<form>` that is submittable even on browsers without JavaScript support is said to *gracefully degrade*).

Nowadays, however, it is far more common to have the frontend portion of a web application built almost entirely with JavaScript and expressed within a single *page*. These are often termed SPAs. Instead of having the user naturally navigate around a website, loading up new pages within the browser upon each action, the SPA will instead rewrite the current page's content and the current browser address. SPAs are therefore dependent upon the user's browser supporting JavaScript and potentially other APIs too. SPAs typically do not gracefully degrade, although it is best practice (and good sense!) to provide a series of fallbacks so that the entire audience can receive functionality.

The proliferation of the SPA can be attributed to both developer experience and user experience boosts:

- **Architecture (DX)**: There is a nicer *separation of concerns* between the frontend client and the backend API layer. This can lead to a cleaner architecture that helpfully delineates *business logic* from UI. Having one code base that governs both the rendering and dynamic enhancement can vastly simplify things as well.
- **State persistence (UX)**: Users can navigate and execute actions within a web application without having to lose in-page state, such as populated input fields or scroll-position. Additionally, the UX can include multiple different panes, modals, or sections that populate independently and can be persisted regardless of other actions taken.
- **Performance (UX)**: The bulk of HTTP resources can be loaded just once within the user's browser, increasing the performance of any further actions or navigations within the application. That is, after the initial load of the application, any further requests can be optimized to be simple JSON REST responses with no unnecessary boilerplate markup so the browser spends less time re-parsing or re-rendering boilerplate HTML, CSS, and JavaScript.

The growing demands on web applications and the proliferation of the SPA have meant that programmers have come to rely much more on browser APIs, especially the DOM, to create rich and dynamic experiences. The painful truth, however, is that the DOM was never intended to cater to the creation of rich desktop-like experiences. Because of this, there have been many growing pains in bringing the DOM up to scratch with current demands. Additionally, there has been a slow and iterative process of creating frameworks that enable the development of rich experiences atop a platform that was not originally designed for them.

One of the most obvious ways in which the DOM (and browser APIs generally) does not meet the current demands of SPAs is experienced when trying to *bind the DOM to data*. We will now explore this topic in more depth.

DOM binding and reconciliation

One specific challenge that multiple frameworks have attempted to solve over the years is the *binding* of the DOM to data. We briefly discussed data-binding in the last chapter's section on MVVM. Any GUI needs to have a way of having its displayed pixels reflect its underlying data.

Via the DOM, we can dynamically create specific elements and place them as we wish. The user can then impose their intent on the application by interfacing with these elements, usually via input fields and buttons. These user actions, which we bind to via DOM events, may then affect a change in underlying data. This change needs to be reflected in the DOM. This *back-and-forth* is usually termed *two-way-binding*. Historically, to achieve this, we would manually create a DOM tree, set up event listeners on elements, and then manually mutate those DOM elements when any underlying data (or *state*) changed.

 A reminder: *State* is the current *situation* of a program: everything the user sees and everything that underlies what they see. The *state* of a given application may be represented in more than one place, and these representations may become out-of-sync. We can imagine a scenario in which the same data is displayed in two places but is not consistent.

The challenge in manually fiddling with the DOM ourselves is that it doesn't scale very well without some kind of abstraction. It is easy enough to take a piece of data and derive a DOM tree from that data, but having the DOM tree tied to changes within the data and having the data tied to user-derived changes in the DOM (for example, clicking on buttons) are quite burdensome things to implement.

DOM reconciliation

To illustrate this challenge, consider a simple shopping list in the form of an array composed of individual items as strings:

```
const shoppingList = ['Bananas', 'Apples', 'Chocolate'];
```

Deriving a DOM tree from this data is quite simple:

```
const ul = document.createElement('ul');
shoppingList.forEach(item => {
  const li = ul.appendChild(document.createElement('li'));
  li.textContent = item;
});
document.body.appendChild(ul);
```

This code would produce the following DOM tree (and append it to <body>):

```
<ul>
  <li>Bananas</li>
  <li>Apples</li>
  <li>Chocolate</li>
</ul>
```

But what happens if our data changes? And what would happen if there were <input> via which users could add new items? To accommodate these things, we would have to implement an abstraction to hold our data and raise events (or invoke callbacks) whenever the data changes. Additionally, we'd need some way of tying each individual data item to a DOM node. If the first item, "Bananas" were to be changed to "Melons", then we should only make the minimum mutations necessary to the DOM to reflect that change. In this case, we would want to replace the first <li> element's inner text node's data property (in other words, the actual text contained within the text node):

```
shoppingList[0] = 'Melons';
ul.children[0].firstChild.data = shoppingList[0];
```

This type of change, in abstract terms, is known as *DOM reconciliation* and involves reflecting any changes made to data within the DOM. There are broadly three types of reconciliation:

- **Update**: If an existing data item is updated, then the corresponding DOM node should be updated to reflect the change
- **Deletion**: If an existing data item is removed, then the corresponding DOM node should also be removed
- **Creation**: If a new data item is added, then a new DOM node should be created, appended to the correct place in the live DOM tree, and then linked as the corresponding DOM node for that data item

DOM reconciliation is a relatively simple process. We could easily create `ShoppingListComponent` ourselves with the ability to update/add/remove items, but it would be very highly coupled to the structure of the data and the DOM. The logic pertaining just to a singular update may involve, as we've seen, the specific mutation of a text node's content. If we want to change our DOM tree slightly or the structure of our data, then we have to significantly refactor our `ShoppingListComponent`.

React's approach

Many modern libraries and frameworks have sought to make this a less burdensome process by abstracting the DOM reconciliation process away behind a declarative interface. A good example of this is React, which allows you to declare your DOM tree declaratively using its JSX syntax within your JavaScript. JSX looks like regular HTML with the addition of interpolation delimiters ({ . . . }) where regular JavaScript can be written to express data.

Here, we are creating a component that produces a simple `<h1>` greeting populated with an uppercase `name`:

```
function LoudGreeting({ name }) {
  return <h1>HELLO { name.toUpperCase() } </h1>;
}
```

The `LoudGreeting` component could be rendered to `<body>` like so:

```
ReactDOM.render(
  <LoudGreeting name="Samantha" />,
  document.body
);
```

And that would result in the following:

```
<body>
  <h1>HELLO SAMANTHA</h1>
</body>
```

We might implement a `ShoppingList` component in the following way:

```
function ShoppingList({items}) {
  return (
    <ul>
    {
      items.map((item, index) => {
        return <li key={index}>{item}</li>
      })
    }
    </ul>
  );
}
```

And then we could render it in the following way, passing our specific shopping list items in our invocation of the component:

```
ReactDOM.render(
  <ShoppingList items={["Bananas", "Apples", "Chocolate"]} />,
  document.body
);
```

This is a simple example but gives us an idea of how React works. The true magic of React is in its ability to selectively re-render the DOM in reaction to changes in data. We can explore this in our example by changing data in reaction to a user action.

React and most other frameworks give us a straightforward mechanism of event-listening so that we can listen for user events in the same manner as we would conventionally. Via React's JSX, we can do the following:

```
<button
  onClick={() => {
    console.log('I am clicked!')
  }}
>Click me!</button>
```

In our case of the shopping list problem domain, we want to create <input />, which can receive new items from users. To accomplish this, we can create a separate component called ShoppingListAdder:

```
function ShoppingListAdder({ onAdd }) {
  const inputRef = React.useRef();
  return (
    <form onSubmit={e => {
      e.preventDefault();
      onAdd(inputRef.current.value);
      inputRef.current.value = '';
    }}>
      <input ref={inputRef} />
      <button>Add</button>
    </form>
  );
}
```

Here, we are using a React Hook (called useRef) to give us a persistent reference that we can re-use between component renders to reference our <input />.

React Hooks (typically named use[Something]) are a relatively recent addition to React. They've simplified the process of keeping persistent state across component renders. A re-render occurs whenever our ShoppingListAdder function is invoked. But useRef() will return the same reference on every single call within ShoppingListAdder. A singular React Hook can be thought of as the *Model* in MVC.

To our ShoppingListAdder component, we are passing an onAdd callback, which we can see is called whenever the user has added a new item (in other words, when the <form> submits). To make use of a new component, we want to place it within ShoppingList and then respond when onAdd is invoked by adding a new item to our list of food:

```
function ShoppingList({items: initialItems}) {

  const [items, setItems] = React.useState(initialItems);

  return (
    <div>
      <ShoppingListAdder
        onAdd={newItem => setItems(items.concat(newItem))}
      />
      <ul>
        {items.map((item, index) => {
          return <li key={index}>{item}</li>
        })}
```

```
      </ul>
    </div>
  );
}
```

As you can see, we are using another type of React Hook called `useState` to persist the storage of our items. `initialItems` can be passed into our component (as an argument) but we then derive a set of persistent items from these that we can mutate freely across re-renders of our component. And that's what our `onAdd` callback is doing: it is adding a new item (entered by the user) to the current list of items:

Calling `setItems` will, behind the scenes, invoke a re-render of our component, causing `<li>Coffee</li>` to be appended to the live DOM. Creations, updates, and deletions are all handled similarly. The beauty of abstractions like React is that you don't need to think of these mutations as distinct pieces of DOM logic. All we need to do is derive a component/DOM tree from our set of data and React will figure out the precise changes needed to reconcile the DOM.

To ensure we understand what's going on, when a piece of data (*state*) is changed via a Hook (for example, `setItems(...)`), React does the following:

1. React re-invokes the component (re-renders)
2. React compares the tree returned from the re-render with the previous tree
3. React makes the essential granular mutations to the live DOM for all of the changes to be reflected

Other modern frameworks borrow from this approach as well. One nice side-effect of DOM reconciliation mechanisms built into these abstractions is that, via their declarative syntax, we can derive a deterministic tree of components from any given data. This is in stark contrast to the imperative approach, within which we must manually select and mutate specific DOM nodes ourselves. The declarative approach gives us a functional purity that enables us to produce outputs that are deterministic and idempotent.

As you may recall from `Chapter 4`, *SOLID and Other Principles*, **functional purity** and **idempotence** give us standalone testable units of predictable input and output. They allow us to say *X input will always result in Y output*. This transparency aids tremendously in both the reliability and the comprehensibility of our code.

Building large web applications, even with the reconciliation puzzle out of the way, is still a challenge. Every component or view within a given page needs to be populated with its correct data and needs to propagate changes. We'll be exploring this challenge next.

Messaging and data propagation

When building a web application, you'll quickly run into the challenge of getting different *parts* or *components* within your page to talk to each other. At any single time, your application should be representing the exact same set of data. If something changes, either via user action or some other mechanism, that change needs to be reflected in all of the appropriate places.

This problem occurs at different scales. You may have a *chat* application where an entered message needs to be propagated to all participants as fast as possible. Or you may have a piece of data that needs to be represented several times within the same application view and hence all of these representations need to be kept in sync. For example, if a user changes their forename in a *profile settings* pane, then this should reasonably update other places in the visible application where their forename appears:

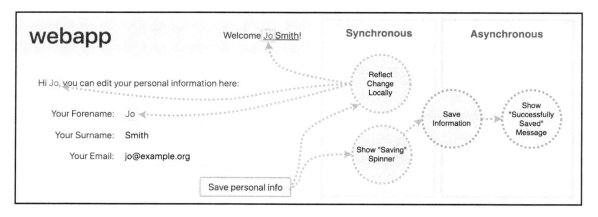

In a conventional non-SPA, the **Save personal info** button would simply submit a `<form>` and the page would then fully reload and a brand new chunk of markup with the updated state would be sent down from the server. Within an SPA, it is slightly more complicated. We would need to both submit the data to the server and then somehow update only the relevant portions of the page with the new data.

To solve this problem, we have to think carefully about the flow of data or *state* within our application. The challenge is reflecting the *source of truth* for the relevant data as soon as possible in all of the places it needs to be represented. To achieve this, we need a way for different parts of our code base to talk to each other. There are a couple of paradigms we can use here:

- **Event-oriented**: This means having specific global events that can be emitted and listened to (for example, `userProfileNameChange`). Any component or view within a page can then bind to this event and react accordingly by updating its content. The *state*, therefore, exists at the same time in many different areas (amongst various components or views).
- **State-oriented**: This means having a global state object that contains the single *source of truth* for the user's forename. This state object, or parts of it, can be recursively passed down through a component tree, meaning that, upon any change, the entire component tree is *fed* with the new state. The *state* is therefore centralized yet propagated whenever a change occurs.

If we consider a user changing their forename via `<input />`, we can envisage the following distinct paths of data flow to all components that depend upon the forename data:

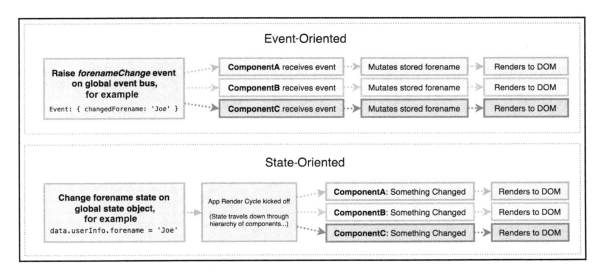

Fundamentally, these approaches achieve the same thing: they render data to the DOM. The crucial thing that differs is how the change, in this case, a mutation of the forename, is communicated throughout the application and where the data resides at any one time:

- The **event-oriented** paradigm has data living in several places at once. So, if, for whatever reason, one of those places fails to bind to the mutation of that event, then you can end up with out-of-sync data representations.
- The **state-oriented** paradigm only has one canonical representation of the data and effectively *pipes* it to the relevant views or components, so that they are always hydrated with the latest version.

The state-oriented paradigm is the increasingly more prevalent approach as it enables us to think in a clearer way about our data and its representations. We can say that we have a single representation of the data and that we derive components (or UI) from that data. It's a functionally pure approach since a component is really just a deterministic *mapping* of data to a given UI. Since any given component only cares about its input data, it doesn't need to make too many assumptions about the context it lives within. For example, we may have a UserInfo component, with an expected input of four values:

```
{
  forename: 'Leah',
  surname: 'Brown',
  hobby: 'Kites',
  location: 'Edinburgh'
}
```

Since this component does not rely on any global events or other contextual assumptions, it can be easily isolated. This aids not only in comprehension and maintainability but also enables us to write simpler tests. The UserInfo component can be extracted and tested by itself, with no inter-dependencies with the application in which it will eventually reside.

React is a popular framework for expressing this state-oriented paradigm, but many other frameworks are following suit. In React, combined with JSX, we may express our UserInfo component like so:

```
function UserInfo({ forename, surname, hobby, location }) {
  return (
    <div>
      <h1>User Info</h1>
      <dl>
        <dt>Forename:</dt> <dd>{forename}</dd>
        <dt>Surname:</dt>  <dd>{surname}</dd>
        <dt>Hobby:</dt>    <dd>{hobby}</dd>
        <dt>Location:</dt> <dd>{location}</dd>
      </dl>
```

```
      </div>
    );
  }
```

Here, we can see that this component's output is merely a mapping of its input. Such a simple case of I/O can easily be tested and reasoned about. The beauty of this harks back to the **Law of Demeter** (**LoD**), which we covered in `Chapter 4`, *SOLID and Other Principles*, which tells us that the `UserInfo` component has no business knowing where its data comes from or where it is used; it only needs to fulfill its singular responsibility: from its four inputs, it simply needs to provide us with a DOM hierarchy—clean and beautiful.

There is, naturally, a lot more complexity in real-life web applications that we have not been able to draw out with our forename example. However, if we remember the basics of separating concerns, and building views or components that are well isolated and functionally pure, then there are few challenges we won't be able to solve cleanly.

Frontend routing

When building web applications, we will likely need to mutate the address the user sees within the browser to reflect the current resource being accessed. This is a core tenet of how browsers and HTTP work. An HTTP address should represent a resource. And so, when the user wishes to change the resource they are viewing, the address should correspondingly change.

Historically, the only way of mutating the current URL within the browser would be for the user to navigate to a different page via an `<a href>` or similar. When SPAs started to become popular, however, JavaScript programmers needed to get creative. In the early days, a popular *hack* would be to mutate the hash component of a URL (`example.org/path/#hash`), which would give the user the experience of traversing a traditional website where each navigation or action would result in a new address and a new entry in the browser's history, hence enabling the use of the back-and-forward buttons in the browser.

 The approach of mutating the #hash of a URL was famously used in Google's Gmail application when it launched in 2004 so that the address bar in the browser would accurately express what email or view you were currently looking at. Many other SPAs followed suit.

A few years later, thankfully, the History API found its way into browsers and is now the standard for mutating the address in response to navigations or actions within an SPA. Specifically, this API allows us to manipulate the browser session history by pushing new *states* or replacing current ones. For example, when a user expresses a wish to change to the About Us view within a fictional SPA, we can express this as a new state pushed to their history, like so:

```
window.history.pushState({ view: 'About' }, 'About Us', '/about');
```

This would immediately change the address in the browser to '/about'. Typically, the calling code would also instigate the rendering of the associated view. Routing is the name given to these combined processes of rendering the new DOM and mutating the browser's history. Specifically, a router takes responsibility for the following:

- Rendering the view, component, or page that corresponds to the current address
- Exposing an interface to other code so that navigation can be instigated
- Listening for changes to the address made by the user (the popstate event)

To illustrate these responsibilities, we can create a simple router for an application that very simply displays Hello {color}! atop a background of that very color for any color represented in the path of the URL. Hence, /red will render a red background with the text, Hello red!. And /magenta will render a magenta background with the text, Hello magenta!:

And here is our implementation of colorRouter:

```
const colorRouter = new class {
  constructor() {
    this.bindToUserNavigation();

    if (!window.history.state) {
      const color = window.location.pathname.replace(/^\//, '');
      window.history.replaceState({ color }, color, '/' + color);
```

```
    }
    this.render(window.history.state.color);
  }
  bindToUserNavigation() {
    window.addEventListener('popstate', event => {
      this.render(event.state.color);
    });
  }
  go(color) {
    window.history.pushState({ color }, color, '/' + color);
    this.render(color);
  }
  render(color) {
    document.title = color + '!';
    document.body.innerHTML = '';
    document.body.appendChild(
      document.createElement('h1')
    ).textContent = 'Hello ${color}!';
    document.body.style.backgroundColor = color;
  }
};
```

 Notice how we're using the *Class Singleton pattern* here (as introduced in the last chapter). Our `colorRouter` abstraction is well-suited to this pattern as we need specific construction logic and we want to present a singular interface. We could have also used the **Revealing Module** pattern.

With this router, we can then call `colorRouter.go()` with our color and it'll change the address and be rendered as expected:

```
colorRouter.go('red');
// Navigates to `/red` and renders "Hello red!"
```

There is, even in this simple scenario, some complexity in our router. When the user originally lands on the page via conventional browsing, for example, perhaps by typing `example.org/red` into the address bar, the state of the history object will be empty, as we have not yet informed that browser session that `/red` is tied to the piece of state, `{ color: "red" }`.

To populate this initial state, we need to grab the current `location.pathname` (/red) and then extract the color from it by removing the initial forward-slash. You can see this logic in the `colorRouter` constructor function:

```
if (!window.history.state) {
  const color = window.location.pathname.replace(/^\//, '');
  window.history.replaceState({ color }, color, '/' + color);
}
```

For more complex paths, this logic can start to get quite complex. In a typical router, many different patterns of paths will need to be accommodated for. As such, usually, a URL parsing library will be used to properly extract each part of the URL and allow the router to route that address correctly.

It's important to use a properly constructed URL parsing library for use in production routers. Such libraries tend to accommodate all of the edge-cases implicit in URLs, and should ideally be compliant with the URI specification (*RFC 3986*). An example of this would be `URI.js` (available on npm as `uri-js`).

Various routing libraries and routing abstractions within larger frameworks have emerged over the years. They are all slightly different in the interface they present to the programmer. React Router, for example, allows you to declare your independent routes as a series of React components via JSX syntax:

```
function MyApplication() {
  return (
    <Router>
        <Route exact path="/" component={Home} />
        <Route path="/about/:employee" component={AboutEmployee} />
    </Router>
  );
}
```

Vue.js, a different framework, provides a unique routing abstraction of its own:

```
const router = new VueRouter({
  routes: [
    { path: '/', component: Home }
    { path: '/about/:employee', component: AboutEmployee }
  ]
})
```

You may notice that, in both examples, there is a URL path specified as
/about/:employee. The colon followed by a given token or word is a common way to
designate that a specific portion of the path is dynamic. It's typical to need to dynamically
respond to a URL that contains a piece of identifying information concerning a specific
resource. It's reasonable that all of the following pages should produce different content:

- /about/john
- /about/mary
- /about/nika

It would be incredibly burdensome to specify these all as individual routes (and near
impossible with large datasets), so routers will always have some way of expressing these
dynamic portions. The hierarchical nature of URLs is usually also mirrored in the
declarative APIs provided by routers and will typically allow us to specify a hierarchy of
components or views to render in response to such hierarchical URLs. Here's an example of
a routes designation that could be passed to the Router service of Angular (another
popular framework!):

```
const routes = [
  { path: "", redirectTo: "home", pathMatch: "full" },
  { path: "home", component: HomeComponent },
  {
    path: "about/:employee",
    component: AboutEmployeeComponent,
    children: [
      { path: "hobbies", component: EmployeeHobbyListComponent },
      { path: "hobbies/:hobby", component: EmployeeHobbyComponent }
    ]
  }
];
```

Here, we can see that AboutEmployeeComponent is attached to the path of
about/:employee and has sub-components that are each attached to the sub-paths of
hobbies and hobbies/:hobby. An address such as /about/john/hobbies/kayaking
would intuitively render AboutEmployeeComponent and within that would render
EmployeeHobbyComponent.

You can probably observe here how intertwined a router is with rendering. It is indeed
possible to have standalone routing libraries, but it's far more typical for frameworks to
provide a routing abstraction themselves. This allows us to specify our routes alongside a
view or component or widget, or whatever abstraction our framework provides for
rendering things to the DOM. Fundamentally, although different on the surface, all of these
frontend routing abstractions will achieve the same result.

Another real-world challenge that many JavaScript programmers will expose themselves to, whether they're predominately working on the client side or server side, is that of dependency management. We'll begin exploring this next.

Dependency management

Loading JavaScript within the context of a single web page used to be simple. We could simply place a couple of <script> tags somewhere within the document's source and call it a day.

Over the years, however, the complexity of our JavaScript has grown tremendously, alongside the demands of our users. Alongside this, our code bases have grown as well. It was, for a period, natural to just keep adding more and more <script> tags. At a certain point, though, this approach falters. Apart from the burden of multiple HTTP requests being made on every page load, this approach also made it hard for programmers to juggle their dependencies. JavaScript was typical, in those days, to spend time carefully ordering <script> placements so that, for any particular script, its dependencies were in place before it itself loaded.

It was not uncommon to see HTML markup like this:

```html
<!-- Library Dependencies -->
<script src="/js/libs/jquery.js"></script>
<script src="/js/libs/modernizr.js"></script>

<!-- Util Dependencies -->
<script src="/js/utils/data.js"></script>
<script src="/js/utils/timer.js"></script>
<script src="/js/utils/logger.js"></script>

<!-- App Widget Dependencies -->
<script src="/js/app/widgets/Nav.js"></script>
<script src="/js/app/widgets/Tile.js"></script>
<script src="/js/app/widgets/PicTile.js"></script>
<script src="/js/app/widgets/PicTileImage.js"></script>
<script src="/js/app/widgets/SocialButtons.js"></script>

<!-- App Initialization -->
<script src="/js/app/init.js"></script>
```

This approach was expensive from a performance perspective as the browser had to fetch every resource before continuing to parse and render the remaining document. Large collections of inline scripts in the <head> of an HTML document were hence considered an anti-pattern as they would block the user from being able to use the website for a significant amount of time. Even moving scripts to the bottom of <body> wasn't ideal as browsers would still have to load and execute them serially.

Predictably, our increasingly complex applications started to outgrow this approach. Developers needed more performance and a finer level of control over script loading. Thankfully, over the years, various improvements have been made in how we manage dependencies, how we bundle them, and how we then serve our code bases to the browser.

In this section, we'll explore the improvements that have occurred over the years and will seek to understand what the current best practices are, as well.

Module definition – then and now

Before 2010 (*approximately*), there were very few agreed upon methods of loading large and complex JavaScript code bases within the browser. Soon, however, developers created the **Asynchronous Module Definition (AMD)** format. This was the first popular attempt at a standard that prescribed the definition of modules within JavaScript. It included both the ability to declare dependencies on each module and an asynchronous loading mechanism. This was a vast improvement upon the slow and blocking nature of multiple inline <script> tags.

RequireJS was a popular library that supported this format. To use it, you only needed to place a single entry point <script> in your document:

```
<script data-main="scripts/main" src="scripts/require.js"></script>
```

The data-main attribute here would specify the entry point of our code base, which itself would then load the initial set of dependencies and initialize the application, like so:

```
requirejs([
  "navigationComponent",
  "chatComponent"
], function(navigationComponent, chatComponent) {
    // Initialize:
    navigationComponent.render();
    chatComponent.render();
});
```

Each dependency would then `define` itself and its own dependencies, like so:

```
// The Navigation Component AMD Module
define(
  // Name of the module
  'navigationComponent',

  // Dependencies of the module
  ['utilA', 'utilB'],

  // Definition of the module returned from function
  function (utilA, utilB) {
    return /* Definition of navigationComponent */;
  }
);
```

This is similar in spirit to modules as now specified in the ECMAScript specification, except AMD is not related to any particular language syntax. It was entirely a community-driven effort to bring something like modules to JavaScript.

The fact that AMD prescribed that each module was defined within a callback, to which dependencies could be passed, meant that loading utilities such as RequireJS could load all dependencies asynchronously and then invoke the callback when it was done. This was a significant boost to frontend JavaScript at the time because it meant we could quite easily load massive dependency graphs in a way that eased the process of writing the code (less dependency juggling) and enabled the code to be loaded into the browser in a non-blocking and more performant fashion.

At a similar time to AMD, a new standards-driven effort started to emerge called **CommonJS**. This sought to make the `require(...)` syntax a standard in various non-browser environments, with the hopeful, eventual intention of such syntax being supported on the frontend as well. Here's an example of a CommonJS module (this may appear familiar if you're accustomed to programming in Node.js):

```
const navigationComponent = require('components/navigation');
const chatComponent = require('components/chat');

module.exports = function() { /* exported functionality */ };
```

This became the standard in various non-browser environments such as Node.js, SproutCore, and CouchDB. It was also possible to compile your CommonJS modules into browser-consumable scripts similar to AMD using the CommonJS Compiler. Sometime after this, around 2017, **ES Modules** emerged. This gave us language support for `import` and `export` statements, effectively solving the historical challenge of *how to define modules* in JavaScript:

```
// ES Modules

import navigationComponent from 'components/navigation';
import chatComponent from 'components/chat';

export default function() { /* do stuff */ };
```

In Node.js, such modules must have filename suffixes of `.mjs` instead of `.js` so the engine knows to expect `import` and `export` and not the conventional CommonJS module definition syntax. In the browser, such modules can be loaded by using `<script type="module">`. However, even with ES Modules supported in browsers, it's still arguably preferable to build and bundle your JavaScript into conventional non-modular script tags. This is due to factors of performance and compatibility across browsers. Not to worry though: we can still use ES Modules when writing our code! Tools such as Babel can be used to compile and bundle the latest JavaScript syntax into JavaScript that is compatible across many environments. It's typical to set up a tool such as Babel as part of your build and development process.

npm and package.json

In the past, there was no package manager available for the JavaScript community. Instead, individuals and organizations would typically release code themselves, enabling developers to manually download the latest releases. With the introduction of Node.js and npm, this all changed. Finally, there was a central repository of packages available to pull into our projects with ease. This wasn't only useful for server-side Node.js projects but also entirely frontend projects as well. The emergence of npm is likely one of the most significant events that precipitated the maturation of the JavaScript ecosystem.

Nowadays, every project that heavily involves JavaScript will set out its manifest in a top-level `package.json` file, usually specifying, at the very least, a name, a description, a version, and a list of versioned dependencies:

```
{
  "name": "the-fruit-lister",
  "description": "An application that lists types of fruits",
```

```
    "version": "1.0",
    "dependencies": {
      "express": "4.17.1"
    },
    "main": "app/init.js"
}
```

There are a variety of available fields you can use in `package.json` so it's worth exploring the npm documentation to understand all of them. Here's a rundown of the most common ones:

- `name`: The name of the package is perhaps the most important thing. If you plan to publish the package to npm, then this name will need to be unique.
- `description`: This is a brief description of your module, to help developers understand its purpose. More detailed information is typically placed in a README or README.md file.
- `version`: This is a **Semantic Versioning (SemVer)** compatible version (of the form, `[Major].[Minor].[Patch]`, for example, `5.11.23`).
- `dependencies`: This is an object that maps every dependency package name to a version range. The version range is a string that has one or more space-separated descriptors. Dependencies can also be specified as a tarball/Git URL.
- `devDependencies`: This is identical in function to `dependencies` except for the fact that it is intended only for dependencies that are required during development, such as code quality analyzers and testing libraries.
- `main`: This can refer to the module ID that is the primary entry point to your program. For example, if your package were named `super-utils`, and someone installed it and then did `require("super-utils")`, then your `main` module's export object would be returned.

 npm assumes that your package and any packages you rely on follow the rules of SemVer, which uses a pattern of `[Major].[Minor].[Patch]` (for example, `1.0.2`). SemVer prescribes that any breaking changes must result in the *major* portion incrementing, whereas backward-compatible feature additions should result in only the *minor* portion incrementing, and backward-compatible bug fixes should result in the *patch* portion incrementing. Full details can be found at https://semver.org/.

Running npm install in the directory where package.json resides will cause npm to download the versions of dependencies that you have specified. When declaring dependencies, by default, npm will do so with a caret (^) attached, meaning that npm will pick the latest available version that complies with the major version specified. So, if you specify ^1.2.3, then anything up to 1.99.99 (and so on) may validly be installed.

There are several fuzzy *version ranges* that you can use:

- version: Must match version exactly
- >version: Must be greater than version
- >=version: Must be greater than or equal to version
- <version: Must be less than version
- <=version: Must be less than or equal to version
- ~version: Approximately equivalent to version (increment patch portion only)
- ^version: Compatible with version (increment minor/patch portions only)
- 1.2.x: 1.2.0, 1.2.1, and so on, but not 1.3.0 (x means anything here)

Arguably, the greatest issue with npm is that the unchecked introduction of new packages and their granularity in terms of functionality has led to projects with incredibly large and unwieldy dependency graphs. It's not unheard of for there to be individual packages that only export a singular narrow utility function. For example, in addition to a generic *string utility* package, you may also find a specific string function as a package of its own, such as *uppercase*. These packages are not inherently problematic—many of them serve useful purposes—but having an unwieldy dependency graph can lead to problems of its own. Any popular package that either is compromised or has not followed SemVer religiously can result in a propagation of issues across the JavaScript ecosystem, eventually affecting your project.

 To help to prevent bugs and security issues, it is highly recommended to specify your dependencies with fixed versions and update dependencies manually only when you have checked their respective changelogs. Nowadays, some tools can help you to keep dependencies up to date without sacrificing security (for example, *dependabot*, owned by GitHub).

It's recommended to use a dependency management system that ensures the integrity of downloaded packages with cryptographic hashes (a checksum that would highlight malicious changes), to ensure that the package you end up executing is definitely the one you intended to install and has not been compromised or damaged during transmission. Yarn is an example of such a system (see `https://yarnpkg.com`). It is effectively a more secure and efficient abstraction atop npm. In addition to being more secure, Yarn has the added benefit of avoiding inconsistent package resolution, which is when two installs of a given code base's dependencies will result in a potentially different set of downloaded dependencies (due to the potentially fuzzy nature of npm's version declarations). Such inconsistencies can result in the same code base behaving differently across two instances (a massive headache and harbinger of bugs!). Yarn stores the current *locked* dependency graph and corresponding versions and checksums in a `yarn.lock` file, which would look like this:

```
# THIS IS AN AUTOGENERATED FILE. DO NOT EDIT THIS FILE DIRECTLY.
# yarn lockfile v1

array-flatten@1.1.1:
  version "1.1.1"
  resolved
"https://registry.yarnpkg.com/array-flatten/-/array-flatten-1.1.1.tgz#9a5f6
99051b1e7073328f2a008968b64ea2955d2"
  integrity sha1-ml9pkFGx5wczKPKgCJaLZOopVdI=


. . .
```

Here, we see just one dependency but there'd usually be hundreds if not thousands as it would have to include not only your direct dependencies but also dependencies of those dependencies.

Dependency management is a topic that has had much written about it, so if you look online, there is no shortage of opinions and solutions. Fundamentally, as our concern is clean code, we should go back to our principles. Foremost, what we should seek in both our dependency systems and the dependencies themselves is reliability, efficiency, maintainability, and usability. In the context of dependencies, when it comes to maintainability, we are interested in both our ability to maintain code that consumes and depends upon the dependency and the ability for the dependency's maintainers to keep the dependency up to date and bug-free.

Bundling and serving

In the land of JavaScript, around the same time as AMD and CommonJS started to emerge, the rise of command-line bundlers and build tools was also on the rise. This gave us the ability to bundle large dependency graphs into singular files that could be loaded with a single `<script>`. The proliferation of build tools such as GruntJS and gulp.js meant that, slowly, the JavaScript we wrote as programmers could be oriented to cleanliness and comprehension and not the loading idiosyncrasies of browsers. We could also begin to take advantage of spin-off languages and subsets such as CoffeeScript, TypeScript, and JSX. Such JavaScript adaptations could easily be compiled and then bundled into fully operable JavaScript sent down to the browser.

The world that we have now is one in which build and bundling tools are incredibly common. There are several specific build tools, such as Grunt, gulp.js, webpack, and Browserify. Additionally, developers can easily use the npm `scripts` directive to create shortcuts to common command-line instructions.

Generally, building involves any preparations that need to occur on development code bases to make them production-ready. This can include anything from linting your CSS to bundling your JavaScript. Bundling, specifically, is concerned with the compilation and collation of large dependency graphs (of JavaScript files) into single JavaScript files. This is necessary so that we can serve our JavaScript code bases to the browser in the most performant and compatible way. Bundling utilities will usually output a file with a hash of the file's content as part of the filename, for example, `main-f522dccf1ff37b.js`. This filename can then be dynamically or statically inserted into a `<script>` tag within your HTML to be served to the browser:

```
<script src="/main-f522dccf1ff37b.js"></script>
```

Having a hash of the file's contents in the filename ensures that browsers always load the updated file and do not rely on a previously cached version of it. These files are usually *minified* as well. *Minification* involves parsing your JavaScript and producing a functionally identical but much smaller representation of it where all possible measures have been taken to take up less space, such as shortening variable names and removing whitespace and newlines. This is used in combination with HTTP compression techniques (such as `.gzip`) to ensure that the transmission over HTTP from a server to a client is as small and quick as possible. Usually, you will have distinct *development* and *production* builds since some build steps, such as minification, would make development (and debugging!) harder.

Serving bundled JavaScript to the browser is usually done with a singular `<script>` tag referencing the bundled JavaScript filename, placed at somewhere within the HTML that you serve to the browser. There are several important performance considerations when selecting an approach. The most important metric is how quickly, from the time of the initial request, a user can start using the application. When loading up superWebApp.example.com, we can imagine the following possible latencies experienced by the user:

- **Fetching resources**: Each resource fetch may involve a DNS lookup, an SSL handshake, and the completion of an HTTP request and response cycle. Responses are usually streamed, meaning that the browser may begin parsing a response before it is completed. Browsers typically make a moderate amount of requests concurrently.
- **Parsing HTML**: This involves the browser parsing every tag name and iteratively building up a DOM representation of the HTML. Some encountered tags will cause a new fetchable resource to be enqueued, such as `<img src>`, `<script src>`, or `<link type="stylesheet" href>`.
- **Parsing CSS**: This involves the browser parsing every ruleset within any fetched CSS. Referenced resources such as background images will only be fetched later if the corresponding element is found to exist on the page.
- **Parsing / compiling JavaScript**: Following the fetching of each JavaScript resource, its contents will be parsed and compiled, ready to execute.
- **Rendering HTML with CSS applied**: This will ideally occur only once, when all CSS has been loaded. If there are asynchronously loaded CSS or other aesthetic resources (such as typefaces or images), then there may be several repaints/re-renders before the page can be considered fully rendered.
- **Executing JavaScript**: Depending on the location of the corresponding `<script>`, a piece of JavaScript will execute and may then mutate the DOM or perform its own fetches. This can potentially block any other fetching/parsing/rendering from occurring.

It's usually preferable to have the execution of your JavaScript occur last, when the browser has done everything else. However, this is not always ideal. Some JavaScript may be necessary to load vital resources, and so it should be executed as early as possible so those HTTP fetches can occur concurrently with the rest of the browser's preparatory work.

Placement of your primary bundled `<script>` (your `main` code base) is vital in determining when your JavaScript will be fetched, when it will execute, and what the state of the DOM will be when it executes.

Here's a rundown of the most popular `<script>` placements and their respective advantages:

- `<script src>` **within** `<head>`: This script will be fetched as soon as `<script>` is encountered during parsing. Fetching and execution will occur in serial order and will block other parsing from occurring. This is considered a bad practice as it needlessly blocks the continued parsing of the rest of the document (and hence increases the latency of the page load, from the user's perspective).
- `<script src>` **at the end of** `<body>`: This script will be fetched as soon as `<script>` is encountered during parsing. Fetching and execution will occur in serial and will block other parsing from occurring. Usually, parsing can be considered mostly complete as `<script>` is the very last thing in `<body>`.
- `<script src defer>` **within** `<head>`: This script will be enqueued for fetching as soon as `<script>` is encountered during parsing, and this fetch will occur concurrently with the parsing of the HTML at a time that is convenient for the browser. The script will only execute once the entire document is parsed.
- `<script src async>` **within** `<head>`: This script will be enqueued for fetching as soon as `<script>` is encountered during parsing, and this fetch will occur concurrently with the parsing of the HTML at a time that is convenient for the browser. The execution of the script will occur immediately following its fetch and will block continued parsing.

Having `<script defer>` in `<head>` is usually preferable as it can be fetched as soon as possible, it won't block parsing, and it'll only be executed once parsing has completed. This tends to give the user the fastest experience if you're serving up one singular bundled script and gives your JavaScript a completely parsed DOM that it can manipulate and render within immediately.

Serving JavaScript to the browser is a simple thing, in truth. It is only complicated by the need for us to have our web applications perform quickly for the benefit of users. Increasingly complex JavaScript code bases produce increasingly large bundles, and so loading these bundles takes time. Hence, the loading performance of your JavaScript is something you'll likely need to take seriously and spend time investigating. Performance is something easily forgotten but incredibly important.

Another similarly easily forgotten topic in the JavaScript ecosystem is security, and that's what we'll now be exploring.

Security

Security is a vital part of a reliable code base. From the user, there is an implicit assumption that any given piece of software will act according to its functional expectations and will not lead to the compromise of their data or devices. *Clean code* considers security as it does other functional expectations—as a vital requirement that should be carefully fulfilled and thoroughly tested.

Since JavaScript is predominantly used in a networked situation—either on the server side or client side, it is forever fraught with the possibility of security vulnerabilities. And the fact that browsers are, effectively, sandboxed vehicles of *remote code execution* means that our end users are susceptible to just as much risk as we are. To protect ourselves and our users, we need to have a diverse understanding of the types of vulnerabilities that exist and how to counteract them. There are reams and reams of intimidating information about security vulnerabilities in the wild. We cannot hope to cover all of them in this book, but hopefully, if we explore a couple of the common vulnerabilities, then we'll be more generally cautious and aware and can begin to understand the types of measures we should put in place.

Cross-Site Scripting

Cross-Site Scripting (**XSS**) is a vulnerability that enables attackers to inject their own executable code (usually JavaScript) into the frontend of a web application so that browsers will execute as if it were trusted. There are many ways XSS can manifest but these can all be boiled down to two core types:

- **Stored XSS**: This involves an attacker somehow saving executable code within seemingly innocuous data to a web application that is persisted and then rendered back to other users of the web application. A primitive example of this is a social media website that allows me to specify my name as HTML (for example, `<em>James!</em>`) but without preventing the inclusion of potentially dangerous executable HTML, allowing me to specify a name such as `<script>alert('XSS!')`....
- **Reflected XSS**: This involves an attacker sending a victim to a URL whilst sending their executable payload along with the request, either in the URL, an HTTP header, or the request body. This executable payload is then executed when the user lands on the page. An example of this would be a search page that reflects a query back to the user (a common feature of any search page) but does so in a way that fails to escape HTML, meaning that the attacker need only send their victim to `/search?q=<script>alert('XSS!')`....

The way that either stored or reflected payloads are rendered within a page is crucial here. Traditionally, XSS vectors were limited to the server-side rendering of unescaped user-entered HTML. So, if Bob sets his social media account name to `<script>alert("Bob's XSS")...`, then when Bob's page is requested from the server, the markup returned will include that `<script>` ready to be parsed and executed by the browser. Nowadays, however, SPAs and websites that involve client-side rendering are far more common, meaning that instead of the server being at fault for allowing unescaped HTML into the document's markup, it is the client (the JavaScript code base) that is at fault for rendering dangerous content directly into the DOM. XSS attacks that rely on client-side rendering are hence often called **DOM-based XSS**.

XSS payloads can come in a variety of forms. It's very rarely as simple as a `<script>` tag. Attackers use a variety of complex encodings, archaic HTML, and even CSS to embed their nefarious JavaScript. Cleansing XSS from strings is therefore not trivial and it is instead recommended to place **no trust whatsoever** in user-entered content.

We can imagine a scenario in which our JavaScript code base has a `UserProfile` component that renders the name and profile information of any user. Upon initialization, this component requests its data from a REST endpoint that looks like `/profile/{id}.json`, returning the following JSON:

```
{
  "name": "<script>alert(\"XSS...\");</script>",
  "hobby": "...",
  "profielImage": "..."
}
```

This component then renders the received name to the DOM via `innerHTML`, without escaping or cleansing its contents:

```
class UserProfile extends Component {
  // ...
  render() {
    this.containerElement.innerHTML = `<h1>${this.data.name}</h1>`;
    this.containerElement.innerHTML += `<p>Other profile content...</p>`;
  }
}
```

All users who render the `UserProfile` component are liable to execute arbitrary (potentially damaging) HTML. This would be an issue whether the arbitrary HTML comes from a reflected or a stored source.

The prevalence of common JavaScript frameworks that abstract DOM rendering means that an attacker need only find a vulnerability within a library or framework to attack thousands of different websites. Most frameworks, thankfully, by default, have interpolation mechanisms that force inserted data to be rendered as text, not HTML. React, for example, will always produce text nodes for any data inserted via JSX's interpolation delimiters (curly braces). We can see this in effect here:

```
function Stuff({ msg }) {
  return <div>{msg}</div>
}

const msg = '<script>alert("Oh no!");</script>';
ReactDOM.render(<Stuff msg={msg} />, document.body);
```

This results in the data containing `<script>` to be literally rendered as text, so that the resulting `innerHTML` of the `<body>` element is this:

```
<div>
  <script>alert("Oh no!");</script>
</div>
```

Because the potentially dangerous HTML was rendered as text, no execution can occur and the XSS attack is prevented. This isn't the only way that an XSS attack can occur though. It's common for client-side frameworks to have templating solutions that rely on inline `<script>` tags, like so:

```
<script type="text/x-template">
  <!-- VueJS Example -->
  <div class="tile" @click="check">
    <div :class="{ tile: true, active: active }"></div>
    <div class="title">{{ title }}</div>
  </div>
</script>
```

This is a convenient way of declaring templates to be used in the later rendering of specific components, but such templates are often used in combination with server-side rendering and interpolation, and such a combination is liable to XSS if an attacker can force a dangerous string to be interpolated by the server into the template, like so:

```
<!-- ERB (Rails) Template -->
<script type="text/x-template">
  <!-- VueJS Template -->
  <h1>Welcome <%= user.data.name %></h1>
</script>
```

If `user.data.name` contains nefarious HTML, then there is nothing that our JavaScript can do on the client side to prevent the attack. By the time we render our code, it may even be too late.

In modern web applications, we have to be wary of XSS, either stored or reflected, rendered on both the server and the client. It's a mind-bending combination of possible vectors, so it's crucial to ensure that you're employing a combination of countermeasures:

- Never trust user-entered data. Ideally, do not allow users to enter any HTML. If they can, then use an HTML parsing library and whitelist specific tags and attributes that you trust.
- Never place untrusted data in an HTML comment, a `<script>` element, a `<style>` element, or where an HTML tag or attribute name should appear (for example, `<HERE ...>` or `<div HERE=...>`). If you must, place it within an HTML element and ensure it is fully escaped (for example, `&` → `&amp;` and `"` → `&quot;`).
- If inserting untrusted data into regular (non-JavaScript) HTML attributes, escape all ASCII values less than `256` with the `&#xHH;` format. If inserting into a regular HTML element's contents, then escaping the following characters is sufficient: `&`, `<`, `>`, `"`, `'`, and `/`.
- Avoid inserting untrusted data into areas where JavaScript is executed, such as `<script>x = 'HERE'</script>` or `<img onmouseover="x='HERE'">`, but if you absolutely must, ensure that the data is escaped so that it cannot break out of its quotes or its containing HTML.
- Instead of embedding JavaScript-readable data in a `<script>`, use JSON to transmit data to the client, either via a request or by embedding it in a no-op element such as `<div>` (ensuring it's fully HTML-escaped!) and then extracting and deserializing it yourself.
- Use an appropriately restrictive **Content Security Policy (CSP)** (we will explain this in the next section).

These countermeasures are not exhaustive, so it's advisable to also have a thorough readthrough of the **Open Web Application Security Project's (OWASP)** Cross-Site Scripting Prevention Cheatsheet: `https://cheatsheetseries.owasp.org/cheatsheets/Cross_Site_Scripting_Prevention_Cheat_Sheet.html`.

Content Security Policy

As an added security measure, it's important to also configure an appropriate CSP.

CSP is a relatively new HTTP header that is available on all modern browsers. It is *not* universally supported or respected, so it should not be depended upon as our sole defense against XSS. Nonetheless, if correctly configured, it can prevent the majority of XSS vulnerabilities. Browsers that don't support CSP will fall back to their default behavior of the same-origin policy, which itself provides a level of crucial security.

 The same-origin policy is a vital security mechanism employed by all browsers that restricts the ability of documents or scripts when accessing some resources from other origins (origins match when they share the same protocol, port, and host). This policy means that, for example, JavaScript within `leah.example.org` cannot fetch `alice.example.org/data.json`. With the advent of CSP, it is, however, possible for `alice.example.org` to express a level of trust and provide such access by disabling the same-origin policy just for `leah.example.org`.

The `Content-Security-Policy` header allows you to specify where different types of resources are allowed to be loaded from. It is essentially an origin whitelist that the browser will validate all outgoing requests against.

It can be specified as a regular HTTP header:

```
Content-Security-Policy: default-src 'self'
```

Or it can be specified as a `meta` tag:

```
<meta http-equiv="Content-Security-Policy" content="default-src 'self'">
```

The format of the value is one or more policy directives, separated by semicolons, where each policy directive starts with the `fetch` directive. These designate the type of resource (for example, `img-src`, `media-src`, and `font-src`), or the default (`default-src`) that all directives will fall back on if they're not separately specified. The fetch directive is followed by one or more space-separated sources, where each source specifies where resources can be loaded from for that resource type. Possible sources include URLs, protocols, `'self'` (to refer to the document's own origin), and more.

Here are some examples of CSP values with explanations for each one:

- `default-src 'self'`: This is the maximally restrictive directive that declares that only resources from the same origin as the document itself can be loaded within the document (whether from `<img>`, `<script>`, XHR, or anything else). No other origins are allowed.
- `default-src 'self'; img-src cdn.example.com`: This directive declares that only resources from the same origin as the document itself can be loaded, except in the case of images (for example, `<img src>` and CSS-declared images), which can be loaded from the origin, `cdn.example.com`.
- `default-src 'self' *.trusted.example.com`: This declares that only resources from the same origin *or* resources from `*.trusted.example.com` are valid.
- `default-src https://bank.example.com`: This declares that only resources from the SSL-secured origin, `https://bank.example.com`, can be loaded.
- `default-src *; script-src https::`: This declares that resources can be loaded from any valid URL except in the case of `<script src>`, which must load its resources from an HTTPS URL.

What an appropriately restrictive CSP is will depend entirely upon your specific web application, what kind of user-generated content you may be dealing with, and the sensitivity of the data you deal with. Having an appropriate CSP not only protects you from creating potential vectors of XSS (by loading from potentially compromised origins) but can help to counteract executing XSS vulnerabilities as well. CSP defends against XSS in the following specific ways:

- CSP disables `eval()` and other similar techniques from working. These are common vectors for XSS, especially in legacy browsers where such methods have been used to parse JSON. You can explicitly enable `eval` via the `'unsafe-eval'` source if you so desire.
- CSP disables inline `<script>` and `<style>` tags, the JavaScript protocol, and inline event handles (for example, `<img onload="..." />`). These are all common XSS vectors. You can explicitly enable these by specifying `unsafe-inline` as a source for the relevant fetch directives, but it's recommended to instead load your scripts and styles from external sources so the origins can be validated against your CSP whitelist by the browser.
- As a last-ditch effort, CSP, if well configured, can prevent currently executing XSS from loading its own malicious resources or calling home with compromised data, limiting its ability to do damage.

Subresource Integrity

Subresource Integrity (**SRI**) is a security feature within browsers that allows us to verify that the resources they fetch are delivered without any unexpected manipulation or compromise. Such manipulation could potentially occur where the asset is served from (for example, your CDN is hacked) or during network transmission (for example, a middleman attack).

To verify your script, you must provide an integrity attribute that contains the name of a hashing algorithm (such as `sha256`, `sha384`, or `sha512`) and then the hash itself. Here's an example:

```
<script src="//cdn.example.com/foo.js"
integrity="sha384-367drQif3oVsd8RI/DR8RsFbY1fJei9PN6tBnqnVMpUFw626Dlb86YfAP
Ck2O8ce"></script>
```

To generate that hash, you can use OpenSSL's CLI as follows:

```
cat FILENAME.js | openssl dgst -sha384 -binary | openssl base64 -A
```

In addition to using the integrity attribute on `<script>`, you can use it on `<link>` for the verification of CSS style sheets. To enforce SRI, you can use the helpful CSP header:

```
Content-Security-Policy: require-sri-for script; require-sri-for style;
```

Doing this will ensure that any scripts or style sheets that exist without an integrity hash will fail to load. Once fetched, if the provided integrity hash does not match the hash of the received file, then it will be ignored (as if it wasn't fetched). Using SRI together with CSP gives you a considerable defense against XSS.

Cross-Site Request Forgery

Cross-Site Request Forgery (**CSRF**) is when commands, usually in the form of HTTP GET or POST requests, are transmitted from a user without their intent, by malicious code. A primitive example would be if a banking website at `bank.example.com` had an API endpoint that allowed logged-in users to transfer a given amount to a specified account number. The endpoint might be as follows:

```
POST bank.example.com/transfer?amount=5000&account=12345678
```

Even if users were authenticated via a session cookie on the `bank.example.com` domain, a malicious website could easily embed and submit `<form>` directing the transfer to their own account, like so:

```
<form
  method="post"
  action="//bank.example.com/transfer?amount=5000&account=12345678">
</form>
<script>
  document.forms[0].submit();
</script>
```

Regardless of what HTTP method is used by the endpoint or what kind of request body or parameters it accepts, it is liable to a CSRF attack unless it ensures that the request comes from its own website. This problem is partially solved by the same-origin policy inherent to browsers, which prevents some types of requests from taking place (such as a JSON POST request via XHR or PUT/DELETE requests), but there is nothing inherent in the browser to prevent a user innocently clicking a link to a website or submitting a form that forges a malicious POST request. These actions are, after all, the entire purpose of the browser.

Since there is no inherent mechanism of the web that prevents CSRF, developers have come up with their own defenses. One common mechanism to prevent CSRF is with a CSRF token (which should really be called an **Anti-CSRF Token**). This is a generated key (random, long, and impossible to guess) that is sent down to the client with each regular request while also being stored on the server as part of the user's session data. The server will then require the browser to send that key along with any subsequent HTTP requests to verify the source of each request. So, instead of just two parameters, our `/transfer` endpoint will now have a third, the token:

```
POST bank.example.com/transfer?
  amount=5000&
  account=12345678&
  token=d55lv90s88x9mk...
```

The server can then verify that the provided token exists on that user's session data. There are many libraries and frameworks that simplify this. There are also a variety of adaptations and configurations of this basic token mechanism. Some of them will only generate a token for a given amount of time, or a given request cycle, whereas others will provide a singular token for that user's entire session. There are also a variety of ways for the token to be sent downstream to the client. The most common is within the response payload as part of the document markup, usually in the form of a <meta> element in <head>:

```
<head>
  <!-- ... -->
  <meta name="anti-csrf-token" content="JWhpLxPSQSoTLDXm..." />
</head>
```

This can then be grabbed by JavaScript and sent with any subsequent GET or POST requests made dynamically by the JavaScript. Or in the case of a conventional website without client-side rendering, the CSRF token can be sent downstream directly embedded in the <form> markup as a hidden <input>, which naturally forms part of the form's eventual submission to the server:

```
<form>
  <input
    type="hidden"
    name="anti-csrf-token"
    value="JWhpLxPSQSoTLDXm..." />

  <!-- Regular input fields here -->

  <input type="submit" value="Submit" />
</form>
```

If your web application is susceptible to XSS, then it is also inherently susceptible to CSRF, as the attacker will usually have access to the CSRF token and hence be able to masquerade any requests they make as legitimate, and the server won't be able to tell the difference. So, strong anti-CSRF measures are not sufficient on their own: you must have countermeasures for other potential vulnerabilities as well.

Whatever anti-CSRF measure you use, the crucial need is for every request that mutates a user's data or carries out a command to be verified as coming from a legitimate page within the web application itself and not some maliciously crafted external source. To get a more thorough understanding of CSRF and the available countermeasures, I recommend reading and fully digesting **OWASP's CSRF Prevention Cheatsheet**: https://cheatsheetseries. owasp.org/cheatsheets/Cross-Site_Request_Forgery_Prevention_Cheat_Sheet.html.

Other security vulnerabilities

XSS and CSRF only touch the surface of the types of attacks that we should be prepared for. Defending against all possible vulnerabilities is incredibly challenging and usually unrealistic, but we'd be foolish to not write code that is resilient against the most prevalent ones. A good general understanding of the types of vulnerabilities that exist can help us to be generally cautious in the code we write.

XSS, as explored, is a very diverse vulnerability with many possible vectors of attack. But we can defend against it in a general way by consistently and correctly discerning between trusted and untrusted data. We can limit the possibility of untrusted data wreaking havoc by placing it in only very specific places, correctly escaping it, and ensuring that we have an appropriately restrictive CSP. Likewise, with CSRF, there are countless ways for an attacker to perform it, but having a solid Anti-CSRF Token mechanism will save you from most of them. All we can hope for in the realm of security, given our limited resources, is that we can have coverage against the majority of popular attacks.

Here's a rundown of some other popular vulnerabilities that are worth being aware of:

- **SQL or NoSQL injections**: Any user-submitted data that is expressed via a SQL or NoSQL query can, if not correctly escaped, provide an attacker with access to your data and the ability to read from, mutate, or destroy it. It's similar to XSS in that both are forms of *injection attacks*, and so our defense against it, again, comes down to identifying untrusted data and then correctly escaping it.

- **Authentication/password attacks**: An attacker can gain unauthorized access to a user's account by guessing their password, brute-forcing combinations, or using a rainbow table (a database of common password hashes). Generally, it is advisable to not create your own authentication mechanisms, but instead to rely on trusted libraries and frameworks. You should always ensure that you're using a secure hashing algorithm (such as *bcrypt*). A good resource is OWASP's **Password Storage Cheat Sheet** (`https://cheatsheetseries.owasp.org/cheatsheets/Password_Storage_Cheat_Sheet.html`).

- **Dependency hijacking**: An attacker can gain access over your server-side or frontend code base by hijacking one of your dependencies. They may gain access to an npm package that exists in your dependency graph (search online for the *left-pad incident*) or compromise a CMS or CDN that you use to store JavaScript assets. To counteract these types of vulnerabilities, ensure that you use a secure package management system such as Yarn, try to use fixed version patterns in your `package.json`, always check changelogs, and on the frontend, have an appropriately restrictive CSP to prevent any malicious code from calling home.

There is always the possibility of an attack, and so we need to build that risk into our system designs. We cannot expect to be immune to these vulnerabilities, but when they do occur, we can ensure that we can fix them quickly, communicate transparently with affected users, and ensure that we carefully consider how we can prevent such vulnerabilities from occurring again.

Whether we're creating a framework for developers or a UI for non-technical users, the consumers of our code will always expect it to behave securely. This expectation is increasingly being encoded into law (for example, in EU law, the **General Data Protection Regulation (GDPR)**), so it's crucial to take it seriously and spend a good amount of time on learning and prevention. The practice of security is yet another example of how clean code is not only about our syntax and design patterns but about the very significant ways that our code affects our users and their everyday lives.

Summary

In this chapter, we have explored a variety of real-world challenges—topics that any JavaScript programmer may find themselves exposed to both within the browser and on the server. Writing clean code in JavaScript is not only about the language itself but about the web ecosystem that it exists within and the demands that this brings. Through our explorations of the DOM, routing, dependency management, and security, we have hopefully gained an insight into the technicalities of the problem domains that JavaScript often deals with, and an appreciation for the many frameworks, libraries, and standards-driven APIs that exist to help us to deal with these problems.

In the next chapter, we'll delve into the art of writing clean tests, a vitally important task, not only because it gives us confidence in our own code, but because it ensures the kind of reliability that users rightfully expect from our software.

Section 4: Testing and Tooling

In this section, we'll learn about the various ways we can foster and defend a cleaner JavaScript code base with testing and tooling. Specifically, we'll learn how to write good tests that will protect us against regressions and unclean code. By doing this, we'll learn about various tools and automation processes that we can use to deliver higher-quality code in a team environment.

This section contains the following chapters:

- Chapter 13, *The Landscape of Testing*
- Chapter 14, *Writing Clean Tests*
- Chapter 15, *Tools for Cleaner Code*

13
The Landscape of Testing

At the beginning of this book, we set out the primary tenets of clean code. Among these was reliability. There truly is no greater way to confirm reliability than to expose your code base to continued and multivariate usage. This means having real users sit in front of your software and use it, for real. Only via this type of exposure can we understand whether our code truly fulfills its purpose. However, it is usually unreasonable, and possibly even dangerous, to conduct such real-life tests constantly. If code is changed, it is possible for a piece of functionality that a user relies on to falter or regress. To prevent such cases, and to generally confirm that our expectations are met, we write tests. Without a good suite of tests, we are passively and arrogantly closing our eyes and hoping that nothing goes wrong.

In this chapter, we'll be covering the following topics:

- What is a test?
- Types of testing
- **Test-Driven Development (TDD)**

What is a test?

A software test is an automated procedure that makes assertions about a piece of code and then reports the success of those assertions back to you. A test may make assertions about anything from an individual function to the behavior of an entire feature.

Tests, much like the rest of our code, deal in layers of abstraction and granularity. If we were to test a car abstractly, we may simply seek to assert the following attributes:

- It has four wheels
- It has a steering wheel
- It drives
- It has a working horn

Obviously, this is not a very useful set of assertions for car engineers, as these attributes are either incredibly obvious or insufficiently described. The assertion It drives is important, but without extra detail, all it expresses is a generic business-oriented objective. It's similar to a project manager asking for a software engineer to ensure that a user-login portal, for example, can allow users to log in successfully. It is the engineer's job to not only implement the user-login portal but to derive working tests that successfully investigate the truth of the assertion users can log in successfully. And it is not always easy to derive good tests from generic statements.

To correctly engineer a test, we must take the generic and abstract requirements and distill them to their granular and unabstracted details. In the case of us asserting that our car *has a working horn*, for example, we can distill it like so:

> *When the driver raises at least one hand and directs the hand to depress by 2 cm the center of the steering wheel for a period of 1 second, a loud sound of fixed frequency at 400 Hz will be emitted by the car at approximately 107 decibels for 1 second.*

When we start to add crucial detail to our assertions, they become useful to us. We can use them as both guides of implementation and confirmations of functionality. Even with this added detail though, our statement is only an assertion or a *requirement*. Such requirements are a useful step in the design of software. In fact, we should be very reluctant to even begin implementing software until we have such levels of specificity.

If a client were to ask you to implement a payment form, for example, it would be wise to gather the exact requirements: what types of payments shall it accept? What other customer information requires collection? What regulations or constraints are we beholden to in our storage of this data? These expanded requirements then become the yardstick via which we, and the client, will measure completeness. It follows naturally that we can then implement these requirements as individual tests to confirm their existence in the software.

A good testing methodology will involve tests for all distinct parts of a code base and will provide the following benefits:

- **Prove fulfillment**: Tests allow us to prove to ourselves and our stakeholders that expectations and requirements are fulfilled.
- **Have confidence**: Tests allow us and our colleagues to have confidence in our code base—both that it works correctly and that it can accommodate changes without faults arising unbeknownst to us.
- **Share knowledge**: Tests allow us to share vital knowledge about how parts of our code operate together. In a sense, they are a form of documentation.

There are many second-order effects of a good testing methodology as well. The increased confidence in the code base by your colleagues will mean you can be more productive and make more significant changes more quickly, cutting costs and pain in the long run. The sharing of knowledge can enable both your colleagues and your users to perform their actions quicker, with more understanding and less overhead in time and expense. The ability to prove fulfillment enables teams and individuals to better communicate the value of their work to stakeholders, managers, and users.

Now that we've discussed the obvious benefits of tests, we can discuss how we should go about authoring them. At the core of every test is a set of assertions, so we'll now explore what we mean by assertion and how we can use assertions to encode our expectations.

The simple assertion

There are many tools, terms, and paradigms of testing. The existence of so much complexity can seem intimidating but it's important to remember that, at the core, testing is really just about making assertions about how something works.

Assertions can be made programmatically by expressing either SUCCESS or FAILURE depending on a specific outcome, as in the following example:

```
if (sum(100, 200) !== 300) {
  console.log('SUCCESS! :) sum() is not behaving correctly');
} else {
  console.log('FAILURE! :( sum() is behaving correctly');
}
```

Here, we will receive a our FAILURE! log if our sum function is not giving the expected output. We can abstract this pattern of success and failure by implementing an assert function, like so:

```
function assert(assertion, description) {
  if (assertion) {
    console.log('SUCCESS! ', description);
  } else {
    console.log('FAILURE! ', description);
  }
}
```

This can then be used to make a series of assertions with added descriptions:

```
assert(sum(1, 2) === 3, 'sum of 1 and 2 should be 3');
assert(sum(5, 60) === 65, 'sum of 60 and 5 should be 65');
assert(isNaN(sum(0, null)), 'sum of null and any number should be NaN');
```

This is the fundamental core of any testing framework or library. They all have a mechanism for making assertions and reporting both the success and failure of those assertions. It is also normal for testing libraries to provide a mechanism to wrap up or contain related assertions and, together, call them a *test* or *test case*. We can do something similar by providing a test function that allows you to pass a description and a function (to contain assertions):

```
function test(description, assertionsFn) {
  console.log(`Test: ${description}`);
  assertionsFn();
}
```

We can then use it like so:

```
test('sum() small numbers', () => {
  assert(sum(1, 2) === 3, 'sum of 1 and 2 should be 3');
  assert(sum(0, 0) === 0, 'sum of 0 and 0 should be 0');
  assert(sum(1, 8) === 9, 'sum of 1 and 8 should be 9');
});

test('sum() large numbers', () => {
  assert(
    sum(1e6, 1e10) === 10001000000,
    'sum of 1e6 and 1e10 should be 10001e6'
  );
});
```

The produced testing log from running this would be as follows:

```
> Test: sum() small numbers
> SUCCESS! sum of 1 and 2 should be 3
> SUCCESS! sum of 0 and 0 should be 0
> SUCCESS! sum of 1 and 8 should be 9
> Test: sum() large numbers
> SUCCESS! sum of 1e6 and 1e10 should be 10001e6
```

From a technical perspective, the pure action of authoring assertions and simple tests is not too challenging. Writing a test for a singular function is rarely hard. However, to write entire test suites and to thoroughly test all parts of a code base, we must utilize several more complicated testing mechanisms and methodologies to help us out.

Many moving parts

To recall the car analogy, let's imagine that we have a car sitting in front of us, and we wish to test its horn. The horn is not a standalone piece of machinery. It is embedded within the car and dependent on a power source separate to itself. In fact, what we may discover is that we must first start the car up via the ignition before the horn will work. And the success of an ignition is itself dependent upon several other components, including a working ignition switch, fuel in the tank, a working fuel filter, and a non-drained battery. The functionality of the horn is therefore dependent upon a series of many moving parts. So, our test of the horn becomes not only a test of the horn itself but effectively a test of almost the entire car! This is not ideal.

To get around this issue, we could hook the horn up to a separate power supply just for testing purposes. By doing this, we are isolating the horn, enabling the test to only reflect the functionality of the horn itself. In the testing world, this **stand-in** power supply we're using might be called a **stub** or a **mock**.

In the software world, both *stubs* and *mocks* are a type of stand-in abstraction for the *real* abstraction that provides appropriate outputs without carrying out the real work of the replaced abstraction. An example would be a `makeCreditCardPayment` stub, which returns `SUCCESS` without creating a real-world payment. This would be used in the context of testing e-commerce functionality, possibly.

Our approach of isolating the power supply of the horn is unfortunately flawed. Even if our test is successful—and the horn works—we haven't guaranteed that the horn will still work when hooked up to the real power supply within the car. The isolated test of the horn is still, arguably, useful because it tells us about any failures within the horn's specific circuitry and mechanism, but it is not sufficient on its own. We need to test how the horn will work when it is embedded in the real-life situation of having to depend on other components. In software, we call such real-life tests **integration tests** or **end-to-end tests**, while the isolated tests are typically called **unit tests**. An effective testing methodology will always include both types:

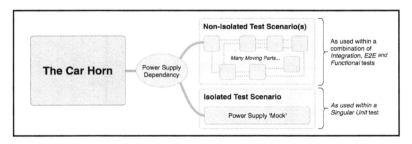

There is a risk when isolating individuals parts for testing, of creating an unrealistic scenario in which you end up not actually testing the true functionality of a code base, but instead testing the efficacy of your mocks. Here, in our car analogy, isolating the horn by supplying it with a *mock* power supply enables us to purely test the horn's circuitry and sound-making mechanism and gives us a clear path to debugging issues if the test fails. But we need to complement this test with several integration tests so that we can be confident that the entire system works correctly. Even if we have a thousand unit tests for all parts of a system, there is no guarantee of a working system without testing the integration of all of these parts.

Types of testing

To ensure a thoroughly tested code base, we must engage in different types of testing. As touched on already, the *unit* test enables us to test isolated parts, while the various combinations of parts can be tested via either **integration**, **functional**, or **E2E** tests. It's useful first to understand what we mean when we talk about a *part* or a *unit*.

When we talk about a unit of code, there is admittedly a fuzziness to the concept. Typically, it will be a piece of code that has a singular responsibility within a system. When a user wishes to perform an action via our software, they will, in fact, be activating a series of parts of our code, all working together to give the user the output they desire. Consider an app in which users can create and share images. A typical user experience (a flow or journey) may involve a few distinct steps that all involve different parts of the code base. Every action the *User* performs, often without them knowing, will encapsulate a series of code actions:

1. (User) Create a new image by uploading a photo stored on the desktop:
   1. (Code) Upload the photo via `<form>`
   2. (Code) Save photo to a CDN
   3. (Code) Show the bitmap within `<canvas>` so that filters can be applied

2. (User) Apply a filter to the image:
   1. (Code) Apply the filter via `<canvas>` pixel manipulation
   2. (Code) Update image stored on the CDN
   3. (Code) Re-download saved image

3. (User) Share the image with friends:
   1. (Code) Find the user's *friends* in the database
   2. (Code) Add the image to each friend's feed
   3. (Code) Send the *push notification* to all friends

Together, all of these steps, combined with all other steps a user could potentially take, can be considered a system. And a fully-tested system might involve **unit** tests for each individual step, **integration** tests for each pair of steps, and **functional** or **End-to-End (E2E)** tests for every combination of steps that together form a *user flow* or *user journey*. We can visualize the types of tests that may need to exist as part of a system as follows:

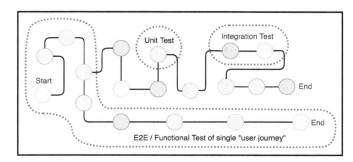

Here, we can see one **Start** point and two **End** points, indicating two distinct *user journeys*. Each dot can be thought of as a single area of responsibility or *unit* that is activated as part of these journeys. As you can see, a unit test is only concerned with a single area of responsibility. The integration test is concerned with two (or more) neighboring areas that integrate. And an E2E or functional test is concerned with all of the areas involved in a singular user journey. In the former example of our image-sharing app, we can imagine that we may have specific unit tests for actions such as uploading a photo to the CDN or sending push notifications, an integration test that tests the integration of the friends database, and an E2E test that tests the entire flow from creating to sharing a new image. Each of these testing methodologies would be vital in ensuring a truly well-tested system, and each has its own unique benefits as well as pitfalls and challenges to overcome.

Unit testing

As we described with our car analogy, a unit test is a test that deals with an isolated *unit* of code. This will usually be either a singular function or module that will make one or more simple assertions about the operation of the code.

Here are some examples of singular unit test scenarios:

- You have a `Button` component that should contain the value `Submit My Data` and should have a class of `btn_success`. You can assert these characteristics via a simple unit test that checks the attributes of the produced DOM element.

- You have a task-scheduling utility that will perform a given action at the requested time. You can assert that it does so by giving it a task to perform at a specific time and then checking for the successful execution of that task.
- You have a REST API endpoint of `/todo/list/item/{ID}` that retrieves a specific item from a database. You can assert that the route works correctly by mocking the database abstraction (providing fake data) and then asserting that requesting the URL returns your data correctly.

There are several benefits of testing individually-isolated units of code:

- **Completeness**: A given unit will typically have a small number of clearly defined requirements. As such, it's easy to ensure that you're testing the full gamut of a unit's functionality. All input variations can be tested quite easily. The very limits of each unit can also be tested, including the often complex minutiae of how something operates.
- **Reportability:** When a given unit test fails, you can quite easily discern the exact nature and circumstance of the failure, meaning quicker debugging and fixing of the underlying problem. This is in contrast to integration tests, which, as we will discover, may have far more generic reporting that doesn't indicate the exact point of failure in the code.
- **Comprehension:** Unit tests are a useful and self-contained form of documentation for given modules or functions. The narrowness and specificity of unit tests help us to fully understand how something works, easing maintainability. This is especially useful when there isn't up-to-date documentation elsewhere.

Completeness here is similar to the popular concept of *test coverage*. The crucial difference is that while coverage is about maximizing the amount of code within a code base that is tested, completeness is about maximizing the coverage of each individual unit, so that the entire input space of the unit is expressed. Test coverage, as a metric, only tells us whether things are tested, not whether they're well-tested.

There are, however, challenges that come unit-testing as well:

- **Mocking correctly**: Creating properly isolated unit tests sometimes means we have to constructs mocks or stubs of other units, as discussed in our former car analogy. It's sometimes challenging to create realistic mocks and to ensure that you're not introducing new areas of complexity and potential failures.

- **Testing realistic inputs**: Writing unit tests that provide a wide variety of realistic inputs is key although it can be challenging. It's quite easy to fall into a trap of writing tests that appear to give confidence but in fact don't test the kinds of situations that would arise when the code is in production.
- **Testing true units and not combinations**: If not carefully constructed, unit tests can begin to bloat and become integration tests. Sometimes, a test can seem very simple on the surface but in fact depends on a series of integrations beneath the surface. To re-use our car analogy, an example of this would be if we were to attempt to make a simple unit test asserting the sound of the car horn without first isolating its circuitry. We'd unknowingly be creating an E2E test.

The unit test, as the most granular type of test, is vital to any code base. It is perhaps easiest to think of it as a type of double-entry bookkeeping system. When you make a change, you must reflect that change via an assertion. This implementation-then-testing cycle is best done in proximity—one after the other—perhaps via TDD, which will be discussed later. The unit test is your way of confirming to yourself that you truly wrote the code you intended to write. It provides a level of certainty and reliability that your team and stakeholders will be hugely grateful for.

Integration testing

Integration testing, as the name suggests, deals with integrations of distinct *units* of code. An integration test will provide a more useful signal about how your software will operate in production than simple unit tests. In our car analogy, an integration test might assert the functionality of the horn, based on how it operates with the car's own power supply, instead of providing a mock power supply. It may however still be a partially isolated test, ensuring it does not involve all components within the car.

Here are a couple of examples of possible integration tests:

- You have a `Button` component that should add an item to a list when clicked. A possible integration test would be to render the component in the real DOM and check that a simulated `click` event correctly adds the item to the list. This tests the integration between the `Button` component, the DOM, and the logic that determines when items are added to the list.
- You have a REST API route of `/users/get/{ID}`, which should return user profile data from the database. A possible integration test would be to create a genuine database entry with ID of `456` and then request that data back via `/users/get/456`. This tests the integration between the HTTP routing abstraction and the database layer.

There are quite a few advantages of integrating modules and testing their behavior together:

- **Get better coverage**: Integration tests have one or more integrated modules as their test subject, and so by having such tests, we can increase our 'test coverage' throughout our code base, meaning we are increasing the amount of our code that is exposed to tests and therefore increasing the likelihood that we'll be able to catch faults.
- **Clearly see faults**: Emulating, at least in part, the integration of modules that we would see in production enables us to see real integration faults and failures as they may naturally occur. A clear view of these faults enables us to iterate with fixes quickly and retain a reliable system.
- **Expose bad expectations**: Integration tests allow us to challenge the assumptions we may have made when building individual units of code.

So, while unit tests give us a narrow and detailed view of the input and output of specific modules and functions, integration tests allow us to see how all of these modules work together and, by doing so, provide us with a view into potential problems of integration. This is incredibly useful, but there are traps and challenges to writing integration tests:

- **Isolating integrations** (avoiding big bang tests): When implementing integration tests, it is sometimes easier to avoid isolating individual integrations and instead just test a large part of the system with all of its integrations intact. This is more akin to an E2E test and is certainly useful, but it's important to also have isolated integrations so you can get granular insight into potential failures.
- **Realistic integrations** (for example, database server and client): When picking and isolating integrations to test, it is sometimes difficult to create realistic circumstances. An example would be testing how your REST API integrates with your database server but instead of having a separate database server for testing purposes, you just have a local one. This is still an insightful test but because it does not emulate the remoteness of the database server (that would exist in production) you may get a false sense of confidence. There may be failures lurking, undetected.

The integration test provides vital insight at the crucial points of interfacing and I/O that govern how all of the individual parts of a code base work together as a system. Integration tests often provide the most signal about potential faults in a system, as they are both usually quick to run and highly transparent upon failures (unlike potentially clunky E2E tests). Naturally, integration tests can only tell you things about the points of integrations they encapsulate. For more complete confidence in the functionality of a system, it's always a good idea to employ E2E testing.

E2E and functional testing

E2E testing is a more extreme form of integration test where, instead of testing individual integrations between modules, we'll test the entire system, usually by executing a series of actions that would happen in reality to produce a given result. These tests are sometimes also called **functional tests** because they are interested in testing areas of functionality from the user's perspective. Well-constructed E2E tests give us confidence that our entire system is working correctly, but are most valuable when combined with more granular unit and integration tests so that faults can be more quickly and precisely identified.

Here's a quick lowdown of the benefits of writing E2E tests:

- **Correctness and health**: E2E tests give you a clear insight into the general health of a system. Since many individual parts will effectively be tested via the typical E2E test, its success can give you a good indication that things are okay in production. Granular unit or integration tests, while very useful in their own way, don't give you this kind of systemic insight.
- **Realistic effects**: Via E2E tests we can tryout more realistic circumstances, emulating the way our code will run in the wild. By emulating the flow of a typical user, an E2E test can highlight potential issues that more granular unit or integration tests might not reveal. An example of this would be when there are race conditions or other timing issues that can only be revealed when a code base is made to run as one consolidated system.
- **More holistic view**: E2E tests give developers a holistic view of a system, enabling them to reason more accurately about how distinct modules work together to produce a working user flow. This can be incredibly valuable when trying to build a full understanding of how a system operates. Much like both unit and integration tests, E2E tests can serve as a form of documentation.

There are challenges involved in crafting E2E tests, however:

- **Performance and time costs**: E2E tests, because they involve the activation of many individual pieces of code immersed in realistic environments, can be quite expensive in terms of time and hardware resources. The time that E2E tests take to run can impede development, and so it's not rare for teams to avoid E2E tests for fear of a slowed development cycle.

- **Realistic steps**: Accurately emulating real-life circumstances in an E2E test can be a challenge. Using fake or made-up situations and data can still provide a realistic enough test but can also provide you a false sense of confidence. Since E2E tests are scripted, it's quite common to not only rely on fake data but to have actions conducted in an unrealistically fast or direct manner, missing out on possible insights you could gain by creating more human circumstances (repeat after me: *always think of the user*).
- **Complex tooling**: The point of an E2E test is to realistically emulate a user flow as it would exist in the wild. To accomplish this, we need good tooling that enables us to set up realistic environments (for example, headless and scriptable browser instances). Such tooling can be buggy or complicated to use and can introduce yet another variable to the testing process that can result in unrealistic failures (tools can give you false signals about whether things are really working).

E2E testing, although challenging to get right, can provide a level of insight and confidence that is hard to get from only unit and integration tests. In terms of automated testing procedures, E2E testing is the closest we can reasonably get to getting our software in front of real users. It is the least granular and most systemic way of discerning whether our software works in the way our users expect it to, which, after all, is what we're most interested in.

Test-Driven Development

TDD is a paradigm in which we write tests before implementation. In doing so, our tests end up informing and affecting the design of our implementation and its interface. By doing this, we begin to see tests as not only a form of documentation but a form of specification. Via our tests, we can designate how we wish something to work, writing assertions as if the functionality existed, and then we can iteratively build out the implementation such that all of our tests eventually pass.

To illustrate TDD, let's imagine that we wish to implement a word-counting function. Before implementing it, we can begin to write some assertions about how we wish for it to work:

```
assert(
  wordCount('Lemonade and chocolate') === 3,
  '"Lemonade and chocolate" contains 3 words'
);

assert(
```

```
  wordCount('Never-ending long-term') === 2,
  'Hyphenated words count as singular words'
);

assert(
  wordCount('This,is...a(story)') === 4,
  'Punctuation is treated as word boundaries'
);
```

This is a rather simple function and so we've been able to express most of its functionality in just three assertions. There are naturally other edge cases but we've pieced together enough expectations that we can begin to implement the function. Here is our first attempt:

```
function wordCount(string) {
  return string.match(/[\w]+/g).length;
}
```

Immediately running this implementation via our small test suite, we receive the following results:

```
SUCCESS! "Lemonade and chocolate" contains 3 words
FAILURE! Hyphenated words count as singular words
SUCCESS! Punctuation is treated as word boundaries
```

The `Hyphenated words` test is failing. TDD, by its nature, expects iterative failure and refactor to bring an implementation inline with a test suite. Given this particular failure, we can simply add a hyphen to our regular expression's character class (between the [...] delimiters):

```
function wordCount(string) {
  return string.match(/[\w-]+/g).length;
}
```

This produces the following test logs:

```
SUCCESS! "Lemonade and chocolate" contains 3 words
SUCCESS! Hyphenated words count as singular words
SUCCESS! Punctuation is treated as word boundaries
```

Success! Via incremental iteration, although simplified for the sake of illustration, we have implemented something via TDD.

As you may have observed, TDD is not a particular type or style of test, but rather it is a paradigm for *when*, *how*, and *why* we go about testing. The traditional view of testing as an afterthought is limited and often can force us into a position where we simply don't have time to write a good test suite. TDD, however, forces us to lead with a solid test suite, giving us a few notable benefits:

- It guides implementation
- It prioritizes the user
- It forces complete test coverage
- It forces single responsibility
- It enables quick problem domain discovery
- It gives you immediate feedback

TDD is an especially useful paradigm when getting started with testing as it will force you to take a step back before implementing something and really consider what you're trying to do. This planning stage is really helpful in ensuring that our code fully aligns with user expectations.

Summary

In this chapter, we introduced the concept of testing and how it relates to software. While brief and introductory, these foundational concepts are crucial if we're going to approach testing with an aim toward reliability and maintainability. Testing, like many other concerns in the software world, can be liable to cargo culting, so it's crucial to retain a perspective on the fundamentals and the theory behind the tests we write. Testing, at its core, is about proving expectations and protecting against faults. We've covered the differences between unit, integration, and E2E tests, discussing both the advantages and challenges inherent in each.

In the next chapter, we'll look into how we can take this knowledge and apply it to crafting clean tests alongside real-life examples. Specifically, we will cover what measures and guiding principles we can use to ensure that our tests and the assertions within them are reliable, intuitive, and maximally useful.

Writing Clean Tests 14

In the last chapter, we covered the theory and principles underlying software testing. We delved into the benefits and challenges inherent in unit, integration, and E2E testing. In this chapter, we will take this knowledge and apply it to some real-world examples.

It's not sufficient to simply understand what testing is and see its merits from a business perspective. The tests we write form a significant part of our code bases, and should hence be crafted in the same careful manner as all other code we write. We want to craft tests that not only give us confidence that our code works as intended, but are themselves reliable, efficient, maintainable, and usable. We must also be wary of writing overly complex tests. Doing so can trap us in a situation where our tests increase the burden of understanding and lead to more overall complexity and flakiness in the code base, reducing overall productivity and satisfaction.

If wielded with care and caution, tests can give code bases a clarity and cleanliness that enables users and colleagues to carry out their work with greater speed and quality. In the following sections, we'll explore the best practices to stand by and potential pitfalls to avoid when writing tests.

In this chapter, we will cover the following topics:

- Testing the right thing
- Writing intuitive assertions
- Creating clear hierarchies
- Providing final clarity
- Creating clean directory structures

Testing the right thing

One of the most important considerations when writing any test, whether a granular **unit test** or a far-reaching **E2E test**, is the question of *what* to test. It's entirely possible to test the wrong thing; doing so can give us false confidence in our code. We may write a huge test suite and walk away grinning, thinking that our code now fulfills all expectations and is utterly fault-tolerant. But our test suite may not test the things we think it does. Perhaps it only tests a few narrow use cases, leaving us exposed to many possibilities of breakage. Or perhaps it conducts tests in a way that is never emulated in reality, leading to a situation where our tests don't protect us from failures in production. To protect us against these possibilities, we must understand what we truly wish to test.

Consider a function that we've written to extract phone numbers of a specified format from arbitrary strings. The phone numbers can be in a variety of forms, but will always have between 9 and 12 digits:

- 0800-144-144
- 07792316877
- 01263 109388
- 111-222-333
- 0822 888 111

Here is our current implementation:

```
function extractPhoneNumbers(string) {
  return string.match(/(?:[0-9][- ]?)+/g);
}
```

We decide to write a test to assert the correctness of our code:

```
expect(
  extractPhoneNumbers('my number is 0899192032')
).toEqual([
  '0899192032'
]);
```

The assertions we use are vital. It's important that we are testing the right thing. With our example, this should include exemplar strings that contain a complete variety of input: strings that contain phone numbers, strings that contain no numbers, and strings that contain a mixture of phone numbers and non phone numbers. It's far too easy only to test the positive cases, but it is in fact equally important to check for the negative cases. In our scenario, the negative cases include situations where there are no phone numbers to be extracted and hence may consist of strings such as the following:

- `"this string is just text..."`
- `"this string has some numbers (012), but no phone numbers!"`
- `"1 2 3 4 5 6 7 8 9"`
- `"01-239-34-32-1"`
- `"0800 144 323 492 348"`
- `"123"`

Very quickly, when composing such exemplar cases, we see this true scope of complexity that our implementation will have to cater to. Incidentally, this highlights the tremendous advantage of employing **Test-Driven Development** (TDD) to define expectations firmly. Now that we have a few cases of strings containing numbers that we *do not* wish to be extracted, we can express these as assertions, like this:

```
expect(
  extractPhoneNumbers('123')
).toEqual([/* empty */]);
```

This currently fails. The `extractPhoneNumbers('123')` call incorrectly returns `["123"]`. This is because our regular expression does not yet make any prescriptions about length. We can easily make this fix:

```
function extractPhoneNumbers(string) {
  return string.match(/([0-9][- ]?){9,12}/g);
}
```

The added `{9,12}` part will ensure that the preceding group (`([0-9][- ]?)`) will only match between 9 and 12 times, meaning that our test of `extractPhoneNumbers('123')` will now correctly return `[]` (an empty array). If we repeat this testing-and-iteration process with each of our exemplar strings, we will eventually arrive at a correct implementation.

The key takeaway from this scenario is that we should seek to test the complete gamut of inputs that we may expect. Depending on what we're testing, we can usually say there's always a limited set of possible scenarios that any piece of code we write will cater to. We want to ensure that we have a set of tests that analyze this range of scenarios. This range of scenarios is often called the **input space** or **input domain** of a given function or module. We can consider something well-tested if we expose it to a representative variety of inputs from its *input space*, which, in this case, includes both strings *with* valid phone numbers and those *without* valid phone numbers:

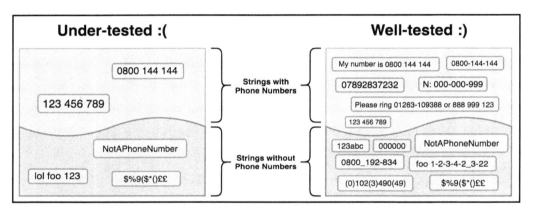

It's not necessary to test every possibility. What's more important is to test a representative sample of them. To do this, it's essential first to identify our *input space* and then partition it into singular representative inputs that we can then individually test. For example, we need to test that the phone number "012 345 678" is correctly identified and extracted, but it would be pointless for us to exhaustively test the variations of that same format ("111 222 333", "098 876 543", and so on). Doing so would be unlikely to reveal any additional errors or bugs in our code. But we should definitely test other formats with different punctuation or whitespace (such as "111-222-333" or "111222333"). It's additionally important to establish inputs that may be outside of your expected *input space*, such as invalid types and unsupported values.

A full understanding of your software's requirements will enable you to produce a correct implementation that is well tested. So, before we even begin writing code, we should always ensure that we know exactly what it is we're tasked with creating. If we find ourselves unsure what the full *input space* might be, that's a strong indicator that we should take a step back, talk to stakeholders and users, and establish an exhaustive set of requirements. Once again, this is a strong benefit of test-led implementation (TDD), where these deficits in requirements are spotted early and can hence be resolved before costs are sunk into a pointless implementation.

When we have our requirements in mind and have a good understanding of the entire *input space*, it is then time to write our tests. The most atomic part of a test is its assertions, so we want to ensure we can effectively craft intuitive assertions that communicate our expectations well. This is what we'll be covering next.

Writing intuitive assertions

The core of any test is its assertions. An assertion prescribes exactly what we expect to occur, and so it is vital not only that we craft it accurately but that we craft it in a way that our expectation is made utterly clear.

A single test will usually involve several assertions. And a test will typically follow the form of: *given an input of X, do I receive an output of Y?* Sometimes, establishing *Y* is complex and may not be constrained to a singular assertion. We may want to introspect *Y* to confirm that it is truly the desired output.

Consider a function named `getActiveUsers(users)`, which will return only the active users from a set of all users. We may wish to make several assertions about its output:

```
const activeUsers = getActiveUsers([
  { name: 'Bob', active: false },
  { name: 'Sue', active: true },
  { name: 'Yin', active: true }
]);

assert(activeUsers.length === 2);
assert(activeUsers[0].name === 'Sue');
assert(activeUsers[1].name === 'Yin');
```

Here, we have clearly expressed our expectations for the output of `getActiveUsers(...)` as a series of assertions. Given a more fully-featured assertion library or more complex code, we could easily constrain this to a singular assertion, but it's arguably clearer to separate them.

Many testing libraries and utilities provide abstractions to aid us in making assertions. The popular testing libraries, Jasmine and Jest, for example, both provide a function called `expect`, which supplies an interface with many *matchers*, each individually allowing us to declare what characteristics a value should have, as in the following examples:

- `expect(x).toBe(y)` asserts that x is the same as y
- `expect(x).toEqual(y)` asserts that x is equal to y (similar to abstract equality)

- `expect(x).toBeTruthy()` asserts that x is truthy (or `Boolean(x) === true`)
- `expect(x).toThrow()` asserts that x, when invoked as a function, will throw an error

The exact implementation of these matchers may vary from library to library, and the abstraction and naming provided may also vary. Chai.js, for example, provides both the `expect` abstraction and a simplified `assert` abstraction, allowing you to assert things in the following fashion:

```
assert('foo' !== 'bar', 'foo is not bar');
assert(Array.isArray([]), 'empty arrays are arrays');
```

The most important thing when crafting an assertion is to be utterly clear. Just as with other code, it is unfortunately quite easy to write an assertion that is incomprehensible or hard to parse. Consider the following assertion:

```
chai.expect( someValue ).to.not.be.an('array').that.is.not.empty;
```

This statement, due to the abstractions provided by Chai.js, has the appearance of a human-readable and easily understandable assertion. But it is actually quite difficult to understand exactly what's going on. Let's consider which of the following this statement might be checking:

- *The item is not an array?*
- *The item is not an empty array?*
- *The item has a length greater than zero and is not an array?*

It is, in fact, checking that the item is both not an array and that it is non-empty—meaning that, if the item is an object, it'll check that it has at least one property of its own, and if it's a string, it'll check that its length is greater than zero. These true underlying mechanics of the assertion are obscured and so, when exposed to such things, programmers may be left in a state of either blissful ignorance (*thinking the assertion works as they wish it to*) or painful confusion (*wondering how on earth it works*).

It may be the case that what we wished to assert all along was simply whether `someValue` was both not an array but was *array-like*, and as such, had a length greater than zero. As such, we can lend clarity using Chai.js's `lengthOf` method in a new assertion:

```
chai.expect( someValue ).to.not.be.an('array');
chai.expect( someValue ).to.have.a.lengthOf.above(0);
```

To avoid any doubt and confusion, we could, alternatively, assert more directly without relying on Chai.js's sentence-like abstractions:

```
assert(!Array.isArray(someValue), "someValue is not an array");
assert(someValue.length > 0, "someValue has a length greater than zero");
```

This is arguably far clearer as it explains to the programmer the exact check that is taking place, eliminating the doubt that could arise with a more abstract assertion style.

The crux of a good assertion is its clarity. Many libraries provide fancy and abstract mechanics of assertion (via the `expect()` interface, for example). These can create more clarity, but if over used, they can end up being less clear. Sometimes, we just need to **Keep it Simple, Stupid** (**KISS**). Testing code is the worst possible place in which to get fancy with egotistic or mis-abstracted code. Simple and straightforward code wins every time.

Now that we've explored the challenge of crafting intuitive assertions, we can slightly *zoom out* and have a look at how we should craft and structure the tests that contain them. The next section reveals *hierarchies* as a helpful mechanism to communicate meaning through our test suites.

Creating clear hierarchies

To test any code base, we would likely need to write a large number of assertions. Theoretically, we could have a long list of assertions and nothing else. However, doing this may make it quite difficult to read, write, and analyze the reports of tests. To prevent such confusion, it is common for testing libraries to provide some scaffolding abstractions around assertions. For example, BDD-flavoured libraries such as Jasmine and Jest supply two pieces of scaffolding: the `it` block and the `describe` block. These are just functions to which we pass a description and callback, but together, they enable a hierarchical tree of tests that makes it far easier to comprehend what's going on. Testing a `sum` function using this pattern might be done like so:

```
// A singular test or "spec":
describe('sum()', () => {
  it('adds two numbers together', () => {
    expect( sum(8, 9) ).toEqual( 17 );
  });
});
```

Behaviour-Driven Development (BDD) is a style and methodology of testing that, similar to TDD, enforces a regime where we write tests first and implementation second. More than this, however, it focuses on the importance of *behaviors* over *implementation,* since behaviors are easier to communicate and are more important from the perspective of the user (or stakeholder). BDD-style tests will hence usually use language such as *Describe X » It does Y when Z occurs...*

Non-BDD libraries tend to surround groups of assertions with simpler infinitely-nestable test blocks, like so:

```
test('sum()', () => {
  test('addition works correctly', () => {
    assert(sum(8, 9) == 17, '8 + 9 is equal to 17');
  });
});
```

As you can see, the naming of the BDD-flavored it and describe terms can help us to craft descriptions for our test suites that read like full English sentences (for example *Describe an apple » It is round and sweet*). This isn't enforced but gives us a useful nudge toward better descriptions. We can also infinitely nest describe blocks so that our descriptions can reflect the hierarchical nature of the thing we're testing. So, for example, if we were testing a math utility called myMathLib, we may imagine the following test suite with its various sub-suites and specifications:

- Describe myMathLib:
    - Describe add():
        - It can add two integers
        - It can add two fractions
        - It returns NaN for non-numeric inputs
    - Describe subtract()l:
        - It can subtract two integers
        - It can subtract two fractions
        - It returns NaN for non-numeric inputs
    - Describe PI:
        - It is equal to PI at fifteen decimal places

This hierarchy naturally reflects the conceptual hierarchy of the abstraction we're testing. The reporting provided by the testing library will usefully reflect this hierarchy. Here's an example output from the **Mocha** testing library in which every test of myMathLib passes successfully:

```
myMathLib
  add()
    ✓ can add two integers
    ✓ can add two fractions
    ✓ returns NaN for non-numeric inputs
  subtract()
    ✓ can subtract two integers
    ✓ can subtract two fractions
    ✓ returns NaN for non-numeric inputs
  PI
    ✓ is equal to PI at fifteen decimal places
```

Individual assertions come together to form tests. Individual tests come together to form test suites. Every test suite provides us with clarity and confidence regarding specific units, integrations, or flows (within E2E tests). The composition of these test suites is vital to ensuring that our tests are simple and comprehensible. We must take the time to think about how we will express the conceptual hierarchy of whatever we're testing. The test suites we create also need to be intuitively placed within the directory structure of our code base. This is what we'll explore next.

Providing final clarity

It can be said that the goal of testing is simply to describe what you have done. By describing, you are forced to assert your assumed truths about how something operates. When these assertions are executed, we can then discern whether our descriptions, our *assumed truths*, correctly reflect reality.

In the act of description, we must choose our words carefully so that they express our meaning clearly and comprehensibly. Tests are one of our last *defenses* against obscurity and complexity. Some code is unavoidably complicated, and we should ideally craft it in a way that reduces its obscure nature, but if we can't fully do this, then it is the role of tests to clear up any remaining confusion and provide the *final* point of clarity.

The key to clarity while testing is to focus purely on the perspective of the person who must read through the tests (or their logged outputs). Here are some specific points of clarity to remain aware of:

- **Use names** of tests to accurately describe what the test does, being overly descriptive if necessary. For example, instead of *test that the* `Navigation` *component renders*, consider saying *test that the* `Navigation` *component renders all navigations items correctly*. Our names can also communicate the conceptual hierarchies of our problem domains as well. Recall what we said about it in the *Consistency and hierarchy* section in `Chapter 5`, *Naming Things is Hard*.

- **Use variables** as vessels of meaning. When writing tests, it is a good idea to be overly explicit with variable names or even to use variables where they may not be necessary, to fully communicate your intent. For example, consider how `expect(value).toEqual(eulersNumber)` is more understandable than `expect(value).toEqual(2.7182818)`.

- **Use comments** to explain odd behaviors. If the code you're testing does something in an unexpected or unintuitive manner, then your tests may themselves appear unintuitive. As a last resort, it is important to provide additional context and explanation with comments. Be wary, however, of stale comments that don't get updated alongside the code.

Consider the following test for `AnalogClockComponent`:

```
describe('AnalogClockComponent', () => {
  it('works', () => {
    const r = render(AnalogClockComponent, { time: "02:50:30" });
    expect(rendered.querySelector('.mm-h').style.transform)
      .toBe('rotate(210deg)');
    expect(rendered.querySelector('.hh-h').style.transform)
      .toBe('rotate(-30deg)');
    expect(rendered.querySelector('.ss-h').style.transform)
      .toBe('rotate(90deg)');
    expect(/\btheme-default\b/.test(rendered.className)).toBe(true);
  });
});
```

As you can see, this test makes several assertions about the `transform` CSS property of specific elements. It's possible to make an informed guess as to what these are, but the clarity could definitely be improved. To make this cleaner, we can use better names to reflect what we're testing, separate the tests to represent the different concepts being tested, use variable names to provide clarity about what values we're making assertions about, and use comments to explain any possibly unintuitive things:

```
describe('AnalogClockComponent', () => {

  const analogClockDOM = render(AnalogClockComponent, {
    time: "02:50:30"
  });

  const [
    hourHandTransform,
    minuteHandTransform,
    secondHandTransform
  ] = [
    analogClockDOM.querySelector('.hh-h').style.transform,
    analogClockDOM.querySelector('.mm-h').style.transform,
    analogClockDOM.querySelector('.ss-h').style.transform
  ];

  describe('Hands', () => {

    // Note: the nature of rotate/deg in CSS means that a
    // time of 03:00:00 would render its hour-hand at 0deg.

    describe('Hour', () => {
      it('Renders at -30 deg reflecting 2/12 hours', () => {
        expect(hourHandTransform).toBe('rotate(-30deg)');
      });
    });
    describe('Minute', () => {
      it('Renders at 210 deg reflecting 50/60 minutes', () => {
        expect(minuteHandTransform).toBe('rotate(210deg)');
      });
    });
    describe('Second', () => {
      it('Renders at 90deg reflecting 30/60 seconds', () => {
        expect(secondHandTransform).toBe('rotate(90deg)');
      });
    });
  });

  describe('Theme', () => {
    it('Has the default theme set', () => {
```

```
      expect(
        /\btheme-default\b/).test(analogClockDOM.className)
      ).toBe(true);
    });
  });

});
```

You'll likely observe that the *cleaner* way is far longer, but when it comes to testing, it is truly best to bias yourselves toward such lengthy descriptiveness. Being over-descriptive is better than being under-descriptive because, in the latter case, your colleagues are left with a deficit of information, scratching their heads and making a possibly incorrect guess about functionality. When we provide a generous amount of clarity and explanation, we are helping a wider diversity of colleagues and users. If we are obscure and terse, however, we are specifically limiting the set of people who can understand our code, and hence limiting its maintainability and usability.

Now that we have explored the craft of exposing *final clarity* via a well-structured test suite, we can *zoom out* once more and discuss how we might communicate the purpose and types of tests we're writing via our directory structures and file naming conventions.

Creating clean directory structures

Our test suites should usually be constrained to individual files, to delineate areas of concern for our programmer-colleagues. Organizing these test files to form a coherent part of a larger code base can be a challenge, though.

Imagine a small JavaScript code base with the following directory structure:

```
app/
  components/
    ClockComponent.js
    GalleryComponent.js
  utilities/
    timer.js
    urlParser.js
```

It's quite typical to place tests relating to particular code in sub-directories close to where that code resides. In our example code base, we may create the following `tests` sub-directories to contain unit tests for our `components` and `utilities`:

```
app/
  components/
    ClockComponent.js
```

```
    GalleryComponent.js
    tests/
       ClockComponent.test.js
       GalleryComponent.test.js
  utilities/
     timer.js
     urlParser.js
     tests/
        timer.test.js
        urlParser.test.js
```

Here are some additional notes regarding conventions, which, as we should know by now, are vital in increasing the familiarity and intuitiveness of a code base and hence its overall cleanliness:

- Tests are sometimes called specs (*specifications*). A spec is typically no different to a test, although, as a name, it is slightly more favored in the BDD paradigm. Use whichever you're comfortable with.

- It's common to see test files suffixed with .test.js or .spec.js. This is so your test-runner can easily identify which files to execute, and it is a helpful reminder to our colleagues as well.

- It's not rare to see test directories with naming patterns involving underscores or other atypical characters, for example, __tests__. These naming patterns are usually used to ensure that such tests are not compiled or bundled as part of your main source code and are easily discernible by our colleagues.

- E2E or integration tests are more commonly placed at a higher level, which alludes to their dependency on multiple parts. It's quite common to see a high-level e2e directory (or some adaptation). Sometimes, integration tests are named individually and stored at a high level; other times, they are interspersed with unit tests throughout a code base.

Once again, hierarchy is key here. We must ensure that the hierarchy of our directories helpfully mirrors the conceptual hierarchy of our code and its problem domain. As an equal and important part of a code base, a test should be placed carefully and appropriately within a code base, not as an afterthought.

Summary

In this chapter, we have applied our theoretical knowledge of testing to the practical craft of constructing real, working, and clean test suites. We looked at some of the pitfalls that exist in doing so, and we highlighted the important qualities to strive for, such as clarity, intuitive naming, and following conventions.

In the next chapter, we will be looking into a variety of tools we can use to help us to write cleaner code, from linters to compilers, and beyond!

Tools for Cleaner Code
15

The tools we use have a massive impact on the habits we fall into when writing code. When coding, just as in life, we want to gather good habits and avoid bad habits. An example of a good habit would be writing syntactically valid JavaScript. To help us enforce this good habit, we can use a linter to inform us when our code is invalid. We should consider each tool in this way. What good habit does it inspire? What bad habit does it discourage?

If we recall our original tenets of clean code (*R.E.M.U*) we can observe how various tools help us abide by them. Here's just a small collection of tools that would be of service to the four tenets:

- **Reliability**: Testing tools, user feedback, error loggers, analytics, linters, static typing tools, and languages
- **Efficiency**: Performance measurement, analytics, user feedback, UX reviews, ecological costing (for example, *carbon footprint*)
- **Maintainability**: Formatters, linters, documentation generators, automated builds, and continuous integration
- **Usability**: Analytics, user feedback, documentation generators, accessibility checkers, UX reviews, and *hallway testing*

Tools that inspire good habits work by augmenting our *feedback loops*. A feedback loop is whatever eventually makes you realize that you need to make a change. Perhaps you introduced a bug that caused an error to be logged. Perhaps your implementation is unclear and a colleague complained. If tools can catch these situations early, then it can speed up our feedback loop, enabling us to work faster and to a higher level of quality. In the following diagram, we illustrate **Our Feedback Loop** and how it is fed by information from tools at each stage of development:

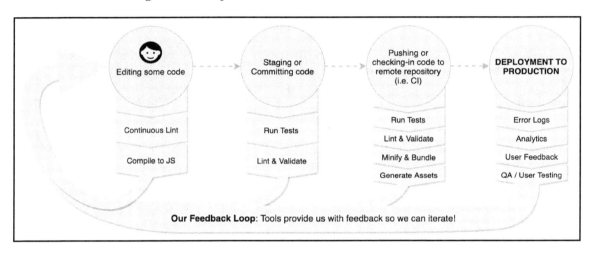

Throughout our stages of development, there are many avenues of feedback. There are linters to tell us when our syntax is problematic, static type checkers to confirm we are using types correctly, and tests to confirm our expectations. Even after deployment, this feedback continues. We have error logs that indicate failure, analytics that tell us about user behavior, and feedback from end users and other individuals informing us about breakages or areas for improvement.

 Different projects will operate in different ways. You may be a solo programmer or 1 of 100 programmers dedicated to a specific project. Regardless, there will likely be various stages of development, and the possibility of feedback exists at every stage. Tooling and communication is vital to an effective feedback loop.

In this chapter, we'll be covering a small selection of the tools that can help us in building good habits and a positive feedback loop. Specifically, we're going to cover the following:

- Linters and formatters
- Static typing
- E2E testing tools
- Automated builds and CI

Linters and formatters

A **linter** is a tool used to analyze code and discover bugs, syntax errors, stylistic inconsistencies, and suspicious constructs. Popular linters for JavaScript include *ESLint*, *JSLint*, and *JSHint*.

Most linters allow us to specify what types of bugs or inconsistencies we would like to look for. *ESLint*, for example, will allow us to specify a global configuration for a given code base in a root-level `.eslintrc` (or `.eslintrc.json`) file. In it, we can specify the version of the language we are using, which features we are using, and which linting rules we would like to be enforced. Here's an example `.eslintrc.json` file:

```
{
  "parserOptions": {
    "ecmaVersion": 6,
    "sourceType": "module",
    "ecmaFeatures": {
      "jsx": true
    }
  },
  "extends": "eslint:recommended",
  "rules": {
    "semi": "error",
    "quotes": "single"
  }
}
```

Here's an explanation of our configuration:

- `ecmaVersion`: Here, we are specifying that our code base is written in the ECMAScript 6 (2016) version of JavaScript. This means that the linter will not complain if it sees you are using ES6 features. It will, however, complain if you use ES7/8 features, as you would expect.

- `sourceType`: This specifies that we are using ES modules (imports and exports).
- `ecmaFeatures`: This informs ESLint that we wish to use JSX, a syntax extension that allows us to specify XML-like hierarchies (this is used considerably in component frameworks like React).
- `extends`: Here, we specify a default ruleset of `"eslint:recommended"`, which means that we're happy for ESLint to enforce a recommended set of rules. Without this, ESLint would only enforce the rules we specify.
- `rules`: Lastly, we are configuring the specific rules we wish to set on top of the recommended configuration:
  - `semi`: This rule relates to semicolons; in our override, we are specifying that we wish for an error to be produced in the case of a missing semicolon in case of a mere warning.
  - `quotes`: This rule relates to quotes and specifies that we wish for single quotes to be enforced, meaning that the linter will warn us if it sees double quotes in our code.

We can try our configuration out by writing a piece of code that intentionally breaks the rules:

```
const message = "hello"
const another = `what`

if (true) {}
```

If we install and run ESLint on this code (within bash: > `eslint example.js`), then we'll receive the following:

```
/Users/me/code/example.js
  1:7  error  'message' is assigned a value but never used
  1:17 error  Strings must use singlequote
  1:24 error  Missing semicolon
  2:7  error  'another' is assigned a value but never used
  2:17 error  Strings must use singlequote
  2:23 error  Missing semicolon
  4:5  error  Unexpected constant condition
  4:11 error  Empty block statement

8 problems (8 errors, 0 warnings)
4 errors and 0 warnings potentially fixable with the `--fix` option.
```

This details all of the errors in the syntax according to our configured rules. As you can see, it details the rule that was broken and the line the problem was found on. ESLint and other linting tools can be incredibly helpful in finding hard-to-spot syntax errors, some of which may, if left untouched, lead to difficult to debug functional bugs in the future. Linting also gives the code more consistency, enabling programmers to feel a sense of familiarity and endure less cognitive burden, as would be the case in a code base with many different syntax conventions.

ESLint also includes a facility for fixing a subset of these syntax errors via its `--fix` option, although you may have noticed that only a subset of errors can be fixed this way. Others will need to be done manually. Thankfully, though, there are a number of more advanced tools available to help us out. Formatters, such as **Prettier** and **Standard JS**, will take our syntactic preferences and make active changes to our code to ensure that it remains consistent. This means that programmers don't have to burden themselves with specific syntactic rules, or endlessly change code in response to linters. They can write code in the manner they desire, and when they're done, the formatter will change the code to conform to the agreed upon syntax conventions or warn the programmer if there is a severe or invalid syntax error.

To illustrate, let's run Prettier with its default configuration on a simple piece of code:

```
function reverse( str ) {
    return ( String( str ).split( '' ).reverse().join( '' ) );
}
```

When running the preceding code through Prettier, we receive the following:

```
function reverse(str) {
    return String(str)
        .split("")
        .reverse()
        .join("");
}
```

As we can see, Prettier has removed and changed some of our syntactic habits to its configured conventions. Namely, it has exchanged single quotes for double quotes, it has removed redundant parentheses, and it's made significant changes to the whitespace. The magic of formatters is that they take the pain away from the programmer. They do the work of correcting minor syntactic habits, leaving the programmer free to pursue more important work. The general trend in the industry is away from simple linters and toward more fully featured tools that combine both linting and formatting.

The decision over what syntactic conventions to abide by is configurable and entirely up to you. There are many strongly held opinions about this, but the most important tenet to uphold is consistency. I personally prefer single quotes to double quotes, for example, but if I'm working in a code base where double quotes are the established convention, then I'll have no qualms about changing my habits. Most of the time, syntactic preferences are just subjective and inherited norms, so what's important is not which norm we use, but whether or not we all abide by it.

Many of the norms we have grown used to within the JavaScript language have been guided by its dynamically typed nature. For example, we have become used to having to check manually for specific types in order to provide meaningful warnings or errors within our interfaces. For many, these norms have been challenging to adapt to, and they have grown desperate for a higher level of confidence in the types they use. Thus, people have brought various static typing tools and language extensions to JavaScript. We'll be exploring these next, and while we do, take note of how such static typing tools might change or improve your personal development feedback loop.

Static typing

As we've explored at length, JavaScript is a dynamically typed language. If wielded carefully, this can be a great benefit, allowing you to work quickly and permit a level of flexibility in your code that enables colleagues to work with it less painfully. However, there are situations in which dynamic types can create the possibility of bugs and needless cognitive burdens for programmers. Statically typed compiled languages, such as Java or Scala, force the programmer to specify the types they are expecting at the point of declaration (or infer the type by how it is used, prior to execution).

Static typing has the following potential benefits:

- The programmer can **have confidence in the types** they'll be dealing with, and thus, can make a number of safe assumptions about the capabilities and characteristics of their values, easing development.
- The code can be statically type-checked prior to execution, meaning that **potential bugs can be caught** easily and are not liable to specific (and accidental) arrangements of types.
- The maintainers and users of the code (or its APIs) have a **clearer set of expectations** to operate under and are not left guessing what may or may not work. The specification of types can itself serve as a sort of documentation.

Even though JavaScript is dynamically typed, there have been efforts to give JavaScript programmers the benefits of a static typing system. Two pertinent examples of this are Flow and TypeScript:

- **Flow** (`https://flow.org/`) is a static type checker and language extension to JavaScript. It allows you to annotate types using its own specific syntax, although it isn't considered a distinct language of its own.
- **TypeScript** (`http://www.typescriptlang.org/`) is a superset language of JavaScript, developed by Microsoft (meaning that valid JavaScript is always valid TypeScript). It is a language unto itself, with its own syntax for type annotations.

Both Flow and TypeScript allow you to declare the types that you are declaring, either alongside variable declarations or parameter declarations within functions. Here's an example of declaring a function that accepts `productName` (`string`) and `rating` (`number`):

```
function addRating(productName: string, rating: number) {
  console.log(
    `Adding rating for product ${productName} of ${rating}`
  );
}
```

Both Flow and TypeScript generally allow the annotation of types following a declaration identifier in the `IDENTIFIER: TYPE` form, where `TYPE` can be any of `number`, `string`, `boolean`, and many more. They do differ in many ways though, so it's important to investigate both. Naturally, both Flow and TypeScript, and most other static type checking technologies for JavaScript, will require a *build* or *compilation* step in order to work, as they include syntax extensions.

Be aware that static typing is not an elixir. The cleanliness of our code is not only constrained to its ability to avoid type-related bugs and difficulties. We have to *zoom out*, in our perspective, and remember to consider the user and what they're trying to achieve via our software. It's quite common to see passionate programmers get lost in the minutiae of their syntax but forgo the bigger picture. So, to change tack slightly, we'll now explore *E2E testing tools*, as E2E testing can be as significant in its effect on the quality of a code base as the typing system or syntax we use, if not more!

E2E testing tools

In the last few chapters, we explored the benefits and types of testing, including an overview of E2E testing. The testing libraries we typically use to build test suites and make assertions rarely include E2E testing facilities, so it's necessary for us to find our own tooling for this.

The aim of an E2E test is to emulate user behavior upon our application and to make assertions about the application's state at various stages of user interaction. Typically, an E2E test will test a specific user flow, such as *user can register new account* or *user can log in and buy product*. Whether we're using JavaScript on the server side or the client side, if we're building a web application, it will be hugely beneficial to carry out such testing. To do so, we need to use a tool that can artificially create the user environment. In the case of a web application, the user environment is a browser. And thankfully, there are a large number of tools that can either emulate or run real (or *headless*) browsers that we can access and control via JavaScript.

A **headless** browser is a web browser without a graphic user interface. Imagine the Chrome or Firefox browser, but without any visible UI, entirely controllable via a CLI or a JavaScript library. Headless browsers allow us to load up our web application and make assertions about it without having to pointlessly expend hardware capabilities on rendering a GUI (meaning we can run such tests on our own computers or *in the cloud* as part of our *continuous integration/deployment* process).

An example of such a tool is **Puppeteer**, a Node.js library that provides an API to control Chrome (or Chromium). It can run either headless or non-headless. Here's an example in which we open a page and log its `<title>`:

```
import puppeteer from 'puppeteer';

(async () => {
  const browser = await puppeteer.launch();
  const page = await browser.newPage();
  await page.goto('https://example.com');

  const titleElement = await page.$('title');
  const title = await page.evaluate(el => el.textContent, titleElement);

  console.log('Title of example.com is ', title);

  await browser.close();
})();
```

Puppeteer provides a high-level API that allows the creation and navigation of browser pages. Within this context, using a `page` instance, we can then evaluate specific client-side JavaScript via the `evaluate()` method. Any code passed to this method will be run within the context of the document, and will, therefore, have access to the DOM and other browser APIs.

This is how we're able to retrieve the `textContent` property of the `<title>` element. You'll have noticed that much of Puppeteer's API is asynchronous, meaning that we have to either use `Promise#then` or `await` to wait for each instruction to complete. This may be bothersome, but considering the fact that the code is running and controlling an entire web browser, it makes sense that some tasks are asynchronous.

E2E testing is rarely embraced because it is perceived as being difficult. While that perception was accurate at one point, it is no longer so. With APIs like that of Puppeteer, we can easily launch our web application, trigger specific actions, and make assertions about the results. Here's an example of using Jest (a testing library) with Puppeteer to make an assertion about the text within the `<title>` element at `https://google.com`:

```
import puppeteer from 'puppeteer';

describe('Google.com', () => {

  let page;

  beforeAll(async () => {
      const browser = await puppeteer.launch();
      page = await browser.newPage();
      await page.goto('https://google.com');
  });

  afterAll(async () => await browser.close());

  it('has a <title> of "Google"', async () => {
    const titleElement = await page.$('title');
    const title = await page.evaluate(el => el.textContent, titleElement);
    expect(title).toBe('Google');
  });
});
```

Fetching a page, parsing its HTML, and producing a DOM that we can make assertions about is a very complex process. Browsers are incredibly effective at doing this, so it makes sense to utilize them in our testing process. After all, it is whatever the browser sees that will dictate what the end user sees. E2E tests give us realistic insights into potential breakages, and it's no longer hard to write or run them. They are immensely powerful for the clean coder especially, as they let us see the reliability of our code from a more user-oriented perspective.

As with many of the tools we've explored, E2E testing may be best integrated into our development experience via automation. We'll now explore this in brief.

Automated builds and CI

As we have highlighted, there are a large number of tools available to help us write clean code. These tools can be activated manually, usually via a **command-line interface** (**CLI**) or sometimes within our IDEs. Usually, however, it is prudent to have them run as part of our various stages of development. If using source control, then this process will include a *commitment* or *staging* process and then a *pushing* or *checking-in* process. These events, when combined with the simple act of making changes to files, represent the three vital development stages that our tooling can use to generate their outputs:

- **Upon changes to files**: It is typical for JavaScript (or CSS) transpilation or compilation to occur at this stage. For example, if you're writing JS that includes the JSX language extension (React), then you're likely relying on *Babel* to constantly compile your JS hybrid to valid ECMAScript (see Babel's `--watch` command flag). It's also common to have linting or other code formatting occur when files are mutated.
- **Upon committing**: It is typical for linting, testing, or other code validation to occur at the pre- or post-commit stage. This is useful in that any invalid or broken code can be flagged before it is pushed. It's not rare for asset generation or compilation to also occur at this stage (for example, generating valid CSS from SASS, an alternative style sheet language).
- **Upon pushing**: It is typical for all processes (linting, testing, compilation, generation of assets, and so on) to occur within a remote machine when new code has been pushed to either a feature branch or the master branch. This is called **continuous integration** and allows programmers to see how their code would run when combined with their colleagues' code before deploying to production. Examples of tools and services that are used for CI include **TravisCI**, **Jenkins**, and **CircleCI**.

It can greatly ease development to have your tooling activate automatically, however, this isn't a requirement. You can lint your code, run tests, transpile your CSS, or generate compressed assets all via the CLI, without having to fuss with automation. You may find this to be slower though, and it's more likely that your tooling will be used inconsistently amongst your team if it is not standardized into a set of automations. It may be the case, for example, that your colleague always runs tests before transpiling SCSS to CSS, while you tend to do it the other way round. This can result in inconsistent bugs and *it works on my machine* syndrome.

Summary

In this chapter, we have discovered the usefulness of tooling, highlighting its power to improve our feedback loops, and how it empowers us to write cleaner code. We have explored a number of specific libraries and utilities as well, giving us a flavor of what types of tools exist and the various ways in which our abilities and habits as programmers can be augmented. We've tried out linters, formatters, static type checkers, and E2E testing tools, and we've seen the merits of tooling at every stage of development.

The next chapter begins our journey into the art and science of collaboration; a vital ingredient for anyone who wants to write clean code. We'll begin with an exploration of how we can write clear and understandable documentation.

Section 5: Collaboration and Making Changes

In this section, we'll cover the vital skills that are involved in collaborating and communicating with other people and how to navigate the need to refactor your code. In doing so, we'll discuss documentation, strategies of collaboration, and how to identify and advocate for change in your team, organization, or community.

This section contains the following chapters:

- Chapter 16, *Documenting Your Code*
- Chapter 17, *Other Peoples' Code*
- Chapter 18, *Communication and Advocacy*
- Chapter 19, *Case Study*

Documenting Your Code **16**

Documentation has a bad reputation. It is hard to find the motivation to write it, it's a nuisance to maintain, and our exposure to it over the years has convinced us that it is one of the driest and dullest methods of knowledge transfer. It doesn't have to be this way, though!

If we choose to focus entirely on the users, then our documentation can be simple and pleasant. To do this, we must first consider who the users of our documentation are. What do they want? Every user, whether a GUI end user or a fellow programmer, begins the journey of using our software with a task in mind. It's our duty, both within the software and through its documentation, to enable them to perform their task with as little pain and confusion as possible. With this in mind, in this chapter we'll explore what it might mean for us to construct such pain-free documentation. We'll specifically be covering the following:

- Aspects of clean documentation
- Documentation is everywhere
- Writing for non-technical audiences

Aspects of clean documentation

The purpose of documentation is to communicate **what a piece of software does** and **how to use it**. We can split the characteristics of clean documentation into four aspects: a clean piece of documentation communicates the **concept** of the software, provides a **specification** of its behaviors, and contains **instructions** for how to perform specific actions. And it does all of this with a focus on **usability**. By the end of this section, we will hopefully understand the vital importance of *the user* in the craft of building *clean* documentation.

Documentation is something most people don't think about a lot. It's usually an afterthought. My task in this chapter is to convince you that it can be, and should be, so much more than this. As we step into these *aspects*, forget what you know about documentation – start with a fresh canvas and see if you come away with revelations of your own.

Concept

A clean piece of documentation will communicate the underlying *concept* of the software. It'll do this by explaining what the software's purpose is in a way that allows potential users to see how they might make use of it. This can be considered the educational part of documentation: setting out the terminology and paradigms that will allow the reader to easily comprehend the other parts of the documentation and the software it describes.

To properly express the concepts of a piece of software, it's necessary to step inside the shoes of your users, seeing things from their perspective and communicating with them on their terms:

- **Determine your audience**: Who are they and what's their general technical proficiency?
- **Determine their understanding of the problem domain**: How much do they already know about this specific software project, API, or code base?
- **Determine the right the level of abstraction and best analogies**: How can you communicate in a way that makes sense to them and integrates well with their current knowledge?

Writing good documentation is a process of considering the user and then crafting the appropriate abstractions for them. You'll hopefully notice how incredibly similar this is to the process of crafting clean code. There are, in fact, very few differences. When building documentation, we are crafting a tool that the user can use to accomplish a specific set of tasks. It is our responsibility to craft it in such a way that users can easily accomplish their end goals without being overwhelmed by the sheer volume and complexity of the software:

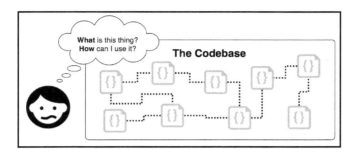

Consider a project that has taken several weeks to complete. It is a **JavaScript (JS)** library called `SuperCoolTypeAnimator` that other programmers can use to create typeface transitions. It allows them to display to the user a block of text that is animated from one typeface to another (for example, from Helvetica to Times New Roman). It's a rather complex code base that calculates these transitions manually. The depth of its complexity has meant that you, the programmer, have discovered far more about ligatures, serifs, and path interpolation than you ever thought possible. After months of being immersed in this increasingly deep problem domain, it is understandably challenging for you to share the perspective of a user who has not had your level of exposure. Thus the first draft of your documentation might start in the following way:

SuperCoolTypeAnimator is an SVG glyph animation utility that allows the creation and frame-by-frame manipulation of transitions between source glyphs and their respective target glyphs, calculating appropriate transitional anchors on the fly.

Let's compare that to the following alternative intro:

SuperCoolTypeAnimator is a JS library that allows you to animate small pieces of text from one typeface to another typeface with ease.

As introductions, the latter is far more widely understandable and will allow even non-expert users to immediately understand what the library does. The former introduction, while informative, may result in current and potential users feeling confused or alienated. The entire purpose of the software we build is to abstract away complexity, wrapping it up in a neat and simplified way. Belaboring our users with complexity should be done with regret and consideration: it is usually the *last* resort.

 The *concept* that we are attempting to communicate in our documentation concerns, above all, how our software can *help* the user. For them to understand how it can help them, we need to describe it in a way that meshes with their current understanding.

Another factor highlighted by the two introductions is their usage of special terminology (such as *glyph* and *anchor*). The usage of such domain-specific terminology is a balancing act. If your users have a good understanding of the *typeface/font* problem domain, terms such as *glyph* and *typeface* may be appropriate. There is, arguably, a high likelihood that users interested in your library are also aware of such concepts. But the use of more nuanced terms such as *transitional anchors* may be a step too far. This is likely a term that you have used within your abstraction to describe a highly complex area of implementation. It is a useful term to you, and perhaps to anyone wishing to make changes to the library, but it is perhaps less useful to users of the library. Therefore, it would be wise to avoid it in our documentation's introduction.

Specification

As well as providing a concept for the software, good documentation will also provide a *specification*, detailing the specific characteristics and behaviors of the interfaces provided by your software. This part of the documentation details the contract that the user or programmer can expect to have when using the software.

The *specification* should ideally be the simplest part of the documentation to write, for the following reasons:

- **It's literally in the code**: The specification of behavior is contained within the code and its tests, usually making it quite simple to manually write up this information as documentation. However, if it is difficult to write, then that indicates an underlying complexity in your code and its interfaces that perhaps should be fixed as a priority.
- **It's possible to automatically generate**: There exist many documentation generators that either rely on static-typing annotations or comment annotations (for example, *JSDoc*). These allow you to generate documentation for entire interfaces via a CLI or build tool.
- **It follows a fixed format**: A specification will follow a straightforward format that is simple to author. It usually contains headings for individual endpoints or method signatures, and a sentence explaining each argument.

The overriding purpose of providing a specification is to answer specific questions that a user might have about the operation of your code:

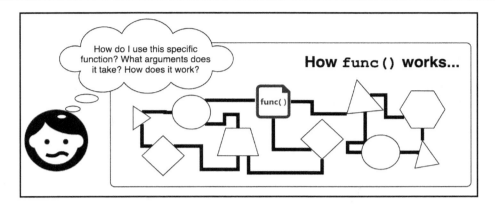

The following is an example of a specification for a function called removeWords.

```
removeWords( subjectString, wordsToRemove );
```

This function will remove the specified words from the specified subject string, returning a new string to you. A word here is defined as a string of characters bound by word boundaries (\b). For example, specifying an "I like apple juice" subjectString and ["app", "juice"] for wordsToRemove would remove only "juice", as "app" exists in the subject but is not bound by a word boundary. The following are the arguments:

- subjectString (String): This is the string that the specified words will be removed from. If you do not pass a String type, then the value you pass will be cast to a String.
- wordsToRemove (Array): This is an array containing words that you wish to remove. A null or empty array will cause no words to be removed.

As you can hopefully tell, this specification is a purely technical explanation of a function's behavior. It tells the user exactly what arguments they must provide and what output they'll receive. When writing the specification portion of your documentation, the most important qualities to abide by are clarity and correctness. Be wary of the following traps:

- **Not enough information to allow usage**: It's important to provide enough information about your implementation so that another programmer, with no knowledge of your software, can begin to make use of it. It's insufficient to only specify types of arguments, for example. Provide extra information if the knowledge domain is especially obscure.

- **Incorrect or out-of-date information**: Documentation can easily fall out of date or be incorrect. This is why it's quite common to generate documentation automatically from annotated code. That way, the chances of information being incorrect or out of date are lessened considerably.
- **Lack of examples**: It's common to only list modules, methods, and argument signatures, without providing any examples. If doing this, the chance of confusion and pain is far higher, so it's always worth providing sensible examples or linking readers to more tutorial-like documentation.

The specification is arguably the most important part of your documentation, as it explains, in clear terms, the behavior of every part of your software's relevant APIs. Ensure that you take the same care and diligence when documenting your code as you would when writing it.

Instruction

In addition to *concept* and *specification*, a clean piece of documentation will *instruct* a user in how to accomplish common tasks. These are commonly termed *walkthroughs, tutorials, how-tos*, or *recipes*.

Primarily, a user, regardless of whether they are a programmer or end user, is concerned with how to get from where they are to where they want to be. They are interested in knowing what steps to take. Without instructions for common use cases, they'll be left desperately piecing together what they know about your software from intuitions or other pieces of documentation. Consider a book about cookery that only details the ingredients and their behaviors when cooked, but doesn't contain any specific recipes that combine ingredients in a specific order. That'd be a challenging cooking book to make use of. While it may provide a highly detailed set of culinary information, it doesn't help users answer their actual questions:

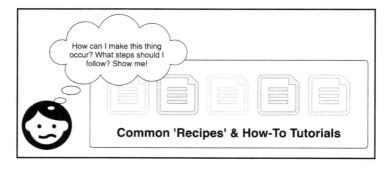

When composing instructions, whether they're in the form or video tutorials or written walk-throughs, it is important to consider what use cases are most prevalent or challenging for your users. As with many things in life, you can only reasonably cater for the bulk of prospects, not all of them. It is unreasonable to create tutorials for every single possible use case. And likewise, it is unreasonable, from a user's perspective, for you to only provide a singular tutorial for the most common use case. It is wise to strike a compromise and have a small collection of tutorials that each express:

- **Upfront expectations and prerequisites**: A set of instructions should specify what expectations the author has about the reader's hardware, software environment, and capabilities. It should also say if there is anything the reader should prepare before beginning the following steps.
- **Specific steps that a reader can emulate**: Instructions should have a number of specific steps that users can follow to reach their desired goal. The user should not have to use too much (or any) initiative when following these steps; the steps should clearly and exhaustively outline exactly what the user needs to do, with code examples if possible. It should also be obvious to the user that they have successfully completed each step (for example, *you should now receive X output*).
- **An achievable and observable goal**: Instructions should work toward a goal that can be observed by the user. It would be upsetting for the last step of a tutorial to say *this won't currently work, due to X or Y, but you would usually expect to see Z*. Ensure that your software is operating in such a way that the tutorial can be completed to its very end and the user can come away having gotten closer to whatever their overarching goal is.

 Don't just tell a user what to do. Tell them what they're accomplishing at each stage, and why it matters. That is, don't just tell me to put salt in the dish, tell me why it needs salt!

The instructional part of documentation is probably the most challenging. It requires us to take on the role of teacher and see things from another person's position of relative ignorance. Maintaining focus on the person we're teaching, the user, is absolutely vital. This feeds quite nicely into our final aspect of clean documentation: usability.

Usability

Usability is the final component in clean documentation. Just like our software, our documentation must be concerned with users and their specific needs. The previous three aspects (*concept, specification, instruction*) have focused on content, while *usability* is purely about the way in which we express that content. It's vitally important not to overwhelm or confuse user when they learn about your software:

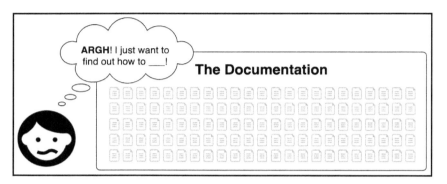

There are many ways we can confuse and overwhelm. Among them are these the following:

- **Too much content**: This can overwhelm a user who may only want to perform some specific and narrow task. They may not see the point in crawling through reams of documentation just to implement their simple task.
- **Too little content**: If a user wishes to do something that is not documented sufficiently, then they are left with few options. They either have to hope that there is community-driven documentation somewhere or that the interfaces are understandable enough to decipher without help.
- **Internal inconsistency**: This is common when there are different areas of documentation that have been updated at different times. A user is left wondering which document or example is correct and up to date.
- **Lacking structure**: Without structure, a user cannot easily navigate through or gain a conceptual understanding of, the entire software. They are left crawling through the details without able to get a clear *big picture*. Hierarchy is important in software, so it's important to reflect this in our documentation.
- **Difficult to navigate content**: Without good UX/UI considerations, documentation can be very hard to navigate through. If it is not centralized, searchable, and accessible, then navigation suffers and users are left in a state of confusion and pain.

- **Lacking presentation**: Alongside navigation, another crucial UX component within documentation is its aesthetic and typographic layout. A well laid-out document is a breeze to read through and learn from. It is entirely reasonable to *design* documentation. It should not be a dry *dumping ground* of endless prose, but a beautiful educational experience!

In `Chapter 2`, *The Tenets of Clean Code*, we went into great detail on what *usability* means. We discussed how it was not only about intuitive design and accessibility, but also about the consideration of *user stories*—specific tasks that users wish to carry out and how to accommodate these. Documentation is no different to any other interface that we provide; it must solve the user's problems. Consider how you may design documentation to cater for these example user stories:

- *As a user*, I wish to understand what this framework does and how I might apply it to my project
- *As a user*, I wish to find out how I can install this framework into my Node.js project
- *As a user*, I wish to understand the best practices when using this framework
- *As a user*, I wish to understand how to build a simple example app using this framework

 Every user is different. Some users will prefer to read through a long and technical document, others will prefer short self-contained tutorials. Consider the different learning styles that people have (visual, aural, social, solitary, and so on). Some learn by studying things at length; others learn by *doing*.

We may consider building different styles of documentation for the different types of information a user seeks. More specification-oriented information (for example, *how does this specific framework function work?*) may be best suited to a traditional long-form document format, while more instruction-oriented information (for example, *how can I build an app with this framework?*) may be best suited to rich media (for example, a video tutorial).

Due to the many types of information a user may seek, and all the different individual users we are catering for, it is absolutely worth dedicating significant time to planning, designing, and executing clean documentation. It should never be an afterthought.

Now that we're explored our four aspects of clean documentation, let's explore the incredible gamut of available mediums we can employ to express our documentation. We do not have to employ only a single dull, scrollable document: there are dozens of other ways we can inform and educate our users and colleagues.

Documentation is everywhere

If we generously define documentation as *a way of learning about a piece of software,* we can observe that there are dozens of different mediums of documentation that exist. Many of them are implicit or accidental; others are more intentionally crafted, either by the creator(s) of the software or the expert community that has gathered around it:

- Written documentation (*API specifications, conceptual explanations*)
- Explanatory images and diagrams (for example *flowcharts*)
- Written tutorials (*walk-throughs, recipes, how to do X*)
- Rich media introductions and tutorials (*videos, podcasts, screencasts*)
- Public Q&As or issues (for example *GitHub issues that explain how to fix something*)
- Community-driven Q&As (for example *StackOverflow*)
- Independent communication between programmers (*online or offline*)
- Meet-ups, conferences, and seminars (*owner or community-driven*)
- Official support (*paid support lines, emails, in-person sessions*)
- Educational classes (*in-person or online*, for example *Coursera*)
- Tests (*that explain concepts, flows, and expectations*)
- Good abstractions (*that help to explain concepts*)
- Readable and familiar code (*that can be easily understood*)
- Structure and delineations (*directory structure, project names,* and so on)
- Intuitively designed interfaces (*educating usage via good design*)
- Error flows and messages (for example *X not working? Try Z instead.*)

It's worth considering how all these mediums care catered for. When the official documentation does not help to solve a user's problem, what other pathways will they explore before abandoning your software altogether? How can we channel a user's difficulty or questions towards a solution as quickly and fluidly as possible? If a user is unlikely to read an entire specification document, then what other mediums can we create for them?

Writing for non-technical audiences

As we have seen, when writing documentation, there is a need to adapt the language used to the audience. To do this, we must have a good picture in our mind of who the audience is, what their current level of knowledge is, and what they're trying to accomplish. A notorious challenge for programmers is communicating with less technical or non-technical people. This is a very common and crucial part of their role as a creator of software. Whether communicating with end users at specific points in a UX, or collaborating with non-technical stakeholders, there is a need to tailor our communication to the audience. To do this, we should do the following:

- **Pick the right level of abstraction**: It's crucial to find a level of abstraction that is fully understood by the audience. Use their roles and proficiencies to inform the analogies you use to explain things. For example, if you were talking to a patient about a piece of medical software, you might prefer to say *please add your medical information* instead of *please populate the medical profile fields*.
- **Avoid overly-technical terminology**: Avoid words that mean nothing to the audience. Use regular language to explain detailed concepts. For example, you might talk about *visual enhancements* instead of *CSS modifications*.
- **Get constant feedback**: Ensure you are being understood by checking with your audience. Don't assume that people understand you just because they don't explicitly say otherwise. Consider user-oriented prompts in your documentation or software (for example, *was this message helpful? [YES] [NO]*)

Communicating with non-technical individuals may appear to be a distinct challenge, but it is no different from communicating with anyone else. As we should be doing all the time, we just need to *meet the person where they're at* and communicate according to their current understanding of the problem domain.

Summary

In this chapter, we have explored the difficult art of authoring clean documentation, breaking it down into the four vital aspects of clean documentation: *concept, specification, instruction,* and *usability*. We've discussed the challenge of correctly identifying our audience and how to craft our communications to suit them. This knowledge will not only be useful in crafting formal documentation, but also in our everyday communications with stakeholders and within our software when it needs to communicate with users.

In the next chapter, we move swiftly on to the unique challenge of dealing with other peoples' code. What happens when we, on the receiving end of potentially poor documentation or unintuitive code, need to be productive? We'll find out.

Other Peoples' Code 17

Humans, being complex and fickle, create complex and fickle things. However, dealing with other people and their code is an unavoidable part of being a programmer. Whether we deal with libraries and frameworks constructed by someone else or inherit entire legacy code bases, the challenges are similar. The first step should always be to seek an understanding of the code and its paradigms. When we have a full understanding of the code, we can begin to interface with it in a clean way, enabling us to create new functionality or make improvements on top of existing work. In this chapter, we'll be exploring this topic in more detail and, through the lens of clean code, considering how we can individually take actions to make other people's code less of a pain to deal with.

In this chapter, we will cover the following topics:

- Inheriting code
- Dealing with third-party code

Inheriting code

When we join a new team or take on a new project, we are usually inheriting a large amount of code. Our ability to be productive in these inherited code bases is dependent on our understanding of them. So, before we even seek to make the first change, we need to build in our minds a conceptual model of how things work. It's not necessary for it to be exhaustive and complete, but it must enable us, at a very minimum, to make a change and understand exactly what effect that change may have on all the moving parts of the code base.

Exploring and understanding

Understanding a code base fully is not strictly necessary to make use of it nor to make changes to it, but if we don't have a sufficient understanding of the complexity of all its interrelated parts, then we can fall into a trap. The trap occurs when we, believing we have a good understanding, start making changes. Without understanding the full effects of our actions, we can end up wasting time, implementing things poorly, and producing accidental bugs. Therefore, it is vital that we become properly informed. To do this, we must first gauge how complete or incomplete our *view* is of the complexity of the system or code base.

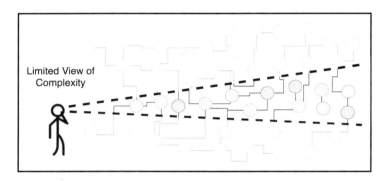

Often the things we cannot see are completely unknown to us, and we are therefore unaware that we lack any understanding at all. This is encapsulated by the common expression *we don't know what we don't know*. It's therefore helpful, when exploring a new code base, to proactively and enthusiastically push to discover and highlight our areas of ignorance. We can do this by following a three-step process:

- **Gather available information**: Talk to informed colleagues, read documentation, use the software, internalize the conceptual structures and hierarchies, and read the source code.
- **Make informed assumptions**: Fill the gaps of what you aren't sure about with informed assumptions. If you're told that the app has a registration page, you can intuitively assume that this means user registration involves typical personal data fields such as name, email, password, and so on.
- **Prove or disprove assumptions**: Seek to prove or disprove your assumptions by inquiring the system directly (for example, writing and executing tests), or asking someone who is informed (for example, a colleague who has experience of the code base).

There are a few specific approaches that are worth employing when it comes to creating and expanding an understanding of a new code base. These include making a flowchart, internalizing the timeline of changes, stepping through the code with a debugger, and confirming your assumptions via tests. We'll explore each of these individually.

Making a flowchart

One useful method we can employ almost immediately when encountering a new code base is to populate a mind map or flowchart that highlights not only the things we know but the things we aren't yet sure about. Here's a simplified example of such a diagram for a piece of medical software I once worked on:

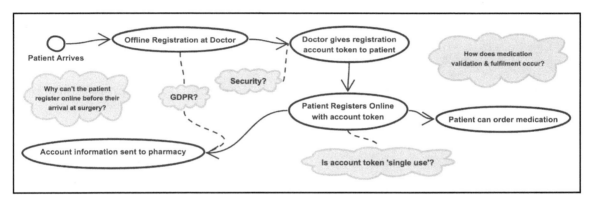

As you can see, I have tried to outline my *current* understanding of the user flow and have also added questions or areas of confusion I am personally experiencing in the *cloud* annotations. Over time, as my understanding grows, I can add to this flowchart.

People learn in a huge variety of ways. This visual aid may be more useful for some people but less for others. There are also countless ways of composing such flowcharts. For the goal of personal understanding, it is best to *use whatever works for you.*

Finding structure and observing history

Imagine you're faced with a large JavaScript application code base that includes several specialized types of *views* or *components*. We've been tasked with adding a new drop-down to one of the payment forms within the application. We do a quick search through the code base and identify a number of different dropdown-related components:

- GenericDropdownComponent
- DropdownDataWidget
- EnhancedDropdownDataWidget
- TextDropdown
- ImageDropdown

They're confusingly named and so we'd like to get a better understanding of them before making changes or utilizing them. To do this, we can just open the source code of each component to establish how it may relate to the others (or how it does not relate).

We end up discovering that TextDropdown and ImageDropdown, for example, both appear to inherit from GenericDropdownComponent:

```
// TextDropdown.js
class TextDropdown extends GenericDropdownComponent {
  //...
}

// ImageDropdown.js
class ImageDropdown extends GenericDropdownComponent {

}
```

We also observe that both DropdownDataWidget and EnhancedDropdownDataWidget are sub-classes of TextDropdown. The naming of the *enhanced* drop-down widget might confuse us, and it may be something that we seek to change in the near future, but, for now, we'll need to hold our breath and just work on doing the work we've been tasked with.

Avoid getting side tracked when you're completing a task within a legacy or unfamiliar code base. Many things may appear odd or wrong, but your task must remain the most important thing. Early on, it is unlikely that you have the level of exposure to the code base that would be necessary to make informed changes.

By stepping through each dropdown-related source file, we can build up a solid understanding of them without having to make any changes. If the code base employs source control, then we can also *blame* each file to discover who originally authored it and when. This can inform us how things have changed over time. In our case, we discover the following timeline of changes:

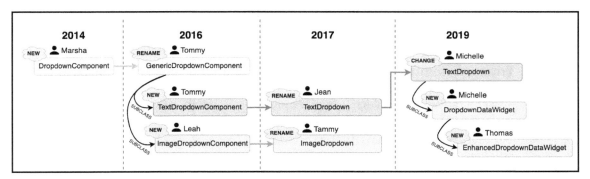

This is incredibly helpful to us. We can see how, originally, there was only one class (named `DropdownComponent`), which later got changed to `GenericDropdownComponent` with two sub-classes, `TextDropdownComponent` and `ImageDropdownComponent`. Each of these got renamed to `TextDropdown` and `ImageDropdown`. Over time, these various changes illuminate the *why* of how things are at the present time.

When looking at a code base, we often make an implicit assumption that it was created *all at once* and with complete foresight; however, as our timeline illustrates, the truth is far more complex. Code bases change over time in reaction to new needs. The set of people who work on a code base also changes, and each individual will inevitably have their own way of solving problems. Our acceptance of the slowly evolving nature of every code base will help us to come to terms with its imperfections.

Stepping through the code

When building an understanding of a singular piece of code within a large application, we can use tooling to debug and study how it functions. In JavaScript, we can simply place a `debugger;` statement, and then execute the part of the application that we know activates that particular code. We can then step through the code, line by line, to answer the following questions:

- **Where is this code called?** A clear expectation of how an abstraction is activated can help us to build up a model of the *flow* or *order* of the application in our head, enabling us to make more accurate judgements about how to fix or change certain things.

- **What is passed to this code?** An example of what input an abstraction receives can help us to build up a clear concept about what it does, and how it expects to be interfaced with. This can directly guide our usage of the abstraction.

- **What is outputted by this code?** Seeing the output of an abstraction, partnered with its input, can give us a really solid idea of what it does, computationally, and can help us to discern how we may wish to go about using it.

- **What levels of misdirection or complexity exist here?** Observing complex and tall stack traces (meaning that, *functions that are called by functions that are called by functions, ad infinitum...*) can indicate that we may have difficulty in navigating and understanding the flow of control and information within a certain area. This would tell us that we may need to augment our understanding with additional documentation or communication with informed colleagues.

Here is an example of doing so in a browser environment (using Chrome Inspector):

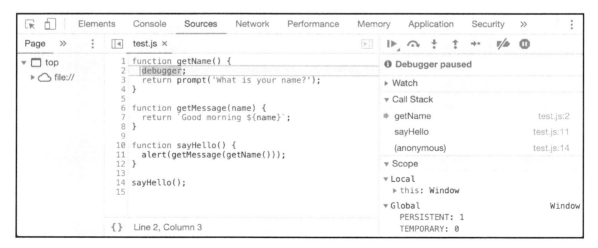

You can use Chrome's debugger even if you're implementing server-side JavaScript in Node.js. To do this, use the `--inspect` flag when executing your JavaScript, for example, `node --inspect index.js`.

Using a debugger like this can present us with a *call stack* or *stack trace*, informing us of what path was taken through the code base to get to our `debugger;` statement. If we are trying to understand how an unfamiliar class or module fits into the larger picture of a code base, this can be very helpful.

Asserting your assumptions

One of the best ways to expand our knowledge of unfamiliar code is to write tests to confirm that the code behaves in the way we believe it does. Imagine we are given this piece of obscure code to maintain:

```
class IssuerOOIDExtractor {
  static makeExtractor(issuerInfoInterface) {
    return raw => {
      const infos = [];
      const cleansed = raw
        .replace(/[_\-%*]/g, '')
        .replace(/\bo(\d+?)\b/g, ($0, id) => {
          if (issuerInfoInterface) {
            infos.push(issuerInfoInterface.get(id));
          }
          return `[[ ${id} ]]`;
        })
        .replace(/^[\s\S]*?(\[\[.+\]\])[\s\S]*$/, '$1');
      return { raw, cleansed, data: infos };
    };
  }
}
```

This code is only used in a couple of places, but the various inputs are dynamically generated in a difficult-to-debug area of the application. Additionally, there is no documentation and absolutely no tests. It is quite unclear exactly what this code does, but, as we study the code line by line, we can begin to make some basic assumptions and encode these assumptions as assertions. For example, we can plainly see that the `makeExtractor` static function itself returns a function. We can specify this truth as a test:

```
describe('IssuerOOIDExtractor.makeExtractor', () => {
  it('Creates a function (the extractor)', () => {
```

```
        expect(typeof IssuerOOIDExtractor.makeExtractor()).toBe('function');
    });
});
```

We can also see some type of regular expression replacement occurring; it seemingly looks for patterns where the letter o is followed by a string of digits (\bo(\d+?)\b). We can begin to explore this extraction functionality by writing a simple assertion in which we give the extractor a string matching that pattern:

```
const extractor = IssuerOOIDExtractor.makeExtractor();

it('Extracts a single OOID of the form oNNNN', () => {
  expect(extractor('o1234')).toEqual({
    raw: 'o1234',
    cleansed: '[[ 1234 ]]',
    data: []
  });
});
```

We can add additional assertions as we slowly discover what the code does. We may never arrive at 100% understanding, but this is OK. Here, we're asserting the fact that the extractor is able to correctly extract multiple OOIDs present within a single string:

```
it('Extracts multiple OOIDs of the form oNNNN', () => {
  expect(extractor('o0012 o0034 o0056 o0078')).toEqual({
    raw: 'o0012 o0034 o0056 o0078',
    cleansed: '[[ 0012 ]] [[ 0034 ]] [[ 0056 ]] [[ 0078 ]]',
    data: []
  });
});
```

When running these tests, we observe the following successful results:

```
    PASS ./IssuerOOIDExtractor.test.js
    IssuerOOIDExtractor.makeExtracator
      ✓ Creates a function (the extractor) (3ms)
    The extractor
      ✓ Extracts a single OOID of the form oNNNN (1ms)
      ✓ Extracts multiple OOIDs of the form oNNNN (1ms)
```

Note how we're still not entirely sure what the original code does. We have only scraped the surface, but in doing so, we are building a valuable foundation of understanding that will make it far easier for us to interface with or change this code in the future. With each new successful assertion, we get closer to a complete and accurate understanding of what the code does. And if we commit these assertions as a new test, then we are also improving the test coverage of the code base and providing assistance for future colleagues who may have been similarly confused by the code.

Now that we have a solid grasp of how to explore and understand an inherited piece of code, we can now look into how we might *make changes* to that code.

Making changes

Once we have a good level of understanding about an area of a code base, we can begin to make changes. Even at this stage, however, we should be cautious. We are still relatively new to the code base and the system it relates to and so we're probably still unaware of many of its parts. Any change could potentially create unforeseen effects. To move forward we must, therefore, go slowly and considerately, ensuring our code is well designed and well-tested. There are two specific methodologies we should be aware of here:

- The delicate *surgical* process of making isolated changes in an unfamiliar setting
- The confirmation of changes via tests

Let's explore these, one by one.

Minimally invasive surgery

When changes are needed in an area of the code base that is old or unfamiliar, it can be useful to imagine that you are performing a kind of *minimally invasive surgery*. The aim in doing this is to maximize the positive effect of a change while minimizing the footprint of the change itself, ensuring not to damage or have too much impact on other parts of the code base. The hope with doing this is that we will be able to produce the necessary changes (*upsides*) without exposing ourselves too much to the possibility of breakages or bugs (*downsides*). This is also useful when we aren't sure whether the change is entirely necessary, so we want to only expend minimal effort on it initially.

Let's imagine that we have inherited a `GalleryImage` component that is responsible for rendering singular images. There are many places in our web application where it is used. The task is to add the ability for videos to be rendered when the URL of the asset indicates that it is a video. The two types of CDN URLs are as follows:

- `https://cdn.example.org/VIDEO/{ID}`
- `https://cdn.example.org/IMAGE/{ID}`

As you can see, there is a clear difference between image and video URLs. This gives us an easy way of differentiating how we render these pieces of media on the page. Ideally, it is reasonable to say that we should implement a new component named `GalleryVideo` to handle this new type of media. A new component like this would be able to cater uniquely to the *problem domain* of a video, which is notably different from that of an image. At the very least, a video must be rendered via a `<VIDEO>` element, while an image must be rendered via `<IMG>`.

We discover that many of the situations where `GalleryImage` is used are not well tested and some rely on obscure internal implementation details that would be difficult to discern in bulk (for example, it would be hard to do a find and replace if we wanted to change all `GalleryImage` usages).

Our available options are as follows:

1. Create a *container* `GalleryAsset` component that itself makes a decision about whether to render a `GalleryImage` or `GalleryVideo` based on the CDN URL. This would involve having to replace every current usage of `GalleryImage`:
   - Time estimate: **1-2 weeks**
   - Footprint across the code base: **Significant**
   - Possibility of unforeseen breakages: **Significant**
   - Architectural *cleanliness*: **High**

2. Add a condition within `GalleryImage` that optionally renders a `<video>` instead of an `<img>` tag based on the CDN URL:
   - Time estimate: **1-2 days**
   - Footprint across the code base: **Minimal**
   - Possibility of unforeseen breakages: **Minimal**
   - Architectural *cleanliness*: **Medium**

In ideal circumstances, if we consider the long-term architecture of the code base, it is clear that the first option of creating a new `GalleryAsset` component is the best one. It gives us a clearly defined abstraction that intuitively caters to the two cases of images and videos and also provides us with the possibility of adding different asset types in the future (for example, *audio*). It will, however, take longer to implement, and carries quite a significant amount of risk.

The second option is far simpler to implement. In fact, it may only involve the following four-line change set:

```
@@ -17,6 +17,10 @@ class GalleryImage {
  render() {

+    if (/\/VIDEO\//.test(this.props.url)) {
+      return <video src={this.props.url} />;
+    }
+
     return <img src={this.props.url} />

  }
```

This is not necessarily a good long-term choice, but it gives us something we can immediately ship to users, fulfilling their needs and the needs of our stakeholders. Once shipped, we can then plan future time to complete the larger necessary change.

To reiterate, the value of a *minimally invasive* change like this is that it reduces the immediate downsides (*risks*) to the code base in terms of implementation time and potential breakages. Obviously it is vital to ensure that we are balancing short-term gains with long-term. Often, stakeholders will pressure programmers to implement a change quickly, but if there is no *technical dept* or reconciliation process, then all of these *minimally invasive* changes can gather into quite a terrifying beast.

To ensure that the code we change is not too delicate or liable to future regressions, it is wise to write tests alongside them, encoding our expectations.

Encoding changes as tests

We've already explored how we can write tests to discover and specify current functionality, and, in previous chapters, we discussed the obvious benefits of following a **Test-Driven-Development** (**TDD**) approach. It follows that we should, when operating in an unfamiliar code base, always confirm our changes via cleanly written tests.

Writing tests alongside your changes is definitely a need when there are no existing tests. Writing the first test in an area of code can be burdensome in terms of setting up libraries and necessary mocks, but it is absolutely worth it.

In our previous example of introducing the capability of rendering videos to GalleryImage, it would be wise to add a simple test to confirm that <VIDEO> is correctly rendered when the URL contains the "/VIDEO/" substring. This prevents the possibility of future regressions and gives us a strong level of confidence that it works as expected:

```
import { mount } from 'enzyme';
import GalleryImage from './GalleryImage';

describe('GalleryImage', () => {
  it('Renders a <VIDEO> when URL contains "/VIDEO/"', () => {
    const rendered = mount(
      <GalleryImage url="https://cdn.example.org/VIDEO/1234" />
    );
    expect(rendered.find('video')).to.have.lengthOf(1);
  });
  it('Renders a <IMG> when URL contains "/IMAGE/"', () => {
    const rendered = mount(
      <GalleryImage url="https://cdn.example.org/IMAGE/1234" />
    );
    expect(rendered.find('img')).to.have.lengthOf(1);
  });
});
```

This is a rather simple test; however, it completely encodes the expectations we have after making our changes. When making small and self-contained changes or larger systemic changes, it's so incredibly valuable to verify and communicate our intent via tests like these. As well as preventing regressions, they aid our colleagues in terms of immediate code review, and the entire team in terms of documentation and general reliability. As such, it's quite normal and preferable to have a team mandate or policy that says *you cannot commit a change if it does not come with a test*. Enforcing this will, over time, create a code base that produces more reliable functionality for users and is more pleasant to work with for fellow programmers.

We've now completed the section on *Inheriting code*, and so you should have a good foundational knowledge of how to deal with such a situation. Another challenge in dealing with *other people's code* is the selection and integration of third-party code, meaning libraries and frameworks. We'll explore this now.

Dealing with third-party code

The landscape of JavaScript is filled with a myriad of frameworks and libraries that can ease the burden of implementing all types of functionality. In Chapter 12, *Real-World Challenges*, we had a look at the difficulties involved in including external dependencies in our JavaScript projects. The modern JavaScript ecosystem provides a rich variety of solutions here, and so dealing with third-party code is far less burdensome than it was before. Nonetheless, the nature of having to interface with this code hasn't really changed. We must still hope that our selected third-party library or framework provides an interface that is intuitive and well-documented, and functionality that fulfills our requirements.

When dealing with third-party code, there are two crucial processes that will define the ongoing risks or benefits we receive. The first is the *selection* process, where we make a choice as to which library to use, and the second is our integration and adaptation of the library into our code base. We'll now go over both of these in detail.

Selection and understanding

Picking a library or framework can be a risky decision. Pick the wrong one and it can end up driving much of the architecture of your system. Frameworks are especially notorious for this because, by their nature, they dictate the structure and conceptual underpinning of your architecture. Picking the wrong one and then seeking to change it can be a considerable effort; one that involves changes to almost every single piece of code within an application. As such, it is vital to practice the skill of careful consideration and selection of third-party code:

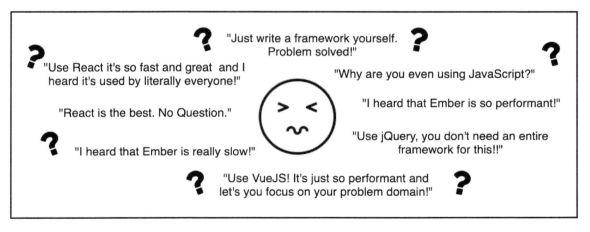

There are a number of useful considerations we can make in order to help us in the process of selection:

- **Functionality**: The library or framework must fulfill a set of fixed functional expectations. It's important to specify these in a sufficiently detailed way so that different options can be quantifiably compared.
- **Compatibility**: The library or framework must be mostly compatible with the way the code base currently works, and must be able to integrate in a way that it is technically simple and easy to understand for colleagues.
- **Usability**: The library or framework must be easily usable and understandable. It should have good documentation and a level of intuitiveness that allows immediate productivity without pain or confusion. The consideration of what occurs when you have a problem or question related to usage is also under the umbrella of usability.
- **Maintenance and security**: The library or framework should be maintained and have a clear and trusted process for reporting and resolving bugs, especially those that may have security ramifications. The changelogs should be exhaustive.

> The four criteria here can be informed, as well, by heuristics such as *who is the project backed by?*, *how many people are making use of the project?*, or *am I familiar with the team who built it?*. Be warned though, these are only heuristics and so are not perfect ways of measuring the suitability of *third-party code*.

Even using these four criteria, however, we may fall into traps. If you'll recall, in Chapter 3, *The Enemies of Clean Code*, we discussed the most notable *Self* (or *ego*) and *The cargo cult*. These are also relevant when selecting third-party code. Remember to specifically watch out for the following:

- **Powerful opinions**: It's crucial to separate ourselves from the decision process as much as possible, and to be very wary of our ignorances and biases. Programmers are well known for their opinionated nature. It's important in these moments to step back from ourselves and reason with pure logic about what we believe would be best. It's key to give everyone a voice as well, and to weigh people's opinions and anecdotes according to their own merits, not according to their seniority (or other personal characteristics).

- **The popularity cult**: Don't get too swayed by popularity. It's easy to get drawn into a popular abstraction due to the size and zealotry of its community, but once again, it is vital to take a step back and consider the merits of the framework in isolation. Naturally, popularity may indicate an ease of integration and more abundant learning resources, so in that way, it is reasonable to talk about, but just be wary of using popularity as a sole indicator of superiority.

- **Analysis paralysis**: There are a lot of choices out there, so it is possible to end up in a situation where you are seemingly unable to make a choice out of fear of making the wrong one. Most of the time, these decisions are reversible, so it's not the end of the world to make a less than optimal choice. It's easy to end up in a situation where a lot of time is being used up deciding which framework or library to pick when it would be far more efficient to just pick *anything* and then iterate or pivot according to changing needs at a later point.

The key thing when making decisions about third-party libraries is to fully appreciate their eventual effects on the code base. The amount of time we sink into making a decision should be proportional to their potential effects. Deciding on a client-side framework for component rendering may be a rather impactful choice as it may prescribe a significant portion of the code base, whereas, for example, a small URL-parsing utility does not have a great impact and can be easily swapped out in the future.

Next, we can discuss how we might integrate and encapsulate a piece of third-party code, following a well-informed selection process.

Encapsulating and adapting third-party code

The downside of picking a third-party abstraction, especially a framework, is that you can end up changing your code base to suit the arbitrary conventions and design decisions of the abstraction's authors. Often, we are made to *speak the same language* of these third-party interfaces, instead of having them *speak our language*. Indeed, in many cases, it may be the abstraction's conventions and design that is appealing to us, and so we are more than happy for it to drive the design and nature of our code base. But, in other situations, we may want to be more protected from our chosen abstractions. We may want the option to easily swap them out for other abstractions in the future, or we may already have a set of conventions that we prefer to use.

In such cases, it may be useful to encapsulate these third-party abstractions and deal with them purely through an abstraction layer of our own. Such a layer would typically be called an *Adapter*:

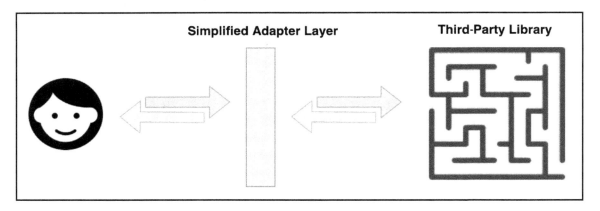

Very simply, an *Adapter* will provide an interface that we design, and will then delegate to the third-party abstraction to accomplish its tasks. Imagine if we wished to use a URL-parsing utility called YOORL. We've decided it works perfectly for our needs, and has complete compliance with RFC 3986 (the URI standard). The only issue is that its API is rather burdensome and verbose:

```
import YOORL from 'yoorl';
YOORL.parse(
  new YOORL.URL.String('http://foo.com/abc/?x=123'),
  { parseSearch: true }
).parts();
```

This would return the following *Object*:

```
{
  protocol: 'http',
  hostname: 'foo.com',
  pathname: '/abc',
  search: { x: 123 }
}
```

We would prefer it if the API was far simpler. The length and complexity of the current API, we feel, would expose our code base to needless complexity and risk (the risk of calling it the wrong way, for example). Using an *Adapter* would allow us to wrap up this non-ideal interface into an interface of our own design:

```
// URLUtils.js
import YOORL from 'yoorl';
```

```
export default {
  parse(url) {
    return YOORL.parse(
      new YOORL.URL.String(url)
    ).parts();
  }
};
```

This means that any modules within our code base can now interface with this simplified *Adapter*, insulating them from the unideal API of YOORL:

```
import URLUtils from './URLUtils';

URLUtils.parse('http://foo.com/abc/?x=123'); // Easy!
```

Adapters can be thought of as *translation mediums*, allowing our code base to *speak the language* of its choice, not having to be slowed down by the arbitrary and inconsistent design decisions of third-party libraries. This not only aids the usability and intuitiveness of the code base but also enables us to very easily make changes to the underlying third-party library without having to change many lines of code at all.

Summary

In this chapter, we have explored the tricky topic of *other people's code*. We've considered how we can deal with legacy code that we inherit; how we can build our understanding of it, how we can debug and make changes without difficult, and how we can confirm our changes with a good testing approach. We've also covered the difficulty of dealing with third-party code, including how to select it and how to interface with it in a risk-averse way via the *Adapter* pattern. There are plenty of other things that we could have spoken about in this chapter, but hopefully the topics and principles we have been able to explore have given you a sufficient understanding of how to navigate other people's code with an eye toward a clean code base.

In the next chapter, we will cover the topic of communication. It may not appear relevant but communication, both within our workplaces and toward our users, is an absolutely vital skill for the programmer, and without it there is little possibility of clean code. We'll specifically be exploring how to plan and set requirements, how to collaborate and communicate with colleagues, and how to drive change within our projects and workplaces.

Communication and Advocacy

18

We do not write code in isolation. We are embedded in a highly chaotic social world in which we must communicate with other people constantly. Our software itself will, via its interfaces, be part of this communication. Furthermore, if we operate within a team, a workplace, or a community, we are liable to the challenges of effective communication.

The most significant way in which communication has an effect on our code bases is in the setting of requirements and the raising of issues and feedback. Software development is essentially one very elongated feedback process, where every change is precipitated by a communication:

Solve the problem	**Understand the problem**
Business Requirements Feature Requests Bug Reports	Understand and diagnose issues Investigate the problem domain Talk to users and stakeholders
Gain user feedback	**Build the solution**
Receive bug reports / feature requests Receive analytics and other data Explore improvements and experiment	Design the software Write code to implement it Build-in feedback mechanisms

In this chapter, we'll learn how to effectively collaborate and communicate with others, how to plan and set requirements, some common collaboration pitfalls, and their solutions. We'll also learn how to identify and raise larger issues that are preventing us from writing clean JavaScript. Throughout this chapter, we will hopefully begin to appreciate our individually vital roles in the feedback cycle of software development.

In this chapter, we'll see the following topics:

- Planning and setting requirements
- Communication strategies
- Identifying issues and driving change

Planning and setting requirements

One of the most common communication struggles resides in the process of deciding what to actually build. Programmers will typically spend a lot of time meeting with managers, designers, and other stakeholders to transform a genuine user need into a workable solution. Ideally, this process would be simple: *User has [problem]; We create [solution]. End of story!* Unfortunately, however, it can be far more complicated.

There are numerous technical constraints and biases of communication that can make even seemingly simple projects turn into punishingly long struggles. This is as relevant to the JavaScript programmer as any other programmer, for we now operate at a level of systemic complexity that was previously only the domain of enterprise programmers wielding Java, C#, or C++. The landscape has changed, and so the humble JavaScript programmer must now be prepared to pick up new skills and ask new questions about the systems they build.

Understanding user needs

Establishing user needs is vital but it is often taken for granted. It's typical for programmers and other project members to assume they understand a certain user need without really digging into the details, so it's useful to have a process to fall back on. For each ostensible *need* or *problem*, we should ensure that we understand the following aspects:

- **Who are our users?**: What characteristics do they have? What devices do they use?
- **What are they trying to do?**: What actions are they trying to carry out? What's their ultimate goal?
- **How do they currently do it?**: What set of steps are they currently taking to reach their goal? Are there any notable issues with their current method?
- **What problems do they experience doing it this way?**: Does it take a long time? Is it cognitively expensive? Is it difficult to use?

At the beginning of the book, we asked ourselves to consider why we wrote code, and we explored what it means to truly understand the nature of our problem domain. Ideally, we should be able to step inside the shoes of our users, experience the problem domain ourselves, and then craft working solutions from firsthand experience.

Unfortunately, we are not always able to talk directly to our users or walk in their shoes. Instead, we may rely on intermediates such as project managers and designers. And so, we are dependent upon their communication efficacy to relay the user needs to us in a way that allows us to build a correct solution.

Here we see how the needs of our users, combined with the technical and business constraints, flow into an idea that is built into a solution and iterated upon. The translation of **User Needs** to **Idea** is vital, as is the process of feedback that allows us to iterate and improve upon our solution:

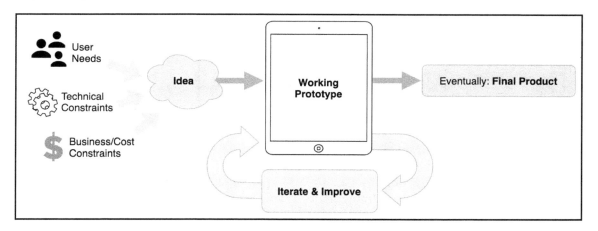

Since user needs are crucial to the process of development, we have to think carefully about how we balance these with other constraints. It is usually impossible to build the ideal solution, catering well to every single user. Almost every piece of software, whether presented as a GUI or API, is a compromise in which the average user is well catered to, inevitably meaning that the edge case users are left being only partially served by the solution. It's important to consider how we can adequately accommodate as many users' needs as possible, delicately balancing constraints such as time, money, and technical capability.

Following our understanding of user needs, we can begin to design and implement prototypes and models of how a system may work. We'll briefly discuss the process of doing this next.

Quick prototypes and PoCs

Software, and especially the web platform, provides us with the benefit of a quick build cycle. We can go from concept to UI in a very short amount of time. This means that ideas can be brought to life during the process of brainstorming, almost in real time. We can then place these prototypes in front of real users, get real feedback, and then iterate quickly towards an optimal solution. Truly, the forte of the web platform—the triad of HTML, CSS, and JavaScript—is that it allows a quick and hacky solution that can be iterated on easily, and can work on multiple platforms and devices:

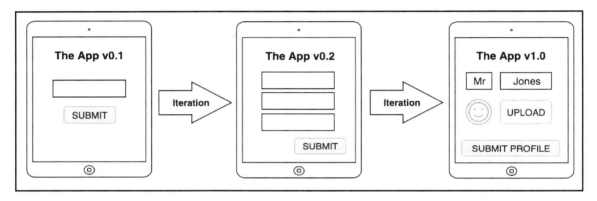

It's easy to get weighed down by the variety and complexity of JavaScript frameworks and libraries; the sheer burden of them can force us to move at a much slower pace. That's why, when prototyping, it's often better to stick to a simpler stack that you already understand well. If you're accustomed to a framework, or if you are prepared to sink some time into learning, then it is worth utilizing one of many available skeletal boilerplate starter repositories as your starting point. Here are some examples:

- React boilerplate (github.com/react-boilerplate/react-boilerplate)
- Angular bootstrap boilerplate (github.com/mdbootstrap/Angular-Bootstrap-Boilerplate)
- Ember boilerplate (github.com/mirego/ember-boilerplate)
- Svelte template (github.com/sveltejs/template)

These each offer a relatively simple project template that you can use to very quickly set up a new prototype. Even though the tooling used within each one involves multiple build tools and framework options, the setup cost is minimal and so the time it takes to start tackling the real problem domain of your project is kept very short. There are, naturally, similar boilerplates and example applications you can find for server-side Node.js projects, isomorphic web applications, and even robotic or hardware projects.

Now that we've explored the technical process of planning and setting requirements, we can move on to discover some vital communication strategies that'll help us collaborate with others on our code bases.

Communication strategies

We intuitively know that communication is vital to an effective project and a clean code base, yet it is annoyingly common to find ourselves in situations such as the following:

- We don't feel listened to
- We don't feel we've got our point across
- We feel confused as to a topic or plan
- We feel out of the loop or ignored

These difficulties come about because of cultures and practices of poor communication. This is not only an issue for morale and general fulfillment in our work but can also become a huge issue for the cleanliness of our code bases and the reliability of the technology we build. To foster a clean code base, we must focus on the underlying communication practices that we employ. A good set of communication strategies and practices are incredibly useful in ensuring a clean code base, specifically helping us with the following:

- Ensuring good feedback with colleagues
- Receiving correct bug reports
- Actioning improvements and fixes
- Receiving user requirements and wishes
- Announcing changes or issues
- Agreeing on conventions and standards
- Making decisions about libraries and frameworks

But how do we actually accomplish good communication? We are inherently biased toward our own socialized communication practices, so it can be difficult to change or even see that we have issues with our communication. For this reason, it is useful to identify a set of communication strategies and pitfalls that can re-bias us towards better and higher signal communication.

High signal communication is any piece of communication that compresses a lot of highly valuable or insightful information in a minimally noisy fashion. Expressing a bug report in a brief and highly objective paragraph may be an example of high signal, while expressing it as a three-part essay with rhetoric and opinion thrown in is an example of low signal.

Listen and respond

Whether in online or offline conversations, it is quite easy to fall into a trap where we end up talking *over* each other instead of *to* each other. A good and useful conversation is one where the participants are truly listening to each other, instead of merely awaiting their turn to talk.

Consider the following conversation between **Person #1** and **Person #2**:

- **Person #1**: *We should use the React framework for this, it has a proven track record.*
- **Person #2**: *I agree about its track record. Shall we explore any other options, weighing up their pros and cons?*
- **Person #1**: *React is really fast, well-documented, and the API is really usable. I love it.*

Here **Person #1** is not paying attention to what **Person #2** is saying. Instead, they are just continuing with their existing train of thought, reiterating their preference for the React framework. It would be more conducive to good teamwork and a healthier project if **Person #1** made an effort to listen to **Person #2**'s points and then respond specifically to them. Compare the preceding conversation with the following one:

- **Person #1**: *We should use the React framework for this, it has a proven track record.*
- **Person #2**: *I agree about its track record. Shall we explore any other options, weighing up their pros and cons?*
- **Person #1**: *That'd be a good idea, what other frameworks do you think we should consider?*

Here, **Person #1** is being receptive, and not purely talking *over* **Person #2**. This shows a much-needed sensitivity and conversational attention. This may seem obvious, or even inane, but you may be surprised how often we end up speaking over each other and the costs it inflicts us with. Consider taking an observational role in your next meeting, observe instances where people fail to properly pay attention, listen, or respond. You may be surprised by its prevalence.

Explain from the user's perspective

In almost every piece of online or offline communication you have in regards to a code base, the user should be the most important thing. The purpose of our work is to fulfill the expectations of the user and deliver to them a user experience that is intuitive and functional. This is relevant, regardless of whether our end-product is a piece of consumer software or a developer API. The user remains our priority. It is, however, incredibly common to find ourselves in situations where there is a decision to be made and we don't know how to make it; we end up relying on gut instinct or our own biased beliefs. Consider the following:

- Of course users should have to fulfill our password strength requirements
- Of course our API should be strictly type-checked
- Of course we should use a dropdown component for country selection

These may seem like fairly unobjectionable statements, but we should always seek to qualify them from the perspective of the user. If we cannot do this, then there's a strong possibility that the decision holds no water and should be challenged.

For each of the preceding statements, we can defend our reasoning as follows:

- **Of course users should have to fulfill our password strength requirements**: Users with stronger passwords will end up being more secure against brute-force password attacks. While we as a service need to ensure secure storage of passwords, it is the user's responsibility, and very much in their interest, to ensure a strong password.
- **Of course our API should be strictly type-checked**: A strictly type-checked API will ensure that users get more informative warnings about incorrect usage and can thus reach their desired goal sooner.
- **Of course we should use a dropdown component for country selection**: A dropdown is an established convention that users have come to expect. We could always augment this with an autocompletion feature as well.

Notice how we are expanding upon our of course statements with reasoning that relates specifically to the user. It's easy for us to walk around making assertions about how things should be without actually backing up our claims with strong reasoning. Doing this can lead to pointless and badly argued opposition. It is better to always reason about our decisions from the user's perspective so that, if there is an argument, we are arguing based on what's best for the user and not merely what opinions are most popular, or held most strongly. Always explaining from the perspective of the user also helps to instill a culture where we and our colleagues are constantly thinking about the user, regardless of whether we're programming a deeply specialized API or developing a generic GUI.

Have small and focused communications

Similar in spirit to the *single responsibility principle* that we use when coding, our communications should ideally only be about one thing at a time. This greatly improves understanding among participants and will ensure that any decisions that are made relate specifically to the matter at hand. Additionally, keeping meetings or communications short ensures that people will be able to pay attention for the entire duration. Long meetings, just like long emails, eventually cause boredom and irritation. And with each topic or tangent added, the chances of each item being individually resolved dwindles massively. It's important to remember this when raising issues and bugs as well. Keep it simple.

Ask stupid questions and have wild ideas

There's a tendency, especially in professional environments, to feign a great level of confidence and understanding. This can be to the detriment of knowledge transfer. If everyone is pretending to be masterful, then nobody will take the humble position that's required to learn. It's so valuable to be honest (and even stupid) in our lines of questioning. If we're new additions to a team or are confused about an area of a code base, it's important to ask the questions we truly have so that we can build the understanding necessary to be productive and reliable in our tasks. Without this understanding, we'll flail about, probably causing bugs and other problems. If everyone in a team takes a position of feigned confidence, the team will very quickly become ineffective, with nobody able to resolve their questions or confusions:

This type of questioning we want to aim towards can be called **open questioning**; a process in which we maximally divulge our ignorances so that we may gain as much understanding as possible in a given area. And similarly to such open questioning, we can say there is also **open ideating**, wherein we maximally explore and divulge any ideas that we have with the hope of some subset being useful.

Sometimes it's the ideas left unsaid that are the most effective. Generally, if you feel an idea or question is too stupid or wild to say, it's usually a good idea to say it. The worst-case scenario (the downside) is that it is an inapplicable or obvious question or idea. But the best-case scenario (the upside) is that you've either gained understanding, asked a question that many people had on their minds (and thus aided their understanding), or have come up with an idea that drastically transforms the efficacy of the team or the quality of the code base. The upsides of being open are assuredly worth the downsides.

Pair programming and 1:1s

Much of a programmer's time is taken up by the isolated pursuit of writing code. This is, to many programmers, their ideal situation; they are able to block out the rest of the world and find fluid productivity, writing logic with speed and fluency. One risk of this isolation, however, is that vital knowledge of a code base or system can accrue in the minds of the few. Without being distributed, there is a risk that the code base will become increasingly specialized and complex, limiting the ability of newcomers and colleagues to navigate it with ease. For this reason, it is essential to consider how to transfer knowledge effectively between programmers.

As discussed previously in the book, we already have a number of formal ways to transfer knowledge regarding a piece of code:

- Via documentation, in all its forms
- Via the code itself, including comments
- Via tests, including unit and E2E variants

Even though these mediums, if built correctly, can be effective in relaying knowledge, there appears to always be a need for something else. The basic human convention of ad hoc communication is a method that has stood the test of time and still remains one of the most effective methods.

One of the best ways to learn about a new code base is through **pair programming**, an activity in which you sit alongside a more experienced programmer and collaborate together on bug fixes or feature implementations. This is especially useful for the unfamiliar programmer, as they are able to benefit from the existing knowledge and experience of their programming partner. Pair programming is also useful when there is an especially complex issue to solve. Having two or more brains tackling the problem can drastically increase problem-solving ability and limit the possibility of bugs.

Even outside of pair programming, generally having a Q&A or teacher-student dynamic can be very useful. Setting aside time to talk to individuals who have the knowledge you desire and asking them pointed but exploratory questions will usually yield a lot of understanding. Do not underestimate the power of a focused conversation with someone that has the knowledge you desire.

Identifying issues and driving change

A large part of being a programmer is identifying issues and fixing them. As part of our work, we employ many different moving parts, many of which will be maintained by other teams or individuals, and as such, we'll need to be effective in identifying and raising issues with code and systems that we don't have a full understanding of. Much like anything we do as programmers, the way in which we articulate these issues must take into consideration the target audience (user) of the issue or bug report that we're expressing. When we begin to see these pieces of communication as user experiences in their own right, we'll start to be genuinely effective communicators.

Raising bugs

Raising bugs is a skill. It can be done poorly or effectively. To illustrate this, let's consider two issues on GitHub. Each of them raise the same issue but do so in drastically different ways. This is the first variant:

This is the second variant:

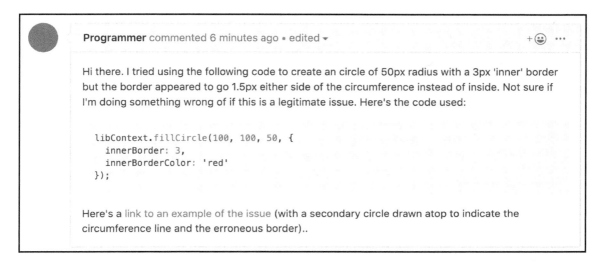

As a maintainer of this code base, which bug report would you prefer to receive? Obviously the second. Yet we see, time and time again, thousands of bug reports and raised issues on open source projects that not only fail to accurately relay the issue at hand but are impatiently worded and disrespectful of the time and efforts of the project owner.

Generally, when raising a bug it is best to include, at minimum, the following information:

- **Problem summary**: You should briefly summarize the problem being experienced in regular prose so that the issue can be quickly understood and triaged (possibly by someone who is not adept at diagnosing or fixing the exact issue).
- **Steps taken**: You should show the exact code that could be used to reproduce the actual behavior that you receive. The reader of your bug should be able to take your shared code or input parameters and reproduce the behavior themselves.
- **Expected behavior**: You should demonstrate what you would expect the behavior or output to be, given the input.
- **Actual behavior**: You should demonstrate the incorrect output or behavior that you observed.

Here's an example of such a bug report for a fictional `sum()` function:

- **Problem summary**: `sum()` does not behave intuitively when given null inputs
- **Steps taken**: Called `sum(null, null)`
- **Expected behavior**: `sum(null,  null)` should return `NaN`
- **Actual behavior**: `sum(null, null)` returns `0`

It may also be useful to include information about the environment in which the code is running, including hardware and software (for example, *MacBook 2013 Retina, Chrome version 43.01*). The entire purpose of raising a bug is to communicate an unexpected or incorrect behavior with a level of accuracy and detail that'll allow a swift resolution. If we limit the amount of information we provide, or are outright rude, we drastically decrease the probability of our issue being resolved.

Apart from the specific steps we should take when raising issues, there is also a wider question around how we should drive and inspire systemic change in a piece of software or a culture. We'll be exploring this next.

Driving systemic change

A bug is usually considered a self-contained technical issue with a piece of hardware or software. There are, however, larger or more systemic issues that we face every day, and these can be expressed in terms of a culture or in terms of the everyday conventions and patterns that we employ throughout a system. Here are some fictional examples of issues from within a typical IT consultancy:

- We tend to use typefaces throughout our designs that are inaccessible
- We have a hundred different standards for how to write good JavaScript
- We seem to always forget to update third-party dependencies
- We don't feed back into the open source community

These issues are slightly too broad or subjective to be expressed as definitive *bugs*, so we'll need to explore other means to surface them and get them resolved. It may be useful to think of such systemic issues as opportunities for growth instead of *bugs*, as this can vastly affect how on-board people are with your proposed changes.

Broadly, the steps involved in creating systemic change are as follows:

1. **QUALIFY: Articulate the problem with specific examples**: Find examples that demonstrate the problem you're trying to describe. Ensure that these examples plainly show the issue and aren't too complex. Describe the problem in a way that makes sense even to people that aren't fully immersed in the *problem domain*.

2. **FEEDBACK: Gather feedback from other people**: Gather thoughts and suggestions from other people. Ask them open questions such as *What do you think about [...]?*. Accept the possibility that there is no problem, or the problem you're encountering is best viewed in some other way.

3. **IDEATE: Collaborate on possible solutions**: Source ideas on possible solutions from multiple people. Don't try to reinvent the wheel. Sometimes the simplest solutions are the best. It's also highly likely that systemic issues cannot be solved in a purely technical way. You may need to consider social and communicative solutions.

4. **RAISE: Raise the problem alongside possible solutions**: Depending on what the problem is, raise it to the appropriate people. This may be via a team meeting, a 1:1 chat, or online communication. Ensure that you are raising the issue in a non-confrontational way and with a focus on improvement and growth.

5. **IMPLEMENT: Collaboratively pick a solution and begin work**: Presuming that you are still considering this problem is worth pursuing, you can begin to implement the most preferred solution, possibly in an isolated and *Proof of Concept* kind of way. For example, if the problem being tackled was *We have a hundred different standards for how to write good JavaScript,* then you could begin to collaboratively implement a singular set of standards using a linter or formatter, reaching out for feedback along the way, and then slowly updating older code to align with these standards.

6. **MEASURE: Check in frequently on the success of the solution**: Get feedback from people and seek quantifiable data to discern whether the selected solution is working as expected. If it isn't, then consider going back to the drawing board and exploring other solutions.

One of the traps in creating systemic change is to wait too long or to be too cautious in approaching the problem. Gaining feedback from others is really valuable, but it is not necessary to depend entirely upon their validation. It's sometimes hard for people to step outside their perspective and see certain issues, especially if they're very accustomed to how things are currently done. Instead of waiting for them to see things your way, it may be best to go ahead with an isolated version of your proposed solution and later prove its efficacy to them.

When people reactively defend how things are currently done, they are typically expressing the **status quo bias**, which is an emotional bias that prefers the current state of affairs. In the face of such a reaction, it is very normal for people to be unwelcoming of a change. So be cautious of placing too much value in others' negative feedback about your proposed change.

Many of the things we wish to change within the technologies and systems we work with every day are not easily solved. They may be complex, unwieldy, and often multi-disciplinary problems. Examples of these types of problems are easily found on discussion forums and community feedback surrounding standards iteration, such as with the ECMAScript language specification. Rarely is an addition or change to the language accomplished simply. Patience, consideration, and communication are all needed to solve these problems and move ourselves and our technologies forward.

Summary

In this chapter, we have tried to explore the challenge of effective communication in a technical context, and have broadly discussed the communicative process involved in taking a problem from the ideation stage to the prototype stage. We have also covered the task of communicating and advocating for technological change, whether in the form of bug reports or raising broader issues concerning systemic problems. Programmers are not just the authors of code; they operate as part of the systems they are building, as crucial agents in the iterative feedback cycles that result in clean software. Understanding the considerable roles we play in these systems and feedback cycles is hugely empowering and begins to get to the crux of what it means to be a clean JavaScript programmer.

In the next and final chapter, we will be bringing together everything we have learned in the book so far, exploring a new problem domain via a case study. That'll conclude our exploration into clean code in JavaScript.

19
Case Study

In this book, we have discussed a litany of principles, walked through almost every aspect of the JavaScript language, and have discussed, at length, what constitutes *clean code*. This has all been working toward a final destination where we are fully equipped to write beautiful and clean JavaScript code that tackles real and challenging problem domains. The pursuit of clean code, however, is never complete; new challenges will always arise that make us think in new and paradigm-shifting ways about the code we write.

In this chapter, we'll be walking through the process of creating a new piece of functionality in JavaScript. This will involve both client-side and server-side parts, and will force us to apply many of the principles and knowledge we've gathered throughout the book. The specific problem we'll be tackling has been adapted from a real-life project that I was responsible for, and while we won't be going into every nook and cranny of its implementation, we will be covering the most important parts. The completed project is available for you to view on GitHub at the following link: `https://github.com/PacktPublishing/Clean-Code-in-JavaScript`.

In this chapter, we're going to cover the following topics:

- **The problem**: We'll define and explore the problem
- **The design**: We'll design a UX and architecture that solves the problem
- **The implementation**: We'll implement our design

The problem

The problem we'll be solving relates to a core part of our web application's user experience. The web application we'll be working on is a frontend to a large plant database with tens of thousands of different species of plants. Among other functionality, it allows users to find specific plants and add them to collections so that they can keep track of their exotic greenhouses and botanical research inventories. The illustration is shown as follows:

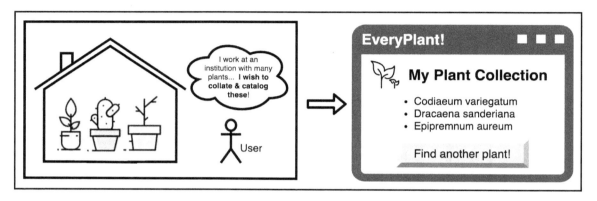

Currently, when users wish to find a plant, they must use a search facility that involves entering a plant name *(the full Latin name)* into a text field, clicking **Search**, and receiving a set of results, as shown in the following screenshot:

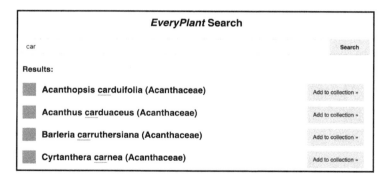

For the purposes of our case study, the plant names only exist as their full Latin names, which includes a family (for example, **Acanthaceae**), a genus (for example, **Acanthus**), and a species (for example, **Carduaceus**). This highlights the challenges involved in catering to complex problem domains.

This works well enough, but following some user focus groups and online feedback, it has been decided that we need to offer a better UX for users that enables them to more quickly find the plants they're interested in. Specific points that were raised are as follows:

- I find it burdensome and slow to find species sometimes. I wish it were more immediate and flexible, so that I didn't have to keep going back and making a change to my query, especially if I've spelled it incorrectly.
- Often, when I know the name of a plant species or genus, I'll still get it slightly wrong and get no results. I'll then have to go back and adjust my spelling or search elsewhere online.
- I wish I could see the species and genuses come up as I type. That way I can more quickly find the appropriate plant and not waste any time.

There are a number of usability concerns expressed here. We can distill them into the following three topics:

- **Performance**: The current search facility is slow and clunky to use
- **Error correction**: The process of having to correct typing errors is annoying and burdensome
- **Feedback**: It would be useful to get feedback about existing *genuses/species* while typing

The task is now becoming clearer. We need to improve the UX so that users are able to query the database of plants in a way that is faster, provides more immediate feedback, and lets them prevent or correct typing errors along the way.

The design

After some brainstorming, we decided that we can solve our problem in quite a conventional way; we can simply transform the input field into one that provides an auto-suggestion dropdown. Here's a mockup:

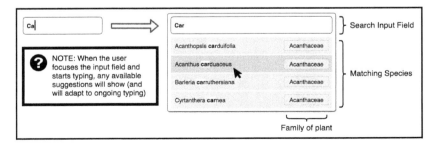

This auto-suggestion dropdown would have the following characteristics:

- When a term is typed, it will display a prioritized list of plant names that contain that term as a prefix, for example, searching for `car` will yield the result `carnea` but not `encarea`
- When a term is selected either by click, the arrow (up/down), or *Enter* key, it will run a specified function (which may later be used to add selected items to the user's collection)
- When no matching plant names can be found, the user will be told with a notice such as `No plants with that name exist`

These are the core behaviors of our component, and in order to implement them, we'll need to consider both client-side and server-side parts. Our client will have to render `<input>` to the user, and as they type, it will have to dynamically adjust the list of suggestions. The server will have to provide to the client a list of suggestions for each potential query, while taking into consideration the fact that results will need to be delivered quickly. Any significant latency will drastically reduce the benefit of the user experience that we're trying to create.

The implementation

It just so happens that this new Plant Selection component will be the first piece of significant client-side code within our web application, and as such, it's important to note that our design decisions will impact not only this specific component but also any other components we consider building in the future.

To aid us in our implementation, and considering the possibility of other potential additions in the near future, we've decided to adopt a JavaScript library to assist in the manipulation of the DOM, and a supporting toolset that enables us to work swiftly and to a high-level of quality. In this instance, we've decided to use React on the client side, with webpack and Babel to aid in compilation and bundling, and Express on the server side for HTTP routing.

The Plant Selection application

As discussed, we've decided to build our *Plant Selection* functionality as its own self-contained application with both a client (the React component) and a server (the plant-data API). Having this level of isolation allows us to focus purely on the problem of selecting plants, but there's no reason that this couldn't be integrated into a larger code base at a later time.

Our directory structure is roughly as follows:

```
EveryPlantSelectionApp/
├─── server/
│   ├─── package.json
│   ├─── babel.config.js
│   ├─── index.js
│   └─── plantData/
│       ├─── plantData.js
│       ├─── plantData.test.js
│       └─── data.json
└─── client/
    ├─── package.json
    ├─── webpack.config.js
    ├─── babel.config.js
    ├─── app/
    │   ├─── index.jsx
    │   └─── components/
    │       └─── PlantSelectionInput/
    └─── dist/
        ├─── main.js (bundling target)
        └─── index.html
```

In addition to reducing complexity for us (the programmers) the separation of server and client means that the server-side application (that is, the Plant Selection API) can be run on its own distinct server if necessary, while the client can be served up statically from a CDN, requiring only the server-side's address in order to access its REST API.

Creating the REST API

The server of `EveryPlantSelectionApp` is responsible for retrieving the plant names (the plant *families*, *genuses*, and *species*) and making them available to our client-side code via a simple REST API. To do this, we can use the `express` Node.js library, which enables us to route HTTP requests to specific functions, easily delivering JSON to our client.

Here's the skeletal beginnings of our server implementation:

```
import express from 'express';

const app = express();
const port = process.env.PORT || 3000;

app.get('/plants/:query', (req, res) => {
  req.params.query; // => The query
  res.json({
    fakeData: 'We can later place some real data here...'
  });
});

app.listen(
  port,
  () => console.log(`App listening on port ${port}!`)
);
```

As you can see, we're implementing just one route (`/plants/:query`). This will be requested by the client whenever a user enters a partial plant name into the `<input/>`, so that a user typing `Carduaceus` may produce the following set of requests to the server:

```
GET /plants/c
GET /plants/ca
GET /plants/car
GET /plants/card
GET /plants/cardu
GET /plants/cardua
...
```

You can imagine how this may result in a larger number of expensive and possibly redundant requests, especially if a user is typing quickly. It's possible that a user will type `cardua` before any of the previous requests can complete. For that reason, when we come around to implementing the client side, it'll be appropriate for us to use some kind of request throttling (or request debouncing) to ensure that we're only making a reasonable number of requests.

Request throttling is the act of reducing the overall amount of requests by only allowing a new request to be performed at a specified time interval, meaning that 100 requests spanned over five seconds, throttled to an interval of one second, would produce only five requests. **Request debouncing** is similar, though instead of performing a single request on every interval, it'll wait a predesignated amount of time for incoming requests to stop being made before enacting an actual request. So, 100 requests over five seconds, debounced by five seconds, would only produce a single final request at the five second mark.

In order to implement the `/plants/` endpoint, we need to consider the most optimal way to search through the names of over *300,000* different plant species for matches. To accomplish this, we'll be using a special in-memory data structure called a **trie**. This is also known as a *prefix tree* and is very common to use in situations where autosuggestion or autocompletion needs to occur.

A trie is a tree-like structure that stores chunks of letters that appear next to each other as a series of nodes attached by branches. It's much easier to visualize than to describe, so let's imagine that we need a trie based on the following data:

```
['APPLE', 'ACORN', 'APP', 'APPLICATION']
```

Using that data, the produced trie might look something like this:

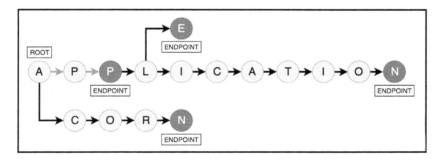

As you can see, our dataset of four words has been represented as a tree-like structure where the first common letter, `"A"`, serves as the root. The `"CORN"` suffix branches off from this. Additionally, the `"PP"` branch (forming `"APP"`), branches off, and the last `"P"` of that then branches off to `"L"`, which itself then branches off to `"E"` (forming `"APPLE"`) and `"ICATION"` (forming `"APPLICATION"`).

This may seem convoluted, but given this trie structure, we can, given an initial prefix typed by a user like `"APPL"`, easily find all matching words (`"APPLE"` and `"APPLICATION"`) by simply stepping through the nodes of the tree. This is far more performant than any linear search algorithm. For our purposes, given a prefix of a plant name, we want to be able to performantly display every plant name that the prefix may lead to.

Our specific dataset will include over 300,000 different plant species, but for the purposes of this case study, we'll only be using species from the `Acanthaceae` family, which amounts to around 8,000 species. These are available to use in the form of JSON as follows:

```
[
  { id: 105,
    family: 'Acanthaceae',
    genus: 'Andrographis',
    species: 'alata' },
  { id: 106,
    family: 'Acanthaceae',
    genus: 'Justicia',
    species: 'alata' },
  { id: 107,
    family: 'Acanthaceae',
    genus: 'Pararuellia',
    species: 'alata' },
  { id: 108,
    family: 'Acanthaceae',
    genus: 'Thunbergia',
    species: 'alata' },
  // ...
]
```

We'll be feeding this data into a third-party trie implementation called **trie-search** on NPM. This package has been selected because it fulfills our requirements and seems like a well-tested and well-maintained library.

In order for the trie to operate as we desire, we'll need to concatenate the *family*, *genus*, and *species* of each plant into a singular string. This enables the trie to include both the fully qualified plant name (for example, `"Acanthaceae Pararuellia alata"`) and the split names (`["Acanthaceae", "Pararuellia", "alata"]`). The *split* name is automatically generated by the trie implementation we're using (meaning it splits strings on whitespace, via the regex `/\s/g`):

```
const trie = new TrieSearch(['name'], {
  ignoreCase: true // Make it case-insensitive
});
```

```
trie.addAll(
  data.map(({ family, genus, species, id }) => {
    return { name: family + ' ' + genus + ' ' + species, id };
  })
);
```

The preceding code enters our dataset into the trie. Following this, it can be queried by simply passing a prefix string to its `get(...)` method:

```
trie.get('laxi');
```

Such a query (for the prefix, `laxi`) would return the following from our dataset:

```
[
  { id: 203,
    name: 'Acanthaceae Acanthopale laxiflora' },
  { id: 809,
    name: 'Acanthaceae Andrographis laxiflora' },
  { id: 390,
    name: 'Acanthaceae Isoglossa laxiflora' },
  //... (many more)
]
```

So, with regard to our REST endpoint, `/photos/:query`, all it needs to do is return a JSON payload that contains whatever we get from `trie.get(query)`:

```
app.get('/plants/:query', (req, res) => {
  const queryString = req.params.query;
  if (queryString.length < 3) {
    return res.json([]);
  }
  res.json(
    trie.get(queryString)
  );
});
```

To separate our concerns a little better and to ensure we're not mixing too many different layers of abstraction (in possible violation of The Law of Demeter), we can abstract away our trie data structure and plant data to a module of its own. We can call this `plantData` to communicate the fact that it encapsulates and provides access to the plant data. The nature of how it works, which happens to be via an in-memory trie data structure, does not need to be known to its consumers:

```
// server/plantData.js

import TrieSearch from 'trie-search';
import plantData from './data.json';
```

```
const MIN_QUERY_LENGTH = 3;

const trie = new TrieSearch(['fullyQualifiedName'], {
  ignoreCase: true
});

trie.addAll(
  plantData.map(plant => {
    return {
      ...plant,
      fullyQualifiedName:
        `${plant.family} ${plant.genus} ${plant.species}`
    };
  })
);

export default {
  query(partialString) {
    if (partialString.length < MIN_QUERY_LENGTH) {
      return [];
    }
    return trie.get(partialString);
  }
};
```

As you can see, this module returns an interface that provides one method, `query()`, which our main HTTP routing code can utilize to deliver the JSON result for `/plants/:query`:

```
//...
import plantData from './plantData';
//...
app.get('/plants/:query', (req, res) => {
  const query = req.params.query;
  res.json( plantData.query(partial) );
});
```

Because we have isolated and contained the plant-querying functionality, it is now far easier to make assertions about it. Writing some tests that target the `plantData` abstraction will give us a high level of confidence that our HTTP layer is using a reliable abstraction, minimizing the potential bugs that can crop up within our HTTP layer itself.

At this point, since this is the first set of tests we'll be writing for our project, we'll be installing Jest (`npm install jest --save-dev`). There are a large number of testing frameworks available, with varying styles, but for our purposes, Jest is suitable.

We can write tests for our `plantData` module in a file intuitively located alongside it and named `plantData.test.js`:

```
import plantData from './plantData';

describe('plantData', () => {

  describe('Family+Genus name search (Acanthaceae Thunbergia)', () => {
    it('Returns plants with family and genus of "Acanthaceae Thunbergia"',
() =>{
      const results = plantData.query('Acanthaceae Thunbergia');
      expect(results.length).toBeGreaterThan(0);
      expect(
        results.filter(plant =>
          plant.family === 'Acanthaceae' &&
          plant.genus === 'Thunbergia'
        )
      ).toHaveLength(results.length);
    });
  });

});
```

There are a large number of tests within `plantData.test.js` that aren't included here for the sake of brevity; however, you can view them in the GitHub repository: `https://github.com/PacktPublishing/Clean-Code-in-JavaScript`.

As you can see, this test is asserting whether an `Acanthaceae Thunbergia` query intuitively returns plants that have a fully qualified name containing these terms. In our dataset, this will only include plants that have an `Acanthaceae` family and a `Thunbergia` genus, so we can simply confirm that the results match that expectation. We can also check that partial searches, such as `Acantu Thun`, also intuitively return any plants that have either *family, genus,* or *species* names beginning with `Acantu` or `Thun`:

```
describe('Partial family & genus name search (Acantu Thun)', () => {
  it('Returns plants that have a fully-qualified name containing both
"Acantu" and "Thunbe"', () => {
    const results = plantData.query('Acant Thun');
    expect(results.length).toBeGreaterThan(0);
    expect(
```

```
      results.filter(plant =>
        /\bAcant/i.test(plant.fullyQualifiedName) &&
        /\bThun/i.test(plant.fullyQualifiedName)
      )
    ).toHaveLength(results.length);
  });
});
```

We confirm our expectations here by asserting that every returned result's
`fullyQualifiedName` matches the regular /\bAcant/i and /\bThun/i expressions. The
/i expression indicates case sensitivity. The \b expression here represents a word
boundary so that we can ensure that the `Acant` and `Thun` substrings appear at the
beginning of individual words and are not embedded within words. For example, imagine
a plant called `Luathunder`. We don't want our autosuggestion mechanism to match such
instances. We only want it to match prefixes, as that is how users will be entering plant
families, *genuses*, or *species* into <input /> (from the start of each word).

Now that we have a well-tested and isolated server-side architecture, we can begin to move
onto the client side, where we will be rendering the plant names provided by
/plants/:query in response to the user typing.

Creating the client-side build process

Our first step, on the client, is to introduce *React* and a supporting toolset that can aid us in
development. In the old days of web development, it was, and arguably still is, entirely
possible to build things without complicated tools and build steps. In times past, we were
able to simply create an HTML page, include any third-party dependencies inline, and then
begin writing our JavaScript without having to worry about anything else:

```html
<body>
  ... Content
  <script src="//example.org/libraryFoo.js"></script>
  <script src="//example.org/libraryBaz.js"></script>
  <script>
    // Our JavaScript code...
  </script>
</body>
```

Technically we can still do this. Even when using modern frontend frameworks such as React, we could opt to just include it as a `<script>` dependency and then write vanilla JavaScript inline. However, by doing this, we would not be receiving the following advantages:

- **Newer JavaScript syntax** (ES 2019 and beyond): The ability to use modern JavaScript syntax and have it compiled to JavaScript that is safe to use in all environments/browsers.
- **Custom syntax and language extensions**: The ability to use language extensions (such as JSX or FlowJS) or other languages that compile to JavaScript (such as TypeScript or CoffeeScript).
- **Dependency tree management**: The ability to specify your dependencies easily (for example, using an `import` statement) and have these automatically reconciled and combined into a bundle, without having to manually fiddle with the `<script>` tags and versioning nightmares.
- **Performance improvements**: Intelligent compilation and bundling can provide meaningful HTTP and runtime performance gains by reducing the overall footprint of your JavaScript and CSS.
- **Linters and analysers**: The ability to use linters and other forms of analysis on your JavaScript (and your CSS and HTML), giving us a detailed insight into code quality and prospective bugs.

Fundamentally, the very nature of web applications is more complicated now, especially on the frontend. For our purposes of creating an autosuggestion component, we need to ensure that we've got a good foundation of tools and build steps so that ongoing development can be seamless and simple. This can create a headache when setting things up but is worth it in the long run.

In order to compile our JavaScript (including React's JSX), we'll be using *Babel,* which can take our JavaScript and convert it into widely supported regular JavaScript syntax. To add Babel as a dependency within `EveryPlantSelectionApp/client`, we can use npm to install it and its various preset configurations:

```
# Install babel's core dependencies:
npm install --save-dev @babel/core @babel/cli

# Install some smart presets for Babel, allowing us to not have
# to worry about which specific JS syntax we're using:
npm install --save-dev @babel/preset-env

# Install a smart preset for React (i.e. JSX) usage:
npm install --save-dev @babel/preset-react
```

Babel will manage the compilation of our JavaScript to a syntax that is widely supported. But in order to make these files ready for delivery to a browser, we need to bundle them into a singular file that can be delivered by itself within our HTML like so:

```
<script src="./ourBundledJavaScript.js"></script>
```

To accomplish this, we will need to use a bundler, such as webpack. Webpack can carry out the following tasks for us:

- It can compile the JavaScript via Babel
- It can then reconcile each module, including any of its dependencies
- It can produce a singular bundled JavaScript file that includes all dependencies

In order to use webpack, we need to install several related dependencies:

```
# Install Webpack and its CLI:
npm install --save-dev webpack webpack-cli

# Install Webpack's development server, which enables us to more easily
# develop without having to keep re-running the build process:
npm install --save-dev webpack-dev-server

# Install a couple of helpful packages that make it easier for
# Webpack to make use of Babel:
npm install --save-dev babel-loader babel-preset-react
```

Webpack also requires its own configuration file, named `webpack.config.js`. Within this file, we must tell it how to bundle our code and whereabouts in our project we want the bundled code to output to:

```
const path = require('path');

module.exports = {
  entry: './app/index.jsx',
  module: {
    rules: [
      {
        test: /\.(js|jsx)$/,
        exclude: /node_modules/,
        use: {
          loader: 'babel-loader',
          options: {
            presets: ['@babel/react']
          }
        }
      }
    ]
```

```
  },
  devServer: {
    contentBase: path.join(__dirname, 'dist'),
    compress: true,
    port: 9000
  },
  output: {
    filename: 'main.js',
    path: path.resolve(__dirname, 'dist'),
  }
};
```

This configuration is essentially telling webpack the following:

- Please begin at `EveryPlantSelectionApp/client/app/index.jsx`
- Please use Babel to compile this module and all its dependencies that end in `.jsx` or `.js`
- Please output the compiled and bundled file to `EveryPlantSelectionApp/client/dist/`

Lastly, we need to install React so that we're ready to create our plant selection component:

```
npm install --save react react-dom
```

It may seem like this is a lot of work just to render a basic UI component, but what we've actually done is created a foundation upon which we can accommodate many new features, and we've created a build pipeline that will make it easier to ship our development code base to production.

Creating the component

Our component's job is to display an enhanced `<input>` element that will, when focused, react to what the user types by rendering a dropdown-style list of available options that the user can then select from.

As a primitive outline, we can imagine the component as containing `<div>`, `<input>` into which the user can type, and `<ol>` to display the suggestions:

```
const PlantSelectionInput = () => {
  return (
    <div className="PlantSelectionInput">
      <input
        autoComplete="off"
        aria-autocomplete="inline"
```

```
      role="combobox" />
    <ol>
      <li>A plant name...</li>
      <li>A plant name...</li>
      <li>A plant name...</li>
    </ol>
  </div>
 );
};
```

 The `role` and `aria-autocomplete` attributes on `<input>` are used to instruct the browser (and any screen readers) that the user will be provided with a set of predefined choices when typing. This is of vital importance to accessibility. The `autoComplete` attribute is used to simply enable or disable the browser's default autocompletion behavior. In our case, we want it disabled as we are providing our own custom autocompletion/suggestion functionality.

We only want `<ol>` to display when `<input>` is focused. In order to accomplish this, we'll need to bind to both the focus ad blur events of `<input>` and then create a distinct piece of state that can track whether we should consider the component open or not. We can call this piece of state `isOpen`, and we can conditionally render or not render `<ol>` based on its Boolean value:

```
const PlantSelectionInput = () => {
  const [isOpen, setIsOpen] = useState(false);
  return (
    <div className="PlantSelectionInput">
      <input
        onFocus={() => setIsOpen(true)}
        onBlur={() => setIsOpen(false)}
        autoComplete="off"
        aria-autocomplete="inline"
        role="combobox" />
      {
      isOpen &&
        <ol>
          <li>A plant name...</li>
          <li>A plant name...</li>
          <li>A plant name...</li>
        </ol>
      }
    </div>
  );
};
```

React has its own conventions around state management, which may look rather bizarre if you've not been exposed before. The const [foo, setFoo] = useState(null) code creates a piece of state (called foo), which we can change in response to certain events. Whenever this state changes, React would then know to trigger a re-render of the related component. Flick back to Chapter 12, *Real-World Challenges*, and look at the *DOM binding and reconciliation* section for a refresher on this topic.

The next step is for us to bind to the change event of <input> so that we can take whatever the user has typed and trigger a request to our /plants/:query endpoint in order to discern what suggestions to show the user. First, however, we want to create a mechanism via which the request can occur. In the React world, it suggests modeling this functionality as a *Hook* of its own. Remembering that Hooks are, by convention, prefixed with a *use* verb, we could call this something like usePlantLike. As its sole argument, it can accept a query field (the string typed by the user), it can return an object with a loading field (to indicate the current loading state) and a plants field (to contain the suggestions):

```
// Example of calling usePlantsLike:
const {loading, plants} = usePlantsLike('Acantha');
```

Our implementation of usePlantsLike is thankfully quite simple:

```
// usePlantLike.js

import {useState, useEffect} from 'react';

export default (query) => {
  const [loading, setLoading] = useState(false);
  const [plants, setPlants] = useState([]);

  useEffect(() => {
    setLoading(true);
    fetch(`/plants/${query}`)
      .then(response => response.json())
      .then(data => {
        setLoading(false);
        setPlants(data);
      });
  }, [query]);

  return { loading, plants };
};
```

Here, we are using another *React* state management pattern, `useEffect()`, to run a specific function whenever the `query` argument changes. So, if `usePlantLike` receives a new `query` argument, for example, `Acantha`, then the loading state will be set to `true` and a new `fetch()` will be instigated, the result of which will populate the `plants` state. This can be difficult to wrap one's head around, but for the purposes of the case study, all we really need to appreciate is the fact that this `usePlantsLike` abstraction is encapsulating the complexity of issuing the `/plants/:query` requests to the server.

It is wise to separate rendering logic from data logic. Doing so ensures a good hierarchy of abstraction and separation of concerns, and enshrines each module as an area of *single responsibility*. Conventional MVC and MVVM frameworks helpfully force this separation, while more modern rendering libraries such as React give you a little more choice. So here, we've chosen to isolate the data and server-communication logic within a React Hook, which is then utilized by our component.

We can now use our new React Hook whenever the user types something into `<input>`. To do this, we can bind to its `change` event and every time it's triggered, grab its `value`, and then pass it as the `query` argument to `usePlantsLike` in order to derive a new set of suggestions for the user. These can then be rendered within our `<ol>` container:

```
const PlantSelectionInput = ({ isInitiallyOpen, value }) => {

  const inputRef = useRef();
  const [isOpen, setIsOpen] = useState(isInitiallyOpen || false);
  const [query, setQuery] = useState(value);
  const {loading, plants} = usePlantsLike(query);

  return (
    <div className="PlantSelectionInput">
      <input
        ref={inputRef}
        onFocus={() => setIsOpen(true)}
        onBlur={() => setIsOpen(false)}
        onChange={() => setQuery(inputRef.current.value)}
        autoComplete="off"
        aria-autocomplete="inline"
        role="combobox"
        value={value} />
    {
      isOpen &&
        <ol>{
          plants.map(plant =>
            <li key={plant.id}>{plant.fullyQualifiedName}</li>
          )
```

```
        }</ol>
      }
    </div>
  );
};
```

Here, we've added a new piece of state, `query`, which we set via `setQuery` within the `onChange` handler of `<input>`. This `query` mutation will then cause `usePlantsLike` to issue a new request from the server and populate `<ol>` with multiple `<li>` elements, each representing an individual plant name suggestion.

And with that, we have completed the basic implementation of our component. In order to make use of it, we can render it in our `client/index.jsx` entry point:

```
import ReactDOM from 'react-dom';
import React from 'react';
import PlantSelectionInput from './components/PlantSelectionInput';

ReactDOM.render(
  <PlantSelectionInput />,
  document.getElementById('root')
);
```

This code attempts to render `<PlantSelectionInput/>` to an element with a "root" ID. As outlined previously, webpack, our bundling tool, will automatically bundle our compiled JavaScript into a singular `main.js` file and place it in `dist/` (that is, distribution) directory. This will sit alongside our `index.html` file, which will serve as a user-facing portal to our application. For our purposes, this only needs to be a simple page that demonstrates `PlantSelectionInput`:

```
<!DOCTYPE html>
<html>
<head>
  <title>EveryPlant Selection App</title>
  <style>
    /* our styles... */
  </style>
</head>
<body>
  <div id="root"></div>
  <script src="./main.js"></script>
</body>
</html>
```

We can place any relevant CSS within the `<style>` tag here in `index.html`:

```
<style>
.PlantSelectionInput {
  width: 100%;
  display: flex;
  position: relative;
}
.PlantSelectionInput input {
  background: #fff;
  font-size: 1em;
  flex: 1 1;
  padding: .5em;
  outline: none;
}
/* ... more styles here ... */
</style>
```

 In larger projects, it's wise to come up with a scaled CSS solution that works well with many different components. Examples that work well with *React* include *CSS modules* or *styled components*, both of which allow you to define CSS scoped just to individual components, avoiding the headache of juggling global CSS.

The styling of our component is not particularly challenging as it is just a list of textual items. The main challenge is in ensuring that, when the component is in its fully opened state, the list of suggestions appears atop any other content on the page. This can be achieved by relatively positioning the `<input>` container and then absolutely positioning `<ol>`, visualized here:

thunb	
Dischistocalyx thunbergiiflora	Acanthaceae
Dyschoriste thunbergiiflora	Acanthaceae
Dischistocalyx thunbergiiflorus	Acanthaceae
Tetraglochidium thunbergiiflorum	Acanthaceae

This concludes the implementation of our component, but we should also implement a
basic level of testing (at least). To accomplish this, we'll be using Jest, a testing library, and
its snapshot matching functionality. This will enable us to confirm that our React
component produces the expected hierarchy of DOM elements and will protect us from
future regressions:

```jsx
// PlantSelectionInput.test.jsx

import React from 'react';
import renderer from 'react-test-renderer';
import PlantSelectionInput from './';

describe('PlantSelectionInput', () => {

  it('Should render deterministically to its snapshot', () => {
    expect(
      renderer
        .create(<PlantSelectionInput />)
        .toJSON()
    ).toMatchSnapshot();
  });

  describe('With configured isInitiallyOpen & value properties', () => {
    it('Should render deterministically to its snapshot', () => {
      expect(
        renderer
          .create(
            <PlantSelectionInput
              isInitiallyOpen={true}
              value="Example..."
            />
          )
          .toJSON()
      ).toMatchSnapshot();
    });
  });

});
```

Jest helpfully saves the produced snapshots to a __snapshots__ directory and then
compares any future executions of the tests against these saved snapshots. In addition to
these tests, we'll also be able to implement regular functional, or even E2E tests that can
encode expectations such as *When the user types, the list of suggestions updates correspondingly.*

This concludes our construction of the component and our case study. If you have a look at our GitHub repository, you can see the completed project, play with the component, run the tests yourself, and you can fork the repository to make your own changes too.

Here's the link to the GitHub repository: `https://github.com/PacktPublishing/Clean-Code-in-JavaScript`.

Summary

In this, the final chapter, we have explored a real-world problem through the lens of the principles and learnings that we have gathered throughout the book. We posed a problem that users were encountering and then designed and implemented a user experience that solved their problem in a clean way. This included both server-side and client-side pieces, enabling us to see, from start to finish, what a self-contained JavaScript project may look like. Although we haven't been able to cover every single detail, I hope that this chapter has been helpful in cementing the core ideas behind *clean code* and that you now feel better prepared to write clean JavaScript code to tackle all types of problem domains. One core tenet I hope you can take away with you is simply this: **focus on the user**.

Other Books You May Enjoy

If you enjoyed this book, you may be interested in these other books by Packt:

Building Forms with Vue.js
Marina Mosti

ISBN: 978-1-83921-333-5

- Learn all about the basics of creating reusable form components with the Vue framework
- Understand v-model and how it plays a role in form creation
- Create forms that are completely powered and generated by a schema, either locally or from an API endpoint
- Understand how Vuelidate allows for easy declarative validation of all your form's inputs with Vue's reactivity system
- Connect your application with a Vuex-powered global state management
- Use the v-mask library to enhance your inputs and improve user experience (UX)

Web Development with Angular and Bootstrap - Third Edition
Sridhar Rao Chivukula, Aki Iskandar

ISBN: 978-1-78883-810-8

- Develop Angular single-page applications using an ecosystem of helper tools
- Get familiar with Bootstrap's new grid and helper classes
- Embrace TypeScript and ECMAScript to write more maintainable code
- Implement custom directives for Bootstrap 4 with the ng2-bootstrap library
- Understand the component-oriented structure of Angular and its router
- Use the built-in HTTP library to work with API endpoints
- Manage your app's data and state with observables and streams
- Combine Angular and Bootstrap 4 with Firebase to develop a solid example

Leave a review - let other readers know what you think

Please share your thoughts on this book with others by leaving a review on the site that you bought it from. If you purchased the book from Amazon, please leave us an honest review on this book's Amazon page. This is vital so that other potential readers can see and use your unbiased opinion to make purchasing decisions, we can understand what our customers think about our products, and our authors can see your feedback on the title that they have worked with Packt to create. It will only take a few minutes of your time, but is valuable to other potential customers, our authors, and Packt. Thank you!

Index

E

efficiency
  about 32
  effects 34
  space 34
  time 32, 33
ember boilerplate
  URL 486
End-to-End (E2E) testing
  about 421, 422
  advantages 421
  disadvantages 421
  tools 445, 446, 447
ES Modules 391
Event Emitter 323
Event Loop 318
event-oriented paradigm 382
execution context 271
exponentiation operator 225, 226
expression 148, 264, 265

F

fallthrough 292, 308
falsy primitives 118, 119
familiarity 37, 38
fault tolerance 29
Flow
  URL 445
for statement
  about 298
  conventional for statement 299, 300, 301
  for...in construct 301, 302, 303
  for...of construct 303, 304
for...in construct 301, 302, 303
for...of construct 303, 304
formatters 441, 443, 444
fragility 36, 37
function declaration 156, 275, 276
function expressions 157
functional programming principles 86, 87
functional purity 88, 89, 379
functional testing 421, 422
functions, bindings
  arguments 153, 154

execution context 150, 151
  new.target 152, 153
  super keyword 151, 152
functions
  about 146, 147
  bindings 149
  names 154, 155, 156
  syntactic contexts 148, 149

G

General Data Protection Regulation (GDPR) 408
generator function 166, 167
grapheme clusters 126
greater than operator 237
grouping 258, 259

H

headless browser 446
hierarchy 103, 105, 106
Hungarian notation
  about 99, 107, 108
  advantages 107
  disadvantages 108

I

idempotence 88, 379
if statement 296, 297, 298
Immediately Invoked Function Expression (IIFE)
  160, 161, 162, 364
immutability 90
imperative 282
imperative form 109
imperative programming
  versus declarative programming 281, 282, 283,
  284, 286
implementation 500
imposter syndrome 56
in operator 240, 241
increment operator 245
input domain 428
input space 428
instability 29
instanceof operator 240
instances
  detecting 199

www.ingramcontent.com/pod-product-compliance
Lightning Source LLC
LaVergne TN
LVHW081507050326
832903LV00025B/1410